MAGILL'S
LITERARY ANNUAL
2002

MAGILL'S
LITERARY ANNUAL
2002

*Essay-Reviews of 200 Outstanding Books
Published in the United States during 2001*

With an Annotated Categories List

Volume Two
M-Z

Edited by
JOHN D. WILSON
STEVEN G. KELLMAN

SALEM PRESS
Pasadena, California   Hackensack, New Jersey

LIBRARY OF CONGRESS CATALOG CARD NO. 77-99209
ISBN 1-58765-066-5

FIRST PRINTING

PRINTED IN THE UNITED STATES OF AMERICA

MAGILL'S
LITERARY ANNUAL
2002

MILOSZ'S ABC'S

Author: Czesław Miłosz (1911-   )
First published: Abecadło Miłoza, 1997, and *Inne
    Abecadło*, 1998, in Poland
Translated from the Polish by Madeline G. Levine
Publisher: Farrar, Straus and Giroux (New York).
    313 pp. $24.00
Type of work: Essays

~

*A collection of short essays, arranged alphabetically by
subject matter, by the Lithuanian-Polish poet and Nobel
Prize winner Miłosz*

~

Czesław Miłosz, one of the most highly respected writers of the twentieth century, has accumulated the wealth of a lifetime in his book *Milosz's ABC's*. He suggests he has written this book "instead of a novel, instead of an essay on the twentieth century, instead of a memoir." Indeed, the book encompasses each of these genres in turn, offering the reader a rare glimpse into the life of a great poet living out his life in the twentieth century.

Milosz's ABC's is a collection of short entries covering a wide variety of topics. As the title suggests, *Milosz's ABC's* is arranged alphabetically by subject, much the way an encyclopedia is structured. Generically, the ABC book has its roots in Poland, and since Miłosz writes only in Polish, the choice of the genre seems fitting. There are both joys and difficulties in this choice, however. The structure of the book is from the outside; that is, there is no organic connection between essays that appear next to each other. Their titles simply follow each other in the alphabet. Consequently, the book sometimes seems fragmented and without direction, one random entry following another. On the other hand, the juxtapositions of widely varying topics often open interesting connections between two or more seemingly unrelated topics. In this way, the book sometimes comes close to resembling poetry, where the unexpected image butts up against some other unlikely idea. The reader's comfort with randomness will probably affect the response to the book. Those readers needing clear, logical transitions will not find them and may be disconcerted by the leaps between entries. Those readers who delight in the unexpected twist of the text will find the abecedarian approach filled with surprise and serendipity.

Miłosz writes biographies of people he knows and of people he does not know, historical essays about Poland and the world, literary criticism, philosophical treatises, and a variety of other less well-defined pieces. Each piece is firmly grounded in the twentieth century (with a few exceptions, such as the entry on the nineteenth century American poet Walt Whitman), and the totality of the book captures a sense of a recently departed past.

*Internationally acclaimed poet,
essayist, and novelist Czesław Miłosz
was born in Lithuania in 1911 and
grew up in Poland before coming to
the United States in 1960. He won
the Nobel Prize in Literature in
1980.*

As a reader, it would be possible to build one's own path through the book, perhaps reading all the biographies first, then examining the philosophy. Another reader might choose to dip into the book at random spots, creating a different set of juxtapositions. Yet another reader might start at the beginning and work through the essays to the last page. Each of these choices would produce a particular kind of reading, different from that produced by another choice.

Miłosz chooses to begin his book with an entry on Ludwik Abramowicz, the publisher of *The Wilno Review*, an important influence on Miłosz's early years. In this first entry, Miłosz also introduces his memories of and love for the town in which he grew up. This first essay, then, sets up a number of themes to which Miłosz will return: Wilno, Poland, the twentieth century, and memory.

Miłosz also addresses the horror of the twentieth century in a number of essays. In "Anus Mundi," an expression that means "the world's anus," he reflects on Auschwitz, Poland, and the role of art and poetry in the face of such evil. In addition, he responds to philosopher Theodor Adorno's statement that "it would be an abomination to write lyric poetry after Auschwitz." Miłosz himself lived in Poland, the place a German described as "anus mundi" in 1942, and wrote lyric poetry throughout. He counters Adorno's statement with one of his own, that "gentle verses written in the midst of horror declare themselves for life; they are the body's rebellion against its destruction." For Miłosz, poetry offers comfort, and as such must be written in spite of the horror of human existence.

Miłosz writes not only of Polish historic and literary figures, he also includes some Americans in his ABC's. Two poets who receive very different treatment are Robert Frost and Walt Whitman. Miłosz takes Frost to task for hiding his biography behind the guise of the New England farmer. Indeed, Miłosz goes so far as to say that he does not like Frost's poetry. Whitman, on the other hand, receives the highest praise from Miłosz: "The 'divine literatus' had conquered the distance between the 'I' and the crowd, had devoured religions and philosophies, so that instead of contradictions, mortality and immortality both fit into his poetry, a leaf of grass and eternity." Whitman's presence can be felt in many of the essays in this book; it seems as though he is a benchmark against which Miłosz measures other poets.

As favorable as Miłosz is to some of the subjects of his essays, he is just as brutal to others. He opens an essay about French feminist Simone de Beauvoir with the words, "I never met her, but my antipathy for her has not lessened even now, after her death when she is rapidly slipping away into the land of small-print footnotes to the history of her epoch." Miłosz thus not only seems to slash at Beauvoir personally, he also attacks her work and her place in history. While it is entirely possible to attack Beauvoir on a number of fronts, Miłosz's sentiments seem almost petty. Although he states in the essay that he holds feminists in the highest regard, one cannot help but wonder about misogyny, particularly given that he ends the essay as he begins it, closing with the words, "A nasty hag."

Miłosz's best writing appears in the essays that deal with abstract concepts, such as time or truth. In these, he is able to transcend his personal feelings about one person or another, as interesting as those personal feelings may be. In the essay "Time," for example, he connects the concept with human life, and with all that is human. Language itself moves in time. In considering time, he also returns to memory, "the memory of people who lived and died." This memory tells him that he, too, is controlled by time, and that soon, he will be gone, too. As a consequence, the essay has a palpable sadness to it that is perhaps present because of the reader's awareness of Miłosz's age.

Any writer of memoir must confront the inevitable duplicity of memory, the way that the years shift and change the recollection of events long past. Miłosz is at his best at these moments. Here is where the voice of the poet seems strongest, in that near-melancholy of a long life lived fully, with time inevitably closing in. He struggles to get at the truth of his life, his century, his persona. In what is surely the finest essay in the book, "Truth," Miłosz tackles what has become one of the great battlegrounds of the postmodern age. He notes that "[d]espite the attacks on the very concept of truth, such that faith in the possibility of an objective discovery of the past has been destroyed, people continue to write memoirs fervently to demonstrate how it was, in truth." Miłosz is humble in his own effort; he says that he has tried hard to be honest, but he also calls it "my" twentieth century, implying that the truth residing in the twentieth century of Miłosz might be very different for some other person. The last lines in the essay are among the most beautiful in the book, as Miłosz considers the connections among all the people who come in contact with one another:

> We exist as separate beings, but at the same time each of us acts as a medium propelled by a power we do not know well, a current of the great river, as it were, through which we resemble each other in our common style or form. The truth about us will remind us of a mosaic composed of little stones of different value and colors.

The final passages in the book appear as an envoi in the closing pages. This essay is called "Disappearance," and like Miłosz's reflections on time, this essay takes as its subject memory, life, death, and transition between worlds. "People disappear," Miłosz writes, "as do animals, trees landscapes, and as everyone knows who lives long enough, the memory of those who once were alive disappears, too." In some ways, these lines echo the theme of *ubi sunt* (where has it all gone?) that echoes through so much English poetry. In the last pages, Miłosz seems almost overwhelmed with the certainty of his own death. He ponders the question of what kind of life, if any, there is after death, and he considers the boundaries between the world, noting that only poets willing to go to hell and back communicate with the dead. For Miłosz, the twentieth century weighs heavily. The weight, he writes, is "a host of voices and the faces of people whom I once knew, or heard about, and now they no longer exist." These voices and faces, Miłosz asserts, use him "in order to return among the living for a brief moment." He understands himself as a man of the twentieth century who somehow remained to tell the tale, using the time to come to terms with the people and places of his life. Like Samuel Taylor Coleridge's Ancient Mariner, Miłosz returns to share with readers what the past century has wrought.

Milosz's ABC's is at times difficult, at times charming, at times heartbreaking. For readers unfamiliar with the history of Poland, many of the names and events Miłosz refers to will be unfamiliar. This can be disconcerting, because Miłosz writes with a confidence that all readers will recognize the names, the places, and the events of which he writes. Miłosz is not to be blamed, of course, for the ignorance of his audience. In addition, there is, at times, the whiff of self-indulgence here, the scent of the self-satisfied writer coming to the close of his life having earned the right to say what he will to readers and listeners, and yet, is this not exactly what Miłosz has achieved? The years of his life were tumultuous, his vision of life large. As witness to the horror of war, as witness to the life and death struggles of his family, friends, compatriots, fellow writers, surely he has much to tell. This would be an important book, if for no other reason than being written by Czeslaw Miłosz, the great voice of Poland in the twentieth century; however, its importance resides in the breadth of history, the vision of culture, and the sheer artistry of language the book encompasses.

Diane Andrews Henningfeld

Sources for Further Study

Commonweal 128 (February 23, 2001): 20.
The New Leader 84 (March/April, 2001): 24.
The New York Times, February 21, 2001, p. E7.
The New York Times Book Review 106 (February 18, 2001): 10.

MONSTRUARY

Author: Julián Ríos (1941-   )
First published: Monstruario, 1999, in Spain
Translated from the Spanish by Edith Grossman
Publisher: Alfred A. Knopf (New York). 225 pp. $25.00
Type of work: Novel
Time: The 1990's
Locale: Berlin, Tubingen, Griesbach, and Bad Petersal,
    Germany; Paris and Enfer, France; London; Brussels;
    and Seville

~

After the Spanish painter Mons destroys a series of
paintings and nearly dies, his life and career are examined
by his closest friend, resulting in a contemplation on the
nature of art and the artist

~

Principal characters:
    VICTOR MONS, a painter
    EMIL ALIA, the narrator, an art critic
    KLAUS HOLZMANN, a sculptor
    UWE (DOUBLE UWE) WACH, a Berlin art dealer
    ANNE KIEFER, an art student loved by Holzmann and Mons
    EDMONDE, Mons's first wife
    EVA LALKA,
    ARMELLE (MÉLUSINE),
    PETRA (PETRUSHKA), and
    UTE (VERONICA), Mons's models, lovers, and muses
    MADAME MAYER/ROSA MIR, an eccentric collector
    FRANK M. RECK, a James Joyce scholar at Brown University
    JOYCE RECK, his wife, a critic
    ARA MONS, the artist's stepsister and first muse
    CARMEN VERDUGO MONS, his mother, a former model
    MARCEL MONS, his adoptive father, a Belgian businessman in Madrid

The nature of art and the artist has long fascinated novelists, especially so in the postmodern age. They wonder where artists, whether painters, composers, or writers, get their inspirations. They ask whether the resulting art is a reflection of their lives, or are their lives irrelevant, as has been the most fashionable literary theory over the past thirty years. (Julián Ríos acknowledges his awareness of such concerns with a passing reference to French structuralist critic Roland Barthes.) *Monstruary* is a commentary on such questions as it presents the works created by a Spanish painter living in Berlin, examining the artist's friends and lovers who have played some part in the

∽

*Born in Galicia, Spain, Julián Ríos
was educated at Madrid University
and has lived in England, Germany,
and France. In 1990, he received the
Columbia University Translation
Award for translating, along with
Richard Alan Francis and Suzanne
Jill Levine, his novel* Larva:
Midsummer Night's Babel *(1991).
He has also translated a James
Joyce children's story into Spanish.*

∽

creation of the paintings and the way he uses
and abuses such relationships. Also acting as a
commentary is Ríos's narrative technique itself,
whereby he presents his disconnected story as a
series of fragments which the reader must piece
together to create something akin to a unified
whole.

Victor Verdugo is an illegitimate nine-year-
old whose father is unknown when, in 1945, his
mother, Carmen Verdugo, marries Marcel Mons,
a Belgian businessman living in Madrid and a
friend and patient of Carmen's physician father.
His mother influences Victor Mons's development as an artist, and his beloved stepsister, Ara,
is the first of several women he loves who serve as inspirations for his art. This information appears early in *Monstruary* and is one of the few instances when Emil Alia,
who narrates most of the novel, presents the details of the artist's life in chronological
order. A critic and one of Mons's closest friends, along with the sculptor Klaus
Holzmann and the art dealer Uwe Wach (known as Double Uwe), Emil writes the catalogues for the painter's exhibitions. He presents Mons's story almost as a series of
catalogues, with each chapter of the novel focusing on a different set of paintings,
friends, and lovers/muses.

Monstruary opens with an "accident" that leaves Mons hospitalized. He has also
destroyed, for no clear reason, the series of paintings which gives the novel its title. It
seems as if Emil's goal is to explain the causes of Mons's destructive behavior, but
Ríos's approach is hardly so conventional. Emil refers to "the enigma" of Mons's "final days and nights in Berlin" but is misleading about the artist's fate. If Mons is an
enigma, Ríos asks, can he truly be understood? Is it the goal of the reader or critic to
understand a work of art fully? Is interpretation even necessary? In the case of Mons,
does his life aid in appreciating his art, or does his art elucidate his life? Rios's point
seems to be that the two are inseparable, and if knowing about the life can help in understanding the art, so much the better. In the case of a real artist, the life would be of
little interest without the art, but Mons is a fictional character whose life is the essence
of Ríos's narrative. Such self-reflecting questions are central to Ríos's highly self-
conscious novel.

Mons's first name recalls Mary Shelley's Dr. Victor Frankenstein, and the painter
is like the scientist who creates an accidental monster except that Mons deliberately
paints monstrous images in his exploration of the demons within humanity. One of his
paintings, *It Isn't Good for the Monster to Be Alone*, depicts what Emil calls a
"Frankensteinized" Adam and Eve, images that look as though they had been carved
by an ax: "Mons had heard the complaint of Dr. Frankenstein's creature: 'I am alone,
terribly alone.' Like the true artist, I told him, who is unique." The artist also resembles Dr. Frankenstein in being unable to control his creations. Unless he keeps or destroys them, Mons's paintings leave him to go out into the world, where anything,

such as wrongheaded interpretation, can occur. Such a lack of control may have contributed, after Emil has begun writing the catalogue following months of work by the artist, to the destruction of the series of monster paintings, an act Mons terms "a mercy killing." The descriptions of Mons's paintings (distorted faces and bodies) recall those of painters Francis Bacon, Balthus (Count Balthazar Klossowski de Rola), Lucien Freud, and R. B. Kitaj, the subject of Ríos's *Kitaj: Pictures and Conversations* (1994).

Mons is so enigmatic that instead of self-portraits he hides his identity within his paintings in images such as a mountain "with the head of a mature bald man, black brows peaked in an M." Mons creates numerous paintings within paintings, and this apparent self-portrait is held by a naked she-devil. Appropriately for someone with a studio in a farmhouse in the French village of Enfer (Hell), Mons is obsessed by devil imagery. In this mountain portrait, the reader may wonder whether Mons intends to imply that women are demons who exert devilish control over his art.

Mons works his way through a series of models/protégées who are also lovers/muses. He may be simply using them for sex and art without truly caring about them. Perhaps this is why his first wife, Edmonde, killed herself. Mons's guilt over his treatment of women, especially Edmonde, comes across in his paintings, but it is an open question whether art is autobiography, psychotherapy, or self-flagellation. Ríos suggests that the multifaceted motivations of the artist and the wide range of possible interpretations are what make art so fascinating.

Even the sympathetic Emil grows puzzled over Mons's attitudes toward some of his women, whom he seems to treat as if they are inanimate objects. Finding Edmonde, an hour and a half after she has slit her wrists, he calmly sketches her so that he can later paint her white face as a death mask. Mons finds his lover Eva Lalka in the arms of a black man, both dead of heroin overdose. He paints Eva as what appears to be "a store window mannequin, inexpressive, or perhaps inanimate, in the black man's arms." (The painting appears in a series entitled *Pornography*.) Mons, the ultimate puppet master, and Holzmann collaborate on some strange marionettes.

Because his mother had been an artist's model in Paris in the early 1930's, Mons paints a large canvas, divided into several paintings, entitled *The Adventures of a Young Model*, some of which depict her in the nude. He is inspired, says his biographer, by "disquieting fantasies and hypotheses." Emil does not look, however, for anything Oedipal in Mons's attraction to his models. Emil can also be an apologist, justifying Mons's attraction to prostitutes with reference to his nomadic life. Streetwalkers and brothel scenes appear frequently in his paintings. Mons is too complex for Emil to make such a banal suggestion as that the painter sees all his women as either mothers or whores.

Mons is not a total monster. Both he and Holzmann have relationships with Anne Kiefer, a young painter. After she is killed in a traffic accident, Mons destroys his nude paintings of her. Mons is haunted by the deaths of so many of his women. It seems significant that Verdugo, his mother's maiden name, is the name of the sword used to execute bulls in bullfights.

When Emil suggests that Mons change the title of the series *Women of My Life* to *Women of My Life and Art*, the painter replies that art is part of life. Mons creates paintings within paintings in part because of his "voyeuristic impulse." This same impulse, the need to experience a reality beyond oneself without becoming part of that reality, is central to the nature of art.

Mons is a mass of contradictions. He opposes interpreting his art, yet he agrees to illustrate a study of James Joyce's epiphanies by his friend Frank Reck. His art is his interpretation of reality as he perceives it: "Mons had the ability to make the most monstrous thing seem natural, the most truthful utterly absurd."

Monstruary is as much about literature as art. Not only is it full of references to literature, but Mons and Emil collaborate on a project inspired by Gustave Flaubert's unfinished *Bouvard et Pécuchet* (1881). They even imagine the characters exploring, on the Internet, the future of literature. In the course of his travels, Emil interviews Robert Coover and John Hawkes, both of whom write postmodernist fiction much like that of Ríos. In its linguistic playfulness, well communicated by translator Edith Grossman, *Monstruary* is reminiscent of the works of Vladimir Nabokov, and there are occasional echoes of his style: "My senior, my seniorita." Reviewers have also compared Ríos to writers such as Italo Calvino, G. Cabrera Infante (the subject of a 1974 study by Ríos), Georges Perec, Raymond Roussel, Arno Schmidt, and Italo Svevo. (The latter is discussed in the novel.)

The uncertainty of knowing anything definite about either art or human behavior is a major concern of *Monstruary*; thus, the novel ends with Mons's decision to begin his monster paintings again. Contemplating Reck's unfinished work on Joyce, Emil reflects that hypotheses about meaning lead only to doubts and further hypotheses. Ríos's fragmentary approach to Mons's sensibility reinforces this view, duplicating the "disconcerting and disconnected" images in the artist's monster paintings. Ríos illustrates how the truth about art or life can never be fully grasped. Such limitation need not, though Mons would disagree, hinder the quest for interpretation.

Michael Adams

Sources for Further Study

Booklist 97 (January 1-15, 2001): 920.
Library Journal 125 (December, 2000): 192.
Los Angeles Times Book Review, April 8, 2001, p. 4.
The New York Times Book Review 106 (March 18, 2001): 25.
Publishers Weekly 248 (January 15, 2001): 50.
The Washington Post Book World, March 25, 2001, p. 15.

MORAL FREEDOM
The Search for Virtue in a World of Choice

Author: Alan Wolfe (1942-   )
Publisher: W. W. Norton (New York). 256 pp. $24.95
Type of work: Current affairs, philosophy, and sociology

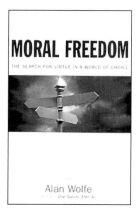

~

An interpretation of the results of interviews with Americans from a wide variety of geographical locations, arguing that while Americans have considered views of certain moral virtues, such views are held without the confidence that they are sustained by an overarching system of moral authority

~

Alan Wolfe, a sociologist and political scientist with a long and distinguished academic publication record, has become one of the United States' premier public intellectuals. Although his earlier works often had the technicality required in the learned professions, they focused on issues central to the "big" conversations: repression of dissent, the Soviet threat, the costs of economic growth, Richard J. Herrnstein and Charles Murray's controversial book *The Bell Curve* (1994), and the relation of moral inquiry in the social sciences. Typical of Wolfe's efforts is *The Human Difference: Animals, Computers, and the Necessity of Social Science* (1994). Directed mainly at the university set, the book examines such critical issues as artificial intelligence, ecology, and sociobiology. *Marginalized in the Middle* (1998) treats immigration, race relations, public education, pornography, and gender politics, all from the perspective of a pragmatic liberalism informed by a wealth of data and sociological theory. In *One Nation, After All: What Americans Really Think About God, Country, Family, Racism, Welfare, Immigration, Homosexuality, Work, The Right, The Left, and Each Other* (1998), Wolfe discusses his work with the "Middle Class Morality Project," an effort to go beyond polling by doing extensive interviews with small but representative groups of Americans. As the title indicates, Wolfe believes that despite the claims of writers who see this society as riven by profound divisions and "culture wars," a more on-the-ground approach reveals Americans as too tolerant and too responsible for such grand battles.

For over two decades, moral philosophers and theologians have paid close attention to matters of moral character and the virtues. In the face of what has seemed to many to be a steady degrading and "de-moralizing" of American culture, interest in Aristotle (384-322 B.C.E.), St. Thomas Aquinas (1224-1274), Josef Pieper (1904-1997) and other "virtue theorists" has intensified. The moral neutrality of public schools has raised the question anew of whether "character education" can be introduced without violating the separation of church and state. Wolfe's *Moral Freedom:*

Alan Wolfe is a professor of political science at Boston College. He is the author of a number of books, including Marginalized in the Middle *(1996) and* One Nation, After All *(1998), and is a contributing editor of* The New Republic *and* Wilson Quarterly.

The Search for Virtue in a World of Choice nicely reflects the state of progress of this discussion. His aim is to learn how Americans actually reflect on a key set of virtues: loyalty, honesty, self-discipline, and forgiveness. In this way, one can gauge both the impact of the academic discussions and the way Americans on their own have evolved "vernacular versions" of virtue theory.

His method is similar to the one used in *One Nation, After All*: Working with a team of eight assistants, he "conducted interviews with people chosen from eight distinct communities, each of which was presumed to represent a particular slice of American experience." The communities were the predominantly gay neighborhoods in San Francisco's Castro district; Atherton, California, a very wealthy Silicon Valley town; Lackland Air Force Base and environs in San Antonio, Texas, where many of the respondents are Mexican American; students from the University of North Carolina at Greensboro; Oakwood, Ohio, a prosperous suburb of Dayton; Tipton, Iowa, "a classic American small town," economically connected to agriculture; Blue Hills, an African American neighborhood in Hartford, Connecticut; and Fall River, Massachusetts, a struggling factory town attractive to recent immigrants. Wolfe also draws from a recent public opinion poll he helped design in cooperation with *The New York Times Magazine*, which probed attitudes on "sex, money, morality, work, children, identity, and God."

Wolfe's method of reporting on the huge volume of data collected here might be called "dialectical interpretation." Thoroughly aware of the long battles between libertarians, liberals, pragmatists, conservatives and neoconservatives, he uses this spectrum as a way to listen carefully to his respondents, most of whom have little awareness of its existence. He then discovers continuities, ironic correspondences, key lines of difference, multiple complexities. Put another way, Wolfe acts as an active moderator and interpreter of a virtual conversation about ethics. This populist method allows Wolfe to make several claims: that the severe polarities of opinion asserted by "culture war" thinkers are not very perceptible at the level of common moral discussion; neither the religious right nor the human-rights left (nor for that matter cultural libertarians) have been able to mobilize opinion in the way that many fear; and "virtue" is not a term Americans use very readily, but they are deeply concerned with right conduct and the practical implications of such matters as a company's loyalty to its employees and the local community.

In chapter 2, "Til Circumstances Do Us Part," Wolfe examines the views of his subject on loyalty, a virtue "presumed to have been lost in America." Yet, he usefully argues, loyalty is a feudal virtue which has never fit well in the highly individualist, competitive society of the United States. While Americans profess to cherish loyalty, they scorn those who do not display the drive to move up—which usually entails moving out. "Upwardly mobile" Americans often evince a secret hostility to those who stay in the same neighborhood and in the same job for most of their lives. Thus, "[d]espite their professions of loyalty, Americans are adept at designing institutions exceptionally adept at discouraging it. Corporations, professional sports teams, and universities reward those most willing to move elsewhere." Accordingly, Wolfe's respondents have evolved a kind of situation ethics when it comes to loyalty in the workplace. Knowing that they cannot count on large enterprises to be loyal to them in any final sense, aware that in order to benefit their families and themselves they must be prepared to quit their jobs, they extend tentative and conditional loyalties to their employers. Surprisingly, Wolfe does not discuss the role of labor unions in providing workers with the security they require to offer more loyalty to the company.

In "Eat Dessert First," Wolfe examines the virtue of self-control, oddly failing to mention its classical name, temperance. Rather, he sets his inquiry against the background of Victorianism. Here he follows the conservative historian Gertrude Himmelfarb, who has argued that nineteenth century Americans took over that moral code almost completely: "Work, thrift, temperance, fidelity, self-reliance, self-discipline, cleanliness, godliness—these were the preeminent Victorian virtues, almost universally accepted as such even when they were violated in practice." Coupled with this moral scheme was the notion that because humans were naturally prone to sin (shortsightedness, egoism, pride, sloth), they require strong institutions to form them in such virtues. Many of those interviewed by Wolfe believe that America has lost all contact with this older wisdom. They worry about permissiveness and shallowness in schools, churches, and families. Consumerism frightens them because not only does it preach an implicit ethic of self-indulgence, it multiplies wants through advertising and ever-more-alluring products. Thus, anyone trying to exercise moderation is involved in "a life and death struggle." The only organizations that support self-sacrifice are military or monastic.

At the same time, Americans believe that self-control can be taken too far. Many speak up for a regime of moderate self-indulgence, implicitly rejecting the Victorian model. They are more inclined to see their fellow citizens as basically good and therefore capable of handling the temptations that come with freedom. They are critical of workaholism and feel that "self-discipline can paradoxically also be a form of self-indulgence, because the highly disciplined person gets that way only by putting his or her needs ahead of others." In this context, the criticism that Americans have rejected the Victorian inheritance by becoming too tolerant and too nonjudgmental needs to be carefully assessed, claims Wolfe. What appears to be toleration bordering on indifference may stem from both egalitarianism and the Christian virtue of humility. Also influential is psychology, which encourages Americans to speak not of character flaws but of "disorders," over which the individual has little or no power.

In this area, Wolfe again defends the common man. America is not an heroic society. Temptations are not those faced by Faust or Greek warriors, so when contemporary Americans "talk of self-discipline and self-indulgence, they think of consumer goods, not God and Satan." While less dramatic, the choices are sufficient "to cause a certain moral vertigo." In this context, Americans should not be too harsh on those who yield to temptations (including drugs), but rather "emphasize the strength it takes to resist any temptations at all."

In succeeding chapters, Wolfe continues to build a picture of America's often improvised morality, its mixture of sources, and the immense complexity of moral situations. Chapter 4, "Honesty, to a Point," stresses that while Americans ardently praise this virtue, few of them are inclined to make it—as did Immanuel Kant—into an absolute. So distrustful are Americans of large, impersonal institutions that many practice a double standard when it comes to truth-telling.

As for politics, Wolfe depicts Americans as realists (rather than cynics), for they recognize that politicians—especially those who serve very diverse constituents—face uniquely difficult challenges to the virtue of honesty. In contrast, they know that business people operate in a quite different moral environment, where honesty is usually the best policy. In a capitalist system, consistent dishonesty normally dooms a firm to extinction. On the personal level, "brutal honesty" in personal relations can be very hurtful and thus should be avoided. Thus, "Americans treat honesty in functional terms. To them honesty is the best policy precisely because it is a policy, something we manage for the sake of getting along somewhat better in the world—and something we can change when circumstances demand a new one."

Wolfe's concluding chapters, "The Moral Philosophy of the Americans" and "The Strange Idea of Moral Freedom" try to sharpen Americans' sense of the historical uniqueness of their moral situation. The intense pragmatism and individualism of Americans means that few surrender themselves to a single system of moral or religious authority. Living in a radically pluralistic society, they are of course free to become Muslims or strict Catholics or cult members. If they do, however, everything around them reminds them that they chose such a course; thus, rather than knowing that Islam, for example, is simply "the way things are," they must let their faith operate in a multifaith environment. Put another way, ultimate moral authority is lodged in the individual.

Wolfe knows that such a stance—spread to an entire society—represents a radical departure. He argues that the old liberal tradition established by John Locke, Thomas Jefferson, John Stuart Mill, and Friedrich Hayek called for much moral restraint and self-discipline. America has gone far beyond this heritage. The impact of Sigmund Freud, Norman O. Brown, Herbert Marcuse, Charles Reich, Michel Foucault, and the self-actualization schools of psychology have brought self-discipline itself under suspicion. Potent too have been the women's movement and gay liberation. This does not mean that the real moral majority tends toward libertinism, anarchy, separatism, or decadence. It does mean that the range of lifestyle models has vastly increased, putting unimaginable pressures on individuals. So far, Americans have on the whole coped well with this new, "inevitable," and "impossible" condition of moral freedom, integrating it into their preexisting skepticism and pragmatism. What the future holds is, however, anyone's guess.

Useful and often profound, Alan Wolfe's *Moral Freedom* will exasperate and puzzle many readers. The alarming last chapter offers a thesis that should have been enunciated at the beginning. The suspicion that it might have been a late addition is reinforced by the singular fact that the subtitle printed on the dust jacket ("The Search for Virtue in a World of Choice") is different from the one on the title page: "The Im-

possible Idea That Defines the Way We Live Now." Further, Wolfe's entire method-
ology is based on a questionable notion about pluralism. Examining "public opinion"
geographically, he overlooks the fact that the Christians, Jews, New Agers, and secu-
larists in each group of interviewees may have much more in common with one another than with each other as "Americans." Catholics, Jews, and Muslims operate
within very different (if related) narratives—and these narratives may have little to do
with the abstraction called "main-stream American moral opinion." Finally, advo-
cates of a virtue/character approach to morality will note that Wolfe has nothing to
say about the role of habit and formation in the virtues. They will rightly wonder why
the classical virtues of courage, temperance, wisdom, and justice receive scant attention in the book.

Leslie E. Gerber

Sources for Further Study

Booklist 97 (March 1, 2001): 1209.
Commentary 111 (May, 2001): 61.
Library Journal 126 (April 15, 2001): 98.
The New York Times Book Review 106 (April 8, 2001): 14.
Publishers Weekly 248 (March 19, 2001): 88.

MOTHER JONES
The Most Dangerous Woman in America

Author: Elliott J. Gorn (1951-   )
Publisher: Hill and Wang/Farrar, Straus and Giroux
   (New York). Illustrated. 408 pp. $27.00
Type of work: Biography
Time: 1837-1930
Locale: The United States and Mexico

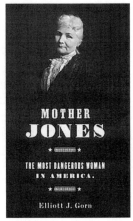

~

A well-researched biography of the grand old lady of the labor movement, an Irish immigrant who devoted her later years to organizing poor and dispossessed workers in harsh conditions

~

Principal personage:
   MARY HARRIS ("MOTHER") JONES, an early U.S. labor organizer

To most twenty-first century readers, the name "Mother Jones" refers to a magazine, if it means anything at all. In the early part of the twentieth century, however, the name Mother Jones was well-known and beloved by the laboring class, and well-known and reviled by many corporate capitalists and government officials. Elliott J. Gorn's book brings alive the life and times of the elderly woman who transcended societal expectations for her gender and class and became an early and influential labor radical.

Mother Jones began life as Mary Harris, second child in a poor family in County Cork, Ireland. As the potato famine that began in Ireland in 1845 spread and worsened, her family joined tens of thousands of others who journeyed on the "death ships" to the United States and Canada. Although they became United States citizens, the Harris family lived mostly in Toronto, which was known as the Belfast of North America for the hostility the majority Protestants showed toward the poor Irish Catholic immigrants. Mary went to normal school (teachers' college), where she was one of only a few Irish students. In her early twenties, she moved to the United States and taught briefly in Michigan, moved to Chicago, where she worked as a dressmaker, then moved to Memphis, Tennessee, to teach again. There, she married George Jones, a member of the International Iron Molders Union, in 1861. They had four children in five years, but George and the children died in the yellow fever epidemic that decimated Memphis in 1867.

Few details of Mary Harris Jones's life in the next decades are known. It appears that she spent several years in California and perhaps even traveled to Europe. For reasons lost to history, Mary Harris became radicalized and reinvented herself in the persona of Mother Jones around the turn of the century. There had been another public figure known by that name in the 1880's—the editor of the Ladies Department of

the *Railroad Brakemen's Journal*. By the end of
the decade, that Mother Jones had disappeared
from the public eye.

The new Mother Jones did not confine herself
to writing poetry and articles for wives of railroad men. She spent the last decades of her life
recruiting union members, especially in the coal
mines, advocating for socialist and other radical
causes, electrifying crowds with her speeches,
organizing marches and demonstrations, and
challenging corporate capitalists and government
leaders on issues of social injustice.

Although her autobiography claims that Mother
Jones first "appeared" in 1877, and at times she
claimed to have been an activist even earlier,
there is no outside confirmation of that persona

∼

*Elliott Gorn was born in Los Angeles
in 1951. After undergraduate work
at the University of California,
Berkeley, he received his Ph.D. in
history at Yale. He taught at Miami
University in Oxford, Ohio, then
joined the faculty at Purdue
University in 1998. Gorn specializes
in nineteenth and twentieth century
U.S. social and cultural history and
has published books on sports,
education, and the history of
violence.*

∼

prior to the 1890's. The first newspaper mention of Mary Jones's involvement in a la-
bor action was with Coxey's Army in 1894; the first newspaper reference to her as
Mother Jones came in a *Chicago Evening Journal* article on the American Railway
Union convention in June 1897.

Coxey's Army was a group of unemployed men who were marching from the Midwest to Washington, D.C., to petition the government to create jobs for the unemployed. Although the marchers were utterly unsuccessful, Mary Jones provided an effective and inspiring support system, giving speeches, raising money and collecting
food, bolstering morale, and—perhaps most important—bringing the men and their
cause to the attention of the public. Mary Jones had found her calling and spent most
of the rest of her life on the road.

Mary Jones's new persona involved not just a new name but a unique identity. To
make herself seem even more grandmotherly, Mary Harris made her Mother Jones
persona several years older than she really was; to reinforce her solidarity with the labor movement, she claimed her birthday was May 1, which had been the international
worker's holiday since 1886. While she always wore old-fashioned, long, black
dresses and had her white hair in a grandmotherly bun, her speeches were laced with
profanities (although mild by today's standards) and she was more than happy to join
the men in a beer or whiskey, enlivening gatherings with off-color jokes and diatribes
against the industrial robber barons. Her appearance often enabled her to enter areas
where she had been banned; as she said in her autobiography, she could slip past soldiers because she looked like "just an old woman going to a missionary meeting to
knit mittens for the heathens of Africa." Strong and unfazed by physical challenges,
she hiked through the hills to coal miners' camps to organize the men, slept wherever
a family could put her up, and was arrested more than once.

As a women, she could not move up in the male hierarchy of the socialist or labor
movements, but as Mother Jones she commanded the hearts and admiration of the
workers, which gave her power she could not have achieved as Mary Jones. Strikes

and labor disputes in which she was an important factor included those of coal miners in Colorado, Pennsylvania, and West Virginia, weavers in Pennsylvania and New Jersey, textile workers in Philadelphia and Alabama, garment workers in New York, brewers in Milwaukee, copper miners in Arizona, and telegraphers in Chicago. She was also involved with the Mexican Revolution and worked for the release of labor leaders jailed in the United States.

Mother Jones was especially successful in involving women and children in labor actions. Some of her marches included small children carrying signs such as "We want to go to school, not to the mines." She organized women not only to join in marches and serve food to strikers, but also to form "mop and broom brigades" to harass strikebreakers and to challenge the mine owners' hired guards and even government troops. Although a working woman, she encouraged women to stay home and raise their children, which she had done herself before her children's deaths. She believed that even the poorest children should be educated, not forced into lives of near-slavery in mines or mills. She appealed to men to prove they were "real men" by joining the union and agitating for decent wages so their families would not be trapped in low-paying, dangerous jobs. She often contrasted the harsh lives of laborers' children with those of the children of the mine owners and even the owners' pampered dogs. She compared the laboring class to slaves of the previous century and was especially flattered when she was compared to John Brown, who was killed for his role as an abolitionist. From her earliest days of organizing, she argued for association based on class, discounting race, religion, and nationality.

Mother Jones was employed for many years by the United Mine Workers (UMW) as a "walking delegate" (an organizer); in 1901, her annual salary was around one thousand dollars, about half that of the union's president. After leaving the United Mine Workers in 1905, she worked as a speaker for the Socialist Party. Tired of the growing middle-class orientation of the Socialists, she left her job with the party in 1912, although she continued to believe in the tenets of socialism. Typically, Mother Jones was more radical and inclined toward socialism than the bureaucrats of the organized labor movement. Such differences often caused friction between her and the union officers, but she continued to be supportive of them until the ascension of John L. Lewis to the presidency of the UMW. Unlike early union leaders, who came from the ranks, worked for a time as organizers, and often returned to the mines, Lewis was solidly middle class and had little, if anything, in common with the men he was to represent.

Mother Jones was briefly associated with the International Workers of the World (IWW), commonly knows as the Wobblies. She was the only woman of the twenty-three original signers of the manifesto calling for all industrial workers to gather into a single union. The class-based focus of the Wobblies was clearly aligned with Mother Jones's ideals; however, she apparently attended only the first two meetings of the group, seldom discussed it, and did not even mention her involvement in her autobiography. Her quick disaffection for the Wobblies probably resulted from their emphasis on utopian ideals over small, practical gains, their tolerance of violence as a means, their increasing factionalization, and the fact that they targeted single men rather than families.

To Mother Jones, the labor movement encompassed religious, political, and especially family values. In her view, the love of the mother bound a family together, and women's inborn maternal feelings should lead naturally to their supporting the union and encouraging their men to join it. As each family was bound up by the love of its mother, the great family of the union was cemented by the love of Mother Jones for her union "children." While she maintained a maternal demeanor, accepted the sentimentally phrased admiration of her followers, and was even compared to Christ at times, she preferred to be thought of as a hell-raiser than a saint. She scoffed at the clergy's lack of commitment to the cause of laborers and was heard to say that it was better to swear than pray.

Her outspoken beliefs and willingness to incite laborers to rise up against their employers brought Mother Jones powerful enemies and negative publicity. One particularly vitriolic attack against her was written by Denver journalist Leonel Ross Campbell under the pseudonym "Polly Pry," published in the antilabor magazine of the same name. In a 1904 article, Polly Pry implied that in the late 1880's, Mother Jones had been known as Mother Harris and run a notorious brothel and gambling house in Denver. Mother Harris, according to the article, took to drink, was arrested several times, lost her business, and went to work in other brothels. Oddly, neither Mother Jones nor many of her closest supporters emphatically denied the charges, although there was never any corroborating evidence to support Polly Pry's story.

As her health failed in the 1920's, Mother Jones was forced to give up her life on the road. During the last decade of her life she wrote an autobiography, but it is as notable for what it leaves out as what it tells. For example, only four pages discuss her personal life before she became involved in the labor movement in her fifties; she does not even mention the names of her four siblings or her four children, nor when her parents died. Her autobiography was of Mother Jones, not of Mary Harris Jones. Even as the story of Mother Jones, it had many omissions, exaggerated some aspects of her life and downplayed others, and often contradicted known facts.

Gorn's book is meticulously researched, with one-quarter of its pages devoted to detailed notes. His sources include not only those that support his theses, but also writers with opposing views. Gorn fills in many of the autobiography's omissions and clarifies much of the sometimes simplistic, sometimes dishonest, information Mother Jones dictated to a friend when her health had failed too much for her to continue her work. The wealth of historical, political, and sociological details make this book valuable not only as a lively biography of a feisty and astonishing woman but also as a treatise on the lives of the common laborers of the time.

Irene Struthers Rush

Sources for Further Study

Booklist 97 (March 15, 2001): 1337.
Library Journal 126 (February 15, 2001): 176.
Mother Jones 26 (March, 2001): 75.

MULLAHS ON THE MAINFRAME
Islam and Modernity Among the Daudi Bohras

Author: Jonah Blank
Publisher: University of Chicago Press (Chicago).
  408 pp. $40.00
Type of work: Religion, anthropology, and current affairs
Time: The late 1990's
Locale: The state of Gujarat and city of Bombay, India,
  and other locales around the globe

~

A young anthropologist and journalist explores the little-known global community of Daudi Bohras, a group of Shia Ismaili Muslims who have consciously chosen to accommodate themselves to selected aspects of modernity while simultaneously reviving their interpretation of Islamic faith

~

In *Mullahs on the Mainframe: Islam and Modernity Among the Daudi Bohras*, Jonah Blank has produced a scrupulously researched and impressively detailed account of the Daudi Bohras, a fascinating and relatively unknown religious community. In doing so, Blank does much more than simply reveal the lives of his subjects. He also undermines inaccurate (and often unkind) stereotypes of Islam and raises issues crucial to the enterprise of organized religion in general, particularly in a world that has passed from the challenging shores of modernity to the positively daunting uncharted seas of postmodernity.

The first half of Blank's study is ethnographic in nature. Blank begins with a rapid-fire history of Islam and the place of the Daudi Bohras in the overall Islamic world. Like other major religions, Islam has fallen prey to schism upon schism. The first major division came soon after Islam's birth in the seventh century C.E.. It involved the controversy over the issue of succession after the death of the prophet Muhammad. Sunni Muslims accepted the authority of the first four caliphs (rulers) following Muhammad. They do not believe that there is a direct link back to the prophet in matters of theology and conduct. They believe, instead, that religious guidance is available to all Muslims through al-Qur'an (the Koran) and the example of the prophet himself. Shia Muslims believe that Ali, the son-in-law of Muhammad, was the prophet's chosen successor, and also that spiritual authority has been passed directly down from Ali through a chain of imams (and their lieutenants) right down to the present. Shia Muslims also believe in the authority of al-Qur'an, but believe that the text and other Islamic laws and directives must be mediated by legitimately chosen spiritual leaders. The Daudi Bohras are Shia Muslims. This alone would make them a relatively small minority among the hundreds of millions of Muslims around the globe, but

Shia Muslims have also experienced episodes of schism. The group studied by Blank constitutes only about one million or so members and is properly designated, according to the World Wide Web site of BOHRA TV, as Shi'a Fatimi Ismaili Tayyibi Daudi Bohra Muslims. Their spiritual leader is the Dai al-Mutlaq. The Dai at the time of Blank's study was Syedna Muhammad Burhannuddin (the title "Syedna Muhammad" meaning "descendant of Muhammad").

Geographically, the largest group of Daudi Bohras are to be found in west central India, in the state of Gujarat and nearby city of Mumbai (formerly Bombay). Blank did field work in both these areas as well as in Karachi, where there is also a sizable Bohra community. Bohras are not limited to South Asia, however. They can be found in well over four hundred communities spread across forty nations. This includes the New York City metropolitan area, where Blank attended a series of lectures given by the Syedna and also interviewed some of the locals.

Jonah Blank is a trained anthropologist who has worked as a news correspondent in India and Pakistan, and also served as a policy advisor on South Asia for the U.S. Senate Foreign Relations Committee. He is the author of Arrow of the Blue-Skinned God: Retracing the Ramayana Through India *(1992).*

The heart of Blank's ethnographic chapters examines the rituals, domestic life, and role of the royalty among the Daudi Bohras, comparing their practices to those of other Muslims as well as non-Muslim Indians. Among the most crucial rituals, and one unique to the Daudi Bohras, is *Mithaq* (often transliterated as "misaq"). *Mithaq* is a requirement for membership in the Daudi Bohra community. The ceremony establishes a covenant between the believer and Allah (God) in which the initiate accepts the obligations placed on one by Allah as well the authority of the Syedna as spiritual guide. *Mithaq* is also seen as a rite of passage to adulthood. Thirteen is a common age for *Mithaq* to take place for girls, fourteen or fifteen for boys. Blank also reviews, in detail, Daudi Bohra rituals regarding marriage, divorce, and death. In addition to these life-stage rituals, Blank catalogues and describes rituals of the Daudi Bohra year, including an especially memorable account of Bohra observance of *Ashura*, a day of atonement in memory of the martyrdom of Imam Husain at Kerbal in the year 680 C.E. Reporting as a participant observer, Blank describes a ceremony of great passion and devotion, featuring a day long fast, marathon kneeling sessions, and the passionate beating of chests. Both as an observer and participant, Blank seems to be truly moved. Blank's account of the Daudi Bohra "royals" is more detached. The administrative, political, and spiritual duties of the Daudi Bohra are carried out by an elite few drawn largely from the Dai's own kin. While this arrangement is a source of some dissent among the Daudi Bohras, as well as criticism from outside the community, Blank is able to locate very little in the way of royal privilege or perks. The royals are economically middle-class and provide important community services.

Overall, Blank's research reveals a flourishing, globally integrated community of believers, one held together by a conscious strategy of cultivating traditional values while employing selected aspects of modernity. More specifically, modern transportation is utilized to allow the Dai to make regular appearances at Daudi Bohra communities around the world, e-mail is used to create an instant communications network uniting geographically disparate groups, and Daudi Bohras, already oriented toward commerce, have been pioneers in the postindustrial information-oriented economy (thus the book's title).

In the second half of Blank's book, he analyzes the maintenance of spiritual and political hegemony among the Daudi Bohras, the specifics of their "orthopraxy" (in terms of dress and economics), their approach to education, and the presence of dissent in the Daudi Bohra community. By "hegemony," Blank means the fact that the Daudi Bohras are subject to central control by the Dai in all matters spiritual and political. This is not to say that the Daudi Bohras are totalitarian or essentially coercive. There is a wide variation of compliance among Daudi Bohras, ranging from seemingly complete devotion to a certain casual minimum. While this minimum, nominal acceptance of the Dai's authority on all matters spiritual and secular sounds ominous, in practice, Daudi Bohras have broad latitude in expressing their faith and making key life choices. In addition, as a tiny minority of the population where ever they happen to be, Daudi Bohras have no (or, at best, very limited) tools for compelling compliance. That said, Blank finds that the hegemonic relationship between elite and followers has played an important role in allowing the Daudi Bohras to flourish during the last third or so of the twentieth century and the beginning of the twenty-first. The revitalization of tradition and strategic, selective embrace of modernity is part of a top-down campaign to perpetuate and strengthen the Daudi Bohra community. Indeed, Blank associates the success of this campaign with the hegemonic aspects of Daudi Bohra social organization. This campaign includes promotion of a dress code (including full beards for men), particularly at public observances; community taxes and interest-free banks; and a system of education based equally on spiritual and secular goals. As idyllic as this might sound, there are dissenters among the Daudi Bohra community. Dissenters object to the monopoly on power held by the royals, the practice of excommunication, and the extension to the Dai of absolute authority over secular matters (they accept this authority on spiritual matters). While Blank attempts to treat these concerns even-handedly, it is clear that he does not take the alleged offenses as seriously as the dissenters themselves, especially since dissenters are perfectly free to establish their own separate orthopraxy.

Blank concludes his book with some lessons to be drawn from the Daudi Bohra experience. As suggested, he sees advantages to the centralized system of authority maintained by the Daudi Bohras. This characteristic has helped to bind Daudi Bohras all over the world into a coherent religious community. At the same time, he believes that flexibility, also, is a crucial factor in explaining the success of the Daudi Bohras: flexibility in accepting different levels of orthopraxy, a broad variety of local customs, and selective embrace of modernity.

Blank also has a larger lesson in mind. He wishes to disabuse his readers of any misconceptions they may have about the nature and dictates of Islam. Specifically, Blank refers to Samuel Huntingdon's 1996 book *The Clash of Civilizations and Remaking of the World Order* as an example of a text suggesting the incompatibility of

Islam with "western" values. In answer, Blank presents the Daudi Bohras: Muslims who have showed that they can deal quite pragmatically and wisely with "western" values. Moreover, Blank makes it clear that the Daudi Bohras are only one example of the rich diversity represented by Islam. Put simply, there is no excuse for identifying the whole or even the essence of Islam with political violence, religious intolerance, or irrational reactionism against economic and technological innovation.

On this last point and throughout the book, Blank is most convincing. His research is methodologically sound, employing direct observation, multiple interviews, case studies, and survey research (both his own and that of other scholars). He is modest in his claims and backs up what he does assert with empirical evidence. In short, Blank maintains an air of detachment appropriate for a scholar as well as a top-notch journalist.

This is not to say that the book is flawless or as reflective as it might be. Though he does make use of a few fascinating case studies, Blank predominantly relies on abstract analysis and statistics. This makes his presentation less colorful and perhaps even less profound than it might have been. Then, too, being an anthropologist and journalist rather than a philosopher, Blank does not explore some of the more esoteric issues raised by his study. What, for instance, is the future of faith in a postmodern world where all values seem to be turning to quicksand? Are the Daudi Bohras fighting a holding action, or does their experience promise a brighter future for all who are concerned with the maintenance of ethical values in a nihilistic world? No matter, readers who are so inclined can explore these questions on their own. They will do so better armed by Blank's well-written and thoroughly informative account of the Daudi Bohras.

Ira Smolensky

Sources for Further Study

Library Journal 126 (May 1, 2001): 90.
The Washington Post Book World, August 12, 2001, p. 4.

MY DREAM OF YOU

Author: Nuala O'Faolain (c. 1942-   )
Publisher: Riverhead Books (New York). 500 pp. $29.95
Type of work: Novel
Time: The late 1990's and the 1840's and 1850's
Locale: Ireland; London, England; many resort locations

~

*The story of an independent Irish journalist, encom-
passing a novella about a love affair between an English-
woman and an Irish servant during the Great Famine*

~

Principal characters:
> KATHLEEN DE BURCA (BURKE), an Irish writer nearing fifty years of age
> SEAMUS "SHAY" MURPHY, a middle-aged Irish gardener living in En-
> gland
> NAN LEECH, a spinster in her seventies, the librarian in Ballygall, Ireland
> BERTIE, proprietor of the Talbot Arms in Ballygall
> DANNY and ANNIE, Kathleen's brother and sister-in-law
> MARIANNE MCCAUSLAND TALBOT, a young English bride transplanted
> to the west of Ireland about 1848
> RICHARD TALBOT, Marianne's husband
> WILLIAM MULLAN, a servant on the Talbot estate

Kathleen de Burca is an Irish expatriate in England, working as a travel writer. The second of four living children in a strict Roman Catholic family, she was raised near the small town of Kilcrennan, Ireland, by a depressed, intimidated mother and an autocratic, English-hating father who was home only on weekends. Estranged from her family and enraged by the lack of freedom for Irish women, she leaves Ireland at the age of twenty, vowing never to set foot on Irish soil again. She does not even return for the funerals of her baby brother or either of her parents.

Shortly after moving to London, Kathleen has a love affair with an English student, Hugo, who throws her out of their apartment when he learns that she has been unfaithful many times. She moves in with a wealthy acquaintance, Caroline, but they become estranged when Caroline falls in love with a heartless and controlling man. By now a writer for a travel magazine, Kathleen rents a small basement flat, from which she regularly travels to vacation spots for her magazine. Although she lives there for many years, it is less of a home than a convenient rest stop between trips. Eschewing commitment and responsibility, she has little communication with her relatives and looks to Alex, her editor, and Jimmy, the magazine's other writer, as her surrogate family. Jimmy and Alex, like Kathleen, have no permanent partners—Alex still lives with his mother and Jimmy has a series of male lovers. Jimmy and Kathleen are more like sister and brother than coworkers. Kathleen even spends holidays with Jimmy and his family in Nebraska, rather than with her sister Nora in New York or her brother Danny and his family, who still live in Kilcrennan, on the farm of their late uncle, Ned. Kathleen's romantic life comprises a series of sexual encounters with strangers she meets on her many trips. Even her career choice reflects her inability to make a commitment; not only does it prevent her from being in one place for any length of time, but travel writing, she says, is the only kind of journalism that does not require belief in anything.

Nuala O'Faolain is one of nine children born in north Dublin, Ireland, to an Irish journalist and his wife. After attending University College, Dublin, she obtained her Ph.D. in medieval literature from University of Hull. She has lectured at university; been a columnist for the Irish Times *for many years; and produced and announced for Radio Telefís Éireann in Ireland. Her first book was* Are You Somebody? The Accidental Memoir of a Dublin Woman *(1998).* My Dream of You *is her first novel.*

Approaching fifty, Kathleen decides to leave the magazine, but with little idea of what to do next. About the same time, Jimmy dies of a heart attack. Having let go of her job and having lost her dearest friend, she gives up her flat, cutting herself loose from England. A legal document from the 1850's, which she has kept since her days with Hugo, inspires her to make a brief trip back to Ireland to do research for a possible book.

The legal document involves the divorce proceedings brought by Richard Talbot against his young wife, Marianne, in which Richard alleges that she has had a long affair with William Mullan, an Irish groom at their mansion, Mount Talbot. The proceedings contain testimony from several servants who claim to have observed familiar conduct between the two. Kathleen is intrigued by the life that would have awaited a young, well-bred English woman transplanted to the desolate west coast of Ireland during the Great Famine, and fascinated by what could have compelled her to have an affair with a servant. Her own life has been ruled by the search for passion, so much so that she cannot imagine how long-married couples can make love. "What's it for, lovemaking, if you love each other already? . . . I couldn't imagine sex that wasn't trying to find something out—that wasn't a venture, an exploration." Still, she cannot argue when Jimmy says she idealizes marriage—she replies "it was no less than a miracle that two separate persons sometimes work side by side, for shared goals, in mutual affection."

Kathleen was raised in a family where her father spoke Irish and reviled the English. Nevertheless, she has spent most of her life living among "the enemy," although she often felt alienated from them and looked down on by them. In England, she went by "Burke," the anglicized form of her last name, de Burca. Her feelings of inferiority begin to heal in Ireland, where she is welcomed as a native daughter come home and comforted by the warmth of the people she encounters. The first is Bertie, who runs the Talbot Arms, the hotel that becomes her home base while she is in Ireland. A widower who relates lovingly to his daughter and her two small sons, Bertie provides a stark contrast to Kathleen's autocratic and distant father. Bertie introduces her to Nan Leech, the town's librarian, who helps Kathleen learn about the tragic lives of the area's natives during the Great Famine, although she disapproves of Kathleen's fascination with the adulterous couple. Ultimately, the two unmarried women develop a strong bond despite their great differences in outlook and behavior.

Leaving Bertie's hotel for a few days, Kathleen meets Shay, an Irishman who also has lived in England his whole adult life. Shay, a gardener, comes to Ireland regularly to help his father in Sligo with his business; his English wife prefers to remain at home with their daughters and grandchildren, who live nearby. To Shay, Kathleen is glamorous and beautiful, although she thinks of herself as plain and unlovable and constantly criticizes her middle-aged body and face. Kathleen follows her usual pattern with men, letting Shay come back to her place and spend the night, but is surprised to find him unlike other men she has been with. Shay, in fact, is the first Irish man with whom she has ever had a sexual relationship. With him, she feels a sense of domestic contentment that is quite unfamiliar, and she is devastated when he leaves the next day. She consoles herself by writing the first part of a book about Marianne Talbot and William Mullan, indulging herself by creating a story of great passion.

The story of Marianne and William had some parallels with her own—Marianne was an expatriate in Ireland, as Kathleen was in England—but Marianne also had much in common with Kathleen's mother, in that both women were powerless in their husbands' homes. More of Kathleen's background is revealed as she digs for facts about Marianne and William and contemplates parts of her own life that she has refused to think about for years, including the cause of her mother's death, the effect her leaving had on her two younger brothers, her infidelities while living with Hugo, her relationships with Jimmy and Alex, and her brief flirtation with her friend Caroline's husband, Ian.

In researching the love story, Kathleen also comes to a deeper understanding of Ireland's Great Famine. Her trips to the bucolic countryside are marred by the telltale signs of those who had lived and died in the bogs just outside Mount Talbot. Through Miss Leech and others, Kathleen begins to comprehend the enormity of the tragedy of the Famine and how it shaped the lives of not only those who emigrated but also the survivors who remained in Ireland. She weaves the privations of the sick and starving Irish living outside the mansions into her love story.

Miss Leech, through a young library student in Dublin, brings Kathleen a new document relating to the divorce proceedings of Marianne and Richard. Written by John Paget, an English gentleman who had visited Marianne and Richard in Ireland, it argued that Marianne never had a relationship with William, but was kept captive and nearly starved by her husband, perhaps raped by an English friend of theirs, and framed so that her husband could divorce her and marry someone who might give him a son. This new evidence does not fit in with Kathleen's vision of a woman compelled by passion to abandon herself and risk ostracism for her love. In subtle ways, her new information about the case, combined with the influence of her new Irish friends, begins to alter the way she sees herself, her dreams for herself, and her feelings about her family.

Her sporadic relationship with Shay begins to grow. He pleads with Kathleen to accept a limited relationship, and she fears that he may her last chance at love or even passion. However, she realizes that all he can offer her is a life of waiting for his next visit. Torn between the desire to settle for what she knows and a yearning for a new, unknown future, Kathleen retreats to an isolated cottage.

My Dream of You is the first novel of well-known Irish journalist Nuala O'Faolain. Part mystery, part history, part coming-of-a-certain-age story, the novel weaves together four stories: Kathleen's current life; her reflections on her past life and family relationships; the actual divorce case of Richard and Marianne Talbot; and "The Talbot Book," the internal novella that contains Kathleen's fictionalized account of the affair. The Talbot story is based on an real divorce case, and sections of the actual documents are scattered throughout the book.

The protagonist, Kathleen, has several similarities to the author. Readers of O'Faolain's 1996 memoir *Are You Somebody?* will find many of the themes she explored there revisited in her first novel—anger at the English repression of the Irish, mixed equally with anger at Ireland's societal repression of women; the search for love clashing with the need for independence; the struggles of an intellectual and talented woman to fashion a satisfying life. O'Faolain's evocative writing brings alive the Irish countryside and the lives of her real and imagined characters. Despite Kathleen's (and the author's) youthful anger at her homeland, her lyrical descriptions of the land and landscape are a love song to the beauty of Ireland.

Irene Struthers Rush

Sources for Further Study

Europe, May, 2001, p. 48.
Publishers Weekly 248 (March 12, 2001): 58.
San Francisco Chronicle, March 21, 2001, p. C2.
The Washington Post Book World, March 25, 2001, p. 4.

MY NAME IS RED

Author: Orhan Pamuk (1952-   )
First published: Benim Adim Kirmizi, 1998, in Turkey
Translated from the Turkish by Erdağ M. Göknar
Publisher: Alfred A. Knopf (New York). 438 pp. $25.95
Type of work: Novel
Time: 1591
Locale: Istanbul

≈

*Part murder mystery, part sexy romance, but mostly an
engaging meditation on the clash of Eastern and Western
artistic traditions*

≈

Principal characters:
> BLACK, former miniaturist who returns from wars hoping to marry his
> cousin, Shekure, whom he has long loved
> SHEKURE, widowed daughter of Enishte Effendi, and Black's cousin
> HAZAN, her brother-in-law and ardent suitor
> ELEGANT EFFENDI, the sultan's gilder, whose murder opens the novel
> ENISHTE EFFENDI, Shekure's father and Black's uncle, in charge of pre-
> paring a secret manuscript for the Sultan, in the style of Western art-
> ists
> MASTER OSMAN, Enishte's rival in the Sultan's court
> STORK, OLIVE, and BUTTERFLY, the Sultan's three miniaturists and
> prime murder suspects
> ESTHER, the silks peddler and go-between for Black, Shekure, and Hazan
> ORHAN and SHEVKET, Shekure's two children
> STORYTELLER, never named or introduced except through the objects he
> gives voice to
> HUSRET, Hoja of Erzuumi, fundamentalist preacher whose followers
> threaten the miniaturists

That *My Name Is Red* is mostly about a character called Black (like the ink on this page) is the kind of irony that characterizes this whole novel, a murder mystery in the manner of Umberto Eco's *Il nome della rosa* (1980; *Name of the Rose*, 1984). Like that book, this is a murder mystery set within a very confined group, not of monks this time, but miniaturists. These painters and craftsmen work for the Ottoman sultan Murad III, illustrating the manuscripts that glorify his victories and rule. Pamuk supplies ample history, as well as a chronology in the back of the book, so the reader knows that 1591 was a twilight period for miniaturists. Murad III was a munificent patron of their art, especially after the empire entered a period of extended peace. However, the golden glow of the era comes from the sun setting on an artistic tradition that had spread, along with the precious secret of red ink, from China across Central

Asia to Turkey over the course of many centuries and countless wars.

Now the miniaturists' traditions are under attack, and murder is the least of their problems. They are a doomed lot, and the book provides a "melancholy elegy to the inspiration, talent, and patience of all the masters who'd painted and illuminated in these lands over the years."

All depictions of humans and animals are considered suspect throughout the Muslim world, which accounts for the primacy of abstract ornamentation in Arabic and Islamic art. In 1591, miniaturists were warned by fundamentalists that on Judgment Day they would be expected to bring their creations to life—or face eternal damnation for challenging the supremacy of Allah's creation. These artists, whose art had roots in China and Persia, tried to rationalize illustration as a development of calligraphy and ornamentation, arguing that "images are the story's blossoming in color." Objects and people are stylized. There is no attempt to depict individuals, they claim, but universals, not people or horses as the artist sees them, but as they are in the mind of Allah.

One of Europe's most prominent novelists, Turkish writer Orhan Pamuk is the author of several novels, including The New Life *(1997) and* The White Castle *(1990). His work, which has been translated into more than twenty languages, is the recipient of major Turkish and international literary awards.*

At the same time that miniaturists are under theological attack, the aesthetic primacy of their work is undercut by the success of Western techniques. The sultan himself is so taken by "Frankish" painting, with its mastery of perspective and portraiture, that he wants to adapt these methods to Ottoman illustrations. The mere idea of this stirs up fundamentalist elements in Istanbul, followers of the Hoja of Erzuumi, who feel that to paint the sultan in such a way would amount to blasphemy.

The Hoja never puts in an appearance, but a mob of his followers finally destroy the coffee shop where the miniaturists congregate. Coffee is bad enough by itself, but coffee shops are dens of every conceivable vice, and this particular one is made unbearable by the presence of a storyteller who mocks the fundamentalists.

This storyteller sits calmly at the heart of this novel, which has no single "storyteller," but a series of narrators, starting with the corpse of the first murder victim. Characters pass the story from one to the next, and back again. They address the reader and point out the inconsistencies and implausibilities of the story, as one would expect in a postmodernist work. It is not just the dead that talk directly to the reader, but the color red, as well as series of drawings—including a dog, a tree, a gold coin, and death—all of which are given voice by the coffeehouse storyteller. It just so happens that these are the same images that the miniaturists were painting for the sultan's secret project (under the supervision of Enishte Effendi, the second victim). Thus, in a way, the novel in the reader's hands *is* the secret project. Pictures are not the only representational art, after all. Storytelling, too, is deeply distrusted because it replaces the Creator's world with the writer's, which is seen as a blasphemous challenge to Allah.

It is nonetheless impossible for humans not to tell stories, and there are many tales within this novel. Aside from the storyteller, whose individual character is always hidden behind the objects he gives voice to (like a good novelist), all the characters repeatedly explain their aesthetic and moral views to each other—and to the reader—by means of tales and fables from the long history of their art. This being a postmodernist work, the morals confuse and conflict. In fact, this novel is as raucous as Pandora's box with opinion and comment, but Pamuk's postmodernism is marked by religious meditation that undercuts fundamentalism. The whole point of postmodernism is that nothing is certain; adding Allah to the mix actually heightens the uncertainty by claiming that there is a fixed and certain center everywhere—and nowhere.

Satan, one of the paintings voiced by the storyteller, says some of the most sensible things in the book, if one can believe Satan. "Of course, good and evil do exist, and the responsibility for drawing a line between the two falls to each of us." Enishte Effendi, wishing to be protected from all fundamentalists, religious or artistic, says "Nothing is pure." But what of the darkness before and after death? "Before the art of illumination there was blackness and afterward there will also be blackness. Through our colors, paints, art, and love, we remember that Allah had commanded us to 'See'!" However, the problem is that the way people see the world changes the way it is depicted—whether in art, religion, or love—and the way it is depicted then changes the way people see the world.

Take romance. One story that is often recounted or referred to here, and often illustrated by miniaturists, is that of the famous lovers Hüsrev and Shirin. Hüsrev woos Shirin by hanging a portrait of himself on a tree where he knows she will see it. Black painted this scene when he first fell in love with Shekure, putting his own likeness in place of Hüsrev's and Shekure's in place of Shirin's. Unlike Frankish painters, Ottoman miniaturists were not supposed to draw likenesses in their illustrations, and there are several fables within the book detailing the dangers of this. In this case, Black was banished from his uncle's home for aspiring to love above his prospects. Yet it was this very painting that kindled Shekure's love for Black and kept the ember alive for the twelve years that he was gone, so that when he returns, she says, "I burned with a love such as they describe in those books we so cherish and adore." All this suggests that love is a construct, not a real experience.

The way of seeing the world changes because of the impure efforts of artists, but Allah understands this. It is those who make idols, even idols out of Allah, who will be punished, not painters, Frankish or Ottoman. "To God belongs the East and the West. May He protect us from the will of the pure and unadulterated." The artistically pure look backward to the artistic tradition for their own immortality as artists. Fundamentalists, on the other hand, look forward, to heaven, for immortality. The better thing, perhaps, would be to look inward, like Master Osman, who blinds himself: "the farthest one can go in illustrating; it is seeing what appears out of Allah's own blackness." Yet even this blackness is not pure: self-blinding refutes the Koran, which says "The blind and the seeing are not equal," by claiming that the illustrator can see as well blind as sighted.

The dispute about the blind and the seeing rises again and again throughout the book, which is not surprising since this quote from the Koran—along with "To God belongs the East and the West"—is one of three that opens the novel. The third is just as relevant: "You slew a man and then fell out with one another concerning him."

Murder opens the book and throws the reader right into the quagmire of human nature and its relation to evil. Black, returning from the long wars that have finally brought peace to the empire, thinks of the sultan's workshop of miniaturists and artisans as a kind of paradise he was ejected from because of love. Black retains some of that original innocence, which is why Shekure loves him, initially, yet he presents his uncle with the brass inkpot—"Purely for red"—that will later be used to kill him.

Chapter 31, "I Am Red," lets red talk for itself, but it is left to the reader to decide why the novel is titled *My Name Is Red*. The story is about Black, but "Life begins with and returns to [red]," and the word "red" peppers every chapter. Red is blood, passion, life, art—all the things driving the artisans of the sultan's court. Red is human nature in all its complexity, and it serves as a corrective to the overemphasis placed by religious fundamentalists on the Word, the stark black Word that cannot tell the whole truth without the blood of ordinary life.

Throughout the novel, the narrative voice is lively and engaging, but the characters are not always easily differentiated, especially in the portions of the book taken up with historical and aesthetic argument. Because of the repetition and overlap, these long stretches often slow the story down. The focus on ideas means, too, that the workshop-centered world of the miniaturist is not rendered as vividly as it could have been. Fortunately, there is considerable drama inherent in the romance, especially since it is not at all certain whether Black will end up with Shekure or in the hands of the Sultan's executioners. Pamuk, who has graced one of the boys with his own name, writes about children very convincingly and uses them to add even more tension to the plot. The story becomes bogged down in so much discussion that, by the end, it may not really matter who the murderer is, but everyone should be happy that Black and Shekure manage to have a long and happy marriage, as these things go.

Unfortunately, miniaturists were not so lucky and were eventually banished, a fact the book is unabashedly laments. "Thus withered the red rose of the joy of painting and illumination that had bloomed for a century in Istanbul. . . . It was mercilessly forgotten that we'd once looked upon our world quite differently."

Philip McDermott

Sources for Further Study

The Christian Science Monitor, October 11, 2001, p. 19.
The Economist 361 (October 27, 2001): 80.
Library Journal 126 (September 1, 2001): 234.
New Statesman 130 (August 27, 2001): 41.
The New York Times Book Review 106 (September 2, 2001): 7.
The New Yorker 77 (September 3, 2001): 92.
Publishers Weekly 248 (August 6, 2001): 58.
The Spectator 287 (August 4, 2001): 29.
The Times Literary Supplement, September 7, 2001, p. 6.

MY WARS ARE LAID AWAY IN BOOKS
The Life of Emily Dickinson

Author: Alfred Habegger (1941-   )
Publisher: Random House (New York). Illustrated.
  764 pp. $35.00
Type of work: Literary biography
Time: 1830-1886
Locale: Amherst, Massachusetts

~

Habegger demonstrates the development of Dickinson as a poet, answers many of the questions her enigmatic life and career raise for readers, and confirms her poetic genius

~

Principal personages:
> EMILY DICKINSON, nineteenth century American poet
> EDWARD DICKINSON, her father
> LAVINIA (VINNIE) DICKINSON, her sister
> AUSTIN DICKINSON, her brother
> SUSAN GILBERT DICKINSON, his wife and Dickinson's best friend
> SAMUEL BOWLES, Dickinson's mentor
> THOMAS WENTWORTH HIGGINSON, Dickinson's first editor
> REVEREND CHARLES WADSWORTH, the love of Dickinson's life
> OTIS PHILLIPS LORD, Massachusetts Supreme Court judge and
> Dickinson's second love

Emily Dickinson was perhaps the greatest poet, and certainly the greatest literary mystery, of the American nineteenth century. How did this diminutive, reclusive spinster write those terse, compact poems containing such insights into self, love, and death? How did a woman who traveled so little in the world outside Amherst, Masssachussets, gain such knowledge of what goes on inside the human heart and the human head? Alfred Habegger is the latest literary detective to take up the challenge which Dickinson's life throws in the face of readers, and his years of research should settle the Dickinson case as far as it can be solved. He will never please all of Dickinson's fans, for the legends surrounding the poet are now centuries deep. Using all the available resources, however—including recently published letters and the new, complete edition of Dickinson's poetry— Habegger reconstructs the most comprehensive life of the poet to date, and reconfirms her poetic preeminence in the process.

What distinguishes Habegger's life of Dickinson is the way he re-creates the historical milieu out of which the poet emerged. If she is a shadowy figure herself, Habegger paints her surroundings in such detail that the poet appears on the page in clear outline (if still clad all in white). Whenever new characters in her life story are introduced, Habegger sketches out their backgrounds and their particular relationships with the poet. Every nineteenth century institution that touched her—education, religion, politics—is described in great detail. Dickinson's own poetry is examined minutely against the background of the social and literary thought of her time. Readers come to understand Dickinson as never before, and her poetry becomes more familiar in the process.

~

Alfred Habegger was formerly a professor of English at the University of Kansas. He is the author of a life of Henry James, Sr., and of Gender, Fantasy, and Realism in American Literature *(1982). He lives with his wife in northeastern Oregon.*

~

In part because of her reclusiveness, Dickinson's life is probably one of the most intriguing stories in American letters. She published only a handful of poems in her own lifetime, but she left behind almost eighteen hundred, often enclosing them (as was the custom in her time) in letters to friends or absent family members. She copied many more in chapbooks she made herself, and hid them away in bureau drawers. Only after her death were they discovered and imperfectly published. She lived in a tight, Calvinistic family, but she often made friends—usually through the correspondences she maintained in thousands of letters—with people everywhere. She had a series of relationships, in both letter and person, with older male mentors, including two adult romances. Her best friend was her brother Austin's wife, Sue, who lived next door to the Dickinson house, but the social fabric of their later relationship was built on concealing Austin's affair with a woman half his age. After Dickinson's death, her sister Vinnie (Lavinia) destroyed many of the letters the poet had received during her lifetime—thus deepening many of the mysteries of her life—and the legends began to grow almost at once. The evidence to counter the myths took longer to produce: the first complete collection of Emily Dickinson's poems was not assembled until 1955, her letters (some of which were altered after her death, probably by her brother Austin to protect the Dickinson family) were not published in anything like a complete edition until 1958, the first adequate biography did not appear until 1974, and the three-volume variorum edition of her poetry (by R. W. Franklin) only appeared in 1998. Habegger's critical study of the poet comes at the first and best possible moment.

The paradoxes of Dickinson's life confront any reader. She was born into a strong New England family with a number of dependencies within it. The dominant figure in that family was her father Edward, who was the head of her household until the poet was forty-four, and who had clear and conventional ideas of women's roles, their necessary subjection to men, and their unfitness as authors. In such a domestic atmosphere, "To publish her poems or proclaim her ambition would have been extremely risky acts" for Dickinson. Habegger sees the difficulty of the poet's position in this family, a kind of dependency that at the same time somehow set her free. "For good or ill, a kind of retardation in growing up was a vital aspect of her poetic vocation." Yet that odd family role also gave her the strength to create her poetry and to play the docile daughter who at times challenged the patriarchal order. As Habegger demonstrates again and again, her poetry was produced within a domestic situation which contained a number of such contradictions.

The problems of the Dickinson legend are only compounded in the relationships the poet developed during her lifetime. Clearly the woman she loved most was her sister-in-law, Susan Gilbert Dickinson, the recipient of dozens of her poems and letters, but that relationship was marked by ambivalence and retreat on both ends, even as it was endlessly stimulating to the poet. (Habegger discounts certain critics' insistence that the relationship was sexual, by showing how much midcentury American culture encouraged the affectionate and sentimental language between women which marks so many of Dickinson's letters.) She had a series of relationships with (mostly older) male mentors, including Samuel Bowles and Thomas Wentworth Higginson, the latter her first editor and a friend who encouraged her to write at the same time as he advised that she not publish her poems in their present form. (His famous letter to his wife after his 1870 visit to Amherst complains, "I never was with any one who drained my nerve power so much. Without touching her, she drew from me. I am glad not to live near her." He adds, however, "She often thought me *tired* & seemed very thoughtful of others.") Later critics have blamed Higginson for suppressing Dickinson, but Habegger shows that the poet herself had little inclination to publish, and that any critic in the middle of the nineteenth century encountering these cryptic, unpunctuated lyrics would probably have had the same reaction as Higginson. Habegger establishes the Reverend Charles Wadsworth as the great love of Dickinson's life, the object in a relationship that was never finalized. Her inability to realize this romance, Habegger shows, revealed to Dickinson the disconnection between her dreams "and the realities of life. Painful and transforming, it brought a final sense of isolation, abandonment, rejection." (Reconstructing this relationship takes the greatest detective work, by the way, because so much of the evidence has been destroyed, first by Dickinson herself, and later by family members and early editors.) At the end of her life she had a second romance, this time with Massachusetts Supreme Court Judge Otis Phillips Lord. Readers need only hear Dickinson's love poetry ("Wild nights—Wild nights!" or "I cannot live with you") to recognize that she had experienced all the stages of adult love and loss.

Habegger's historical approach works best in showing how deeply Dickinson was immersed in the culture of her day: "Sequestered though she was, Dickinson was very much a part of the society of her time." Religious revivals occurred throughout her lifetime, for example, and friends were always trying to convert her, but Dickinson—whose poetry is deeply spiritual, in spite of her religious skepticism (see "Adrift! A little boat adrift!" or "Safe in their alabaster chambers")—kept her own counsel and resisted their attempts. This after all is the poet who could write

> Some keep the Sabbath going to Church—
> I keep it, staying at Home—
> With a Bobolink for a Chorister—
> And an Orchard, for a Dome—
> and
> There's a certain Slant of light,
> Winter Afternoons—
> That oppresses, like the Heft
> Of Cathedral Tunes—

Habegger notes that "one of the biggest mistakes we make with Dickinson is to detach her from the religious currents of the 1850's, without which she could not have become herself." The more than fifty photographs Habegger collects here help to bring those currents into clearer view, by reproducing many of the faces and some of the houses in Dickinson's Amherst world.

Habegger analyses hundreds of Dickinson poems, uncovers her central themes in the process, and shows the stages of her development as a poet. She was a private as opposed to a public writer—a perfect foil for the other major American poet of the nineteenth century, Walt Whitman, whose voice reached for the largest possible audience. She wrote powerfully about pain and suffering, about the loss of friends, about "frustrated desire and energetic fantasizing." At the peak of her creativity, in the early 1860's, she was producing a poem every day or two. Dickinson lives for her readers, Habegger writes, "because she was able to pack grief, gaiety, memory, and so much more in a tight, always fresh, lyric package." Perhaps part of Dickinson's continuing appeal stems from the fact that she sounds like such a contemporary; she wrote "about extreme states: mental anguish, despair, the self as bomb or volcano, the fear that one may be coming apart." Her thought deepened and matured during her poetic career, but she never lost her distinctive and natural power of language. "Even in her last two and a half years, enfeebled by illness and a series of deaths, her voice never sounded old or defeated." Her poetry continues to live for students and other readers, and Habegger's analyses of poems ("Our lives are Swiss—," the poem Habegger uses for his title, "My wars are laid away in books," and so many others) can only deepen appreciation of them, and relate them to her life more clearly. He spends several pages discussing the differences between versions of "Safe in their Alabaster Chambers," for example, to show their role in the poet's tangled relationship with Sue.

Habegger intends his book both for the specialist and the general reader, and succeeds with the latter because he keeps notes and bibliographical information away from his text. (The notes and appendices—including family genealogical charts and an index to first lines of the hundreds of poems quoted in the study—take up more than one hundred pages at the end of the book.) One of the two problems with his study, however, is that specialists will have some difficulty finding and tracking down references they want to explore further. (A reader must know before looking, for example, that the authoritative 1998 Franklin edition of Dickinson's poetry is listed in his references as "*Var*," Thomas Johnson's three-volume 1995 collection of Dickinson's poems as "*Poems*." Other scholarly references in the text appear nowhere in his notes.) The lesser weakness of this study is that Habegger's historically comprehensive view means that it is hundreds of pages into the biography—and after detailed portraits of her parents and grandparents—before readers confront the adult poet. Still, these are the natural consequences of Habegger's goal of trying to produce the most comprehensive life of the poet, and he succeeds in writing the best life of Emily Dickinson to date, and showing once again, as she wrote, that "This was a Poet—It is That/ Distills amazing sense/ From ordinary Meanings—"

David Peck

Sources for Further Study

Booklist 98 (October 1, 2001): 43.
Library Journal 126 (September 1, 2001): 178.
The New York Times Book Review 106 (October 21, 2001): 24.
Publishers Weekly 248 (July 23, 2001): 57.
The Wall Street Journal, November 2, 2001, p. W11.
The Washington Post Book World, November 11, 2001, p. 5.

NEW AND COLLECTED POEMS, 1931-2001

Author: Czesław Miłosz (1911-   )
Publisher: Ecco Press/HarperCollins (New York).
   776 pp. $45.00
Type of work: Poetry

~

This updated edition of the Nobel Prize winner's 1988
Collected Poems *provides ample evidence of Miłosz's place*
among the great poets of the twentieth century

~

It is fair, if not quite generous, to ask whether *New and Collected Poems*, appearing just thirteen years after Czesław Miłosz's monumental *Collected Poems* (1988), amounts to anything more than a well-deserved ninetieth birthday present to one of the twentieth century's greatest poets. The answer is that it does. The simple reissue of the earlier volume from a writer who has been "witness to poetry" and to history would be reason enough to celebrate, but fully one-third of the new volume comprises poems that Miłosz has written since 1987—an amazing feat for a writer who, as he approached ninety, continued not just to write but to write as well as ever. Readers who have aged along with Miłosz will witness no slackening of his poetic powers or any turning away from those most characteristic concerns that have made him one of the most compelling literary figures of the past century. They may lament the lighter typeface that strains the eyes and the decision to drop the 1988 preface, no less indispensable now than it was then, for its brief discussion of both the earlier book's conception and the role that Miłosz's many translators had in it. On the other hand, *New and Collected Poems* adds a brief but excellent introduction, in which Miłosz sums up certain of his views on his poetry— most important, his concern with "tangible reality" and with writing poems that are, although more objective than subjective, nonetheless "infused with personal struggle." The new volume also greatly expands the notes appended to the earlier one. (Unfortunately, the notes for the new poems are both few and spare.) The real reason to rejoice over the publication of *New and Collected Poems* is the poetry itself: seventy years' worth in "pursuit of the Real." "How to tell it all?" Miłosz asks. How to encompass and comprehend "a life unendurable" that was nonetheless endured?

Miłosz first came to notice outside his native land in the 1950's, with his defection from Poland and the publication of his book of criticism *Zniewolony umysł* (1953; *The Captive Mind*, 1953) and the novel *Zdobycie władzy* (1953; *The Seizure of Power*, 1955), which made him an especially attractive as well as articulate figure in (and to) the West during the early years of the Cold War. In fleeing Poland, first for France and later the United States, Miłosz became in fact what he had long been in temperament: exile, wanderer. He became, that is, the twentieth century's representative man: the

Winner of the 1980 Nobel Prize in Literature, Czesław Miłosz has written novels, autobiography, literary history, and translations. However, it is as a poet that he is best known and most highly respected.

detached yet strangely involved—even implicated—as well as helpless *I*, the "Eye," as "universal witness," at once voyager and voyeur.

Forever between two worlds, two conditions, Miłosz anticipates without actually participating in the kind of hybridity that a later generation of postcolonial writers such as Salman Rushdie has celebrated. This basic and irreconcilable doubleness, so closely associated with his exile, becomes the focus of much of his poetry, leaving Miłosz between opposing claims and allegiances, every acceptance tinged with regret, with an intense awareness of the inadequacy of every choice. He exists at, and as, the point where opposites meet: the philosophical and the "flesh-enraptured," the history-saturated Polish-Lithuanian past and the historyless American-Californian present. Exile only exacerbates a doubleness which precedes his actual defection; it is there in the twin realities of his native Polish Wilno/Lithuanian Vilnius and his adopted Warsaw of cafes and ghetto. It is there, early and late, in his oscillating between nature and history on the one hand and broader metaphorical and metaphysical claims on the other. The doubling appears in various forms, from the unbearably concentrated ("a million white fish leaping in agony") to the tantalizingly metaphysical ("And the body is most mysterious,/ For, so mortal, it wants to be pure,/ Liberated from the soul which screams: 'I!'").

For critic Aleksander Fiut, this doubleness, crystallized in Miłosz's phrase "the eternal moment," points to the poet's larger subject, "the drama of the loss of God." Fiut may be putting too fine a Polish and Catholic a face on writing that has come to resonate too widely to be quite so narrowly circumscribed, but his claim is suggestive, especially when read in terms of the complex role that witnessing plays in Miłosz's art: "Though of weak faith, I believe in forces and powers/ Who crowd every inch of the air./ They observe us—is it possible that no one sees us?" The need to witness is balanced here by the need to be witnessed, seen and judged. The "drama of the loss of God" entails the loss of certainty that propels modern humanity into the postmodern condition. The exile as tragic figure, as Wandering Jew, is transmogrified into hapless Peeping Tom doomed to playing the part of helpless witness while drowning in "depths of time," "the eternal moment" itself transmogrified into the historical horror of eternal recurrence, the landscape of Sylvia Plath's bitter, self-lacerating poem, "Daddy," the Poland "scraped flat by the roller of wars wars wars."

Because it is so inextricably bound up with his exile and with the devastation of his native Poland in World War II, Miłosz's poetry is about loss in all its forms. His description of Washington, D.C, in 1949 as "the city which had seemed eternal" is a palimpsest in which the reader catches a glimpse of Warsaw in ruins. It is the desire to "find everything we have lost," as he puts it in one early poem, the desire to "remind us of everything we have lost" as he writes more than thirty years later, that is Miłosz's great theme. Remembrance, in his work, lies between nostalgia and despair. It is only partly the work of Job's servant, whom God has left alive to tell the tale. Rather, it is the more urgent, even desperate work of the guilt-driven survivor addressing "You whom I could not save." The intensity of this loss and this failure imbues Miłosz's poetry with its characteristic power and intensity and makes his preoccupation with his own mortality, beginning in the mid 1970's, seem less narrowly personal than it otherwise would.

Against the wistfulness of a line such as "Nothing lasts, but everything lasts: a great stability," Miłosz posits the counterweight of physical reality, one which is rarely sexual, often natural, and most often, and most evocatively, rendered with the precision of seventeenth century Dutch painting:

> Only this table is certain. Heavy. Of massive wood.
> At which we are feasting as others have before us,
> Sensing under the varnish the touch of other fingers.
> Everything else is doubtful.

The luminous clarity and indisputable presence of Dutch painting is not so much an answer for Miłosz, as an option, albeit an especially attractive one, a consoling presence amidst so much that is "ungraspable" and incomprehensible. "Though he would rather understand than speak," speech, not comprehension, is what he has been given, along with the knowledge that, as he says of Heraclitus, "a moment of consciousness never will change us." At moments such as these, Miłosz's "eternal moment" recalls the scene in French novelist Louis-Ferdinand Celine's *Mort à crédit* (1936; *Death on the Installment Plan*, 1938), in which the narrator tries to stop death by freezing the living in their tracks. Less given to Celine's brand of desperate grotesquerie, Miłosz generally takes a gentler tack: "Only this moment at dawn is real to me.// . . . I cast a spell on the city asking it to last."

For Miłosz, not to "speak" (that is, write) means not to save and thus to contribute to the general devastation: "What is pronounced strengthens itself./ What is not pronounced tends to nonexistence." But what is pronounced itself often falls short. "Beyond the power to name" lies a realm where only faith may go. Thus Miłosz thinks of language, of poetry, as both necessary and insufficient. "Approaching ninety, and still with a hope/ That I could tell it, say it, blurt it out," he is simultaneously haunted by "all I have not said." In the poetry, the heavy burden of Catholic guilt, the need for atonement and the possibility of redemption, is given added historical weight and combined with "the messianic hope of my civilization," that "in Poland a poet is a barometer" as well as a political savior. Miłosz comes in the footsteps of the nineteenth century Polish-Lithuanian poet, patriot, and exile Adam Mickiewicz, but at a time when the poet's role is much reduced. He is too modern to be a latter-day Mickiewcicz but too much the Slavic poet to follow Robinson Jeffers's example and "proclaim . . . an inhuman thing." In his "search for what is most strongly opposed to *smrt"* (the Lithuanian word for "death" is left untranslated), Miłosz steadfastly rejects Jeffers's "inhumanism" but deals with Allen Ginsberg's politically charged poetry very differently: "Allen, you good man, great poet of the murderous century, who persisting in folly attained wisdom./ I confess to you, my life was not as I would have liked it to be." The "shame of failing to be/ what I should have been," as Miłosz puts it in one of his best-known poems, "To Raja Rao," forms one of the strongest currents in the prolific career of a writer "Proud of my strength/ Yet embarrassed by view" from the Berkeley Hills. "Deprived. And why shouldn't you be deprived?/ Those better than you were deprived."

This sense of (relative) deprivation is connected to Miłosz's lifelong search for an enabling form. Miłosz's technical virtuosity, discussed by Donald Davie in *Czesław Miłosz and the Insufficiency of Lyric* (1986), is especially noticeable in *New and Collected Poems*. Miłosz's explorations in form includes songs, lyrics, odes, hymns, narratives, notes and notebooks, prayers and confessions, chronicles, cycles, prose poems, talks, treatises, dialogues, primers, lengthy prose extracts. He uses short lines, long lines, and everything in between, imitates Jeffers, Ginsberg, Philip Larkin, and others. "I have always aspired to a more spacious form," but the formal experiments seem to have as much to do with the insufficiency of individual forms, or of a metaform, as it does with aspiration. In this respect, Miłosz is like the legendary Polish king, Popiel, whom mice have eaten. The Heraclitean rivers of his youth to which Miłosz returns so often in his poetry are at once richly evocative and "shallow," and thus an apt symbol for the poet who even as he hoped, early in his career, "to be redeemed by the gift of arranging words," prepared himself "for an earth without grammar."

Miłosz, Wisława Szymborska, and the late Zbigniew Herbert are the three great Polish poets of the twentieth century. The first two were Nobel Prize winners; the third deserved to be. Miłosz has none of Szymborska's slyly ironic wit, and none of Herbert's fierce political passion. He has not created a distinctive style (as did Szymborska) or a distinctive persona (Herbert's Mr. Cogito). What he has created is a perspective and a predicament. Against the sheer bulk of his poetic achievement— seventy years, 750 pages in a vast variety of forms—Miłosz presents himself not as a messiah, and maybe not quite as a barometer either. Rather, he is the poet as survivor, exile, witness: appalled, ashamed, meditative; expectant, above all elegaic. "I wanted to be like others but was given the bitterness of separation," and given too the opportunity, or responsibility, to make from that bitterness "a few verses, durable."

Robert A. Morace

Sources for Further Study

Artforum 40 (November, 2001): 33.
The Guardian, November 10, 2001, p. 6.
Los Angeles Times Book Review, November 18, 2001, p. 1.
The New York Times, August 26, 2001, p. D13.
The New York Times Book Review 106 (December 2, 2001): 58.
Publishers Weekly 248 (September 3, 2001): 82.

THE NEW BUDDHISM
The Western Transformation of an Ancient Tradition

Author: James William Coleman (1947-   )
Publisher: Oxford University Press (New York).
   265 pp. $25.00
Type of work: Religion and sociology
Locale: The United States and Great Britain

∿

A survey and analysis of the rise and growth of Western Buddhism

∿

Buddhism began with Siddhartha Gautama, who lived in northern India in the sixth or fifth century B.C.E. Tradition says he became "the enlightened one" (the Buddha) after a period of deep meditation under a bodhi tree. The remainder of his long life was devoted to three intertwined teachings: an ethical teaching that one's intentions in this life determined one's future rebirth; a teaching that the nearly endless cycle of rebirth could be ended by enlightenment, by seeing reality as it really was; and a teaching that a state of mindfulness and deep meditation could produce such wisdom.

This wisdom, according to James William Coleman in *The New Buddhism*, is not discursive but experiential. The reality that all is flux, that even a human being is nothing more than constantly changing bundles of experience, means there is no core self to be protected. Clinging ceases and with it suffering (the effect of clinging), and what remains is *nirvana*, a state of unspeakable bliss no longer subject to the karmic laws of cause and effect.

Though in its long history Buddhism has been characterized as world-renouncing, and the development of Buddhist monasticism would seem to affirm such judgment, the reality is far more complex. Varieties of popular Buddhism have emphasized the prospect of a good rebirth by the doing of meritorious deeds or by the chanting of certain phrases. Even some elite Buddhist groups engaged with the world in study, ritual, and politics. "Western Buddhism," Coleman writes, "has drawn its primary inspiration from a relatively narrow spectrum of Asian Buddhism: the meditation-oriented elite Buddhists who do not see monastic renunciation as an essential component of the path to enlightenment."

As Buddhism left India, and all but perished in its homeland, it took root in various forms in Sri Lanka and Burma (where Theravada Buddhism or "the way of the elders" began to flourish), in Tibet (where several sects developed that emphasized esoteric and ritualistic Buddhism), and in China (which saw the rise of the schools of Hua-yen and T'ien T'ai, the development of the popular Pure Land form, and Ch'an Buddhism). In turn, China heavily influenced Buddhism in Korea, Vietnam,

James William Coleman, a professor of sociology at California Polytechnic University, San Luis Obispo, has also published The Criminal Elite: Understanding White-Collar Crime *(1985). A practicing Buddhist, Coleman graduated from the University of California, Santa Barbara, specializing in the sociology of religion.*

and Japan (where Ch'an became Zen). Japan itself produced an innovative form of Buddhism that arose from the teachings of the Japanese monk Nichiren, whose aggressive condemnation of all other forms of Buddhism and worship of a sacred text known as the *Lotus Sutra* made it unique.

Buddhism adapted to new cultural conditions as it spread throughout Asia and continued to do so in Great Britain and the United States. Coleman distinguishes between ethnic Buddhism in the West, part of the cultural tradition brought by Asian immigrants, and the "new Buddhism" which attracts Western adherents, most of whom are "wealthy, liberal, highly educated Anglos." The author's survey of 359 people at seven Buddhist centers, conducted from 1992 to 1996, while not scientific, is nevertheless instructive. The new Buddhism finds adherents among the well-educated middle and upper classes because, Coleman writes, it "is an intellectually challenging religion that demands an extraordinarily high level of dedication and discipline among its members, and, of course, lots of time to devote to spiritual pursuits. Unlike Asian Buddhism, it lacks the emotional appeal of the devotional faiths that history has shown to hold the greatest attraction for those in the less privileged classes."

Though Buddhism was not unknown in the United States and Britain by the end of the nineteenth and the beginning of the twentieth centuries, the so-called Beat Generation of the 1950's, including such notables as the poets Alan Ginsberg and Gary Snyder and novelist Jack Kerouac, brought Japanese Zen to the attention of a larger reading audience. Essayist Alan Watts, allied with the Beats without identifying himself as one, promoted an intellectualized Buddhism in *The Way of Zen* (1957) and many other books. There was a new wave of interest in Zen in the late 1960's and early 1970's, as those in the counterculture sought more stable alternatives to the experiences provided by psychedelic drugs.

Certain other Western students traveled to Asia to study, and brought back what they had learned. Among them were Philip Kapleau, founder of the Rochester, New York, Zen Center; Robert Aitken of Hawaii's Diamond Sangha (*sangha* is the community of Buddhists); and Peggy (Jiyu) Kennett who founded the Shasta Abbey monastery in Northern California. Asian Zen teachers themselves, most notably Thich Nhat Hanh of Vietnam, have also had considerable influence in the West. Shunryu Suzuki, the son of a Zen priest, taught Zen in the United States and founded the first Zen Center there in 1961. He taught that sitting meditation (*zazen*) with the right posture was itself enlightenment. No special state of mind was needed.

In the West, Tibetan Vajrayana (the "diamond vehicle"), more emotionally outgoing and colorful than Zen, was shaped in large part by Chogyam Trungpa. Trungpa came to North America in 1970, founded the Naropa Institute in Boulder, Colorado (which offers degrees in Buddhist studies), and warned of the dangers of what he called "spiritual materialism," which produced only egocentricity under the guise of spiritual attainment. Trungpa was an advocate of "crazy wisdom," a kind of uncomfortable spontaneity. A controversial figure, he "openly had sex with his students, smoked, and drank heavily enough to be characterized as an alcoholic by many who knew him."

The Theravada tradition of southern Asia made its appearance in the West in more secularized fashion. Called Vipassana, this form of Buddhism is promoted by Western teachers as akin to psychotherapy. Sharon Salzberg, Joseph Goldstein, and Jack Kornfield founded the Insight Meditation Center in Barre, Massachusetts. Kornfield left to found the Spirit Rock Meditation Center in Marin County, California.

Finally, the Japanese sect called Soka Gakkai promotes a Buddhism for the masses, emphasizing not meditation but praise of the *Lotus Sutra* which, it is believed, will bring wealth and happiness to the adherent. Unlike other forms of Buddhism Coleman considers, Soka Gakkai in the West is under the direction of one central authority, the parent organization in Japan. Though influential in the West, Soka Gakkai is itself worthy of an entire study, and Coleman mentions it only briefly.

As Buddhism becomes entrenched in the West, Coleman finds signs of increasing eclecticism, a mixing of "insights and approaches of all the Asian Buddhist traditions, often combined with a healthy dose of such things as Sufism, Taoism, the nondualistic schools of Hinduism, and Western psychology." What is more, some Western groups, such as the Springwater Center in New York, have given up Buddhist identification in an effort to overcome clinging, even to Buddhism itself.

Coleman's survey of Buddhist centers in North America is supplemented by formal interviews, personal experience as a practicing Buddhist, and a reading of the relevant literature. The author provides a comprehensive overview of the emerging responses of Western Buddhism to individualistic postmodern (mostly American) culture. If a Buddhist is defined as a person who looks for refuge to the Buddha, the *sangha*, and the *dharma* (the universal truth about reality), then there were perhaps from one to four million Buddhists in the United States by the end of the twentieth century. Involvement varies, from "bookstore Buddhists" to those deeply involved in small Buddhist groups which often sponsor meditation retreats and "*dharma* talks."

As Western Buddhism develops, it poses a challenge not only to more traditional Asian forms but faces its own temptations. Coleman writes that

> One of the great paradoxes of Buddhism is that the respect, prestige, and authority the teacher receives are a powerful encouragement to the very kind of ego attachments that Buddhist practice is expected to help the practitioner transcend. More than a few Western Buddhists have been deeply troubled when, for example, they have seen high-ranking Tibetan teachers being chauffeured around in a limousine, attended by a team of servants, or giving their dharma talks from a golden throne. Traditional cultural forms or ego delusion?

In response, certain Western groups have tried to put less emphasis on the authority of the teacher, and some have worked out policies of shared governance within the community and promulgated codes of ethics.

Western Buddhist centers were rocked by a number of sex-and-power scandals in the 1980's. Perhaps the most significant in terms of its lasting effects on Western Buddhism involved the successor to Chogyam Trungpa. Leadership of Trungpa's *sangha* was given to Osel Tendzin in 1987, who continued the pattern of open sexuality and heavy drinking. The community was split a year later when it was revealed that Tendzin, who had known he was infected with the acquired immunodeficiency syndrome (AIDS) virus, failed to tell his sexual partners and failed to use protection. Coleman writes that "Complete realization is rare indeed, and the actions of even the greatest teachers must be questioned when they appear wrong. Of course, it takes great courage to stand up and challenge a powerful and revered teacher, but those raised in the individualistic culture of Western democracy seem to be uniquely suited to the task."

The new Buddhism has also had to consider the place of women and the family. Traditional Buddhism, while philosophically open to the full equality of women and men in the quest for enlightenment, in practice tended to be patriarchal and sexist. Western Buddhism has taken a far more egalitarian approach and Coleman writes, "The most important transformation Buddhism has undergone, and the one that seems most likely to be a permanent fixture in the West, has been the growing power of women and the trend toward full gender equality."

New forms of practice are also evolving in relation to families with children. Early Buddhism advocated celibacy for its adherents so monks (and nuns) would not be distracted in their practice, and Coleman observes that "most Western Buddhist centers have failed to come up with any viable institutional alternatives to allow the full participation of parents with heavy child-rearing responsibilities." Though Buddhist meditation appears inimical to the life of the family, the author suggests a more careful understanding shows that "[i]f parents seek to bring the attitude of practice into their daily lives, a crying baby can be as much a reminder to come back to the here and now as the great bells of the temples."

Buddhism, however, is more than just the psychology of being "present." Some may come to Buddhism seeking therapeutic answers to personal problems, but that makes Buddhism simply another coping mechanism for the self. Instead, Buddhism's

> most profound teachings do not offer a new identity or a new set of techniques for managing our problems but deconstruct the whole project of the self—to bring us to see the pointlessness of our desperate efforts to construct, maintain, and protect our self-identity that consume so much of our lives. . . . Although self-identity remains, the attachment to it—what Buddhists call self-clinging—and the suffering it causes do not. Self-identity is recognized as simply one more pattern of thought that arises and passes away as conditions dictate.

Coleman finds a bright future for the new Buddhism, which he believes may become part of the Western religious mainstream. While much of traditional Asian Buddhism emphasized the place of social withdrawal in the path toward liberation, Western Buddhism is more socially and politically involved, "a profoundly subversive force in postmodern consumer society."

Written in a popular style, *The New Buddhism* is a sympathetic yet critical guide, a model of engaged objectivity.

Dan Barnett

Sources for Further Study

Library Journal 126 (January 1, 2001): 114.
Publishers Weekly 247 (November 20, 2000): S14.

NEXT
The Future Just Happened

Author: Michael Lewis (1960-   )
Publisher: W. W. Norton (New York). 236 pp. $23.95
Type of work: Technology and current affairs
Time: The 1990's to the present
Locale: The United States and Great Britain

~

*An accessible account of technological forces changing
the present and the future*

~

Principal personages:
JONATHAN LEBED, adolescent stock market
    manipulator
MARCUS ARNOLD, self-taught adolescent legal adviser
DANIEL SHELDON, fourteen-year-old advocate of Gnutella
JUSTIN FRANKEL, inventor of Napster

Michael Lewis's book *Next* explores the types and depth of changes that the spread of computer technology—especially the Internet—has brought to society. Mainly drawing on interviews of teenage boys who were deeply involved in the computer culture, Lewis comes to conclusions that have wide implications for society's future.

In Lewis's view, society and its paid seers were looking at the Internet in the wrong way, concentrating on its seemingly endless ability to create wealth while ignoring its social effects. Although the dot-com-fueled explosion of wealth imploded, the societal changes remain and are unlikely to subside—the genie cannot be put back in the bottle. Lewis subscribes to the school of sociologists who espouse "role theory," which argues that people have no actual self, but only masks they wear in response to varied social situations. The Internet, which has created a new set of social interactions and expectations, affords everyone the opportunity to wear new masks, and thus create new selves—in fact, as many new selves as one has the creativity, time, and energy to invent and maintain.

Lewis asserts it is "wildly disruptive to speed up information," and that the Internet has changed society profoundly and irrevocably, inverting the power between adolescents and adults and altering the balance between insiders and outsiders. As the Internet creates a childcentric economic model, the accompanying technological changes have subtly moved more authority to the hands of children, as any middle-aged parent who has had to ask an eleven-year-old for help resetting a video recorder or troubleshooting a computer knows. Lewis thinks that adults generally are oblivious to how much authority has been ceded to the next generation. Three of his four case studies involve teenage boys who not only wield immense power in their families, but also, he argues, give evidence of a shift in the balance of power in society as a whole. In discussing Jonathan Lebed and his family, he points out that "technology had turned them into a family of immigrants," with the child forced to "translate" for confused and uncomprehending parents.

Lewis's first two cases, Jonathan Lebed and Marcus Arnold, share several similarities: Each was in his mid teens when he came to prominence for his Internet activities; each had created a persona on the Internet that led people to believe he was a subject-matter expert, not a self-taught adolescent; and each received his first computer from computer-illiterate parents who neither understood, nor could control, what their sons were doing on their computers.

Michael Lewis was born in New Orleans in 1960. After receiving a B.A. from Princeton and an M.A. from the London School of Economics, he worked as a bond trader on Wall Street in the mid-1980's. Liar's Poker *(1989), the first of his many books, was based on his experiences in that job.*

Jonathan came into the public eye for manipulating the stock market so expertly that he was investigated by the Securities and Exchange Commission (SEC), finally settling for a fine of $800,000—only part of the money he had made on stocks by the age of fourteen. After researching little-known companies, both through the Internet and from in-person visits, Jonathan bought stock in those he felt would rise in price. Then, using four screen names, Jonathan posted numerous glowing, enthusiastic messages about his stocks on various financial message boards. After a stock went up, Jonathan sold at a profit, then moved on to the next stock, again buying, hyping, and selling. He managed his parent's investments, and many teachers at his high school sought his advice on their stock market accounts.

Lewis does not believe that Jonathan did anything illegal, or anything that is not done regularly by paid stock advisers; his only crime, in Lewis's opinion, was being an unlicensed adolescent. His intelligence, dedication, and tireless researching contributed to his success, but without the Internet he could not have reached the thousands of potential buyers whose financial investments in his chosen stocks enabled him to accumulate such profits. The Internet put Jonathan on a level playing field with persons older and more experienced than he—his readers had no idea he was a teenage boy, and he made sure that they did not find out.

Marcus Arnold's story is similar: A teenager with an interest in law, he posed as a twenty-five-year-old legal expert on AskMe.com. Although most of his legal information came from watching television shows, he soon was rated number three among the legal advisers on AskMe.com, in one two-week stretch answering more than nine hundred questions.

Adolescents also were the driving force for spreading music free through the Internet. Justin Frankel was a teenage student when he wrote software called Winamp that enabled computers to play digital music files. Justin did not charge for his software, but requested that users send him a small payment if possible. By the time Justin was nineteen years of age, the software had been downloaded fifteen million times, and he had made millions of dollars and hired his father to oversee his accounts. Two years later, Justin sold his company to America Online (AOL), reportedly for seventy to one hundred million dollars. Although Justin's status had changed from insider to outsider, in the short run, his behavior continued to be subversive of the system. In March, 2000, Justin posted new software, Gnutella, which enabled peer-to-peer computing, with which users could share anything on each other's computers over the Internet without going through a central server. Although the program was available on the Internet for less than one day before AOL pressured Justin to remove it, it had been downloaded by more than ten thousand people. Not long after it was withdrawn, one its users had figured out the code and it was up and running again.

After Gnutella, computer titans Intel and Sun Microsystems, along with numerous newly started companies, began actively pursuing peer-to-peer computing. No matter how huge the corporate structure, however, the Internet gave the humblest outsider a chance to subvert it from without. For example, in a working-class suburb of England, Lewis found fourteen-year-old Daniel Sheldon, one of many young people devoted to carrying on what Daniel called "the legend that is Gnutella." Daniel had no training in using computers, but within six months was an accomplished programmer and capable of hacking. He astonished Lewis with his ability to participate in several chat rooms, read novels he downloads from the Internet, and search sites for music he could download during his weekly visits to a cyber-cafe with a high-speed connection—all at the same time. His story was similar to those of Jonathan and Marcus: His mother purchased his computer and had no idea what he did on it, but she was proud as well as intimidated when his exploits were recognized by the outer world with a summons from Warner Brothers, threatening to sue him for putting up a Harry Potter fan site on the World Wide Web.

Daniel expressed no interest in making money off his compulsion—like many of his peers, he thinks money is evil and those (such as Justin Frankel) who became rich from their programs were sell-outs. Perhaps it is only fourteen-year-old bravado or naïveté that leads Daniel to say, "'. . . if you're just in it for the money, then you're not really going to have a sense of achievement. That's why real advances aren't made by commercialists. . . .We're out to make a network that benefits us all and isn't governed or monitored or censored by anybody else . . . .'" Despite his ideals, he is a realist: "'I'd like to think I was undermining capitalism, but . . . I very much doubt [that].'" Like Marcus and Jonathan, Daniel is aware that the Internet puts him on equal footing with persons who would never take him seriously in person. He was a decade younger than the de facto leaders of the chat rooms devoted to Gnutella, but programmed and participated on an equal level.

The third section of *Next*, "The Revolt of the Masses," looks beyond the Internet to the interaction between technology in general and the greater society. Lewis focuses on how television helped to create a mass market of like-minded consumers of both entertainment and products, and how advances in television are dramatically altering that symbiosis. Formerly, U.S. consumers sought and found the melting pot of a shared experience; now the experience, like U.S. society in general, more resembles a frenetic patchwork quilt. One device that will accelerate this process if it is widely accepted is the personal television receiver or "black box" (such as TiVo and ReplayTV), which enables viewers to capture shows of interest at any time and watch them without commercials. Unlike video recorders, which have to be set to tape each show, black boxes capture shows based on expressed preferences and let the viewer skip through commercials almost instantaneously, rather than scrolling through with the fast-forward function. The viewer's choices are stored in the black box—in essence, while one watches television, the black box watches back—and the maker of the box can sell information about viewers to companies who want to reach them with targeted messages. As television and computer technology blend together, more tracking of consumer's behavior seems inevitable.

Lewis's last profile is of an eighty-year-old widow, Marion Frost. Unlike Daniel, Marcus, and Jonathan, Marion is not out to change the world through the Internet; rather, she demonstrates how the Internet enters people's homes and changes them and their relationship to the outside world. Marion was one of tens of thousands of people solicited by Knowledge Networks to participate in online surveys on products and politics. Although she is so unknowledgeable about the system they installed on her three-decade-old television that her son has to come to her house and enter her answers to surveys, and although she makes no use of the Web TV or free Internet access and e-mail, she feels a sense of accomplishment from participating in the surveys.

Lewis devotes a brief final chapter to two elder statesmen of the techno-elite. A few pages discuss Danny Hillis, designer of the world's fastest supercomputer in the 1970's, when he was in his twenties. Hillis had come to believe that the quest for faster computing power had destroyed even short-range future planning. In response, he started the Institute of the Clock of the Long Now, to build a clock that would last for ten thousand years. Second was Bill Joy, chief scientist of Sun Microsystems and one of the developers of the Internet programming language Java. Joy had written "Why the Future Doesn't Need Us," published in the April, 2000, issue of *Wired* magazine, positing the destruction of the earth by self-replicating nanobots programmed to do evil. ". . . We are on the cusp of the further perfection of extreme evil, an evil whose possibility spreads well beyond that which weapons of mass destruction bequeathed to the nation-states, on to a surprising and terrible empowerment of extreme individuals," Joy wrote. Lewis's response is that Joy has now become one of the conservative old guard, out to stop the kind of progress and principles on which Joy himself built his career.

Next is well written and quick to read, not a scholarly treatise. There are no references, bibliography, or index. Nevertheless, it provides a great deal of interesting information for the reader to ponder.

Irene Struthers Rush

Sources for Further Study

Book 16 (September, 2001): 79.
Business Week, August 6, 2001, p. 16.
Los Angeles Times, August 31, 2001, p. E3.
Publishers Weekly 248 (July 9, 2001): 60.
The Washington Post Book World, August 12, 2001, p. 5.

NICKEL AND DIMED
On (Not) Getting By in America

Author: Barbara Ehrenreich (1941-   )
Publisher: Metropolitan Books/Henry Holt (New York).
   221 pp. $23.00
Type of work: Current affairs
Time: 1998-2000
Locale: Key West, Florida; Portland, Maine; Minneapolis, Minnesota

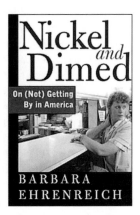

∽

A piece of investigative journalism in which the author takes three low-wage jobs in three cities and demonstrates that hard work alone will not guarantee survival—let alone prosperity—for unskilled service workers in the United States

∽

Over the last decade of the twentieth century, the American economy has been a roller coaster of ups and downs, as the Dow Jones Industrial Average hit record highs and dot-coms soared and then crashed. The summer of 2001 saw rebate checks sent to millions of taxpayers—the fruits of a large government surplus—but a few months later the House and Senate were arguing over economic stimulus packages to get a stalled economy moving again.

A large group of U.S. citizens remain largely untouched by these wide economic swings. Known as the "working poor," these people work long hours at jobs at or near the minimum wage. They do not have savings accounts and retirement funds to worry about, and they do not invest in the stock market. When a new federal plan for welfare reform promised to get able-bodied welfare recipients off the dole and into jobs, social critic Barbara Ehrenreich and a friend, a magazine editor, wondered what sorts of jobs these new workers would find, and whether they could earn enough from them to maintain a basic standard of living. That wondering led to a series of articles in *Harper's* magazine and eventually to *Nickel and Dimed: On (Not) Getting By in America*.

To research the book, Ehrenreich conducted an experiment that is easy to describe: She moved to a new town and found a place to live ("the cheapest that offered an acceptable level of safety and privacy"), paying the first month's rent from her own savings. She accepted the highest-paying job she could find without drawing on her college degrees or her writing skills and lived off what she earned. At the end of the month, she hoped to have enough money saved to pay a second month's rent. Ehrenreich lived a month each in three cities over a time span reaching from 1998 to 2000, working low-end jobs during the day and maintaining a journal on her laptop computer when she could summon the energy at night.

There has been a long tradition of left-leaning writers exploring the lower classes in this way. Two well-known examples came out of the early part of the twentieth century, as Jack London described farm laborers in *People of the Abyss* (1903), and George Orwell looked at urban workers during the Depression in *Down and Out in Paris and London* (1933). Ehrenreich herself has examined issues of class and economy before. In the 1980's she offered reflections on *The Worst Years of Our Lives: Irreverent Notes from a Decade of Greed* (1990). She traced the rise of the professional middle class in the United States in *Fear of Falling: The Inner Life of the Middle Class* (1989). Not only are the aspirations of middle-class America somewhat empty, she concluded, but the middle class is so visible—considered so typical—that lower classes become invisible. With *Nickel and Dimed*, Ehrenreich puts a needed spotlight on one overlooked portion of the lower class, drawing attention to a group of people with whom her readers interact every day, but who are usually ignored. Ehrenreich's aim is not to shed light on her own heroic passage through poverty (she points out that "millions of Americans" do for years what she did for only a month at a time, "and with a lot less fanfare and dithering"), but to illuminate the day-to-day challenges of making ends meet on a low-wage income. The focus is on numbers—the dollars and cents, the minutes and hours—instead of on personalities.

Barbara Ehrenreich is the author of many books and numerous articles for Harper's, The Nation, Time, *and* The New Republic. *She has written frequently about poverty and class issues. Her* Fear of Falling: The Inner Life of the Middle Class *(1989) was nominated for the National Book Critics Circle Award.*

In her introduction, Ehrenreich shows that she has a clear sense of what her experiment can and can not establish convincingly. She is aware of the ways in which she is not typical, aware of the advantages she brings to her new life: education, good health and good health habits, white skin, English fluency, and the knowledge that she can return to her own life at any time. She allows herself a car and an ATM card for real emergencies. She does not have young children who need supervision while she is away at work. Her experience, therefore, is not typical, but probably the best that can be hoped for "in the economy's lower depths."

For her first stop, Ehrenreich moves to Key West, Florida, a small city near her own home. Although she has tried to prepare for what she is about to do, she is immediately stymied. She has guessed that she can earn about seven dollars an hour, and that she should therefore be able to spend five or six hundred dollars on rent. The cheapest place she can find in Key West, however, is a trailer with no air-conditioning, screens, or fans for $675 a month. Ultimately she decides to take a one-room cabin thirty miles out of town, and drive the forty-five minutes back and forth each day. The lack of affordable housing will be a continual problem as subsequent chapters take her from Key West to Portland, Maine, to Minneapolis, Minnesota.

With a home secured for her first month, Ehrenreich finds a job as waitress in a family-style restaurant she calls the "Hearthside," attached to a chain motel. She will work an eight-hour shift and earn $2.43 an hour plus tips. She approaches the job with good cheer, and a kind of dark humor that is labeled "sassy" and "irreverent" in reviews. For the most part, she turns the humor against herself, as she struggles with her own incompetence in the face of demanding and complicated work, but she saves some jabs for arrogant managers and insensitive customers. She quickly discovers that no matter how good a waitress she becomes, she will never be able to afford her next month's rent. Soon she adds a second job, serving food at another restaurant, Jerry's, but can manage two shifts and the long drive back home for only two days. By month's end she has quit the Hearthside, moved to a trailer closer to one job to save driving time and gas money, and taken a second job as a housekeeper in the hotel attached to Jerry's. "I am not tired at all," she claims, "though it may be that there is simply not enough 'I' left to do the tiredness monitoring." After a devastating scene of confused food orders, screaming, and a thrown tray, Ehrenreich leaves—simply leaves, broke, frustrated, and feeling like a failure.

Her next stop is Portland, Maine. Arriving on a Trailways bus with one thousand dollars in her pocket, she settles into a Motel 6 to begin looking for a home and a job. Here she discovers a growing trend in resort areas that have been taken over by wealthy city dwellers' summer homes: There are few places for poor people to live. Although she finds an apartment in a strip motel for $120 a week, she spends well over $300 at the Motel 6 before she can move in. Meanwhile, she begins the process of job hunting, undergoing the same series of humiliating intelligence and personality tests, drug tests, and company pep talks she found in Key West. Again she quickly discovers that she will need two jobs to get by. She joins Merry Maids, a cleaning service that pays her six to seven dollars an hour, and also takes a weekend job as a dietary aide at a nursing home for seven dollars an hour. (According to the National Coalition for the Homeless, in 1998 a worker needed to earn, on average, $8.89 an hour to afford a one-bedroom apartment.) She will not have any days off, but neither will she have the physical strain of working two shifts a day.

By working seven days a week, and eating free meals at the nursing home, Ehrenreich just makes it through the month in Maine. When one of her coworkers is injured on a cleaning job, however, Ehrenreich realizes that there is no money in her budget—or in the injured woman's—for emergency expenses such as medical care. In fact, most of the women she works with are worse off than she is. Some of them live in their cars or with large families in small rooms, never able to save enough for first month's rent, last month's rent, and security deposits required to move into even a modest apartment. Most of them eat far fewer calories per day than the physical exertion of house cleaning demands of their bodies. With housing costs consuming most of their income, they can not afford fresh produce and lean protein, much less further education, home ownership, or other steps toward the middle class.

In Minneapolis, Ehrenreich gets a job in the women's clothing department at a Wal-Mart. Her job is to take newly arrived clothing, or clothing that customers have tried on and rejected, and hang it on the racks. The indignities of Wal-Mart's rules (no talking with coworkers on the job) and her inability to find minimally clean and safe housing she can afford bring out some of her most impassioned writing, as she fantasizes about forming a union or mouthing off to a manager.

No one can match Ehrenreich for seizing upon the sharp detail, the bit of dialogue, that brings a scene into focus. When she leaves narration for diatribe, she is sometimes less effective. Although she is reminded again and again that her skills and her education are irrelevant to the six jobs she takes on for this project, Ehrenreich never quite loses her essential belief that she is in many ways superior to the people she encounters. Occasionally her humor takes on an unpleasant smugness, as when she complains that the residents in a nursing home "smell like they're carrying a fresh dump in their undies," or when she categorizes the buyers of one line of Wal-Mart clothing as "pudgy fourth-grade teachers with important barbecues to attend." While Ehrenreich angrily urges her readers to see her coworkers as bright and hard-working human beings, she consistently objectifies the residents in the nursing home, the owners of the homes that need cleaning, and the customers of restaurants and department stores.

In a final chapter she calls "Evaluation," Ehrenreich summarizes her numerical findings, and issues a final bit of praise for the contributions of low wage-earners, whom she calls the "major philanthropists of our society. They neglect their own children so that the children of others will be cared for; they live in substandard housing so that other homes will be shiny and perfect; they endure privation so that inflation will be low and stock prices high."

By the very fact of writing a book about poverty, Ehrenreich is prisoner to an unavoidable irony, and she knows it: The people she is writing about cannot afford to buy basic medical care, much less spend twenty-three dollars for a hardcover book. Inevitably, although she tries to bridge the gap between "haves" and "have-nots" by conducting her experiment and by sharing it, it is only the "haves" who will read the book and learn its lessons. This might mean that Ehrenreich's calls at the end of the book for workers to rise up, make demands, form unions, and get angry are wasted. However, if the book's readers accept the need for a higher minimum wage and improved low-cost housing opportunities—or even if they simply treat food servers and cleaning staff with more respect—Ehrenreich can be proud of a job well done.

Cynthia A. Bily

Sources for Further Study

The American Prospect 12 (July 30, 2001): 43.
Barron's 81 (August 6, 2001): 37.
Book 16 (May, 2001): 27.
Booklist 97 (April 1, 2001): 1433.
Business Week, May 28, 2001, p. 24.
The Christian Century 118 (August 1, 2001): 30.
The Humanist 61 (September, 2001): 40.
Library Journal 126 (May 1, 2001): 115.
The Nation 272 (June 11, 2001): 52.
Publishers Weekly 248 (May 14, 2001): 67.

NIETZSCHE
A Philosophical Biography

Author: Rüdiger Safranski (1945-   )
First published: Nietzsche: Biographie seines Denkens, 2000, in Germany
Translated from the German by Shelley Frisch
Publisher: W. W. Norton (New York). 409 pp. $29.95
Type of work: Biography and philosophy
Time: 1844-1900
Locale: Europe

～

A well-respected scholar of German philosophy offers a chronologically organized account of Friedrich Nietzsche's dauntingly diverse writings, as well as a chapter on the response to Nietzsche among selected European thinkers and movements

～

Principal personages:
　FRIEDRICH WILHELM NIETZSCHE, seminal nineteenth century German
　　philosopher
　RICHARD WAGNER, famous composer and formative influence on
　　Nietzsche

In *Nietzsche: A Philosophical Biography*, Rüdiger Safranski reviews and offers commentary on the writings of seminal nineteenth century thinker Friedrich Wilhelm Nietzsche (1844-1900). Safranski, a former teacher at the Freie Universität in Berlin before turning freelance author and critic, isolates and discusses key themes and concepts in Nietzsche's work, throws light on Nietzsche's intellectual and aesthetic influences, and draws connections between Nietzsche's life and his work. The book closes with an abbreviated account of some of the uses and abuses that have been made of Nietzsche's ideas since 1890, when Nietzsche ceased writing due to mental illness.

It must first be stated that the biographical aspects of Safranski's book are quite limited. They really only arise in the context of trying to understand Nietzsche's writing. Readers will nevertheless come away with some definite impressions of what Nietzsche's life was like and how it may have affected his work. For one thing, Nietzsche was a lonely individual. His father died early in his life and Nietzsche never felt very well understood by his mother. He appears to have had an essentially hostile relationship with his sister, who later became executor of his work. While Nietzsche enjoyed the friendship of many notables during his lifetime, he did not sustain many of these friendships for very long, often parting on bad terms. As far as is known, Nietzsche never achieved a healthy, long-term, intimate relationship. He was turned down by the two women to whom he proposed, and even these proposals seem to have been awkward and halfhearted. Nietzsche was often physically ill throughout his life and succumbed to mental illness over the last decade of his life. Because of his illnesses, Nietzsche experienced difficulty reading. He was, therefore, aggressive and enthusiastic in his reading, but not comprehensively well-read overall. Nietzsche spent the last part of his writing career as a virtual nomad, moving around between many different locations in Europe and never quite finding a place to call home. Finally, it is significant that Nietzsche's first love was music, not literature. His eloquence as a writer masks the fact that he was unable to express himself forcefully in the medium for which he originally had the highest regard.

∼

Rüdiger Safranski was born in 1945, in Rottweil, Germany. His formal studies have been in German literature, philosophy, history, and art history. Safranski taught for a time at the Freie Universität in Berlin before becoming a full-time writer and critic in 1985. His previous books include Schopenauer and the Wild Years of Philosophy *(1991) and* Martin Heidegger: Between Good and Evil *(1998).*

∼

The balance of Safranski's book is spent on the difficult task of unraveling Nietzsche's philosophy, starting with his diaries and ending with a flurry of activity that ended up being the fragments that would comprise *Der Wille zur Macht* (1901; *The Will to Power*, 1910). One thing that makes this task so difficult is the fact that Nietzsche was a powerful, provocative writer who moved in a mercurial way from topic to topic rather than develop an easily interpretable (or even discernible) philosophical system. Then, too, Nietzsche was given to exaggeration and overstatement—he was, to put it bluntly, willing to sacrifice precision (and consistency) for impact. Finally, it is not clear that Nietzsche's is a finished body of work. He certainly indicated there was more to come. Indeed, there is an air of something adolescent and unfinished about much of Nietzsche's writing. Even in this state, however, there is also an undeniable uniqueness to the work. It is simply too brilliant and stimulating to be ignored.

Well aware of these difficulties, Safranski wades into the material without hesitation or fanfare. He discusses various influences on Nietzsche such as the great composer Richard Wagner, philosopher Arthur Schopenhauer, and radical individualist Max Stirner. More specifically, he shows how Nietzsche's works such as *Die Geburt der Tragödie aus dem Geiste der Musik* (1872; *The Birth of Tragedy out of the Spirit of Music*, 1909), *Also sprach Zarathustra* (1883-1885; *Thus Spake Zarathustra*, 1896), *Jenseits von Gut und Böse* (1886; *Beyond Good and Evil*, 1907), and *Zur Genealogie der Moral* (1887; *On the Genealogy of Morals*, 1896) may have been affected by these figures.

Most central to Nietzsche's development was his contact with the larger-than-life Wagner. As mentioned, Nietzsche's first love was music, and the most prodigious musical force of his time was Wagner. Nietzsche became Wagner's friend and, in today's parlance, his fan. Nietzsche threw his full support behind Wagner's grandiose scheme to create the vitalizing myth of a new and unforeseen culture through his operas. To Nietzsche, modern rationality had killed off not only God ("God is dead"), but the whole set of illusions by which people live and through which the human spirit soars. Wagner's ambitious exploits, in Nietzsche's view, promised at the very least an exciting experiment in recovering the Dionysian (and suprarational) side of the human spirit. In time, Nietzsche broke with Wagner, coming to believe that animating myths could not be simply promulgated on demand. To be effective, myths had to appear to be rooted in the nature of things. Nietzsche also became disenchanted with Wagner's vanity and his obvious questing after celebrity. What remained throughout Nietzsche's work, however, was an acute awareness of the tension between reason and myth, as well as between reason and emotion. In line with the Romantic movement in general, Nietzsche was unwilling to give free rein to reason while ignoring the wilder side of the human psyche. More to the point, he would not allow even philosophy, the main fortress of rationality, to reckon its path by cold intellect alone.

Other themes and concepts treated by Safranski include those of the *übermensch* (overman), the will to power, and eternal recurrence. These are all difficult notions to nail down with any certainty, and it would be too much to expect for Safranski to provide definitive interpretations. He does, however, provide sensible and appropriately profound discussion, quoting Nietzsche effectively and often to make his point. Though he does not oversimplify or sentimentalize the concept, Safranski does a good job of differentiating the *übermensch* of Nietzsche from the Nazi "superman" sometimes evoked in his name. He is also quite forthright about the concept's ambiguity. On the will to power, Safranski does a good job of suggesting possible meanings, including those related to art, religion, and, to the extent Nietzsche was interested, politics. Safranski does make it clear that the will to power was an idea on which Nietzsche was still at work when his intellectual career effectively came to an end. On the notion of eternal recurrence (sometimes rendered as "recurrence of the same"), Safranski seems less sure of himself, probably because Nietzsche himself is so obscure on the topic. Safranski is much better able to elucidate Nietzsche's ideas on morality, particularly with regard to the nonmoral (and perhaps even antimoral) roots of morality, and also the way in which traditional morality has had the effect of transforming people from individuals to "dividuals" torn apart by the war between instincts and conscience. Safranski also ably describes the ambiguous treatment by Nietzsche of the Judeo-Christian tradition, conveying Nietzsche's awe at the tradition's immense influence over history as well as his disgust at its limitations in terms of freeing humanity's full creative juices.

Safranski closes his book with a chapter on the European response to Nietzsche. Ironically, word of Nietzsche's mental health problems did much to make him a celebrity, some how authenticating and amplifying his puzzling but powerfully unique body of work. Up until the 1890's, Nietzsche had a certain limited notoriety. Then, with rumors of his insanity swirling around, he became a fascinating cultural icon. He was a source of inspiration for a trendy school of thought and expression known as *Lebenphilosophie* (philosophy of life). In quite a different vein, German nationalists and anti-Semites somehow found fuel for their cause in Nietzsche's work (with a big assist from his sister and brother-in-law), though Safranski makes it clear that Nietzsche was, at best, a lackadaisical nationalist and an unambiguous "anti-anti-Semite." In addition to these popular renditions of Nietzsche, prominent thinkers and scholars such as Karl Jaspers, Martin Heidegger, and Michel Foucault found inspiration in

Nietzsche for their own intellectual exploits. Nor has Nietzsche receded from his place of importance in the world of ideas. He remains an important figure to intellectuals and even makes his appearance occasionally in popular culture (for example, the phrase, "that which does not kill us makes us stronger," has become part of the everyday wisdom of athletes, business professionals, and others).

Safranski's book ends abruptly. He admits that he does not have the key to solving the enigma that is Nietzsche and also that there is a whole body of American responses to Nietzsche (including on the part of American pragmatists) that he has left virtually unexplored. As such, there is a seeming incompleteness about this book. Safranski whets the reader's appetite and then seems to say, "I do not fully understand Nietzsche or the implications of his work; probably no one can."

There are other limitations of the book as well. Though Safranski quotes liberally from Nietzsche, he does not provide synopses of his work. Indeed, readers who are unfamiliar with Nietzsche's writing will probably have difficulty following the book's rapid tour through his written work. On the other hand, experienced readers of Nietzsche may well find the discussion unsatisfactory since they will probably have their own idiosyncratic interpretations of Nietzsche's rich menagerie of ideas, proclamations, and symbols.

Despite these apparent shortcomings, this is a worthwhile book. The greatest asset Safranski brings to the book is his excellent ability as a writer (ably assisted by Shelley Frisch, who translates from the German). Like Nietzsche, Safranski is quite adept at turning a phrase. Indeed, there is much to be gained from observing the engagement between Safranski and his subject and even in joining the fray ourselves. In addition, there is considerable value to the seemingly impossible comprehensiveness of Safranski's effort. True, there is too much to Nietzsche for all of his wit and wisdom to be captured in a relatively short volume such as Safranski's. On the other hand, the reader gets a good sense of how Nietzsche's ideas evolved over time and is left with the desire to read or reread his books and letters with this broader perspective in mind. Finally, Safranski does a good job of showing that what Nietzsche cared about, that is, the conduct of life when one's ability to believe has been sorely wounded, remains a topic of vital importance in a morally, politically, and aesthetically confusing world.

Ira Smolensky

Sources for Further Study

Booklist 98 (November 15, 2001): 525.
Publishers Weekly 248 (November 12, 2001): 50.

NIGHT OF STONE
Death and Memory in Twentieth Century Russia

Author: Catherine Merridale (1959-   )
Publisher: Viking (New York). Illustrated. 402 pp.
  $29.95
Type of work: History
Time: The twentieth century
Locale: Russia

≈

A powerful, beautifully written study of the moral and cultural effects of mass death on modern Russian society

≈

Catherine Merridale's *Night of Stone: Death and Memory in Twentieth Century Russia* is an evocative meditation on the meaning of life in the face of atrocity and catastrophe. Merridale situates her study in a land where such musings bear especial significance. Russia in the twentieth century experienced a string of disasters, which resulted in a level of mortality not seen in a European country since the days of the Black Death in the fourteenth century. War, famine, and repression took a human toll that probably reached fifty million lives, and the figure arguably could be higher. Such numbers beggar the imagination. The magnitude of Russia's loss threatens to stun commentators into silence. As with the Holocaust perpetrated on the Jews and other "undesirables" by the German Nazis, here one confronts the unutterable abyss of human depravity and is forced to contemplate the yawning, seemingly bottomless capacity of humanity to suffer.

Yet following the Holocaust, some measure of justice, however imperfect, was meted out to the perpetrators of crimes against humanity. Those who died at their hands were widely seen as victims of a uniquely horrible criminal act. There is no such consolation for the survivors of Soviet tyranny. In Russia, victims and victimizers coexist. The former *zeks* of the Gulag and the executioners of the secret police, all legatees of the Soviet Union, collect their pension checks together. Even veterans of World War II, known in Russia as the Great Patriotic War, honored as the vanquishers of fascism, are likewise prisoners of an official forgetfulness. They must act their parts in a preordained script. Proudly displaying their medals, they must suppress dark memories that countervail the glorious tale of throwing back the invader. Like the others, they are pensioners of a failed dream.

The Soviet Union, simultaneously an idyllic experiment, a totalitarian laboratory, and a charnel house, thrust the Russian people into the crucible of a searing modernity. The citizens of the Soviet Union found themselves principals in a horrifying drama, a Faustian attempt to reengineer humankind and society. The seventy-year Soviet interlude profoundly scarred the Russian people. Today the first halt-

ing steps are being taken to calculate the damage. Merridale's book is an honorable contribution to this effort at historical reconstruction.

~

*Catherine Merridale is a senior
lecturer in history at the University
of Bristol in England. She is the
author of books on Russia.*

~

    Catherine Merridale is an accomplished his-
torian, securely ensconced at a British university.
She set out to write a monograph that explored the
intersection between Soviet culture and identity,
evoking something of the texture of a rapidly fading "mentality." She was intrigued
by the Soviet desire to create a "new man" and hoped to uncover the working out of
this ambition through a study of the Soviet way of death. Few systems of belief are
more fundamental to a culture than its attitude toward death. Merridale intended to
expose the ways in which the Soviets wrestled with habits of heart and mind rooted in
centuries of religious practice through research in the archives of the League of the
Militant Godless and the Society for the Dissemination of Scientific Cremation. Such
a scholarly work would have been useful and illuminating. It would have fitted admi-
rably into contemporary trends in historical fashion.

    Merridale's plans were betrayed by her integrity as a scholar. Her professional
quest for the truth led Merridale into new directions. As her work progressed, her
topic began to grow as new questions naturally emerged. Any study of the Soviet attitude toward death compelled some attention to the horrors committed in communism's name. Continuities and innovations in burial customs paled in significance
next to the graves opened by executions, starvation, and combat. It has long been a
cliché that Russians are inured to suffering and death, that they are inherently violent
and brutal. As Merridale notes, Russians themselves say this, attributing the cruelty
manifest in their history to the rigors of the climate and the legacy of centuries of rule
by the barbarous Tartars. As Merridale proceeded in her investigation, as her library
of taped interviews with Russian survivors grew, such glib and all-too-easy answers
seemed increasingly inadequate.

    Merridale has an enormous capacity for empathy; she found herself responding
with a powerful sympathy to the stories that she recorded. What began as an academic
exercise became instead something of an existential journey, a quest into the heart of
darkness. Brimming with more questions than answers, graced by a number of vignettes during which the author describes her encounters with men and women who
defy all the easy generalizations, *Night of Stone* manages to consistently resist the
conventions of historical prose. The result is a book that transcends genre. Epic in
scope, meticulous in detail, *Night of Stone* is a freewheeling overview of modern Russian history. It touches on a wide variety of topics, ranging from late Czarist funerary
rituals to the social consequences of the Soviet Union's war in Afghanistan.

    Merridale begins her study of death and memory in the Soviet Union by looking at
the legacy bequeathed to the Soviets by the Russia of the czars. This legacy was rich
but combustible, a mixture of beauty and squalor, preminiscent of Soviet forms in
some ways but radically different in spirit. Dominating this Russia's understanding of
death and the departed were the teachings and the liturgies of the Russian Orthodox
Church. Peasants were as likely to identify themselves as "Orthodox" as they were

"Russians." The Orthodox Church enveloped death and the afterlife in a dense field of meaning. So ingrained were Orthodox reflexes that early Russian revolutionaries had a hard time weaning themselves from Christian funerals. However, already present in Russian society of the late nineteenth and early twentieth centuries was something of the cruelty and hardness that would be compounded many times during the Soviet years. The authority of landlords weighed heavily on the peasantry. Floggings were common. In turn, peasants occasionally rose against landlords with murderous rage. The czarist government responded to unrest with callous brutality. Executions became so frequent that children made "public execution" into a schoolyard game. Toward the end of this period, Russia's rural Jewish population suffered from violent pogroms countenanced, if not overtly sanctioned, by the government. These pogroms established an ominous precedent for the collective scapegoating and persecution of a targeted minority. Even in times of peace and quiet, life was difficult, and usually short, for Russian peasants. The diseases endemic to poverty made death ever present in peasant villages. Peasants themselves showed little mercy to people accused of a variety of transgressions. Thieves and murderers might be tortured to death. Witches were still burned alive in their huts.

A small but suggestive body of memoirs and folkloric studies gives some insights into the ways Russian peasants responded to death in the centuries prior to the Soviet Union. Merridale is quick to point out that very much remains hidden from us. Few living people remember Czarist times. Even then, if questioned, the emotional residue of threescore and ten years under the Soviets would color their reminiscences. Merridale possesses the courage to admit the essential mysteriousness of life, to acknowledge the difficulty of probing, let alone knowing, the secrets of the human heart. The full truth lies somewhere under the illusions and misunderstandings heaped up by commentators writing from the outside. This does not condemn the historian of ideas to unintelligibility, but it does demand some epistemological humility. Assertions about the manner in which a people understood death must always be qualified and tentative.

Merridale evinces the same modest and realistic spirit in her discussion of the Soviet period. Here the documentary record is rich, and many survivors can still offer their recollections of life under the Communists. Yet, as Merridale learned during the course of her research, even when graced with a wealth of material, the truth of what she sought proved elusive. The cascade of information that has flowed from various archives since the collapse of the Soviet Union has helped enormously in grasping the contours of Russian suffering in this century, but these records and statistics give only the most oblique glimpses into the attitudes of ordinary Soviet citizens. Furthermore, when recording the memories of Russians who had lived through the terrible events of the 1930's and 1940's, Merridale discovered that these people selectively remembered the past, their anecdotes and images fitting patterns of interpretation attuned to their own needs. Indeed, the people that she tape-recorded often fell into an almost automatic, obviously well-rehearsed monologue. Gentle prodding by Merridale might or might not break through her subject's defensive carapace. One of the most compelling of Merridale's interviews was with a woman born into a peasant family singled out for proscription in the 1930's. Her father disappeared. She, her mother, and two brothers found themselves starving in a government camp. A relative showed up and took her away. Thus she lived, while her brothers died. She was trained as an entertainer and traveled with the army during World War II. She gave birth to a son and sent him to her widowed mother in the country. Some years later, her son killed himself in despair. The woman, recollecting all this in an apartment crammed with mementos of her show business career, spent most of her time with Merridale waxing nostalgic over the war years. She was appallingly oblivious to the suffering of her family. Merridale could not approve of this woman, but she could understand her. In the context of the Soviet Union, this woman was a survivor.

All human memory is self-absorbed and self-interested. Individually or collectively, it is a powerful means of coping with experience. For many, memory is a happy avenue into a cherished past. For Russians, memories of the twentieth century are much more problematic. Beginning with World War I, the overthrow of the czar, and the Bolshevik Revolution, Russia endured a series of calamities, each of which took a hideous toll of human life. The Revolution was followed by a devastating civil war. Once the Communists consolidated their power, they launched an ambitious program to build socialism. The initial Five-Year Plan and the collectivization of agriculture cost millions of lives. Millions more died in a famine deliberately engineered by the government. The Soviet dictator Joseph Stalin then proceeded to eliminate any potential rivals for power by unleashing a massive purge of the government and Communist Party. Countless people were executed or condemned to the gulag. World War II led to the deaths of twenty to thirty million Soviet citizens. Another famine followed the war, and more died. The wounds left by this grim history are deep and untreated. During the Soviet period, dwelling on these events and the losses they entailed was discouraged. Soviet psychologists and doctors refused to acknowledge the existence of popular trauma. Russians learned to live with a stiff upper lip. In post-Soviet Russia, memorials to the victims of Stalin's purges are springing up, but these gestures compete with nostalgia for the good old days. It is not at all clear how Russia will come to terms with the past.

Merridale does not make any sweeping claims about death and memory in modern Russia. The dead retain their secrets. Their memory remains ambiguous. In the end, Merridale admits that she is reduced to silence before the unspeakable and unknowable. The great merits of her book are the way in which she illumines the profundity of her subject, and the extraordinary delicacy with which she traces the tortured responses of ordinary Russians to the horrors of their history. *Night of Stone* sheds precious light on modern darkness.

Daniel P. Murphy

Sources for Further Study

Booklist 97 (March 15, 2001): 1337.
Commonweal 128 (September 14, 2001): 30.
The Economist 357 (October 28, 2000): 80.
Library Journal 126 (March 1, 2001): 114.
The Times Literary Supplement, July 13, 2001, p. 28.

NIGHT PICNIC

Author: Charles Simic (1938-   )
Publisher: Harcourt (New York). 86 pp. $23.00
Type of work: Poetry

~

*In his new collection, Simic continues his lifelong explo-
ration of the uncanny hidden within the ordinary*

~

Night Picnic continues to explore the area Charles Simic
has set out for himself: the surface of the ordinary, and the
dreams and nightmares beneath. Few contemporary poets
have had as much influence as Simic on contemporary poetry, and yet he writes superficially quiet poems, dwelling
on simple, recognizable scenes. The technique by which landscape or still life turns to
nightmare is subtle and full of tricks. The poem often seems to be about one thing and
may have a friendly, even nostalgic tone, yet the uncanny has been admitted as early
as the first line. The weirdness grows with the poem and takes over by the end. The effect is often similar to looking for the first time at a painting by René Magritte. Even
the title suggests Magritte's sort of surrealism, where the light and dark are reversed,
and where the expected is balked at every turn.

Simic grew up in Belgrade, Yugoslavia, and his early childhood experiences included wartime evacuations, anxiety, and sudden changes of plans. "My travel agents
were Hitler and Stalin," he said in an interview for *Cortland Review*. He spent time as
a troubled young teenager studying English in Paris, then sailed for America while
still in his teens to rejoin his father, who had left the country earlier. By young manhood he had experienced war, dislocation, family separation, and poverty, and these
experiences are present directly and indirectly in his work. That stability is illusive,
that what you see is usually not what you get, serves as a major theme in his work.

However, the poems do not present broad, sweeping statements. The trademark
Simic poem is cryptic and elusive, focusing intensely on what appears to be a small
scene or even a trivial item that turns out to have massive reverberations. It is part of
Simic's style to be small, separate, enclosed. His poems do not pile up into an epic or
reach out through myth and history to make some summary statement. Each poem is
itself, and can be read and appreciated independently, although reading them all together does give the reader more of a sense of what Simic is doing. There is a sense of
perverse haiku, haiku gone mad, to some of his work, as if the haiku writer had looked
at the subject so long he had looked right through it or maybe melted it with the heat of
his gaze. Hard parts bend, soft parts are frozen and glazed. Shadows fall far from their
source. There is a constant sense of doubleness in his ironic suggestions that what is
most beautiful is ugliest, what is desirable is repellent, the dark cloud and the silver

lining are really one substance. Sometimes this implication is obvious, as in his tale of the window decorator who is putting a Christmas tree and lights in the window of a funeral home, with cotton snow "From the same stash . . ./ You plug ears and noses with." Sometimes the suggestions are more subtle, and might even be missed except for the context of his other poems. Whether subtly or obviously, the poems assert that the surface is a lie.

Simic's quirky vision does not seem to alter much throughout the body of his work. "Fork," one of his earlier poems, perhaps the most frequently anthologized, sets the tone for his oeuvre. The poem begins: "This strange thing must have crept/ Right out of hell./ It resembles a bird's foot/ Worn around the cannibal's neck."

The estrangement of the ordinary, the linking of daily routine with chaotic nightmare, appears in much of his work, including many of the poems in *Night Picnic*. In addition to Magritte, some of his poems may make the reader think of the photographs of Diane Arbus, whose photographs of gritty detail surrounding her subjects turned ordinary clutter and trivial disorder into pathology. Yet while Arbus's photographs tend to evoke sadness, even despair, there is a positive element—as there is in Magritte—to Simic's

Charles Simic has long been a major figure on the American poetry scene. He has published more than twenty books of poetry, as well as translations, memoirs, and essays. His collection of prose poems The World Doesn't End *(1989) received the Pulitzer Prize, and he has received both the Guggenheim Foundation Scholarship and a MacArthur Foundation Fellowship, along with two National Endowment for the Arts Fellowships and a host of other honors.*

work. There are sometimes suggestions of transcendence in the darkness and jumble, although certainly not always. The grotesque is sad and comic; weirdness can be a relief.

Some of the poems in *Night Picnic* are more superficially coherent than is usual with Simic, yet there remains an element of oddness in even the most unified poems. "Book Lice," for instance, begins with the lice: "Dust-covered Gideon Bibles/ In musty drawers of slummy motels,/ Is what they love to dine on." The "pages edged in gold" that are their favorite food are then abandoned in favor of brief descriptions of the rooms' occupants, the bathtub suicide, "Her face already blurring in the mirror" and the "gray-haired car thief" whose windowpane is "Pockmarked with the evening rain." The poem is very simple, yet the images stay with the reader, and the gold Bible pages, the book lice, the sad transients add up to more than the superficial and obvious connections.

Night Picnic provides a sad carnival, as implied by the title, in which the apparent gaiety of the contemporary scene is presented as a kind of disguise. Many of the titles suggest party time: "Firecracker Time," "With Paper Hats Still on Our Heads," "The

Grand Casino," "Couple at Coney Island," "The Avenue of Earthly Delights," and others. The party never fulfills its promise, however. It is over or it never happened or one is not invited, or perhaps the party is underway but it is not a pleasant one. The party poems convey the weird tackiness of pleasure in its various forms, and their images define the false glitter of Vanity Fair. "The Avenue of Earthly Delights" provides "A tangle of tanned arms, breasts/ Bathed in sweat" as well as masks "On a makeshift table/ With empty eye sockets,/ Mouths frozen in a scream . . ." Nothing that the avenue offers is worth taking, and yet it draws the crowd of frenetic celebrants.

Some of the poems are inhabited by disembodied voices that offer oracle-like, ambiguous answers to the problem of cosmic incoherence. "The Grand Casino" may or may not allude to Wallace Stevens's line, "Life is an old casino in a park," but like the Stevens poem it plays with and on the possibility of transcendence. This short poem offers a "casino of the sky/ Lit up with summer stars," which does not respond to the question of what coin fits "the soul's jukebox." The brief, open poem engages the reader's imagination with its minimalist imagery and mingles natural and artificial, tacky and true in its metaphysical question.

One of the more complex, mystical poems is "Tree of Subtleties," which has the characteristic mysterious opposites of the collection and which teases the reader with metaphysical hints and allusions. The tree's leaves are "hinting/ At dark secrets," although the day is bright: "the sun's yellow broom/ Sweeping the corners for leftover gloom." The tree is "weighted with obscurities" and makes the speaker's heart "flutter/ As if St. John of the Cross himself/ Was whispering his verses/ To the white chickens pecking the corn." Everything seems allusion, the bright day, the dark night of the soul, William Blake's tree and William Carlos Williams' white chickens of "The Red Wheelbarrow." The confusion between definite and indefinite is deliberate. The poem firmly resists closure but its images produce powerful, self-annulling feelings as bright and dark, day and night, earth and heaven, precision and obscurity collide.

The presentation of these poems is spare, the tone colloquial. There is no ornamentation to his free verse and all words are needed for the meaning; Ezra Pound would be content. Many poems have a self-cancelling mixture of jollity and horror, and the poems are open-ended in that readers will differ as to which element they find predominant. This collection seems less self-consciously quirky than the earlier ones, although the radical dissonances are still there. Sometimes there appear to be spaces between the images as though they were noted separately, on different occasions, and only later was some kind of strange relationship established between them. This sense of dislocation is there even if the poem seems to be describing a sequence of events, or a single scene. The effect seems to suggest that any coherence, any apparent meaning can collapse without warning, its parts drifting into other constellations.

Some critics have been disappointed with this collection, complaining that Simic's work does not show enough change, development, progress toward some goal, or that his metaphysics is muddy. According to Fred Muratori, "The poems are vignettes, ordinary or quirky scenes displayed at face value, vaguely inviting the reader to extend them beyond their uncertain borders via glancing references to churches, angels, and saints, convenient ciphers meant to suggest a metaphysical dimension more easily implied than articulated." However, transcendence is imprecise by nature, and the notion that poems must move in a particular direction, build some kind of structure which is to be finished only in the mind, is romantic. It is the persistence of Simic's unique vision that makes his poetry noteworthy, and the odd metaphysical bits belong. The uncanny mixes with the ordinary in poem after poem to produce a shock of recognition: The world has these strange coincidences, these odd parallels, and it is a pleasure to find them even when they horrify because they remind the reader that not all truths are literal. Donna Seaman sees this collection more positively: "Nabokovian in his caustic charm and sexy intelligence, Simic perceives the mythic in the mundane and pinpoints the perpetual suffering that infuses human life with both agony and bliss."

The appeal of this collection is enhanced by the reader's sense that this is not quite American poetry, even though it is paradigmatically so. The scenes are often filled with topoi of the United States. In "Firecracker Time," for instance, the speaker is looking at a newspaper story featuring "a Jesus lookalike/ Who won a pie-eating contest in Texas"; other poems allude to Halloween, a maternity ward in Rochester, New York, carnies and hucksters, familiar New York City street scenes, little New England towns, churches of the 1940's or 1950's. Yet while the scenes, the names are American, there are echoes and shadows of other cultures and traditions—the poems' mixed cultural identities are yet another instance of Simic's doubleness.

Janet McCann

Sources for Further Study

Booklist 97 (August, 2001): 2078.
Library Journal 126 (September 1, 2001): 185.
The New York Times Book Review 106 (October 21, 2001): 15.
Publishers Weekly 248 (June 18, 2001): 76.

THE NOONDAY DEMON
An Atlas of Depression

Author: Andrew Solomon (1963-   )
Publisher: Charles Scribner's Sons (New York). 571 pp.
  $28.00
Type of work: Memoirs, medicine, and psychology

～

Solomon's investigation of the mental and physical ill-ness known as depression is a comprehensive work that begins with the author's own breakdown and expands to include a history of the causes, treatments, and conse-quences of this widespread and intractable malady

～

Andrew Solomon readily admits that he is not an obvi-ous candidate for sympathy: "I did not experience depres-sion until after I had pretty much solved my problems. My mother had died three years earlier and I had begun to come to terms with that; I was publishing my first novel; I was getting along with my family; I had emerged intact from a powerful two-year relationship; I had bought a beautiful new house; I was writing for *The New Yorker.*" Yet by offering himself up as Exhibit A, this privileged son of a pharmaceutical company executive, this former student at Yale and Cam-bridge Universities, this member of the New York literary elite proves his fundamen-tal point: Depression is an equal-opportunity illness, striking rich and poor, old and young, accomplished and undistinguished individuals without discrimination. The goal of his ambitious tome is to cast some light into dark corners where most people prefer not to look and to give hope even to those who have no reason to believe hope exists.

Before he gets to hope—"Hope" is, in fact, the title of his last chapter—Solomon surveys the landscape of mental illness in an effort to describe what depression is, what causes it, and how it might be cured. In this effort he ventures far afield. Solo-mon movingly describes his interview with a Cambodian woman who was forced to watch while members of the Khmer Rouge first gang-raped, then killed her twelve-year-old daughter. Although Phaly Nuon exhibits classic signs of depression—rocking and weeping—while she recounts this story, Solomon tells us that after the fall of the dictator Pol Pot, Nuon went on to found an orphanage and a center for de-pressed women, endeavors that have led to talk of a Nobel Peace Prize. Solomon also traveled to Greenland, where he studied depression among the native Inuit, who enjoy free healthcare and education, but who also live in a land that remains dark for a full three months each year. An astronomical 80 percent of this population is said to suffer from depression. In Senegal, on the northwest coast of Africa, Solomon underwent a kind of public exorcism when he participated in an animist ritual called an *ndeup*, designed to rid the native peoples of depression. After spooning with a live ram who is then slaughtered to provide the fresh blood Solomon must wear in order to be freed of his demons, the author concludes that "the *ndeup* impressed me more than many forms of group therapy currently practiced in the United States."

Not all of Solomon's research took place in such exotic locales. Some of the book's most moving sections appear in a chapter called "Poverty," where he introduces women such as "Lolly Washington" of Prince Georges County, Maryland, an abused and indigent mother of eleven children who was set on a course toward depression at age six, when a friend of her alcoholic grandmother began sexually abusing her. Not all the depressive women Solomon describes are so bereft of resources, however: Laura Anderson is blond and beautiful, graced with both a supportive mother and an attentive boyfriend. Once

Andrew Solomon, a regular contributor to The New Yorker, *is the author of* The Irony Tower: Soviet Artists in a Time of Glasnost *(1991), as well as a novel,* A Stone Boat *(1994).* The Noonday Demon *won the 2001 National Book Award for nonfiction.*

again, the exception proves the rule. While it is true that depression disproportionately affects the poor, the reader's last vision of Laura is of a woman so ill that her mind gets stuck like a broken record. As Solomon recalls,

> She was telling me who was who in [her family] photos and she began repeating herself. "That's Geraldine," she said, and then she winced and began again. "That's Geraldine," each time taking longer to pronounce the syllables. Her face was frozen and she seemed to be having trouble moving her lips. . . . We eventually managed to get her upstairs; she was till saying over and over; "That's Geraldine."

So much for depression being an affliction of malingerers. So much for it being a fashionable self-indulgence.

The Noonday Demon lives up to its billing as an "atlas of depression," providing not only contrasting case studies but also statistics, which are more than a little disturbing in and of themselves. Solomon claims that over nineteen million Americans suffer from this illness, and that some sixty million prescriptions were written for antidepressants in the year 1998. Depression, he says, is the leading cause of disability worldwide for persons over the age of five, and if one takes into account diseases such as alcoholism and hypertension, which can mask depression if depression causes them (and it often does), depression may be the most lethal and widespread illness the world has ever known. The incidence of depression is rising, and its onset is occurring at earlier ages. At the turn of the twenty-first century, depression customarily shows up when its victims are around the age of twenty-six, ten years before their parents' generation might have been expected to manifest signs of the illness. While it is true that depression has been around at least since the fifth century B.C.E., when the Greek philosopher and scientist Empedocles described melancholy as the consequence of an excess of black bile, Solomon states flatly that escalation in rates of depression is an inevitable consequence of the pressures of modern life. Interestingly, however, he questions whether a mental state that is so common can actually be called a disease, and in a chapter titled "Evolution," he rehearses the theory that depression is some sort of adaptive mechanism whereby melancholy fosters self-examination, which in turn begets disengagement from hopeless situations or, alternatively, carefully thought-out decisions about how to change one's circumstances.

Such analyses of depression make for intriguing reading, but it is Solomon's bare-all examination of his own experiences that make this more than five-hundred-page book compelling reading. Although his first big breakdown occurred when he was thirty-one, in retrospect Solomon can see that even as a child his course was in some sense rigged. As a child of six, he was overcome with paralytic fear born of a sense that life was permeable, not a hard surface that one could count on for support. As a teenager, his confusion about his sexuality added to his sense of disorientation and instability. During his last year in college, he suffered a minor breakdown when some unknown fear forced him to return prematurely from a European jaunt. It was his mother's diagnosis of terminal ovarian cancer and subsequent death—by suicide, assisted by her family—that seems to have finally pushed Solomon over the edge.

Solomon is careful, however, to explain that there can be no clear distinction between biological predisposition to depression and experiential triggers. He describes the progress of his disease in evocative terms, comparing it to the growth of a parasitic vine that had gradually merged with and choked most of the life out of an ancient oak tree under which he had played as a child: "My depression had grown on me as that vine had conquered the oak; it had been a sucking thing that had wrapped itself around me, ugly and more alive than I. It had a life of its own that bit by bit asphyxiated all of my life out of me." After his mother's death, Solomon experienced steady slippage of his hold on reality, until, shortly before his thirty-first birthday, he fell apart. Unable to sleep, unable to eat, unable even to control his own bowels or to turn over in bed, Solomon was fortunate to be rescued by his father and turned over to a psycho-pharmacologist. With the help of numerous antidepressant medications, he gradually recovered.

Then, like so many others, he stopped taking the drugs. All too predictably, Solomon backslid into depression. This time, however, instead of being gripped by a crushing weight of terror, he became quietly, determinedly suicidal. His realization that he could not go on seemed to him wholly rational, as did the plan he formulated to do away with himself: He would engage in promiscuous unprotected anal sex in an attempt to contract acquired immunodeficiency syndrome (AIDS). AIDS, unlike depression, was a illness that his family and friends could recognize and understand. AIDS, unlike a gunshot to the head, would not devastate them. It would give him an excuse to kill himself.

Solomon did not contract AIDS, but he put a stop to his risky behavior when he realized that he might be infecting others. In the aftermath of his discovery that he was HIV-negative, the fog of his depression lifted. This would not, however, be his last bout with depression. Solomon seems resigned to the fact that he will probably be obliged to keep on taking antidepressants—"swallowing my funeral," as he puts it—for the rest of his life. He is vehement in his support for chemical treatment of depression, but he is also clear that pills alone cannot save its victims. It is as foolish, he argues, to say that depressives have no control over their fates as it is to declare that they can pull themselves back from the brink through sheer willpower. By extension, he says, it is foolish to attempt to treat depression only with either drugs or more traditional talk therapy—both are necessary, as is love.

Solomon remains disturbed by those who continue to ask him when he will be able to chuck his medication. He recalls how one *New Yorker* editor tried joshing him with the flat-footed rhetorical question, "C'mon . . . What the hell do you have to be depressed about?" It is just such attitudes that contribute to what Solomon sees as America's abject failure to address its rising tide of mental illness. While insurance companies pay for the effects of depression—which can include illnesses such as heart disease—they are notably reluctant to pay for psychiatric care. The Puritan heritage that helped foster Christian Science founder Mary Baker Eddy's religious belief that prayer alone can heal body and soul contributed to Solomon's own decision to go off his medication cold turkey. In presenting his own case so unflinchingly—including even such details as his violent assault on a lover whom, in his depressed state, he suspected had betrayed him—he hopes to demonstrate the fallacy that self-help alone can heal depression and related mental illnesses. The expression of violence was, he readily admits, restorative. It did not cure him of depression.

In the end, there is this: Solomon seems to have learned in some sense not just to live with his disability, but to love it. He finds that it has made him nicer, kinder, more sympathetic, less snobbish. In short, the illness that literally brought him to his knees has made him better acquainted with the human condition in all its forms. The one thought that sustained him through his major depression, during which he had to be spoon-fed by his father, was that he wanted to live so that he would be able to return the favor during his father's old age.

Lisa Paddock

Sources for Further Study

Commentary 112 (December, 2001): 38.
Library Journal 126 (April 15, 2001): 118.
The New York Times Book Review 106 (June 24, 2001): 9.
Publishers Weekly 248 (May 14, 2001): 63.

ON BORROWED WORDS
A Memoir of Language

Author: Ilan Stavans (1961-   )
Publisher: Viking (New York). 263 pp. $23.95
Type of work: Autobiography
Time: 1961-2000
Locale: Mexico City; various European, Near Eastern, South American, and African countries; New York; Amherst, Massachusetts

≈

A polyglot writer-scholar describes an odyssey in search of his true literary and linguistic self

≈

Principal personages:
> ILAN STAVANS, the author, a Mexican-born teacher and writer of Jewish extraction
> BELA STAVCHANSKY ("Bobbe Bela"), grandmother of the author
> ABREMELE STAVANS, the author's father, an actor
> DARIÁN STAVANS, the author's brother

Although the subtitle of Ilan Stavans's book promises a linguistic theme, much of the early emphasis falls rather on his family and his travels. A Mexican-born professor of Latin American culture, he is also a writer who has discovered that he is most at home in New York City (to which New England, in his mind, serves as a sort of extended suburb) and most creative in the English language. To arrive at this geographic and linguistic destination, Stavans had to come to terms not only with his Jewish heritage but with the four languages which his ethnicity, his homeland, and his present nation imposed upon him. The ingredients of this book include a candid analysis of three family members, a description of several years of nomadic drifting in early adulthood, and an account of his happy assimilation into the cultural life of New York.

The attention he gives to family might lead the reader to expect an early encounter with an archetypal Jewish mother. Stavans has a Jewish mother, but she is an educated woman, a psychology professor whose significance for him, it must be said, does not equal that of three other family members. He was gifted with an especially influential Jewish grandmother, Bela Stavchansky—Bobbe Bela to her grandchildren. Born in 1909 in a Warsaw suburb, she emigrated to Mexico in 1929 and married a Ukrainian immigrant. In the New World she relinquished both Russian and Polish, in which she was fluent, in favor of the Spanish of her adopted nation and Yiddish, always her language of everyday need. Nevertheless, she wrote and consigned to her grandson Ilan a thirty-seven-page memoir of her life composed in imperfect Spanish, thus raising two puzzles of great importance to him.

One has to do with memory and with the form of autobiography that relies on it most heavily. A memoir, Stavans wryly observes, is "driven by our desire to improve our prospects in human memory," and he found Bobbe Bela's *diario*, as she called it, no exception. Her memory having warred unsuccessfully with her desire to leave the family a flattering account of herself, her children and grandchildren easily enough recognized her fabrications. She consigned the memoir to Ilan, he judges, to inspire him to write his own life. In this book he has striven for an authenticity which Bobbe Bela's effort lacked.

Ilan Stavans has both written and edited short-story collections; he is also the author of nonfiction such as The Hispanic Condition *(1995) and* The Riddle of Cantinflas *(1998). He is Lewis Sebring Professor of Latin American and Latino Cultures at Amherst College.*

Stavans's attitude toward memory is an ambivalent one. Despite the tricks memory can play, and despite the temptation to bend it in the service of the self that one wants to project, it is the faculty that rescues past experience from oblivion. The author has good reason to dread oblivion. Several of his relatives failed to escape the Holocaust, and one great-uncle, who had emigrated to Argentina from Poland, returned to Warsaw as a widower with his children in time to perish with them at Auschwitz. Another great-uncle lost his memory, was institutionalized, and the family ultimately lost track of him. Better an imperfect record of a life than its erasure. Stavans is struck by the title his friend Richard Rodriguez gave to one of his own books: *Hunger of Memory*. Obviously, for Stavans also, memory is food for the soul.

Stavans's own memory, he says, is capacious. Certainly his telling use of detail in his remembrances of times past and his facility at quoting from "somewhere" in this or that writer lends support to his claim. (Nevertheless, he manages to include at least one amusing instance of misremembering in asserting that his Mexican passport lists his height as 1.58 meters and his weight as 170 kilograms. These figures convert to five feet, two inches and 375 pounds, dimensions easily belied by the photograph on the dust jacket of *On Borrowed Words*.) More important than the capacity of Stavans's memory or its lapses, however, is his conviction that memory is a creative faculty capable of conferring significance on "disjointed" and "incongruous" scraps of apparently meaningless life experience.

The other puzzle which his grandmother's memoir posed for him is a problem for polyglots only: to what language should one's most heartfelt experiences be committed? Stavans's choice of language for his most personal writing (he also produces criticism and other essays in Spanish), while less surprising than his grandmother's, is one earned through a process of seemingly aimless drifting about most of the continents of the world and reflecting on the merits of the available tongues.

For a third-generation Mexican from a family interested in maintaining its Jewish traditions, the process actually began much earlier. Unlike most of his classmates at the Jewish school he attended for fifteen years in Mexico, he enjoyed the intensive study of Yiddish. He came to realize how central it had been to Jewish communal life, but he also recognized its limitations as a literary vehicle. Expressive as this spoken language of Central and Eastern European Jews is, its present audience is relatively small and inevitably diminishing. For the sake of one possible alternative, the "classical" Jewish language of Hebrew, the twenty-year-old Stavans journeyed to Israel. Although no Zionist, he was "enchanted" by Hebrew, absorbed it readily, and learned to relish poems by Shlomo Ibn Gabirol and Yehuda Halevi. Not surprisingly, however, he found that the language had less of a hold on him after his sojourn of several months in the Holy Land had ended.

He credits *Moby Dick* (1851), which he read in his mid-twenties after coming to New York, with opening up to him the possibilities of English. He took to copying and assiduously looking up the meanings of the unfamiliar words in Herman Melville's text—a practice that deadened the impact of the novel as literature but vastly enlarged his English vocabulary and brought him to a realization of the possibilities of literary English. As he took to speculating about this discovery, the great Polish novelist Joseph Conrad's account of his own discovery of English as a literary vehicle impressed Stavans profoundly. Conrad, in replying to critics and reviewers who wondered why he wrote neither in his native Polish nor in French, his second language and one familiar to him from an early age, explained that he had not chosen English as his literary vehicle. Rather, he was "adopted by the genius of the language." Like Conrad, Stavans discovered in his maturity that in an alien tongue lurked his true language of self-expression. He regards English as a "precise, almost mathematical" language, an idiosyncratic notion surely. One thinks of Samuel Beckett, who discovered precision, more plausibly perhaps, in French and professed an inability to translate his work accurately into his native English. The extraordinarily large English word stock permits precise choices, but is not the precision in the writer rather than in the language? It is certainly possible to argue that the allusiveness, the connotativeness, of the English language militates against precision.

Results, however, matter most, and Stavans has achieved an English style particularly suited to the probing, questioning utterances so prevalent in *On Borrowed Words*. At the time Stavans realized his similar destiny to write in English, he professed discomfort at his "appalling accent," a defect that apparently did not greatly trouble Conrad, who spoke with a thick Polish accent throughout his life. (Conrad, one suspects, might have faced a larger problem had he written in the current era of virtually mandatory promotional speaking tours.) Accent, however, falls away on the page, and very seldom does Stavans's prose betray anything less than a firm command of idiomatic English.

The second great family influence on Stavans was Bela Stavchansky's second son, Abremele, the author's father. An actor of considerable talent, Abremele, like so many other Jewish performers with difficult Eastern Europe surnames, simplified his: thus, Stavans. His reluctant involvement in a family business limited Abremele's theatrical prospects during his young and handsome years; consequently, he never reached the top rank of his profession and took to piecing out his later stage work with routine television fare, including commercials. The author stresses his closeness to his father, whose career and advice to his son both warned him that an artist's life was liable to involve unwelcome compromises.

The author's debt to his younger brother Darián is less clear. Some of his unpleasant disclosures about his brother's life make sense only if one assumes that his main importance is as a reminder of the perils of destructive behavior. Darián also possessed talent, but not of the verbal sort enjoyed by his father and brother. A stutterer, he early displayed love for and promise in music. Although Stavans never explicitly connects his brother with his own early obsession for a pistol which his father kept (but for which he never bought ammunition), the reader is left to wonder whether his revelations of Darián's suicidal and even murderous tendencies—fortunately not consummated—amounted to a self-check on his own strong passions.

As for the literary influences on Stavans, they are wide-ranging. Aside from *Moby Dick*, he refers familiarly to scores of other books, European and Latin American works predominating. He credits his eventual gravitation to New England with introducing him to other major nineteenth century American writers—Nathaniel Hawthorne, Walt Whitman, Edgar Allan Poe, and Ralph Waldo Emerson—but the present book exhibits few signs of their importance for him. Although now teaching at Amherst College, he does not mention that town's greatest gift to literature, Emily Dickinson. The grand sweep of Whitman's poetry appeals to him, and he pays homage to Jorge Luis Borges and other poets, but admits that he is not particularly a reader of poetry. He favors narrative prose in a stream from the great seventeenth century Spaniard, Miguel de Cervantes Saavedra, down to the present, and has absorbed the techniques of modern prose masters.

The organization of *On Borrowed Words* reflects his interest in the flexible manipulation of chronology in narrative—another Conradian legacy. He begins his book, for example, with an account of his arrival in New York City, artfully leading the reader to suppose that as a recent arrival from Mexico he has been overwhelmed by the Big Apple. Later, the reader learns that Stavans was no wide-eyed provincial when New York and Herman Melville exerted their sway. He had not only visited Israel but lived and worked variously in a number of European countries and had made stops in Africa and South America. The effect is to enhance New York as a particularly nourishing cultural apple.

Along the way, this book might well have focused more attention on the people, the tongues, and the experiences of his New York, less on family members (as distinct from his ethnic heritage, which is extremely important to his purpose). Nonetheless, it ends brilliantly with a poignant anecdote of a woman whom Stavans met in an airport on his way back to New York from Houston. Because she had lost her memory and thus her power of significant speech, his own and two kindly policemen's attempts to help her proved fruitless. Reading *On Borrowed Words* conveys the full horror of such a condition.

Robert P. Ellis

Sources for Further Study

Booklist 97 (August, 2001): 2077.
Library Journal 126 (July, 2001): 92.
The New York Times Book Review 106 (September 16, 2001): 16.
Publishers Weekly 248 (July 2, 2001): 61.

ON HISTORIES AND STORIES
Selected Essays

Author: A. S. Byatt (1936-   )
First published: 2000, in Great Britain
Publisher: Harvard University Press (Cambridge, Mass.).
    196 pp. $22.95
Type of work: Literary criticism

~

In this collection of essays addressed both to the general reader and the literary specialist, an eminent and erudite novelist explores the nature of historical fiction and its popularity among contemporary authors, as well as its connection to a resurgence of interest in narration and storytelling

~

On Histories and Stories brings together two sets of lectures, the Richard Ellmann memorial series at Emory University and the Finzi-Contini talk given at Yale, with a few other related occasional pieces, all of which focus primarily on contemporary literature. In them, the prominent British novelist A. S. Byatt addresses nothing less than the complex connections between reading and writing: reading as it is done by the "amateur" lover of books—whom Virginia Woolf famously called "the common reader"—and the "professional" literary critic; and writing as done by both the literary theorist or specialist and the creative artist. Herself a university teacher and essayist as well as a novelist in the grand tradition of George Eliot in the nineteenth century and of Iris Murdoch and Doris Lessing in the twentieth, Byatt is a blend of all these different types of readers and writers in this volume, where she poses and answers several questions: Why does one practice criticism in the present age, and how should one do it? Why has historical fiction recently undergone a resurgence in popularity, and how might one go about writing it? What accounts for the renewed interest among current authors in the age-old story or tale? Readers will find the core of her argument expounded in the lengthy essay at the center of this collection, "True Stories and the Facts in Fiction."

Byatt situates her comments about why she is drawn to practice criticism in the context of what she sees happening in the academy today. Although she remains tantalized by the Barthesian notion of the reader as writing the text, she is uneasy about what this means for concepts of authorship and authority. Furthermore, she is troubled by the gulf between literary theory and the words in a given text; she might find much of current criticism "clever," with its practitioners adopting the rhetorical flights of fancy and imaginative stance once the province of the writers and artists, but it still "distances" her as a reader. Finally, the current field of literary theory has be-

∽

A. S. Byatt, whose novel Possession
(1991) won England's prestigious
Booker Prize, studied at Cambridge
University, Bryn Mawr College, and
Oxford University. Her other works
of fiction include The Virgin in the
Garden (1978), Still Life (1985),
The Matisse Stories (1993), and
Babel Tower (1996). A former
university teacher, Byatt has also
written several books of literary
criticism, among them Passions of
the Mind (1991).

∽

come overly politicized, subject to the vagaries and whims of group ideologies, and consequently transient. Using an approach that is heavily text-centered (and thus one that will appear determinedly old-fashioned to some), Byatt hopes to "create new paradigms" and "complicate the discussion" by mapping out recent fiction, mainly British, which she does by ranging widely over three dozen writers, from such well-known luminaries as Anthony Burgess and John Fowles, V. S. Naipaul and Muriel Spark, to such lesser-known lights as Penelope Fitzgerald and Ian McEwan, Hilary Mantel and Graham Swift.

In order to do the kind of broad-based criticism that will appeal to both the common reader and the specialist and that Byatt undertakes here, one must first be a voracious reader who immerses oneself in a text by encountering it over and again, listening to it until the words—and all the words from earlier texts that "haunt" and inhabit it—reveal themselves. It is the type of critical reading that depends for its force and authority upon extensive quotation of lengthy passages from the text being studied (sometimes unaccompanied by much commentary); these textual quotations—what Byatt calls "the Thing itself"—are as integral to the literary essay as are "slides in an art historical lecture." Hers is a criticism heavy on wonder and appreciation. The narratives she will analyze and discuss employing this method fall mainly into two categories, historical fiction and the story or tale, both of which she herself has written.

In her choice of historical fiction as her favored subgenre, Byatt distinguishes herself sharply from her own sister, the novelist Margaret Drabble, and other twentieth century writers of "sensibility" such as C. P. Snow and Kingsley Amis, who believe that the proper aim of fiction is to depict, interrogate, and criticize contemporary society. Despite opening herself up to the charge of turning out escapist books, she readily joins the increasing ranks of writers whose subject is the past and whose fictional works coincide with "a complex self-consciousness" among historians "about the writing of history itself;" their awareness that "all history is fiction," that there can be no such thing as an objective reporting of past events, has done nothing less than "restore the narrator" to history—and thus provide a telling example for writers of "fiction as history." Obviously, many of these authors took up historical fiction in order to bring the marginalized to the center, as is true of postcolonialist and immigrant writers such as Salman Rushdie and Timothy Mo.

If the modernist novel from Woolf in England through Michel Butor and his followers in France was marked by stream-of-consciousness, epiphanies, and experimental techniques such as fragmentation and flashbacks, the new historical novel of Byatt and her contemporaries will once again foreground narration, storytelling. Furthermore, it will do so in forms that utilize—or even merge—parody and pastiche, romance and allegory, with maybe some of the secrecy and thrills of popular genre fiction thrown in for good measure. Using Peter Ackroyd's novels as an example—though it would apply equally well to such works of her own as *Possession* (1991), *Angels and Insects* (1993), and *The Biographer's Tale* (2000) in their attempts to recuperate and rescue "complicated" Victorian thinkers from dismissal—Byatt points to a stylistic feature she terms "ventriloquism," as a way, through imitative language, of resuscitating the past so that the readers "hear the Victorian dead." If the modernist texts that eschewed storytelling adopted largely the first-person voice and limited point of view in order to render subjectivity and project a radical skepticism, Byatt herself will favor third-person narration, not because such omniscience somehow apes the gods, but rather because she believes it allows her, paradoxically, to get closer to the interior lives of her characters and keep better control of the external reality, allowing for the weight, gravity, and moral vision that concreteness can alone provide in an age lacking transcendent sanctions.

All of these abstract concepts and ideas are themselves made concrete in an opening triptych of essays entitled "Fathers," "Forefathers," and "Ancestors." In the first, she looks at narratives of World War II and her father's generation, beginning with the late modernists Henry Green and Elizabeth Bowen and the comic chroniclers Evelyn Waugh and Anthony Powell, through Peter Everett and Robert Irwin—who pose questions about the possibility of art and literature in the face of the Holocaust—to Julian Barnes and Pat Barker. She finds the latter's *Regeneration* trilogy the "best and formally much the most interesting," not for its "ideology of the feminization of society brought about by the war," but because of the way in which Barker "avoid[s] the constraints of prescribed feminist subject-matter." In "Forefathers," she focuses her gaze on the more "distant pasts" as analogues for the present and the formal strategies devised for narrating them by authors such as Fowles, William Golding, Mantel, Fitzgerald, and Jeanette Winterson, among others. Finally, in "Ancestors," she turns her attention to how she and those who have come before have read their world by interrogating the way in which Darwinian ideas about human origins affect the subject matter and formal qualities of current fiction that is largely resistant to his questioning of the significance of individual lives. Throughout these essays, she is fascinated by notions of biological time, both linear and cyclic, of determinism and chance or accident, and of cataclysm and indestructability.

The volume's final three essays, "Old Tales, New Forms," "Ice, Snow, Glass," and "The Greatest Story Ever Told," all have to do with what Byatt sees as a renewed interest in storytelling and the tale. The last—which is not, as its title might suggest, about the Bible, but rather about *The Thousand and One Nights* (fifteenth century; English translation 1706-1708), apotheosizes Scheherazade as the archetypal storyteller who, through an inventive imagination, unleashes the power of narrative to almost endlessly postpone death. Yet if she must "narrate or die," it is equally true that in death, everyone's life is elevated to the level of story, affirming the immortality of art for those lacking any other faith. Here and in "Old Tales," which posits a greater interest by European writers in the genre of the tale, Byatt ranges widely over authors such as Rushdie, Karen Blixen (Isak Dinesen), Jorge Luis Borges, Italo Calvino,

Roberto Calasso, and Naguib Mahfouz who have reworked myths, rewritten fairy stories, or who have otherwise borrowed or retold collections of tales that can now be seen as talking back to or in conversation with earlier ones. Valuing the form for its qualities of economy, rhythm, and logic, Byatt traces its influence upon *Possession* and its stories-within-stories, where her intention was "to *feel and analyse* less, to tell more flatly."

Some of Byatt's most astute analysis comes in "Ice, Snow, Glass," where she turns her own critical lens upon two fairy tales, Hans Christian Anderson's "The Snow Queen" and the Grimm Brothers' "Glass Coffin"—the latter of which she herself rewrote as if it came from the pen of Christabel LaMotte, one of her characters in *Possession*. She argues that interpretations of the binaries of red/white, ice/fire, snow/blood, life/death in these two stories have most often resulted in unambiguous readings that valorize the need for the girl to be awakened from a lethargic, lonely, virginal state and rescued by the male for the proper destiny of marriage and happily ever after. Yet Byatt says that, even as a young girl, she herself sensed there was "something secretly good, illicitly desirable" about the dormancy and isolation of the ice princess, whose condition might be "life-giving" as well as "threatening." Here Byatt's aesthetic and her own nonstrident feminism—one that rejects, for example, such things as rewriting fairy tales for no other purpose than to convey "messages of female power"—converge: Happiness may be purchased too dearly, at the expense of a space of one's own and the solitude necessary for the creation of the work of art. It is, finally, the affirmation of the unfragmented and unfettered life and "the perfection of the work" that matter for Byatt above all else.

Thomas P. Adler

Sources for Further Study

Library Journal 126 (February 15, 2001): 168.
New Statesman 129 (December 4, 2000): 51.
The New York Review of Books 48 (May 17, 2001): 16.
The New York Times Book Review 106 (March 18, 2001): 6.
The New Yorker 76 (February 19, 2001): 216.
Publishers Weekly 248 (January 22, 2001): 310.

ORNAMENTALISM
How the British Saw Their Empire

Author: David Cannadine (1950-   )
Publisher: Oxford University Press (New York). Illus-
trated. 264 pp. $25.00
Type of work: History
Time: 1850-1950
Locale: The British Empire

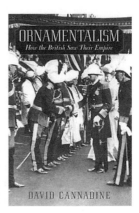

∽

*Cannadine defines two aims in this study: to demon-
strate how Britain's vast empire constituted at its height
one great organic unity, and to discover what the British
Empire actually looked like both to the British at home and
to those overseas*

∽

Of the unity of the British Empire during the period 1850-1950, Cannadine says,
"[T]his remarkable transoceanic construct of substance and sentiment is imperialism
as ornamentalism," and ornamentalism is "hierarchy made visible, immanent and actual . . . with ample available plumage for showing it and for showing off." Readers
will find the "plumage" best illustrated in a photograph of the Prince of Wales wearing an Indian headdress in Banff, Alberta, in 1919, and the corpulence of Sir Robert
Menzies fully clad in absurd regalia is certainly visible and immanent.

Although Cannadine does not deny the Britons' sense of their racial superiority, he
stresses the importance of their vision of a social hierarchy in which the illiterate natives at the periphery were seen as the social counterparts of the working masses in
the metropolitan homeland. When the British thought of their overseas peoples collectively, they often saw them by race, but seen as individuals they were judged
by their social status. Thus, it was not only an Enlightenment belief in the inferiority
of dark-skinned peoples that guided British overseas governance but also a pre-
Enlightenment understanding of "a carefully graded hierarchy of status, extending
in a seamless web from chiefs and princes at the top to less worthy figures at the
bottom." Between the Indian Mutiny of 1857 and Indian independence, British rulers
strove to create both at home and abroad a picture of a "layered" hierarchy unifying
the empire. Cannadine defends this thesis in a series of chapters that distinguish
among the dominions, India, the colonies, and the mandates.

Cannadine points to the hierarchical attitudes revealed in Britons' general contempt for American Indians and African Americans, and he quotes Edmund Burke's
brutal remarks about native peoples. British settlers abroad tried to replicate "on top"
of these lower castes a system of rank like the one they knew at home, inventing

~

*David Cannadine is professor of
history and director of the Institute
of Historical Research at the
University of London. He is the
author of numerous books,
including* The Decline and Fall of
the British Aristocracy *(1990),*
Class in Britain *(1998), and* History
in Our Time *(1998).*

~

such titles as Esquire, Gent, Master, and Honourable to identify everybody's place in a society marked by subordination. Unfortunately for England, the antihierarchical sentiment in the United States overwhelmed the empire's best efforts to sedate its growing colony with titles and plumes, and when the Revolutionary War ended, the British determined that elsewhere in the colonies hierarchy would be "nurtured and supported" as a means of diverting the population from social revolution. The Act of Union of 1800 joined Great Britain and Ireland in a new "imperial-cum-metropolitan unity," and the appointment of a viceroy who lived in splendor in Dublin Castle created the "proconsular prototype" that would eventually preside over India and throughout the Empire. The viceroy was the "cynosure and apex" of an elaborate structure of pomp and ceremony.

The Irish solution was extended to Canada, where the conservative immigrants were susceptible to a rigid social order. In India, where a firmly layered society already prevailed, based not on property but on caste and manners, the British policy was to strengthen the system by fluffing up the native princes and developing a regime of "unprecedented grandeur" catering to the Indian taste for such ceremony. The British saw themselves in a layered society at home and wanted to see their overseas possessions structured in the same way. To encourage intricacies of rank and title, a bloated honors system evolved, with the (English) Order of the Garter, the (Scottish) Order of the Thistle, and a new (Irish) Order of St. Patrick. The Order of the Bath was extended, and the order of St. Michael and St. George was introduced. Cannadine explains: "The result was the consolidation of a pan-British, pan-imperial elite that conquered and governed, unified and ordered, the empire for the first time."

Despite these efforts and despite how the system may have looked to Britons at home, this grand scheme was only a "partial image" of reality. British conservatives in India often scorned the native rulers they perceived as corrupt and loathed the manners they judged barbaric, and surely many colonial subjects understood—and resented—British manipulation. At the same time, Cannadine insists that "from the Indian Mutiny of 1857 to Indian independence ninety years later, the rulers and leaders of the British Empire tried to make that hierarchical system happen, and that hierarchical vision convince." How they went about this challenge is his story.

Britain's four great dominions of settlement—Australia, New Zealand, Canada, and South Africa—were treated as "white men's countries," resulting in the disregard of such "inferior" peoples as the "Hottentots" in South Africa, the Indians and Inuits in Canada, and the Maoris and Aborigines in New Zealand and Australia. The subsequent treatment of these groups was unconscionable, for the Maori of New Zealand were robbed of their land, as were the Xhosa in the Cape and the Zulu in Natal. With the natives shoved to one side, the dominions all developed their own social structures modeled on the homeland example, and some influential Britons even urged transplanting an aristocracy to grow in Canada. Given the Canadian enthusiasm for British traditions of hierarchy, it is not surprising that their governors would be "mimetic monarchs" and that from Melbourne to Toronto, Sydney to Cape Town, as Cannadine puts it, stratified societies evolved with all the accompanying pomp and snobbery.

The situation differed in India, where "analogues of hierarchy" prevailed as the British saw in the caste system a familiar arrangement open to exploitation in maintaining power. The result was that two-thirds of India was ruled by a government that was "simultaneously direct and indirect, authoritarian and collaborationist, but that always took for granted the reinforcement and preservation of tradition and hierarchy." In the remaining third of India, the rajahs and maharajas, the nawabs and nizams, were suddenly welcomed not as petty exploiters but as brothers of a sort, a gentry all their own presiding over five hundred personal fiefdoms and serving as puppet governors for the Raj. To make this system palatable to the locals, the British spoke of these various ruling princes as "native aristocracy" and indulged in spectacular durbars, or meetings between the rulers and the ruled, and cultivated the policy of ornamentalism to its limit by building magnificent lodges and palaces. The vanity of certain viceroys meant that "New Delhi was the setting for the grandest living on earth, with more bowing and curtseying, more precedence and protocol, than anywhere else in the empire, London included."

Collaboration with conventional tribal structures became the British policy as well in its colonies in Malaya, Fiji, Ceylon, Nigeria, Kenya, Uganda, Bechuanaland, Basutoland, and Swaziland. Even though Joseph Chamberlain, the colonial secretary from 1895-1903, wanted to dismiss the native rulers and modernize the colonies, he was overruled. Lord Lugard, high commissioner of Northern Nigeria from 1900-1906, described Britain's practice of indirect rule as, in the words of his biographer, "the most comprehensive, coherent, and renowned system of administration" the empire had achieved. The result of British efforts was a system modeled on the Indian pattern with plenty of "imported proconsular pomp" but not approaching the plumed ornamentalism of the Raj. In fact, to many romantic imperialists, the overseas societies seemed purer and less corrupt than the metropolis, and "indirect rule of dark-skinned races was about admiration rather than condescension." If that sounds a little improbable, consider the remark that in certain aspects "Merrie Africa" may have surpassed "Merrie England."

The British occupied Egypt in 1882, and after World War I the empire took over League of Nations mandates in Jordan and Iraq to pursue what Cannadine terms its "last act of traditional-cum-imperial social engineering." Nineteenth century Britons who had traveled in the Middle East had loathed the "despotic politics and squalid conditions" they had perceived, but half a century later, faced with social turmoil at home, "many anxious and disenchanted patricians" endowed the tyrannical Bedouin chieftains with a romantic splendor. T. E. Lawrence—Lawrence of Arabia—was joined by Winston Churchill in ruing the passing of such dynasties as the Habsburgs, Hohenzollerns, and Romanovs, and admiring the Arab feudal chieftains. Churchill, for instance, admired King Ibn Sa'ud of Arabia, who had signed a treaty in 1927 giving Britain supremacy in the whole area, and he expressed great confidence in Emir Abdullah of Jordan.

In the late nineteenth and early twentieth centuries, the British indulged in a rage for honorifics to satisfy the need of their puppet rulers—Indian princes, Malayan sultans, Sudanese sheikhs, Nigerian emirs—to feel important and equal to their masters. Lord Elgin remarked that "in the colonies, premiers and chief justices fight for stars and ribbons like little boys for toys, and scream at us if we stop them." The number of knights bachelor jumped from 230 in 1885 to 700 in 1914; one of them was the first African to be knighted, Samuel Lewis from Sierra Leone in 1896. Lord Curzon, viceroy of India, may look a bit overdressed wearing the insignia and robes of a knight grand commander of the Order of the Star of India, but no more than the begum of Bhopal adorned with the same insignia. The result of this frenzy of ornamentalism was a "complex and comprehensive titular hierarchy" that, it was hoped, projected a picture of a unified empire.

Cannadine never abandons his thesis but he undercuts it sharply in his chapter titled "Limitations," which admits that the empire was never as homogenized as the government wished it to be. Most Indians were not seduced by ornamentalism, and British fondness for "traditional" India ignored the radical middle-class reform movement growing in Calcutta. Comparable follies plagued British rule in Africa and the Middle East, where social conservatism did not lead to passive acceptance and the empire came to be seen as a hindrance to progress. Many Indian maharajas detested the plumes of ornamentalism as "false and demeaning," an embarrassing circus in which they were expected to perform. In Nigeria and Malaya, the tribal leaders chosen for their independence and intelligence became problem puppets for having just those qualities. The worst messes came in the Middle East, where King Faisal of Iraq was completely unreliable in the 1920's, as was his successor, King Ghazi, whose broadcasting station attacked British rule. Egypt's King Farouk openly sided with the Axis powers in World War II and had to be bullied into supporting the Allies. The "make-believe and illusion" of ornamentalism derived, Cannadine believes, from Britons' naïve views of the cultures they ruled. The hierarchies of the dominions had no traditions, as revealed by the many errors in *Burke's Colonial Gentry*; "timeless" India was actually evolving rapidly; and the Malayan sultans and African chiefs were not what the British supposed them to be. Thus, the "whole paraphernalia of the imperial monarchy" had no substantial underpinning, and the empire was ripe to be split into separate, sovereign nations.

The times were changing. The Irish Free State established in 1922 became an independent republic in 1949, two years after India achieved independence in 1947. Abandonment of the rulers of the Indian native states was criticized by many for the policy's apparent cynicism, a hardness that Cannadine explains as driven by Nehru's thorough contempt for any remnants of the Raj. At her coronation in 1953, Queen Elizabeth II presided over a much diminished Britain, as Canada, Australia, and New Zealand were coming "to stand for national autonomy, open access, social equality, economic modernity, ethnic diversity, and multiculturalism." The African and Middle Eastern states had been inflated by pomp and they collapsed in brave ceremonies, leaving Britons aware that they would have to deal with a different social class. In the last analysis, the British practice of ornamentalism may be best judged as a failure in cultural understanding.

Frank Day

Sources for Further Study

Library Journal 126 (August, 2001): 130.
The New York Times Book Review 106 (August 26, 2001): 17.
The New Yorker 77 (September 24, 2001): 93.

PACIFIC TREMORS

Author: Richard Stern (1928-   )
Publisher: Northwestern University Press (Evanston,
Ill.). 200 pp. $26.95
Type of work: Novel
Time: The 1990's
Locale: Fiji, Los Angeles, San Francisco, and Italy

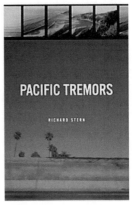

~

*A tale of Hollywood, centering not on the young and
glamorous but on a pair of friends in middle age who try to
retain and recapture the successes of youth*

~

Principal characters:
> EZRA KENERET, a director
> MARCIA KENERET, his wife
> WENDELL SPEAR, English film critic and historian friend of Keneret
> LEET DE LOOR, a Frenchwoman Keneret discovers in Fiji and casts as
> the star of his latest film
> JENNIFER ABARBANEL, Spear's attorney granddaughter

Pacific Tremors is a large-hearted narrative concerned with the human foundation
beneath the glittering Hollywood facade. Stern explores the drive for success and the
narcissism of the movie kingdom, while also considering the timeless verities of human experience. His creations are always more than they appear and their capacities
for tenderness and sympathy dispel Hollywood stereotypes.

The novel begins in Fiji, where sixtyish Ezra Keneret, a director en route from a
failed attempt to secure financing for a film, believes he has found cinema's newest
sensation, Leet de Loor, a young French woman. Keneret is so taken with her, he develops a script treatment and begins shopping around Hollywood for cast, crew, and
financing. His choices, necessitated by his flagging career, are an assemblage of over-
the-hill prospects, long on talent but short on other offers.

A month into the shoot the project unravels when it is discovered that de Loor cannot act, Keneret's cameraman is injured filming the Rodney King riots, and the producer withdraws financing. Keneret is left without his moorings, while his friend and
confidant, Wendell Spear, lives a reclusive life in the Malibu hills as his career begins
its decline. Suddenly displaced and without a job, Leet de Loor works as a stenographer and before long establishes a multimillion dollar business writing vanity biographies for the rich and famous. Jennifer Abarbanel, Spear's granddaughter, rises on the
corporate ladder, is abruptly "downsized" and left at loose ends, and later revives her
career by joining de Loor's thriving enterprise.

On the surface, *Pacific Tremors* would seem to be another in long line of Hollywood novels, and indeed Stern plows some familiar ground by satirizing the shallowness and vanity of the film industry. Keneret's interviews with actors and crew members are hilarious profiles in self-absorption, as each of these hacks imagines himself vital to the industry and Keneret finds himself massaging their fragile egos.

In a certain respect, Keneret finds comfort in the business, delighting, for instance, in being back at a studio where all human needs are miraculously attended to. In explaining filmmaking to the novice de Loor, he tells her that films cannot handle much complexity and that their job is "to make [people] fall in love with the characters, the shadows." Keneret is awed by the subtle power of cinema and aims to exploit its powerful influence on an audience.

Richard Stern is the author of the novels Golk *(1960),* Stitch *(1965),* Other Men's Daughters *(1973), and* Natural Shocks *(1978). He has also published collections of short stories and a memoir,* Sistermony *(1995), which was awarded the Heartland Award for Best Nonfiction Book of the Year. Stern teaches at the University of Chicago, where he has been a faculty member since 1955.*

What was he after? Some heightened yet simplified, at least clarified, depiction of decisive encounters set in artful spaces arranged to speed the pulse of thought, of being, human being, so that the result would be and perhaps stay part of every viewer's own interior book, a guide to and transfiguration of existence. And this for a few dollars, and without—at least physical—risk.

This world of illusion, however, is littered with failure, and like F. Scott Fitzgerald and Nathanael West before him, Stern concentrates on the human wreckage.

His Hollywood is as much prison and asylum as it is dream factory, a place that thrives on failure as much as success. In many ways it is a quintessential small town, where people know each other's business, and Keneret despairs of his new status: "Tomorrow everybody here will know I'm out. Every face will look different. They'll look through me. I'm not there anymore. Transparent. Empty. A nothing. What that writer Ellison said blacks felt in white streets. The visibility so threatening it has to be unseen. Oh, we're a species, we are."

Throughout the novel the integrity and cohesiveness of individual selfhood dissolves under the pressures of professional failure. Before his project is aborted, Keneret accidentally catches a stray glimpse of himself in a mirror and is shocked to find his reflection that of his own grandfather. Age and status "shadow" him, but these reflected images and shadows suggest Keneret's growing dissociation from himself.

His project is an act of personal reclamation; therefore, when the money vanishes the sense of defeat is all the more acute. "Duggan [the producer] had brought him back from film exile, from the grave of not working. Now he'd reburied him, as if

Christ had raised Lazarus so he could throttle him." As he feels himself falling down the arc of his career, Keneret declares he has "no self left" until he performs some inevitable stocktaking.

He finds his answer immediately before him in his wife, Marcia. Twenty years Keneret's junior, she longs to advance to his age and share more of their lives. Watching him at loose ends, she convinces him to work on an autobiographical sketch and engage himself once more, if only vicariously, with his career. Keneret comes to a more profound appreciation of her, describing her as his "lifeline," and realizes a life is more than a career.

Wendell Spear wrestles with his own sense of finitude. Surrounded by Hollywood's despair and what he labels "Pacification"—the "invisible dominance of a Pacific mentality" that leads inevitably to "the actual, not virtual, death of the imagination"—Spear has retreated to his house in the hills, the one thing about Hollywood that brings pleasure and consolation. However, after a canyon fire consumes everything, Spear also finds himself at loose ends. His purpose is found in his enduring love for his granddaughter, Jennifer. As a result of her affection, he eventually reconciles with his estranged daughter just before he succumbs to cancer.

Leet de Loor struggles with her own failure. Deserted by her father during World War II after supporting the Nazi's "final solution," de Loor wanders through life enjoying transitory pleasures but no significant sense of purpose. Apart from being attractive, she is a cipher, and her curious sense of absence dooms her film career. When she inadvertently discovers her father's address in Argentina, she effects a reunion. He reveals no love or affection and is a broken figure, a denounced man who sought relocation and reinvention: "I won't explain my life here now. Much of it has been undoing, forgetting, trying to forget the life I had, the person I was." However, the escape is doomed; he can neither escape the past nor reclaim himself. There is no "I" to recover." Where the other characters delude themselves into thinking that self can be equated with profession, de Loor's father realizes that self is more a profound phenomenon and inextricably bound up with those whom one loves.

The theme of love is central to the book, as Stern examines a range of relationships. Early in the narrative Keneret remarks to himself "that people in the grip of feeling fall into classic poses. You see them actually turn into art." Indeed, Stern's characters are each wrapped tightly in the grip of feeling and as a result become something more refined than their mere personalities. The novel explores love between spouses, between parents and children, between grandparents and grandchildren, between friends, and the love that people have for their professions. Love is provoked by the immediate and tactile but also by memories, which for Keneret are in some cases over fifty years old. He further believes that by knowing more, feeling more, loving more he can become a better director, and thus age only enhances, rather than weakens, ability.

When Jennifer tells Spear of an exhibit where patrons record four-minute messages about love, he gravely ponders what he might say. Laboring over his eventual presentation, Spear considers the works of modern writers such as Philip Roth and John Updike and concludes:

Lovers were each other's motif, outlet, occasion of relief and exaltation, almost second selves, not just theaters of each other's seductive and sexual performances. As for the last, Spear, their reader, realized how limited his own virtuosity had been even when lust and passion dominated every day and night. . . . His feelings, though, had not been banal, or, if banal, still enormous; but he'd never worked up a vocabulary for them.

Jennifer's letter of response is a cry from the heart, so deep and affecting that Spear can look beyond its sentimentality to the purity of its feeling.

However, it is de Loor's father who grimly puts all the novel's loving into context. When he meets his daughter after decades of separation, she assumes—largely because of films and their sentimentality—that the two will fall into each other's arms for a tearful rapprochement. Nothing could be further from the truth: He tells her that he cannot feel much more than guilt. "Love is a choice, not nature," he bluntly confesses. "If you need to hear the word *love* from me, I'll say it, but to feel it, I'd have to undo myself." This choice to love characterizes most of the character's attachments, and the novel's beauty resides in Stern's ability to make those choices believable and compelling.

As de Loor's father reveals, there are fault lines that run under any relationship, and thus the novel's title becomes an ironic commentary not only on life in California but also on human attachments and allegiances. The novel abounds with earthquake and tremor imagery, as characters are repeatedly described falling into literal and figurative abysses, while some even dream of dropping into boiling magma. Humor is never far from some portraits, as one corpulent composer is described as a mountain, who, when he copulates, sends Southern California on quake alert. However, Hollywood is a perfect metaphor for social and personal instability, as everyone's emotional and psychological footing becomes increasingly precarious.

The novel ends with a brief episode during which a pregnant de Loor and her husband are awakened as the ground shifts and she races to save her child. The rumbling transforms not only their sense of time but also their sense of the bizarre. Suddenly they are closer than they have ever been, and Stern's examination of human fragility and affection comes into high relief.

Stern is a master of narrative economy, accomplishing more with a single sentence than seems possible. In an era of metafictional self-reflection, his works, while not exactly straightforward, hark back to an earlier method of storytelling. *Pacific Tremors* glistens with gems of wit and verbal precision and carefully developed, though never sentimental, emotions.

David W. Madden

Sources for Further Study

Booklist 98 (December 15, 2001): 705.
Publishers Weekly 248 (December 3, 2001): 41.

A PAINTED HOUSE

Author: John Grisham (1955-   )
Publisher: Doubleday (New York). 388 pp. $27.95
Type of work: Novel
Time: 1952
Locale: Arkansas

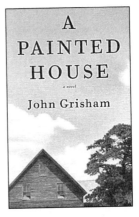

~

In a surprising departure from his highly successful legal thrillers, Grisham writes a realistic novel about life on a cotton farm based on his own memories of an impoverished and overburdened childhood

~

Principal characters:
> LUKE CHANDLER, a seven-year-old boy who narrates the story from an adult perspective
> JESSE CHANDLER, Luke's father
> KATHLEEN CHANDLER, Luke's mother
> ELI "PAPPY" CHANDLER, Luke's grandfather
> RUTH "GRAN" CHANDLER, Luke's grandmother
> HANK SPRUILL, a young temporary farm laborer with a violent disposition
> TALLY SPRUILL, a teenage girl with whom Luke falls in love at first sight

A Painted House is an abrupt and surprising change of pace for legal-thriller author John Grisham, who has been turning out one best-seller after another since 1991 and accumulating countless millions from book sales and movie rights. In this faux memoir inspired by his childhood, he writes about the drudgery and simple pleasures of life on a cotton farm in Arkansas. The narrator, Luke Chandler, is looking back into the past to the time when he was only seven years old and had to work all day in his grandfather's cotton fields, hoeing weeds when the plants were growing and picking the snowy harvest starting in September and sometimes continuing straight through to December. Critics have complained about the ambiguous tone of the narration. Grisham uses simple words and short sentences to create the illusion that it is a seven-year-old talking, but at the same time the incidents are obviously being described by a grown man—someone about Grisham's present age—looking back into the past. The book can hardly be called a coming-of-age novel, because the hero-narrator is still only seven when he concludes his story. Although Grisham has earned a fortune by producing one blockbuster novel after another, he shows a certain ingratiating awkwardness and naïveté in venturing into an entirely new genre.

The Chandlers are poor. They stand halfway up the social ladder between sharecroppers and land owners. They rent eighty acres and are chronically in debt to the landlord and the merchants who sell them cotton seed, spare parts for their old vehi-

cles, and the few staples they cannot raise themselves. Like most one-crop farmers, they are at the
mercy of the weather, the world's economy, and
the mysterious commodities market. When crops
are good the price of a bale of cotton is forced
down by the iron law of supply and demand.
When the price is high it is because droughts or
floods or insects have left the farmers with little
cotton to sell. The Chandlers keep a cow and
chickens, raise pigs, and have a large vegetable
garden. Ironically, these subsistence resources
keep them alive, while their eighty acres of ined-
ible and sometimes unharvestable cotton only
drive them deeper into debt.

*John Grisham, formerly a practicing
lawyer, is the phenomenally
successful author of numerous
novels dealing with legal practice
and politics. Many of his books,
including* The Client *(1993),* The
Pelican Brief *(1992),* The Firm
(1991), and A Time to Kill *(1989),
have been made into high-grossing
films featuring Hollywood's top
stars.* A Painted House *hit the top of
the* New York Times *Bestseller list
shortly after publication.*

In September, 1952, when Luke is seven years
old, nature seems to have given the cotton farmers
a bountiful yield, but they are having trouble rounding up pickers. They finally manage to hire a truckload of hardworking, respectful Mexican braceros and a family of
unruly, unreliable Arkansas hillbillies. The Mexicans move into the barn and the hill
people set up tents in the Chandler's front yard, making an unsightly mess.

Day after day, the entire Chandler family, including Luke's mother and grandmother, along with their temporary helpers, go out into the cotton fields and drag their
long sacks down the rows until they are too heavy to drag further. Then the cotton is
weighed and dumped into a truck to be driven into town to the cotton gin. Even
though Luke is only seven years old, he is expected to put in a full day picking cotton.
His parents and grandparents are desperate to earn enough to pay down their debts
and have something left over to survive another winter. They are nervous about the
weather. Their only source of entertainment is their radio. On the hot, humid nights
they sit outside and listen to the Saint Louis Cardinals baseball games with pleasure
and the weather reports with trepidation.

Luke's mother Kathleen is the only member of the family who understands the futility of their struggle for existence. She wants her husband to get a factory job "up
North" and quit farming for good. Jesse Chandler knows he can make three dollars an
hour assembling Buicks in Flint, Michigan. In 1952 there is little competition from
foreign car manufacturers, and Americans are buying the gaudy gas guzzlers as fast as
they roll off the assembly lines. Jesse has already gone up North several times to keep
the family from starving, but he is reluctant to make the commitment to leave Arkansas forever. For one thing, he feels like a cotton farmer and not a factory hand. It is the
difference between being independent and becoming a cog in a wheel. More importantly, he does not know how his mother and father can get along without him. His
brother Ricky is off fighting in Korea and might never come back to work on the farm.
If he did come back, he might get married, start his own farming operation, or move
away. Ricky has gotten a local girl pregnant. She believes he loves her and will marry
her, although she belongs to a family of lowly sharecroppers. One of the dramatic ele-

ments of Grisham's story has to do with the question of what is happening to Ricky overseas and whether he will ever come home to resume a normal life.

A Painted House is autobiographical, but Grisham obviously realized that a whole book about life on a farm could become monotonous. With his sharply honed professional skill he has inserted fictional elements to make his story dramatic. Hank Spruill commits a brutal murder which the young protagonist actually witnesses. Luke is pressured to keep his mouth shut because the Chandlers cannot afford to lose the labor the Spruills provide. If Hank is arrested, his family will pack up and move away. Furthermore, Hank has repeatedly threatened to disembowel Luke with his switchblade if the boy gives him away and might even murder other members of the Chandler family. Luke's parents, strict Baptists, have taught the boy that he should always tell the truth. Now, in painful isolation, he is learning the conflict between the ideal and the cold reality.

Meanwhile the sadistic Hank Spruill, the only human antagonist in the plot, is deliberately provoking the Mexican laborers. A minor war seems inevitable. Hank finally gets his comeuppance when he attacks one of the braceros on a bridge and ends up floating down the river with a knife wound in his abdomen. Luke, true to his role as the viewpoint character, just happens to be on hand to witness this death duel and has another secret on his conscience for the rest of his life.

The weather is favorable, but there are radio reports of rain and flooding in nearby states. Occasional thunderstorms hold up harvesting for a day or so, but the creeks and the river are still held within their banks. Luke's grandfather hopes to make enough money from this year's crop to pay down some debts. This is the major dramatic question of the loosely structured plot. It is not answered until the very end when the black clouds move in with their full fury and rain finally becomes universal. The creeks dump more and more water into the Saint Francis River. The river overflows its banks and relentlessly floods the lowlands. No more cotton can be salvaged. In addition to sustaining another financial loss, the god-fearing Chandlers are forced to shelter and feed the Latchers, a big family of sharecroppers who have not only lost everything they own but have to be rescued from drowning by boat. One of the Latchers is the teenage mother of Ricky's newborn child.

This disaster in a year of bountiful crops is the last straw for Luke's mother. She has come to hate farming and what Karl Marx once called the idiocy of rural life. She insists that her husband take her and Luke to Michigan, where he can do his parents more good by earning cash money and sending some of it back home. There are painful scenes of separation which echo the real separations that have been going on in the United States since the exodus from country to the cities began around the beginning of the twentieth century.

Some of the dramatic questions which have kept the reader turning the pages never get answered. The reader is left wondering whether Ricky survives the Korean War and whether he comes back to marry pathetic little Libby Latcher. The reader is left to wonder what ever happened to Luke's grandparents. Did they ever finish painting their house? How long did the Latchers with their horde of children continue to live in the Chandler barn? Grisham may be planning to publish a sequel in which he ties up some of the loose ends. Otherwise, the reader will be left to guess that what happened was about the same as what has happened to millions of other rural Americans. Gramps and Gran held on as long as they could and then followed their children to the big city, where they were hapless dependents until they died. Ricky probably survived Korea and returned to America but did not marry Libby. The Latcher children, including Libby's illegitimate son, either died or somehow managed to grow up and moved away, trading serfdom for wage slavery.

Grisham's novel is significant, not only because it represents an interesting departure by one of America's most prominent writers, but because the Chandler's story, like the story of the Joad family in John Steinbeck's *The Grapes of Wrath* (1939), symbolizes what has been happening to America's farm families, who used to represent 90 percent of the population, as the result of technological innovation, economic pressures, free public education, and changing mores. Sharecropping is no longer a viable institution. Small farmers are being driven off the land and replaced by agribusiness. The cities offer opportunities and attractions the younger people cannot resist, and life on the land seems more and more grueling, monotonous, and fruitless. The little farmhouses and barns are being bulldozed, the fences torn down, the land tilled and harvested by gigantic machines that move for miles in one direction before they ever have to turn around. At harvest time the fields are illuminated all night long by the blazing headlights of mechanical monsters that never get tired or hungry.

Grisham's novel is a bittersweet memorial of the way things were in America's bucolic past. Some of his dramatic elements sound derivative. When Luke induces the Mexican migrant workers to help paint his grandfather's house by making them think it is good fun, the incident is so reminiscent of Mark Twain that Grisham rather self-consciously makes Luke's mother say, "Well, if it isn't Tom Sawyer," to which Luke improbably replies, "Who's he?" When Luke is forced to lie about having seen the murder committed by Hank Spruill, the reader is reminded of Tom Sawyer's troubles with Injun Joe. When the Chandlers and Latchers are ruined by the big flood, the reader is reminded of the climax of *The Grapes of Wrath*, especially as there is a newborn infant and a flood involved in the family tragedy.

It is in the genuine little details of daily life, the parts that are true to Grisham's childhood experience, and not in the invented dramatic material, that the novel shines. Grisham is to be commended for turning away, at least temporarily, from his outrageously lucrative, and somewhat redundant, legal thrillers and writing truthful regional literature in the tradition of great American authors such as Hamlin Garland, Sherwood Anderson, Steinbeck, William Faulkner, and Wallace Stegner.

Bill Delaney

Sources for Further Study

The American Spectator 34 (April, 2001): 90.
Booklist 97 (February 1, 2001): 1020.
Library Journal 126 (March 1, 2001): 131.
The New York Times Book Review 106 (March 4, 2001): 31.

PARADISE PARK

Author: Allegra Goodman (1967-   )
Publisher: Dial Press/Random House (New York).
   360 pp. $24.95
Type of work: Novel
Time: 1972-1998
Locale: Hawaii; Jerusalem; Brooklyn; Boston; Cambridge, Massachusetts

~

Sharon Spiegelman's quest for religious enlightenment and satisfying human relationships over a period of twenty-five years and several geographical locations engenders a colorful picaresque novel

~

Principal characters:
   SHARON SPIEGELMAN, the narrator
   MILTON SPIEGELMAN, Sharon's father
   CATHY SPIEGELMAN, Sharon's stepmother
   ESTELLE SPIEGELMAN, Sharon's alcoholic mother
   GARY, Sharon's first lover and dancing partner
   BRIAN WILLIAMSON, an ornithologist at the University of Hawaii
   KEKUI, a Hawaiian student who is Sharon's lover after Gary
   PASTOR MACLAREN, an evangelist who tries to convert Sharon
   BARON and T-BONE (THAD), Sharon's housemates
   WAYNE, a marine who loves Sharon possessively
   EVERETT SIEGEL, a rabbi who tries to return Sharon to Judaism
   DAVID and RUCHEL, a Bialystoker Hasidic couple who befriend Sharon
   RABBI SIMKOVICH, who runs a religious school (Bais Sarah) in Bellevue, Washington, where Sharon studies
   DR. AND MRS. KARINSKY, Bialystoker couple in Brooklyn with whom Sharon lives when she meets Mikhail
   MIKHAIL, Russian émigré pianist and Bialystoker whom Sharon marries
   LENA, Mikhail's Christian aunt on his mother's side

Sharon Spiegelman's first-person narrative begins when she recounts how she and Gary, her dancing partner and lover, leave Cambridge, Massachusetts, for Hawaii, where Gary hopes to work with Brian Williamson, an ornithologist at the University of Hawaii. Gary believes Brian is interested in saving endangered wildlife, but he quickly becomes disillusioned and takes off with another woman for Fiji, leaving Sharon stranded in their hotel with barely enough money to pay their bill. Thus Sharon's quest for identity and meaning in her life begins.

Sharon accompanies Brian and his students to an island to do research on red-footed boobies, but that adventure is short-lived, and she is disappointed when the research paper does not adequately acknowledge her work on the team. Working at a fast food restaurant, she meets Kekui, a college student dropping out of school for a while to earn money. They fall in love, but Kekui's parents disapprove of Sharon both because she is not Hawaiian and because she is not a devout Christian as they are. Sharon and Kekui flee to an island paradise on Molokai, where they live until Kekui feels compelled to return to his people after his father dies.

Allegra Goodman has published the volumes of short stories Total Immersion *(1989) and* The Family Morkowitz *(1997), as well as an earlier novel,* Kaaterskill Falls *(1998). She lives with her family in Cambridge, Massachusetts, and contributes stories to magazines, including* The New Yorker *and* Commentary, *while working on her next book.*

Abandoned once again, Sharon gets another job and meets Wayne, a marine who falls desperately in love with her. He treats her well but is very possessive. On a whaling trip together, Sharon has an extraordinary experience: "The sky swung back in liquid gold, the air mixed with the water. I saw something. It was a whale, but not just a whale. It was a vision of God." The vision is a turning point in Sharon's life, because from then on she is on a religious quest. Her life completely changes. She breaks up with Wayne, who is unsympathetic about her experience, and alters everything else in her life, getting a new job, a new place to live, and new friends.

Sharon's new housemates are Baron and Thad, whom everyone calls T-Bone. They are big men who love to party but are very generous and decent to Sharon. Sharon also gets a cat, whom she names Marlon. She now works for a religious couple, the Lius, who run a jewelry shop in the Ala Moana Shopping Center. They take an interest in Sharon and, together with their pastor, the Reverend MacLaren, try to convert her to Christianity. Sharon is open to the idea and studies hard, feeling some of the love and gentle warmth with which the religion tries to fill her, but ultimately, it does not take, and taking drugs does not help, either. Nevertheless, she is intent on finding God somehow.

Sharon gets a new job at the Good Earth, a health food store, where the manager, Kim, suggests that she go on a retreat to the Consciousness Meditation Center, a 1950's Buddhist ranch. Attracted to their way of life, Sharon gives the monks all her earthly goods, including her grandfather's silver watch that has been a good luck charm for her. This religious experience also fails, and Sharon returns to her house, her friends, and her cat. She gets a new job and a new place to live. Continuing her quest for religious enlightenment, she enrolls at the University of Hawaii as a part-time religious studies major. Her first course is very satisfying, but the second one, by a far less charismatic teacher, is a disaster. She abruptly walks out during a boring lecture by an arrogant professor on St. Augustine. Meanwhile, she hears from Gary, who has become a convert to orthodox Judaism in Jerusalem.

After some correspondence with him, Sharon flies to Jerusalem to meet Gary, hoping they can pick up again, not where they left off but in a new, religious way. Sharon takes instruction at a yeshiva, where she lives among other women, but she finds the strict orthodoxy that Gary has embraced very hard to bear. Thanks to Rabbi Everett

Siegel back in Hawaii, who persuaded her to teach folk dancing to a group of elderly ladies in his synagogue, Sharon has earned enough money for her trip. Rabbi Siegel is also very eager to help Sharon recover her Jewish roots, and it is during one of their conversations that Sharon has another profound religious experience—learning to listen to another person who is reaching out to her. Listening well is something that Sharon, a rather wild, free spirit, has never been able to do, for she has been too self-absorbed most of her life. Before she goes to Jerusalem to meet Gary, Rabbi Siegel teaches Sharon Hebrew and more about Judaism than she has ever known. Though both her parents are Jewish, they are not practicing Jews and have long been divorced. After her alcoholic mother left, Sharon had gone to live with her father, a Boston University professor and dean, and his second wife. Their strict discipline and lack of understanding alienated her, and she eventually became estranged from them as well as from her unstable mother.

After her disastrous trip to Jerusalem, Sharon returns to Hawaii and her dying cat. With Marlon's death, she feels she has hit rock bottom. She has failed her course at the university, and she has neither boyfriend nor ambitions. Then she meets David and Ruchel, a couple deeply immersed in the Bialystoker sect of Hasidic Judaism, who have come to Hawaii to help stimulate Jewish religious life. They interest Sharon in their way of life, and through their efforts get Sharon a full scholarship to the Bais Sarah Institute, a kind of boarding school for women, in Bellevue, Washington. There, under Rabbi Simkovich's tutelage, Sharon learns still more about Judaism and begins to love it deeply. David has already convinced her that she has a "Jewish soul," which is why, he says, she could not fully embrace any of the other religions she has studied. After several months at Bais Sarah, she goes to live with Dr. and Mrs. Karinsky, another Bialystoker couple, in Brooklyn, New York, where Estie, her teacher from Bais Sarah, is about to be married.

At Estie's wedding, Sharon meets Mikhail Abramovich. He is a Russian immigrant and a classical pianist who is trying to earn some money by playing in the band. Sharon and Mikhail, who is also a deeply religious Jew and a Bialystoker, fall in love, much to the delight of the Karinskys. Sharon is not sure about marrying Mikhail, however, even though she loves him. An interview with the rebbe, or leader of the sect, is arranged, and he simply advises Sharon to ask her parents what to do.

Following the rebbe's instruction, Sharon goes to Boston to see her parents. It has been nearly twenty years since she last saw her father and even longer since she has seen her mother. The meeting with her father and stepmother is strained and unsuccessful, as they cannot forgive her many past misdeeds, especially her lying. Sharon then goes to find her mother, who is working in a New Age shop in Provincetown, Rhode Island, and has given up drinking in a sustained attempt to reform her life. Their meeting is more pleasant, but while her mother cannot give Sharon any more advice than to ask if she loves Mikhail, Sharon recalls that her mother and father once loved each other very much, too, and then everything fell apart. Nevertheless, she is not ready to give up on love and goes to find Mikhail in Boston, where he lives with his Aunt Lena.

After visiting with Mikhail and his aunt, Sharon decides that they should get married. A serious complication arises on the eve of their wedding, when the Karinskys learn that Mikhail's mother was a converted Jew, not a Jew by birth. They insist that evidence must be found to determine whether the conversion occurred under the supervision of an orthodox rabbi and was approved by a rabbincal court; otherwise, the conversion would be invalid and Mikhail could not be considered Jewish. Gathering the evidence, even if it could be found, could take six months, but the couple decide not to wait. Though it means leaving the Bialystoker fold, their decision does not involve giving up their strong Jewish faith. They get married and live with Lena in her small apartment in Boston, as Mikhail tries unsuccessfully to enter piano competitions that could help him make a name for himself. He is constantly refused entry, and Lena suspects anti-Semitism may be playing a part in the rejections. Meanwhile, Sharon becomes pregnant.

Desperate to earn a living, Sharon and Mikhail form a small band that performs at weddings and similar occasions. Sharon manages the group, called The Refusniks, and becomes the band's lead singer. The work provides the couple with a modest income so that they are at last able to find a place of their own to live. The novel ends with the birth of their son, whom they name Zohar. At his circumcision ceremony, Sharon's parents attend, and the family is finally reconciled to their erstwhile incorrigible daughter.

Sharon's quest ends there, in a good Jewish family environment, with a devoted husband and their infant son. Gary turns up again, this time in a suit, working for the Jewish Federation's adult education program, the Partnership for Lifelong Learning, which he has codesigned. He, too, has changed once more, now more pessimistic and no longer religiously dedicated, but still clinging to his Jewish identity. Quizzed by her old lover, Sharon explains that besides working for the band, she manages an organic juice store in Brookline, is earning a degree in organic nutrition, and has become an active member in her havurah (a Jewish discussion group). She concludes:

> In general, in my life, you know what the thing is? I stopped looking. The thing I realized was I didn't need to go on looking anymore, and learning this and reading that and taking classes, because God was actually looking for me! So I decided to be a receptor. I've decided to be more of a listener, and a sounding board who is open to God in all the ways he might come—visions, dreams, prophecies, music—in all his myriad forms. Do you know what I mean?

The question, put to a skeptical Gary, is also addressed to the reader, who may or may not know what Sharon means, but can certainly understand and appreciate her long and difficult quest.

Jay L. Halio

Sources for Further Study

Booklist 97 (February 1, 2001): 1039.
The Christian Science Monitor, March 1, 2001, p. 16.
Library Journal 126 (January, 2001): 154.
The New York Times Book Review 106 (March 11, 2001): 10.

PEACE LIKE A RIVER

Author: Leif Enger (1961-   )
Publisher: Atlantic Monthly Press (New York). 313 pp.
$24.00
Type of work: Novel
Time: 1962-1963
Locale: Minnesota and North Dakota

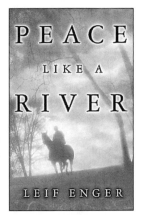

~

*A boy, his sister, and their remarkable father undertake
a wintry journey across the Great Plains in search of their
brother and son, who has fled from justice*

~

Principal characters:
REUBEN LAND, an asthmatic eleven-year-old boy
DAVY LAND, his beloved brother and idol
SWEDE LAND, their sister, a budding writer
JEREMIAH LAND, their father, a hard-working janitor
ISRAEL FINCH and TOMMY BASCA, two teenage thugs
MARTIN ANDREESON, a federal agent who is hunting for Davy
ROXANNA CAWLEY, a nurturing farm woman
JAPE WALTZER, a dangerous fugitive

Peace Like a River is a strange but pleasing coming-of-age book, containing echoes of the picaresque novel and the archetypal quest, with passing references to Homer, the Bible, and historical figures of the American West. Leif Enger immediately establishes a winning voice for his eleven-year-old narrator, Reuben Land, which alternates with the adult Reuben's omniscient but equally relaxed voice. He is a perceptive character, although admittedly self-critical, "beyond my depth and knowing it, yet unable to shut up."

To begin with, Reuben was born "a little clay boy" with ominously swampy lungs, unable to draw breath until his father, Jeremiah, rushed into the hospital room and commanded him to breathe. Even though the infant was without oxygen for twelve minutes, he miraculously suffered no brain damage; but his lungs remain weak into adolescence. Ironically, while Reuben has watched his father walk on air and heal a man's raw face with a single touch, his own asthma remains uncured. Jeremiah can only steam him with salt and baking soda or thump his back to loosen the congestion.

Reuben fully believes he has survived such an inauspicious beginning in order to bear witness to his father's unexplainable miracles, since "no miracle happens without a witness." He does not use the word "miracle" lightly, for real miracles bother people. He is never certain whether his father prays for miracles or whether they just happen.

Before the boy's birth, Jeremiah was studying medicine on the G.I. Bill until he was snatched up by a tornado and deposited unharmed four miles away. This event changed his life. "Baptized by that tornado into a life of new ambitions," he dropped his medical studies in favor of an intense spirituality. His wife, disappointed by his lack of initiative, later abandoned him and their three children. Now he works as a school janitor in the small town of Roofing, Minnesota, and is plagued by frequent, stunning headaches.

Leif Enger graduated from Moorhead State College and worked as a reporter and producer for Minnesota Public Radio for many years. He has coauthored several crime novels with his brother Lin under the pen name of L. L. Enger.

A mild man of conscience, he reads his Bible daily, silently, and without ostentation. A man of prayer and intense conversation with God, he at one point literally wrestles with the Almighty.

Davy, Jeremiah's older son, is in some respects already an adult at sixteen, but unfortunately he possesses an impatient nature. Unlike his father, he prefers to act rather than wait. An accomplished hunter and trapper, he affectionately labels his adoring brother "Natty Bumppo" (after James Fenimore Cooper's famous marksman), following Reuben's first successful hunt; and he is very protective of their little sister, known only as Swede. Swede is precocious and endearing, an enthusiastic but unorthodox cook who sometimes decorates her sugar cookies with frozen peas. She is a widely read and literate child but blunt with the artlessness of childhood. She asks good questions that do not have easy answers.

A passionate fan of Western novels, Swede is in love with the legendary Old West. Astride an old saddle Davy has given her for her ninth birthday, she types spirited poetry with overtones of Robert Service. The dashing Sunny Sundown, hero of her poems, is an upright lawman turned reluctant outlaw. Her real-life hero is the young Teddy Roosevelt, who ranched in North Dakota before becoming president. Reuben, too, admires and envies Roosevelt for his triumph over asthma.

During a school football game two local troublemakers, Israel Pinch and Tommy Basca, corner Davy's girlfriend in the girls' locker room and attempt to molest her. At his janitorial duties, Jeremiah overhears the struggle and chases them off. The girl later reports that his face was mysteriously "luminous" in the darkened room as he whacked the two boys with his broom handle. After the boys threaten his family, the feud escalates. The Lands find their front door covered with tar, which Jeremiah quickly cleans, hoping the matter will end there, but it does not.

While Jeremiah and Reuben attend an evening service at the Methodist church, Swede is abducted and terrorized by Israel and Tommy. Enraged, Davy wants to go after them, demanding, "How many times does a dog have to bite before you put him down?" Instead, his father quietly summons the town policeman, who does nothing. Two nights later, Davy smashes out the windows of Israel's car, a deliberate provocation, and when Israel and Tommy break into his home with a baseball bat, Davy shoots them both. Although he is arrested and jailed for murder, he refuses to plead self-defense, insisting that he intended to shoot.

Reacting to the scandal, the school superintendent decides to "scour that janitor's teeth" by first humiliating Jeremiah and then publicly firing him in in front of a lunchroom full of children. At Davy's trial, a reluctant Reuben testifies as an eyewitness to the shootings until, carried away by self-importance, he unintentionally strengthens the case against his brother. There is little hope that the jury will release Davy, who promptly breaks out of jail, escaping with a horse and a revolver. No one knows where he has gone.

The family's hard times grow harder. Jobless and depressed, Jeremiah becomes seriously ill with pneumonia. His children pound his back to relieve his clogged lungs as their doctor prescribes antibiotics and bed rest. Reuben finds a temporary job tearing down a corncrib, for which he is paid twenty-five dollars, and he is then able to buy food for the household.

Just before Christmas, the family is visited by Martin Andreeson, a federal investigator. Apparently, Davy has crossed the state line. Swede and Reuben are hostile, dubbing Andreeson the "putrid fed," but their father answers all questions regarding Davy with absolute honesty. On Christmas Eve they receive a mixed blessing—word that an acquaintance, a hard-luck traveling salesman, has died, bequeathing his brand new Airstream trailer to Jeremiah. After a friend in North Dakota reports that Davy has been seen, the Lands determine to find him.

As they set out on a modern odyssey, towing the shiny Airstream trailer with their old station wagon, the novel expands its mythic dimensions. Andreeson follows them across the Great Plains in bitter winter weather to a small city park, where a severe headache forces Jeremiah to camp overnight. When the federal agent knocks on their trailer door at dinnertime, Swede steals out to pour maple syrup in his gas tank so he will not follow them again.

They pass through central North Dakota, evading state troopers who strangely enough never see or stop them. They find themselves driving across the frozen prairie on an empty tank, waiting to run out of gas and propane heat for the trailer. Well into the Badlands, a notorious area of bleak buttes and mesas in the western part of the state, they come to a farmhouse with two gasoline pumps in front and a propane tank. The self-reliant owner, Roxanna Cawley, greets them with a newborn goat in her arms. Earth mother and impressive cook, she soon offers them a place to stay the night.

Reuben, who has always feared dying in his sleep if he cannot breathe, is frequently troubled by bizarre dreams. That night he dreams of a ghastly little man who ties up his strangled breath in a skin bag. When his father wakes him, Roxanna is pounding his back to keep him from choking. Overnight, snow transforms the landscape, and the blizzard prolongs their stay until snowplows can free them. Soon Reuben is referring to Roxanna as "a lady you would walk on tacks for." Swede is greatly impressed by her knowledge of multisyllable words and, best of all, by her colorful stories about her great-uncle, a physician and gunsmith who was a friend of the outlaw Butch Cassidy. Jeremiah and Roxanna are falling in love with each other.

Roxanna treats them to a wondrous January picnic in the Badlands, where years ago lightning struck a vein of lignite that is still burning. In this "garden of fire" where "the ground itself seemed coming unstitched," Andreeson again appears to report that Davy is definitely in the area. He begs Jeremiah to search with him before the boy is hurt or killed. The next morning Reuben sights his brother on horseback, watching him, and after dark Davy takes him to his hideout to meet a fellow fugitive, Jape Waltzer.

When Reuben sees the formidable Waltzer, he subconsciously links the man's "eyes from a dead photograph" with the evil little man who carried the skin bag filled with his breath. The boy is terrified. Nevertheless, he continues to ride out secretly with Davy at night in the hope that his brother will return to them. He anguishes over Davy, whose attitude toward the killings is pragmatic: "Say I did regret it; what good does it do? I have to go on from here."

Meanwhile, Jeremiah has begun to court Roxanna, even moving out to the Airstream at night to preserve her reputation. Both good people who deserve happiness, they are transfigured by this gentle courtship. At the same time, Reuben is disturbed by his father's newly cordial relationship with Andreeson, who no longer appears to be an enemy. When the agent suddenly halts all communication, Reuben, fearing for his brother's safety and then for Andreeson's, must decide whether to reveal Davy's whereabouts to their father.

Enger presents a moral dilemma with respect to the character of Davy. The reader is reluctant to view Davy as a hardened outlaw even when his crime, a double murder, is described in detail. Placed in the same ambivalent position as his family, one longs to support him even though he never expresses remorse for what he has done. It is as if the world cannot render a clear-cut judgment of Davy, and perhaps that is the point.

One might be tempted to allegorize this novel, for it could easily slide into abstraction: Jeremiah as the good Christian, a saint, even (as one critic suggests) as God; Davy as the archetypal rebel, beloved even as he sins; the fugitive Jape Waltzer, who is always accompanied by the odor of sulfur, as the Devil. To limit the book in this way would be doing it a disservice, for its very human characters are beautifully drawn. At its center it revolves around the overwhelming power of love—divine, human, and brotherly love, perfect and imperfect—the love that binds this small family together.

Enger's vivid imagery is an attractive feature of *Peace Like a River*. The clink of coffee cups and an overheard conversation may be reassuring noise or "the sounds of hope landing facedown." The book also provides some of literature' s most accurate and claustrophobic descriptions of severe asthma. As Reuben explains, "Sometimes when the breathing goes it goes like that—like smoke filling a closet. . . . Your breaths are sips, couldn't blow out the candle on a baby's cake." In lyrical passages, Enger evokes autumn and winter on the Great Plains ("skies so cold frost paisleyed the gunbarrels"). Here the land itself is always a presence, a sharp reminder of a power far beyond human limitations—immense sky, sweeping prairie, the cold, clean Dakota wind—even the boundless desolation of the fabled Badlands, where the ground is eternally on fire.

Joanne McCarthy

Sources for Further Study

Booklist 97 (May 15, 2001): 1707.
Library Journal 126 (June 15, 2001): 102.
The New York Times Book Review 106 (September 9, 2001): 19.
Publishers Weekly 248 (July 16, 2001): 166.

PERFECT RECALL
New Stories

Author: Ann Beattie (1947-   )
Publisher: Charles Scribner's Sons (New York). 347 pp.
  $25.00
Type of work: Short fiction
Time: 1995-2000
Locale: Maine; New York City; Key West, Florida

~

In this uneven collection of eleven stories, Beattie explores relationships gone awry and the fragile bond of male friendship

~

Principal characters:
> CARLEYVILLE, a Vietnam vet whose life is composed of many minor disasters
> RICHARD HOWARD MANSON, secretary and researcher for world-famous chef Lowell Cartwright
> JANE, whose perfect recall of every situation enables her to chronicle her family's story
> FRAN, a wife who never feels comfortable at her husband's family gatherings
> DEREK, a man whose commitment to his friend Wendell costs him his marriage

Fresh from the success of her new and collected stories *Park City* (1998), Ann Beattie offers up *Perfect Recall* (2001), a collection of eleven stories, all set in the present, but using the 1960's and 1970's as a mythological buttress which many of the characters reference. The stories mark something of a departure from Beattie's earlier stories and novels that offer authentic glimpses into the ambiguity of contemporary relationships. Though some of her earlier skill shows through in stories such as "Mermaids" and the title story "Perfect Recall," this collection is flawed by Beattie's use of obvious plot devices and transparent characterization, which forces the reader to rigid and largely predictable conclusions. Furthermore, Beattie's talent for depicting her cultural milieu with accuracy often sinks into baby-boomer nostalgia in some of these stories. One thematic thread that runs through most of the works, the culture of male friendships, adds a different dimension to the book, but does not form enough of a cohesive thread to keep the collection together.

The first story in the collection, "Hurricane Carleyville," illustrates Beattie's reliance on simplistic characterization and forced resolution. The story chronicles the protagonist Carleyville's passage from somewhere in the Midwest to the home of friends

Ann Beattie has published several collections of stories and novels. Her work has appeared in O. Henry collections and John Updike's Best American Short Stories of the Century *(1999). In addition, Beattie has received a Guggenheim Fellowship, as well as an award in literature from the American Academy of Arts and Letters.*

Jimmy and Fiona in Maine. He travels with a dog, a cat, and an older horse that he pulls in a rickety horse trailer. He is not feeling well. He hits his hand. His truck battery dies. In essence, this man is an emotional and physical mess. When he arrives at his friends' home, they are preparing for a hurricane which threatens the coast. In the process of helping his friends, he lures the husband into a hurricane-turbulent river for a swim, and cuts his arm, requiring thirty-eight stitches. The reader does not have to look far to see that the main character is something of a hurricane himself. Then, in the final pages of the story, Fiona makes the comparison even more explicit when she tells him, "We ought to send *you* outside and let the damned *hurricane* in." This announcement of the symbol detracts from the reading of the story. Instead of being a fully developed character, Carleyville becomes a collection of Dickensian mannerisms that announce the story's "moral" before the story has concluded. This same problem plagues other stories in this collection, sometimes making the point of the work too obvious.

Another story that uses the same problematic technique is "Coydog." Here, Beattie adopts an almost Anne Tyler-like method of sketching a dysfunctional family in a moment of crisis. This eccentric family consists of a number of loveable hangers-on and a matriarch who demands that the family get together for holidays before their actual date so that no one will be injured traveling to the family home. The yard is scattered with wooden cutouts of animals carved by a family friend. Fran, the protagonist of the story, resists attending these gatherings. As the outsider who married into the family, she tries to convince her husband Hank that they should not attend. She seems to have particular differences with his sister, "Dreamy Dora." At this family gathering, Fran makes a negative comment to Dora and she responds rather inappropriately by telling the family that her parents forced her to have an abortion as a young girl and refused to let her marry the man she loved. Later, the family watches a coydog—a crossbreed of coyote and dog—nuzzle the wooden animals in the yard as if they were real and he belonged there with them. As the story ends, Beattie brings the reader to a time several years in the future. It is revealed that Fran and her husband stayed together only four years after this incident. No one recalls Fran's comments or Dora's outburst, only that a coydog believed the wooden animals were real. Just as in "Hurricane Carleyville," Beattie makes the title and the message of this piece too obvious. Fran feels like an outsider and tries to join a family. The coydog tries to befriend the animals, but they are wooden. Fran tries to feel comfortable with the family, but they are not what they seem. Beattie ends the story with an obvious coda: "I remember the day the poor lonesome coydog got a broken heart when it went and fell in love with animals not quite its kind."

When Beattie's stories are not delivering obvious endings, they often deflect the reader from understanding where to focus in the story. This pattern is particularly true of the longest story in the collection, "The Big-Breasted Pilgrim." The narrator, Richard Manson, works as a secretary for a famous chef named Lowell Cartwright. Because Richard spends so much of the early part of the story detailing information about Lowell, his sister Kathryn, and his current girlfriend Daphne, one assumes that Richard's relationship with Lowell and these relatives and friends will be a large part of the story proper. Beattie loads these opening scenes with information about the clothing of the women, as well as details about Richard's life and his relationship with Lowell as a trusted friend and confidante. Then, the plot takes a radical shift when Nancy, a friend of Kathryn, shows up at Lowell's house and Richard immediately begins a romantic liaison with her. The world of Lowell is left behind for most of the second half of the story, with only scattered references to a dinner Lowell is supposed to prepare for Bill and Hillary Clinton in between parties and dates Richard has with Nancy, a hair highlighter from New York. Once more, the reader prepares to settle on this set of circumstances with this new plot as the main point of the story. Then, again, a sudden change occurs as the romantic liaison ends before it really has time to begin, though Beattie has invested almost twenty-five pages in developing this entirely new set of characters and circumstances. Furthermore, the narrator does not seem invested in this new plot. At the end of the story, the focus comes back to Lowell, but only in omission—he has fallen out of a tree and has been seriously injured. Richard sits alone in the house, looking for a wine pull that he fears might have been stolen. Unlike the other stories that had devices to trace the story's conclusion, this story lacks any narrative control. The two different sets of characters and complications might have worked in a longer work, but in fifty pages, Beattie cannot integrate the two plots into a coherent whole. Consequently, the reader never knows where to focus or what is happening—or not happening—to the narrator.

The title story in the collection, "Perfect Recall," also contains a large cast of characters, but in this work, Beattie more deftly distributes the less-rounded characters amongst the essential players of the story. The narrator, Jane, has "perfect recall," and the entire story shows how her memory helps reconstruct her family's saga. Despite the fact that Jane recalls sometimes arcane details about the family—the way her uncle's girlfriend's dog Prince Valiant could balance a hot dog on his nose, for example—the story never digresses from the central characters and their relationships with each other and their children. The central conflict occurs at the end of the story as Jane and her sister Elizabeth must decide whether to tell Elizabeth's stepson that he has inherited an expensive painting from his eccentric uncle Nath's collection. Although this conflict arises late in the story, Beattie successfully integrates past experiences with present situation to make the end resolution seem imaginative and uncontrived.

Probably the best story in the collection, "Mermaids," uses a mixture of these same methods, as well as a first-person limited omniscient narrator, to good effect. In Key West on Christmas Day, an unnamed woman suns herself and begrudgingly looks for the aunt of Miles Hetherly, a friend of hers who has driven three hours to Key West to go fishing with her husband, James. Using internal monologues, Beattie showcases the protagonist's neurotic tendencies. Obsessed with her age and her relationship with her husband, she constantly speaks to herself in the language of self-help books and psychologists. She is a standard example of women of her type. She seems moderately in control of her emotions and relatively happy. Yet, when she meets Miles's Aunt Rose, the protagonist's glib internal monologues belie an anxiousness and depression that surface when she speaks to another sympathetic woman. The reader learns that her husband has had an affair, and she is not happy being left alone on Christmas Day. Later, the protagonist goes to meet her husband and friend's fishing boat, only to discover it is a "pleasure" boat, filled with drunken men and sluttish women dressed in mermaid costumes. Beattie adeptly displays the shifts from the protagonist's earlier belief in herself to this low point of degradation. "Mermaids" represents a high point in this collection, showcasing Beattie's strengths in manipulating point of view and creatively portraying a modern woman in a stressful situation.

The collection as a whole is held together by a repeating focus on male friendships and their fragility in the modern world. In three of the stories, men take on roles as other men's secretaries or confidants. In most of the cases, outsiders in the story presume that the male secretaries are the gay lovers of the wealthier, established men. In "The Infamous Fall of Howell the Clown," the opposite is true: Everyone assumes that Howell is having an affair with a woman, when actually he is gay. Though in most cases the stories speak positively of the need for male friendships and how often they are misunderstood, in "The Women of This World," the male bonding between son and stepfather showcases their fatuous misunderstanding of the women in their life. The men sit home and proclaim their need for perfection, both in wine and in women, while the two women help another woman who has been attacked in her home. Certainly James, the husband in "Mermaids," and his wife's friend Miles Hetherly have made a pact that might seem typical of the carousing, womanizing male. Yet, in "In Irons," Beattie explores the relationship between Eugene and Derek, a male friendship so deeply felt that Derek's wife leaves him because of it; furthermore, Derek does not end the friendship to save his marriage. The two men share a true sense of camaraderie that transcends the sexual and affects Derek more strongly than any other relationship in his life. Beattie may be saying in these stories that men are often deprived of male friendships because of new stereotypes. Many of the men in these stories are restless, needing to move away from women into environments where expectations of success and responsibility take a back seat to more pressing emotional needs.

Taken together, the stories in this collection disclose some interesting insights into the world of male friendships and the women who are involved with them, but they lack Beattie's careful crafting of plot and character. Though her occasional flashbacks to the 1960's and 1970's in the stories show where her work has come from, her inability to represent the present as authentically makes this collection problematic.

Rebecca Hendrick Flannagan

Sources for Further Study

Booklist 97 (November 15, 2000): 586.
Library Journal 125 (December, 2000): 194.
The New York Times, January 2, 2001, p. E9.
The New York Times Book Review 106 (January 14, 2001): 7.
Publishers Weekly 247 (November 20, 2000): 44.
The Wall Street Journal, January 19, 2001, p. W9.

THE PICKUP

Author: Nadine Gordimer (1923-   )
Publisher: Farrar, Straus and Giroux (New York).
   270 pp. $21.00
Type of work: Novel
Time: The late twentieth century
Locale: South Africa and an unnamed desert country

*A young, white South African woman falls in love with
an undocumented Arab immigrant, providing a context for
her growing cross-cultural understanding complicated by
the man's unceasing efforts to emigrate legally from his
poor desert homeland to a developed country*

~

Principal characters:
> JULIE SUMMERS, a public relations officer and fund raiser
> NIGEL ACKROYD SUMMERS, Julie's father
> DANIELLE SUMMERS, Julie's stepmother
> BEVERLY, Julie's mother, who lives in California with her second
>   husband
> DR. ARCHIBALD "UNCLE ARCHIE" SUMMERS, Nigel's brother
> IBRAHIM "ABDU" IBN MUSA, who has entered South Africa illegally
> IBRAHIM'S MOTHER
> YAQUB, Ibrahim's prosperous uncle and his employer
> MARYAM and AMINA, Ibrahim's sisters
> KHADIJA, Ibrahim's sister-in-law
> ZAYD, Ibrahim's brother, who is "lost" in the oil fields

In *The Pickup*, Nadine Gordimer again explores the theme of interracial, inter-
cultural relationships such as those at the center of *The Lying Days* (1953) and *A Sport
of Nature* (1987). Here, however, the context is not apartheid. Rather it is the plight of
the immigrant, especially the illegal immigrant, that draws her attention. What if,
Gordimer asks, a well-to-do young woman, a white South African with Irish and
Scots ancestry living on her own in a kind of bohemian independence, with a wealthy
and well-connected father, were to encounter a young, attractive Arab man working
(illegally) in a menial occupation? What if they are attracted to each other and become
sexually involved? What if they fall in love? What if his illegal status is discovered
and he is ordered (again) to leave the country? In this novel, the human heart is in conflict not only with itself but with the various forces of disparate cultural traditions, including religion, the position of women, the drive to escape the oppression of poverty,
community, and fate, as well the burning desire to be independent. Tied to these social

issues are the themes of identity and selfhood. Identity is set in opposition to nonentity, the search by Julie Summers for her identity is set in opposition to that of the man known as "Abdu" early in the novel. Is one's identity a matter of one's birth, social status, clothing and appearance, race and religion? Can it ever be a matter of choice?

The novel's principal South African settings are the EL-AY Café in Johannesburg and the neighborhoods of its young upwardly mobile habitués, the suburbs where Julie had grown up amongst other wealthy white professionals, the desert village home of Ibrahim ibn Musa, and the working-class streets and shops, in one of which "Abdu" has found work repairing automobiles. In a symbolic scene, Julie first meets Ibrahim as he crawls out from beneath an automobile. The other significant setting is the desert country, Ibrahim's homeland, to which Julie and Ibrahim go after their marriage upon his deportation from South Africa. At first a place utterly foreign to Julie, and fundamentally detested by Ibrahim even though it is his home, the desert and its people become for Julie both a place of beauty and possibility and a people of dignity and identity. It remains for Ibrahim, however, a prison from which he must escape.

Nadine Gordimer was born in Springs, a mining town in Transvaal, South Africa. Her father, a jeweler, was a Latvian Jew who immigrated to South Africa and had a jewelry shop in Springs. Her mother, born in London, immigrated to South Africa with Gordimer's grandfather, a diamond miner. Gordimer was awarded the Nobel Prize in Literature in 1991.

Because the novel's technical narrative point of view focuses more on Julie than any other character, including Ibrahim, and is essentially presented through her eyes with commentary from a sympathetic if somewhat aloof narrator, the novel is about Julie's growth and development. In the beginning she is a young upwardly mobile professional, a public relations officer in a nameless corporation, who depends upon the responses of her friends for much of her identity. These friends are guided by situational ethics and pride themselves on being social liberals, open to encounters, especially sexual encounters, with the Other and generally scornful of traditional ethics, perhaps because of the corruption and bankruptcy of traditional ethics revealed by the historical realities of apartheid. Julie and her friends are little concerned and perhaps ignorant of economics, being largely the children of the northern suburbs of Johannesburg. Their lives are characterized by finding the new hot spots for dancing, drinking, and dining and express an easy and facile liberalism, easy because the struggles to overthrow apartheid are years behind them, and facile because most of them are the children of privilege whose rebellion seems (as presented through Gordimer's narrative stance) more than a touch hypocritical.

As her relationship with Ibrahim grows, however, Julie's character grows and develops in a satisfying manner. After their forced return to his homeland, an unnamed

Arabic country "liberated" to a degree from European colonial domination, a land of desert sands, winds, heat, and traditions startlingly foreign to Julie, she finds herself welcomed first by Ibrahim's little sister and then by other members of his family. She develops a respectful, accepting, and curious attitude toward the realities of the culture and the climate. She finds ways to be of genuine use to her new family and community by teaching English to the children, the women of the family, and the larger community. She develops a firm and mutual friendship with Maryam, Ibrahim's sister, and slowly earns the respect of his mother. She also develops a love for the desert and the shadowy Bedouin who inhabit it. These changes mark one of Gordimer's essential themes—experience of another culture by voluntarily immersing one's self in it instills a deep appreciation of the Other and argues that apparently insurmountable cultural differences can be overcome through dedication, sharing of oneself, and participating respectfully—and honestly—in the customs and traditions of the Other.

However, Julie's education begins very early in her relationship with Ibrahim when he persuades her to take him to meet her family, whom she then sees through his eyes. She reluctantly agrees, and then only in the context of a large gathering hosted by her father, where the attendees are nearly all men and women in high finance and big business, the sort of people whose values she thinks she is embarrassed by and has rejected. She is startled to notice how attentively Ibrahim listens to talk of economics, trade, stock markets, the "intimate language of money," language that embarrasses her because she mistakenly believes that he does not approve of this culture. She has hidden this culture from him, a culture of money and power that she has rejected. She cannot understand his interest in it, although she can understand his interest in the ease with which the honorees of this large party are able to relocate to Australia. Here the contrast between two classes of people is sharply drawn: Those who can emigrate with ease from one country to another (the wealthy, the powerful, and their attendants) because of their wealth, their connections, and their lawyers, and those who, like Ibrahim, even though they may be well educated, are of a class or ethnicity or cultural status regarded unfavorably by other countries and thus denied entry.

Later, when they are living in Ibrahim's home village at the very edge of an infinite desert, he cannot conceive that she might not only endure it but become fascinated with it, with its colors, its realities of heat and dryness, its history, its possibilities, and its nomadic Bedouins. He believes that she will leave him and return to the green country of her home in Johannesburg if he cannot get them out of the desert and into another "green" country. However, unknown to Ibrahim, Julie has become convinced that his desert village is the place where she wants to spend her days, within his family, teaching English to the children and the women of the village, and learning his culture and his language. In return for teaching English to the women and children in the family and a group of their friends, she learns their language—his language—so that she will not sit among them as a deaf-mute. She also writes to her mother in California, asking her to order from an online bookstore a hardback translation of the Koran and to have it sent her by courier. (Ibrahim had encouraged her to reestablish contact with her mother, admonishing her that she was remiss in not keeping a "daughter's contact with a mother.") The verses, *suras*, that she learns to read are those that his mother knows by heart, so that Julie, unknowingly, takes a huge step toward acceptance by the family's matriarch.

When he finally is successful, with the help of letters of recommendation that Julie has gotten from her mother and stepfather in California, in getting immigration visas for them both to the United States, Julie purchases two airline tickets to transport them both to this "promised land." However, the taxi carefully ordered in advance to take them to the airport and his long-sought-for escape departs with only Ibrahim, incredulous and baffled. Julie's decision, while not irrevocable, has a logic to it; it is the result of her search for meaning and identity in her own life, for a genuine connection to a cultural tradition and a place that demands commitment and care.

Julie and Ibrahim in many ways remain mysteries to each other, and, one must believe, to themselves. At the beginning of their relationship, each is attracted to the idea of the exotic, the strange, the Other. Their sexual relationship, a mutual exploration rooted in the most basic impulse and instinct of any species, becomes a metaphor for their individual searches for identity and connection, for an essential verification of their humanness. For Julie, the more deeply she falls in love with this exotic stranger, her "oriental prince" as her EL-AY Café friends call him, the more she questions her habitual values and the more curious she becomes about his country, his culture, his family, and their values. Ibrahim, on the other hand, is consumed with his driving need to escape his culture, to win access to the "promised land" wherever it might be—Australia, Great Britain, South Africa, the United States—whatever developed country might accept him and allow him to pursue his dream of financial and cultural transformation. Thus, he is immune to the opportunities presented (with the promised help of funding from Julie's trust fund) in his own country. He feels trapped in the desert and frustrated in his desire to make something of himself and thus help his family. She feels intrigued, useful, and more authentic in this exotic desert culture and village community than in her cosseted Jo'burg culture.

Certain other characters play significant roles in Julie's transformation, including Ibrahim's sister Maryam and his mother. The mother's rule of the household is unquestioned and her devotion to her religion and her family suggests a kind of timeless stability that Julie contrasts to the instability of her own home: her mother, long divorced from her father and now remarried and living in California; her father, living in splendor with Danielle, his second wife, a kind of "trophy wife." Julie, in short, has lacked a center in her home life; Ibrahim's life, the life that he is busily rejecting, has a center that is attractive to her.

Featuring a spare and remote authorial voice with only occasional interpretative commentary, Gordimer's narrative strategy relies extensively on what narratologists term free indirect discourse to communicate and filter the thoughts and thought processes of her characters with the reader. In addition, Gordimer creates effective scenes and summarizes action with an economical and stylish narrative that is always crisp and clear, at times, almost stark. Her style works well to reveal the emotional conflicts and resolutions of each Other in the shifting sands of human needs.

Theodore C. Humphrey

Sources for Further Study

Booklist 97 (July, 2001): 1949.
Library Journal 126 (August, 2001): 161.
The New York Times Book Review 106 (December 16, 2001): 10.
Publishers Weekly 248 (July 16, 2001): 155.
The Washington Post Book World, September 30, 2001, p. 9.

A PITCHER'S STORY
Innings with David Cone

Author: Roger Angell (1920-   )
Publisher: Warner Books (New York). 290 pp. $24.95
Type of work: Biography
Time: 1963-2001
Locale: Kansas City, Tampa, and New York

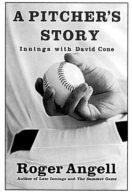

~

A biography of the Cy Young Award-winning pitcher's remarkable career and a study of coping with adversity as the great pitcher faced his most disappointing season

~

Principal personages:
DAVID CONE, pitcher for the New York Yankees
LYNN CONE, his wife
ED CONE, his father
JOE GIRARDI, Yankees catcher
JOE TORRE, Yankees manager
MEL STOTTLEMYRE, Yankees pitching coach
ROGER ANGELL, self-reflexive biographer

Roger Angell, writer and editor for *The New Yorker*, was granted access to Yankees pitcher David Cone during the 2000 baseball season to chronicle that season and pay tribute to one of the great pitchers in baseball history. However, it soon became apparent that the story would play out differently from what either had anticipated. The 2000 season would be the worst of Cone's career, indeed, one of the worst of any of the great pitchers' careers. *A Pitcher's Story* becomes a story of success and failure, injury and rehabilitation, pitching technique and personal resilience. Ironically, the unforeseen turn of events ultimately makes it a more satisfying book.

Angell begins his book with a chapter entitled "Perfection," which focuses on David Cone's single perfect game, one of only sixteen such achievements in baseball history. In many ways it was atypical of his style of pitching and certainly atypical of his disastrous 2000 season. In that July 18, 1999, game against the Montreal Expos, Cone never went to ball three on any batter and threw eighty-eight pitches in nine innings, a remarkably low number considering that he typically had high pitch totals with frequent 3-2 counts on batters. In fact, more characteristic of Cone was his 1992 1-0 shut out of the San Francisco Giants in which he threw 166 pitches: "an insane admixture of prodigality and thrift," according to Angell.

Angell implies that it was stamina—Cone's ability and will to stay in baseball for nineteen years—that increased his odds of reaching perfection. He meditates on the "Sisyphean burden" of fan expectations that baseball heroes carry during a season.

∿

*Roger Angell, the stepson of writer
E. B. White, serves as fiction editor
of* The New Yorker, *a position
formerly held by his mother,
Katharine Angell White. He has
published several baseball
companions as well as collections
of essays about baseball, including
the highly acclaimed* The Summer
Game *(1972).*

∿

His year of studying David Cone opened his eyes to the many factors, including injury, that militate against perfection. He also makes clear that Cone did everything possible in the 2000 season to continue performing at the high level to which he was accustomed. The author of two twenty-win seasons, three one-hitters, and a perfect game, Cone once struck out nineteen batters in a game, won the Cy Young award in 1994, and earned five World Series rings. His personal heroes were pitchers who showed great stamina: those who, over many years, played through pain and over-extended themselves, often with negative long-term physical effects.

The 2000 season, his nineteenth in professional baseball, was a nightmare for Cone. He finished 4-14 with a 6.91 earned run average (ERA); he was removed from the starting rotation in midseason to become reacquainted with pitching basics at the Yankee training facility in Tampa, Florida; then, after he returned to the starting rotation and won three games in August, he suffered a dislocated left shoulder. Barely included on the playoff roster, he was assigned to the bullpen, and threw only five pitches in the World Series. This final appearance, however, both ironic and triumphant, not only indicates the vicissitudes of baseball but also hints at the character necessary to persevere in such a profession. To Angell, Cone's 2000 season epitomized the haphazard, luck-shaped careers of baseball players who take their triumphs and defeats as they come, always hungry for another opportunity, however slight their role may be.

Adversity was not new in Cone's career. Playing minor league baseball early in his second year as a professional, he tore the anterior cruciate ligament of his knee and was lost for the season. Several years later, he broke a finger on his pitching hand that plagued his sinker ball in seasons to come. In 1996, he suffered numbness in his pitching hand due to an aneurysm in his shoulder. "With me it's always been about pain management," he told Angell.

As if this is not enough, pitchers also face mechanical problems unrelated to injury—loss of speed, breaking pitches that do not move sharply enough, pitches that do not work at all—due to almost undetectable changes in timing, weight shifts, and body positioning. In short, Cone had the problem of any athlete: making the body do the mind's bidding. In the 2000 season, for example, he could not get his famous slider to work. According to pitching coach Mel Stottlemyre, pitchers with multiple pitch types might lose track of one of them and never get it back. Cone was not about to be defeated by this problem, however. Throughout his career, he had had easy games and what he called "struggle games." In his estimation, the latter—when one had to adapt to a situation in which he did not have his best pitches—made pitchers great.

If he had not observed him when he was struggling, Angell may not have appreciated so well the excellent qualities of Cone's pitching. From interviews with former teammates and coaches, he learned that Cone was thought of as "a power pitcher with an idea." Not only did he have strength and skill, but he also had a clear plan of attack. His first coach—his father—contributed to his success when he urged his son to stay back over the pitching rubber longer. This "infinitesimal pause" gave him his power and his uniqueness. Joe Girardi, Cone's favorite Yankee catcher, noted his intellectual command of the game. Despite extensive scouting reports on every hitter's strengths and weaknesses, Cone did not follow the game plan literally. Each man at bat, Anqell writes, presented "something fluid and conditional, a cloud chamber of variables" that included the score, the count, the situation, the umpire, and Cone's own particular strengths that game. His former Kansas City teammate, pitcher Bret Saberhagen, and another Yankee catcher, Mike Stanley, both noted his variety of pitches and intelligent deployment of them. His high pitch counts might reflect his experimentation as well as stubborn unwillingness to give in to what a batter can hit.

Without the unusual degree of adversity in the 2000 season, Angell might also not have been able to see so well the character of David Cone, which rose up to confront the disastrous events of the season. In the midst of frustration was the optimistic belief that the next start would prove the bad luck behind him. At thirty-eight years of age—elderly by baseball standards—Cone stubbornly believed that his best games were ahead of him. He had learned professionalism in the face of adversity from the Kansas City Royals in only his second year as a pro. Allowed to rehabilitate his knee in the major league club's facilities, partly because Kansas City was his hometown, Cone had learned to model his behavior after the seriousness of the major leaguers. Angell called this stint of rehabilitation his "college."

Angell suggests that his study of Cone can give readers a newfound respect for baseball players, especially given the doubts raised in recent years about their character. The players strike of the mid-1990's and the phenomenal salaries, not to mention scandals involving off-the-field sexual misconduct and drug use, raised many questions among grumbling fans and lowered attendance figures in major league parks. Cone was in the thick of these problems. He was one of the chief negotiators for the players union during the strike. He was highly paid, earning upwards of $66 million over his career. From 1987 to 1992, he was affiliated with a high-flying New York Mets team that scandalized the public with some of its off-field behavior. His future wife Lynn felt that, in an effort to fit in, Cone became one of the Met "night critters" who prowled the bars seeking drink and women. Even on the minor league level, Cone now believes that he had not been ready for the amount of freedom baseball offered him. Drafted fresh out of high school in 1981 by the Kansas City Royals, he invested his first $17,500 in a cherry-red Z-28 Camaro that he soon traded in because he was unable to make the payments. "I thought I was king of the world. I was a pro ballplayer, eighteen years old, and completely out of control."

To balance the swinging image of the youthful Cone, Angell presents a man who was regretful that his yearly salary at one point was more than his father made in a lifetime, and it eventually gave him great pride to contribute enough to his family that his father would never have to work again. It is also noteworthy that he maintained a relationship with Wheaton College graduate Lynn DiGioia, and she eventually became his wife and staunch advocate. Although Angell also mentions Cone's charity work for children's care, he downplays what he considers a cliché among sports-writers, mentioning the charities players sponsor to balance discussions of high sala-ries. Angell seems to believe that Cone's work ethic and effort on the field were suffi-cient justification of his paycheck and the ultimate measure of any player's integrity. To counter the notion that baseball players are glory hounds, he cites Cone's selfless-ness in the 2000 World Series. Eager to start a game because he sought redemption for a miserable season, he nevertheless offered to use his relief experience in the bullpen, an offer much appreciated by manager Joe Torre. Cone pitched only five pitches of re-lief in the series, albeit in an important encounter with Mike Piazza, the most danger-ous of the Mets hitters.

Despite past glories and the many testimonials to his greatness by friends, team-mates, and coaches, Cone was not the same pitcher in 2000. Already in the midst of a disastrous season, when he came back from the left shoulder injury he was even worse, losing three of four games with an ERA of 14.11. The devastating effects of the injury, not to the pitching arm but to the off arm, underscored for Angell the complexity and fragility of success. He began better to understand pitching in all its "absorbing and ex-cruciating detail." The five masterful pitches to Mike Piazza in the 2000 World Series, getting him out on a pop-up to preserve a 3-2 lead, were not enough of a triumph to justify more than a half-million-dollar offer from the Yankees for 2001. When Orioles phenomenon Mike Mussina agreed to a six-year, $88.5 million deal with the Yankees, Cone was effectively replaced on the roster and moved on to the Boston Red Sox.

A strength of this book is its placing of Cone's personal story in the larger context of major league baseball and modern American society. It ranges widely from Cone's Catholic, working-class upbringing in Kansas City to America's celebrity culture; from Little League fields to the big city bar scene; from fathers coaching their athleti-cally talented children to big leaguers negotiating exorbitant salaries. Instead of showing a simple progression to success, Angell had to alter his book's intent to re-flect the radically changing circumstances of Cone's career. "Instead of an inside look at a wizardly old master at his late last best, this was going to be Merlin falling head-long down the palace stairs . . . ." Cone offered to call the book off, but Angell was in-trigued, failure actually proving more interesting than success. The new plot of the book became Cone's "defeats and his stubborn energy and courage. . . .The more I saw Cone in confusion and pain, the better I liked him."

William L. Howard

Sources for Further Study

Booklist 98 (September 1, 2001: 35.
The Economist 360 (July 7, 2001): 1.
Library Journal 126 (April 15, 2001): 103.
The New York Times Book Review 106 (May 6, 2001): 16.
Publishers Weekly 248 (April 16, 2001): 54.
The Wall Street Journal, April 20, 2001, p. W10.
The Washington Post Book World, May 20, 2001, p. 9.

POEMS, 1968-1998

Author: Paul Muldoon (1951-   )
Publisher: Farrar, Straus and Giroux (New York).
479 pp. $35.00
Type of work: Poetry

～

*Muldoon's collection of his poems written over the last
thirty-five years includes some traditional poems and many
more that challenge the reader to find their meaning*

～

Paul Muldoon is a fascinating and elusive poet whose poems over a thirty-year span have been collected here. They show his development from a fairly traditional Irish poet to a postmodernist language poet who undermines any attempt by his reader to construe meaning. He is also a humorous poet whose mocking and often joking poems poke fun at a number of established positions. He is, in addition, a skilled poet who can construct a strong poetic line and create some dazzling images and metaphors.

The first book in the collection, *New Weather* (1973), shows Muldoon as a conventional poet in the mode of Seamus Heaney. "Wind and Tree," for example, metaphorically traces the connection between humans and trees. The relationship of the trees to each other is described in sexual terms as they "are grinding/ Madly together and together." The Muldoon speaker then adds a realistic note: they are actually "breaking" each other in the connectedness. He is like them, although he would not break the tree. He is, however, already broken and through that "I tell new weather." There is a good deal of irony in the poem, but it is still a lyric and not a language poem.

There are a number of poems about his father in the collection, and "The Waking Father" is one of the best. It begins with father and son catching fish and throwing them back. The imagery describing the place becomes strange and exotic. The fish are "piranhas" and the "river a red carpet." The son asks if the father is dead or alive. If dead, he would turn the course of the river so the father might have a proper burial "bed." There, none could doubt that he was a "king" and could discover in that river bed "the real fish farther down." It is an effective poem that uses some fanciful metaphors, but the images of river and fishing enable Muldoon to pay tribute to and create feeling for the lost father.

Muldoon's next book of poems, *Mules* (1977), rapidly moves away from traditional poetry. "Lunch with Pancho Villa" is an imaginary conversation between the poet and the famous Mexican revolutionary. Muldoon makes a number of references in his poems to Mexico, the American Indians, and the American Southwest. Perhaps these function as exotic place names in contrast to the drabness of Ireland. The poem starts with the poet asking Villa, "Is it really a revolution, though?" He then describes

Paul Muldoon is the author of many well-received books of poetry. In 1999, he was elected professor of poetry at University of Oxford. He also is currently Howard G. G. Clark Professor of Humanities at Princeton University

the accomplishments of Villa as coauthor of a number of pamphlets, such as *Blood on the Rose*. Villa takes a more serious tone as he chastises Muldoon for writing "rondeaux." Villa challenges him to "get down to something true." The Muldoon speaker, however, reveals it is all a game: "Nobody's taken in, I'm sure,/ By such a mild invention." He reveals that the fabrication was given away by the creation of the "preposterous titles" of Villa's books. The last stanza comes back to "'When are you going to tell the truth?'" However, there is no truth about Villa or the Mexican revolution in the poem. What matters is the play between the exotic and ordinary names and characters, and the privileging of imagination over fact.

There are a number of historical poems and some translations from the Irish in this collection, and "Keen" is one of the better ones. The original eighteenth century poem, "*Caoineadh Airt Uí Laoighire*" (known in English as "The Lament for Art O'Leary,") was composed by Eibhlín Dubh Uí Chonaill after her husband, a Catholic, was killed for refusing to sell a prized horse to a Protestant landowner. It begins with the speaker recalling the moment she discovers her husband's death: "I never dreamt you would die/ Till your horse came back to me. . . ." She rides out to find him near a bush, "Without priest or monk/ To preside or pray over you. . . ." He is bleeding and, since "I knew of no way to staunch it./ I cupped my hands and drank it." The "keen" as a mourning ritual in Irish Gaelic culture is more than a vocal lament; it is also a sacrificial drinking of blood in the absence of the rites of the church.

"History" is a poem that focuses not on political events but on sexuality, It begins by asking "Where and when exactly did we first have sex?" He wonders if it was in a city and supplies names that start in Ireland, move on to London, and end up in "Marseilles or Aix?" The final speculation is of time and place. Was it when "you and I climbed into the bay window/ On the ground floor of Aquinas Hall/ And into the room where MacNeice wrote 'Snow,'/ Or the room where they say he wrote 'Snow.'" The difference between fact and a tale is impossible to determine in Muldoon. He continually undercuts any claim to authority or certainty while all is in play.

By the time of *Quoof* (1983), the poems are becoming longer and harder to understand, but they are always playful and fun to read and play with. "The More a Man Has the More He Wants" is twenty pages long, portraying the surrealistic adventures of an unlikely hero named Gallogly. It begins with his beloved abandoning him in "a froth of bra and panties" in Paris. He then undertakes an endless journey to various exotic places. The strangeness of the names and places seem to be at the heart of Muldoon's spoofing of the ordinary and the traditional.

"Meeting the British" is the title poem of his next collection. It is marked by the surreal imagery and non sequitors: "We met the British in the dead of winter./ The sky was lavender." The Muldoon speaker calls out, strangely, "in French." The result of the encounter is that neither the British "General Jeffrey Amherst/ nor Colonel Henry Bouquet/ could stomach our willow-tobacco." This presumably makes the Muldoon speaker into an American Indian rather than an Irishman. The poem ends sardonically: "They gave us six fishhooks/ and two blankets embroidered with smallpox." The encounter between an advanced and a colonized society always seems to involve a fatal exchange, and the use of "embroidered" is very effective in describing the deception of that exchange.

"7, Middagh Street" is a twenty-two page poem that mocks a number of twentieth century poets, especially W. H. Auden and his group. It describes Auden's journeys to Spain and other areas in the 1930's as futile and disappointing. He then has a problem in returning to England not as a hero but merely as "Auden." Muldoon also pokes fun at W. B. Yeats by quoting and mocking some notorious lines of Yeats:

> . . .'Did that play of mine
> send out certain men (*certain* men?)
>
> the English shot . . . ?'
> The answer is 'Certainly not'.
>
> If Yeats had saved his pencil-lead
> would certain men have stayed in bed?

Gypsy Rose Lee, Louis MacNeice, and Chester Kallman appear in the poem, as well as Salvador Dali, who makes some surreal comments. The whole poem refuses to take anything seriously.

Muldoon's next book, *Madoc: A Mystery* (1990), contains the 124-page title poem, on the projected plan by the British poets Robert Southey (1774-1843) and Samuel Taylor Coleridge (1772-1834) to found a pantisocracy near the banks of the Susquehanna River. The project never came to fulfillment, but Muldoon treats it as a reality and the poem describes Coleridge and Southey's encounters with the American Indians in the United States of the early nineteenth century. It is a hilarious poem, but it is difficult to understand, largely because of the wide and often contradictory range of Muldoon's references and allusions. Each section has the title of a philosopher; philosophy is just one of the things that Muldoon is undermining. An example of the humorous undermining can be seen in this complete section:

> [ARCHIMEDES]
> Coleridge leaps out of the tub. Imagine that.

The adventures of Coleridge and Southey intersect with the travels of Meriwether Lewis and William Clark and a number of other historical figures, such as Lord Byron. The title comes from a puzzling discovery:

[PLOTINUS]
Shad waves back, and bends for the mattock
He'll use to dig

a grave for the dog
when it comes to him in a flash—MADOC.

Madoc ap Owein Gwynedd was a legendary Welsh prince believed to have sailed to the west to escape civil war in 1170 and to have discovered North America. According to the legend, he returned to Wales and took seven shiploads of settlers back to this new land. These settlers were believed, by the eighteenth century, to have assimilated with the native population and become a tribe of "Welsh-speaking Indians" who always lived just a little further up the river. The desire of oppressed Welsh intellectuals, stirred by the ideals of the American and French Revolutions, to reunite with their free American brothers and found a *Gwladfa*, or national homeland, devoted to Welsh language and philosophical ideals, was the inspiration for Southey's poem *Madoc* as well as the two poets' Utopian plans. The failed Welsh quests to find the *Madogwys*, believed to be the Mandan Indians, nonetheless provided maps and inspiration for Lewis and Clark's expedition as well. Muldoon uses this tumultuous period of myth and exploration as the raw material for comment on philosophy, colonialism, and Romantic impulses.

There is a poem with a good deal of feeling in Muldoon's next book, *The Annals of Chile* (1994). "Milkweed and Monarch" begins with the poet kneeling at the grave of his mother and father. As he is doing so, tastes of "dill or tarragon" assault him and "he could barely tell one from another. . . ." The grief, however, is for a lost woman and not for his parents. He recalls her talk "while the Monarch butterflies passed over/ in their milkweed hunger." However, the feeling for the absent parents does return at the end of the poem as he contemplates their tomb once more: "as he knelt by the grave of his mother and father/ he could barely tell one from the other." The image of mixing smells in the beginning is forcefully connected to the mixture of the bodies of his parents in their grave.

"Yarrow" is a thirty-nine page poem that is the most resistant to explication. It, as do many other long poems, mixes historical figures and fictional ones in various time periods. Sylvia Plath makes an appearance, as does Jim Hawkins from Robert Lewis Stevenson's *Treasure Island* (1883). The Muldoon speaker joins Jim Hawkins in "plundering the Spanish Main. . . ." The only structural principle is the repetition of "That was the year" in which some events, often bizarre ones, happened.

Hay (1998) is the last book in the collection, and the most interesting group of poems is the "Hopewell Haiku." Muldoon subverts the haiku form by rhyming the first and third lines of every haiku and not observing the syllabic pattern very exactly. In addition, he tends to use the sordid rather than the elegantly beautiful in nature. For example, haiku X:

A crocus piss stain.
"There's too much snow in my life,"
My daughter complains.

Paul Muldoon's career is an interesting example of a poet who began as a traditional lyric poet and then embraced—and surpassed—many of the postmodern and avant-garde movements of his time. Those exotic poems, especially the very long ones, are sometimes hilarious, and often diverting. Muldoon has a perverse sense of humor and it informs many of these poems. The later poems seem to be exercises in subverting meaning. Muldoon must defeat his reader or surrender to him. Many of the poems are not structures but comic collages of discordant materials. The early poems are like those of another Irish poet, Seamus Heaney. However, the later ones place him firmly in the camp of James Joyce.

James Sullivan

Sources for Further Study

Booklist 97 (March 1, 2001): 1220.
The New York Times Book Review 106 (June 10, 2001): 14.
Publishers Weekly 248 (February 12, 2001): 204.

PORTRAIT IN SEPIA

Author: Isabel Allende (1942-   )
First published: Retrato en sepia, 2000, in Spain
Translated from the Spanish by Margaret Sayers Peden
Publisher: HarperCollins (New York). 304 pp. $26.00
Type of work: Novel

∼

This sprawling novel, a companion to Daughter of Fortune, *tells the tale of a wounded young woman whose lost early memories conceal the truth about her family and heritage*

∼

Principal characters:

AURORA DEL VALLE, a young woman of partly Chilean ancestry who was born in San Francisco in 1880
PAULINA DEL VALLE, Aurora's aristocratic grandmother, a woman who violated all the rules of female behavior and made herself a success
FREDERICK WILLIAMS, Pauline's second husband and former servant
MATIAS DEL VALLE, Paulina's son and Aurora's irresponsible father
ELIZA SOMMERS, Aurora's maternal grandmother who raised her until age five (and the protagonist of *Daughter of Fortune*)
TAO CHI'EN, Aurora's beloved maternal grandfather, who died when she was a child
LYNN SOMMERS, Aurora's mother, who died at her birth
LUCKY SOMMERS, Aurora's uncle
DIEGO DOMINGUEZ, Aurora's lover and husband
NIVEA DEL VALLE, wife of Paulina's nephew (and a major character in Allende's 1982 novel *The House of the Spirits*)

Isabel Allende is a controversial and outspoken writer, whose stories blend history and fiction in a breathless rushing narrative of Chilean life. Her true forte is the depiction of women in male regimes who often try invisibly to change the course of events, and whose power is very different in nature from men's power. Born in Peru, Isabel Allende is the niece of Chilean President Salvador Allende, who was assassinated in a bloody coup in 1973. Not long after that, the novelist began to publish essays, memoirs, stories, and plays. "I think I have divided my life [into] before that day and after that day," she once told an interviewer. Many of her novels and stories introduce women of privilege who are sheltered from life by the patriarchal structure, but then circumstances destroy the shelter and force the women to take part in a violent culture and do their best to change it.

Allende's work has been subject to critical attention for its Magical Realism, and also for the use she makes of history. Herself part of Chilean history and witness to much of the bloody revolutionary activity, she gives the political history human faces. Her style is always polyvocal, polyvalent. Allende is famous for the epic family history which connects generations with formative historical events. The families are in some way always matriarchal despite the fact that men rule the outside world with iron fist. The lineage she traces is matriarchal, mystical, intuitive power passing from grandmother to mother to daughter. There is a particular brand of feminism in much of her work, as

∽

Isabel Allende has won numerous awards for her writing, in Chile, the United States, France, Germany, Italy, Mexico, Belgium, and Portugal. Portrait in Sepia *is her seventh novel; she has also written journalism, humor, children's books, plays, and an autobiography.*

∽

men and women are definitely opposites, and the women are almost always morally superior. Yet Allende's contexts make it clear that the gender roles are written for the main characters by the society they inhabit and they do not choose their destinies.

Magical Realism, usually associated with South American writers, introduces fantastic elements into a realistic narrative as though they were just part of the landscape; often there is a combination of fairy-tale elements and Catholicism. In Allende's stories, the fantastic takes the form of clairvoyance and paranormal events; she might claim that she is not using Magical Realism at all but only describing the often overlooked or misunderstood qualities that women, especially women in extreme circumstances, actually possess.

Because her stories are rooted in Chilean history—even when they take place far from Chile—they tend to be violent, bloody, and passionate. The political events themselves, massacres and coups d'état and assassinations, tend to follow lengthy, leisurely explorations of the lives of those they affect, and to come as a surprise, bringing to the reader the reminder that this is myth interwoven with history, and that there is a randomness that is always at play in human events.

Like Allende's other stories, *Portrait in Sepia* is expansive narrative that covers generations and gives a vivid sense of woman's place in a male society which has little understanding for the things of women. This story takes up the characters of her 1999 novel *Daughter of Fortune*. The main character of *Daughter of Fortune*, Eliza Sommers, here is a secondary personage as the grandmother of Aurora del Valle, whom she raises until the age of five and then parts from completely, leaving her in the care of Paulina del Valle. The women portrayed in this narrative are also related to the female characters in *The House of the Spirits*, which extends later in time and takes place in Chile; Aurora is a contemporary of and related to Clara del Valle, one of the main characters in *The House of the Spirits*. Allende has referred to the three novels as a trilogy, but they are so only in the sense of having some overlapping characters and sharing as theme the exploration of women's roles and potential within a society officially run by men and inimical to women's values of stability, family, and love. The novels are separate; they were not written in chronological sequence and do not depend on each other.

Aurora del Valle, the narrator and protagonist of *Portrait in Sepia*, begins by telling of her birth in San Francisco, "a man's city," in 1880. She is now at a kind of plateau in her life, her lover having betrayed her and she herself not knowing where to go next. Unable to remember anything about the first five years of her life, she decides to investigate her own past, knowing that she cannot participate fully in a relationship without some sense of who she is.

Allende's storytelling style is idiosyncratic and vitally effective. There is always an element of suspense, and there is always the awareness of a tale being told, a hint of once-upon-a-time. If the major action is left to history, the more domestic events are narrated in a breathless rush that pulls all of history into the life of one woman, one child. Just when the reader gets used to the characters, they change; the focus passes on from one generation to the next or from one branch of the family to another. *Portrait in Sepia* begins with the birth scene of the narrator, and it is a rough thrust into a troubled world:

> I came into the world one Tuesday in the autumn of 1880, in San Francisco, in the home of my maternal grandparents. While inside that labyrinthine wood house my mother panted and pushed, her valiant heart and desperate bones laboring to find a way out to me, the savage life of the Chinese quarter was seething outside, with its unforgettable aroma of exotic food, its deafening torrent of shouted dialects . . .

Aurora—symbolically named like all Allende's female major characters—pulls at the tag ends of her childhood to find the cause of her nightmares and the reason she cannot remember anything about her early life, and in doing this, she places herself in history. A photographer, she uses photographs as evidence as well as for self-definition. She interviews family members and uses documentary evidence to find out about a past that had by family agreement been erased, and finds out the specifics of her mother's death, her grandfather's death, and the series of events that took her away from her maternal grandparents, the Sommers, to be raised by Paulina del Valle who, when she was widowed, took her granddaughter to grow up in Chile. Here Aurora was protected by her eccentric grandmother from the oppression that stifled most women in this patriarchal society:

> In Santiago, intellectuals gathered in cafes and clubs, and only men were included, based on the belief that women were better off stirring the soup than writing verses. My grandmother's initiative in including female artists in her salon was a novelty that bordered on the immoral.

The granddaughter of two idiosyncratic women who refused to accept society's dictates, Aurora has a good grounding for her own move toward independence.

Much of the novel is simply Aurora's richly detailed account of her memories of growing up, and of the characters and activities of the other major women in her life, especially Paulina del Valle. The men tend to be present only in shadow form, although their activities do much to advance the story by providing obstacles to the women. The implication is that men live entirely in a world of action, and women, of passionate being. Even when their natures and external events cause them to take part in the men's world, the women's passions are what drive them and what come first. When Aurora is betrayed by her lover, she is frozen, and cannot be unfrozen until her whole passionate being is unveiled to her. Another characteristic of the women's lives is their cyclic nature, as events for them seem always to go in circles rather than in linear progression. People and things left behind resurface; events are re-experienced. A third element that distinguishes the women is their intuitive knowledge, which sometimes occurs in the form of clairvoyance, sometimes in understanding of others' feelings, and which tends to be represented by the houses in which they live: structures that have been built onto and changed around at whim, and are more comforting than any conventional home. All in all, the women's world that Allende presents is consistent and fascinating.

What Aurora finds out is horrifying, but it does allow her to know her place in the world, where she comes from and what kind of future is open to her. The birth described in the opening paragraph is followed by the ending of a second birth, of awareness and knowledge, and now Aurora is complete. The epilogue is the narrator's meditation on time, memory, photographs, reality, and fiction. Words and photographs become evidence of existence in the fiction that is memory:

> Through photography and the written word I try desperately to conquer the transitory nature of my existence, to trap moments before they evanesce, to untangle the confusion of my past. Every instant disappears in a breath and immediately becomes the past; reality is ephemeral and changing, pure longing.

The revelations of the ending, when Aurora finally gets back in touch with her maternal grandmother and is told the truth, are a bit disappointing, which is the case sometimes with Allende: Such breathless action, it seems, could only end in an apocalypse that would lead to a new world order, and naturally this does not always happen. What Aurora finds out about her grandfather's death seems anticlimactic. Moreover, the reader might well think that a conspiracy of silence on the part of the family was misplaced—such intuitive, intelligent women as Eliza and Paulina might have seen that to allow their granddaughter to experience displacement and nightmares could be more damaging than telling her the truth. Then, too, the events of Chilean history play a smaller part here than in some of her other works, and her discussion of the social problems in San Francisco that led to her grandfather's death is less incisive than her perspective on Chilean history. Nevertheless, the characters are richly portrayed and the way in which the personal interacts with the political is insightfully described. The action and passion in an Allende novel sweeps the reader into a colorful and vital world that it is hard to envision, from any distance, as a sepia portrait, though the image captures well the freezing effect of taking stills of lives so fast-moving they seem a blur. Allende's popularity is due in part to the appeal she has for different kinds of readers: This is a bodice-ripper as well as a novel of political and social analysis. *Portrait in Sepia* is also a persuasive argument for essentialist feminism, as it is the women who keep the society from self-destruction.

Janet McCann

Sources for Further Study

Booklist 98 (September 1, 2001): 3.
Library Journal 126 (October 15, 2001): 105.
The New York Times Book Review 106 (November 4, 2001): 32.
Publishers Weekly 248 (July 16, 2001): 164.

THE PRICE OF CITIZENSHIP
Redefining the American Welfare State

Author: Michael B. Katz (1939-   )
Publisher: Metropolitan Books/Henry Holt (New York). 469 pp. $35.00
Type of work: Current affairs, economics, history, and sociology
Time: American colonial times to the present
Locale: The United States

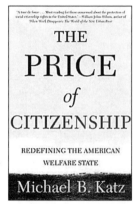

∽

Katz traces the changing architecture of American public and private social programs through an examination of historical roots and changes in legislation and public attitudes

∽

Painstakingly gathering information from numerous studies into one volume, Michael Katz produces a history and criticism of social programs, both private and public welfare. He argues that public policy has been influenced to reduce programs by misrepresentations and the "willful ignorance" of conservatives seeking to trim welfare roles, extend favor to corporations, and advance a particular moral agenda.

Beginning with a prologue entitled "The Invention of Welfare," Katz provides twelve chapters, an epilogue, and eighty-nine pages of notes to support his points. Each chapter focuses on a slightly different aspect of "welfare," which Katz defines as the United States Constitution's provision for the government's advancement of the "well-being" of the entire population. Each chapter gives a historical background to particular topics such as family support, worker's compensation, and employee benefits, and then takes the reader through trends and legislation involving that topic into the late 1990's. The chapters build on each other, reinforcing the trends toward greater economic equality and the abolishment of poverty on through a retreat from these goals and embrace of market models and a new form of Social Darwinism.

Katz is thorough in his use of statistical data, but in some chapters, especially the middle section of the book, the volume of this data becomes nearly overwhelming. Acronyms appear frequently and are similar enough on occasion that the reader must backtrack to find the original, spelled-out version of some program or organization. Although conservative critics have taken aim at Katz's politics and accused him of being a "dinosaur" who fails to accept the will of the public, they never question his facts.

In contrast, Katz exposes the frequent misrepresentation that welfare reformers have used to sway the American public to support changes in policy and programs. He points out the extreme cases, from welfare "queens" to workers' compensation

~

*Michael B. Katz has received
fellowships from the Guggenheim
Foundation, Institute for Advanced
Studies, Shelby Cullom Davis
Center, Russell Sage Foundation,
Woodrow Wilson Center, and Open
Society Institute. He is the Sheldon
and Lucy Hackney Professor in the
department of history at the
University of Pennsylvania and is
the author of several books on
social issues involving class and
education.*

~

defrauders, that are held up as reasons for change, when they are at best a small fraction of offenders, and at worst, only a fiction created by reformers themselves. For example, when reformers in the state of California sought to make changes to workers' compensation laws, an ad campaign aimed at the public featured able-bodied workers who were supposedly receiving benefits. When the law was changed, making it harder to qualify for benefits, less than 1 percent of recipient cases were deemed suspicious, and few of those were investigated. The more likely defrauders of this program, Katz points out, were the workers' compensation "mills"—doctors and clinics who specialized in these cases but rarely helped those workers they charged the system to treat. However, because the changes in the law made it harder to qualify, fewer applicants sought benefits, and the real winners turned out to be employers, who paid less in insurance premiums when fewer employees filed claims against them. Unfortunately, Katz argues, this proved a greater financial savings for these companies than the alternative of improving on-the-job safety and preventing more injuries to their employees, which was the factor that caused drops in workers' compensation claims in previous decades.

Similar tactics have worked to the benefit of employers and the ultimate detriment of workers in other aspects of welfare. Although the granting of small pensions (first offered to American Express workers in 1875) appeared at the end of the nineteenth century, employment benefits did not expand greatly until after World War II. A wage freeze during the early 1940's meant that employers wishing to lure and keep workers could only increase the benefits they offered. Gradually, a "private welfare state" developed that was tied to work, and employers adopted a paternalistic attitude in which they promised to take care of loyal workers through systems of health care and pensions extending into retirement. This private welfare state not only provided incentives for people to work, but also displaced the idea of universal, public welfare from the public arena. Combined with a strong work ethic, this marriage of work and benefits eventually led to the notion of the "undeserving poor," who did not perform work to earn these benefits, but expected to be given them freely.

No social benefits have ever been free and easy to obtain, as conservative critics would have us believe. Recipients have in the past suffered and continue to suffer indignities, moral scrutiny, social stigma, and deferment to obtain the basics of survival. In colonial times, relief was offered to the poor, but some towns made such relief a civic entitlement, and people not considered to belong to the town were driven out rather than helped. Later, into the twentieth century, poor people were forced to enter poorhouses that were purposefully miserable places, to encourage the poor to find any available means, within the law, to escape them.

Such purposefulness is one of the aspects that should disturb citizens the most, especially in uncertain economic times when today's worker can easily become tomorrow's unemployed. There have been many reasons, some articulated and some not, that have caused recipients of any public funds to be stigmatized. After the Industrial Revolution, employers wanted a ready labor market and feared that if relief and benefits could be obtained too easily, they would not have workers to produce goods and would have to pay higher wages to attract workers. This fear was also combined with a fear of moral subversion, which led to a rule of thumb that no one should be able to live as comfortably on relief as they could at the most menial job.

Although Katz uses the term "public welfare" to embrace all social assistance programs, from AFDC (Aid to Families with Dependent Children) to Social Security, he acknowledges that "welfare" generally evokes the image of the single, minority mother, "racializing" poverty. Alarmed by the growth in numbers of unmarried women with children on the welfare rolls, conservative critics have claimed that such programs have encouraged moral corruption, and that by supporting these poor families with higher benefits than the mother could earn at a minimum-wage job, the program has undercut her will to work and failed in its purpose. Thus, a moral issue—unwed motherhood and its inherent problems—eclipses the facts of single-parent poverty and lack of opportunity.

During the 1980's, cities that were squeezed by drops in manufacturing, flight to the suburbs, and decaying infrastructures and saddled with a growing poor population in inner-city neighborhoods sought extreme reforms to their overburdened welfare programs. Katz examines some of the new programs, bolstered by federal dollars, that sought to find work for welfare recipients and bring them back into mainstream society. Not enough was ever done, however, to adequately train these potential workers; to provide safe, affordable childcare options for single mothers or poor families; to find them jobs that paid a livable wage; and to follow up on what became of them when the temporary programs were over and they were cut loose. In many cases, people who left the welfare rolls returned to them within a year, and yet the failure of particular programs was ignored. In fact, Katz claims that programs that actually failed were often lauded and used as justification to attempt the same reforms in other cities across the country.

In more recent times, Katz identifies attempts to run public welfare programs using a market model that supposedly will create a leaner, more efficient operation that will serve the truly needy while eliminating waste. Katz argues that a market model is not appropriate for social programs and has not led to any measurable success. He examines the pressure for privatization in Social Security, which is advanced by false claims that Social Security is in trouble and something must be done about it at once. This has alarmed younger workers into believing that the monies they are paying into Social Security will not be there upon their retirement. Katz explains why these scare stories are not true and points out the potential disasters awaiting ordinary workers, who are not savvy about the stock market and are traditionally conservative investors, if privatization is implemented. The only winners in this scheme would be the private investing firms that will reap billions in fees from handling privatized accounts.

Katz looks at healthcare, uncovering why former president Bill Clinton's national healthcare plan was doomed from the start (too much secrecy made it suspect) and why the rise of health maintenance organizations (HMOs) has, once again, proved a boon to employers and left consumers less than satisfied. The assimilation of healthcare to the market model has not improved healthcare, but in most cases has driven the costs even higher. Katz also discusses the history of Medicare and Medicaid, the most expensive programs of social welfare.

As more people have turned to the stock market to gain wealth in recent decades, the pressure upon corporations to show profits has escalated. This is one reason, among many, that has influenced employers to end the paternalism they once showed to employees and reduce benefits that many working Americans had come to see as entitlements. Downsizing and an increasing dependence upon temporary workers, whom employers do not provide with any benefits, has put more Americans at risk of losing not only their paychecks, but also their health benefits, which are ludicrously expensive to maintain privately. With more social programs slashed at all levels, from local to federal, more people will find themselves falling through holes in the tattered safety net.

Although public welfare has often been legislated nationally, it has always been distributed locally, from state on down through county and city governments. Katz points out that there never was a "golden age" of private support of the poor. Private organizations have never been able to provide help to all the people who need it, and the supplementation of public funds helped filled the empty spaces in the safety net. One of the most unforgivable facts is that reformers gauge the effectiveness of their programs by the decline in numbers on the assistance rolls and do not track the fate of those who no longer qualify for assistance. Do former recipients escape poverty? No studies have been done; no statistics on this exist. The "willful ignorance" shown by reformers is chilling. Katz uses supporting figures to prove his point that welfare has always been the least expensive way to keep people alive. Welfare has never been meant to be a way of life, and the phenomenon of welfare recipients spanning generations is more indicative of the shrinking opportunities workers face than of the rise of a morally corrupt underclass.

This insightful book should be required reading for anyone working in the social services field as well as concerned citizens who have been misled about the realities of programs for the disadvantaged for far too long.

Patricia Masserman

Sources for Further Study

Booklist 97 (April 1, 2001): 1434.
Library Journal 126 (March 15, 2001): 96.
Publishers Weekly 248 (March 12, 2001): 76.
Washington Monthly 33 (June 2001): 60.

A PRIMATE'S MEMOIR

Author: Robert M. Sapolsky (1957-   )
Publisher: Charles Scribner's Sons (New York). 304 pp. $25.00
Type of work: Autobiography and natural history
Time: 1978-2000
Locale: East Africa

～

A primatologist recounts his adventures during twenty years of studying baboons in the Serengeti of East Africa, seeking to understand stress responses in these creatures in order to discover the link between human stress and disease

～

Principal personages:
Robert M. Sapolsky, a primatologist
Rhoda, a half-Masai, half-Kikuyu woman who becomes Sapolsky's first friend among the native Kenyans
Soirowa, a Masai villager living near Sapolsky's camp
Richard and Hudson, two Kenyans whom Sapolsky hires to collect data on the baboons whenever he has to return to the United States
Samwelly, Richard's brother and Sapolsky's research assistant
Lisa, Sapolsky's fiancee

"I joined the baboon troop during my twenty-first year," Robert Sapolsky begins his memoir of twenty years of studying stress in baboons—and in humans, including himself—in East Africa. "I had never planned to become a savanna baboon when I grew up; instead, I had always assumed I would become a mountain gorilla."

Sapolsky is a professor of biology and neurology at Stanford University, a research associate with the Institute of Primate Research of the National Museum of Kenya, and the recipient of a MacArthur Foundation "genius" grant. *A Primate's Memoir*, intoxicating in its flamboyant eloquence and endearing in its occasional self-deprecations, interweaves descriptions of his observations of two generations of baboons in the Serengeti National Park with confessions of his often ill-fated attempts to communicate with the native Masai and other Africans, whose behaviors were far less easy to comprehend. Sapolsky's lively, high-octane personality charges his prose with the same fiery purpose that he brought to his work in 1978 when he first settled in to watch a troop of baboons upon whom he bestowed Old Testament names, such as Solomon, Leah, Aaron, Isaac, Naomi, Rachel, and Benjamin.

Sapolsky was one of the first researchers to chart the effects of chronic stress on the brain both in animals and in humans. He sought to learn how a baboon's social behav-

~

Robert M. Sapolsky is a professor of neuroendocrinology at Stanford University. His earlier books are Stress, the Aging Brain, *and the* Mechanisms of Neuron Death *(1992),* Why Zebras Don't Get Ulcers: A Guide to Stress, Stress-Related Disease, and Coping *(1993), and* The Trouble with Testosterone *(1997).*

~

ior, social rank, and emotional life are related to what diseases it gets, especially stress-related diseases. To measure the symptoms of stress in his baboons, he daily had to shoot one or more with an anaesthetizing dart, carry it back to camp, take samples to measure the blood hormones, stress hormones, antibodies, cholesterol, and other indicators of health, and then release the ape, all the time making sure that no other males harmed it while the anaesthesia was taking effect. Sapolsky describes the delight he took as he improved in this rare skill:

I am the angel of death. I am the reign of terror, the ten plagues, I am a case of the clap, I am the thing that goes bump in the night, De Shadow, death warmed over. I am the bogeyman with cat eyes waiting until midnight in every kid's clothes closet, I am leering slinky silent quicksilver baboon terror, I am Beelzebub's bill collector. Another baboon successfully darted. Euphoria.

Sapolsky divides his book into four parts, named for the four stages of a baboon's life: "The Adolescent Years," "The Subadult Years," "Tenuous Adulthood," and "Adulthood." Though he does not tell his tale in strict chronological order, and rarely provides the date of the remarkable encounters and endeavors he endured, the reader can follow Sapolsky's own maturation through the chapters as he learns to recognize scams worked by the poverty-ridden Africans upon Americans, learns to understand—a little—the philosophies and kindnesses and deceits of the neighboring Masai, and, most delightfully, learns the personalities of the baboons in the troop that he observes.

A great many of the twenty-nine chapters are concerned with his visits to towns outside the Serengeti, to Nairobi and Mombasa and heavenly Katire, and in one suspenseful, occasionally terrifying, and poignant passage, with his pilgrimage to the Ruwenzoris, the famous Mountains of the Moon, to see the rare mountain gorillas and to visit the grave of legendary primatologist Dian Fossey (1932-1985).

Sapolsky saw much weirder behavior among humans than among his baboons. His research assistant, Samwelly, was at heart an architect and builder, and when not on call would frenziedly build huts all over the campsite; when elephants came to eat the huts, he would steadfastly rebuild them the following day. When Sapolsky came back from watching baboons one day, he found their nearby trickle of a river gone; Samwelly had dammed it up to provide them a lake, which Sapolsky regretfully had to order him to undam.

He visited Kampala, Uganda, to witness the chaos following the overthrow of dictator Idi Amin; was coerced by Rhoda, his first Masai friend, and other village women to drive a blood-spattered "crazy" woman who had killed a goat with her bare hands to a hospital an hour away; he was beaten and robbed by Kenyan soldiers at an army checkpoint after an attempted coup in 1982. He hiked up fifteen-thousand-foot

Mount Karisimbi with a sullen young ranger who, Sapolsky was convinced, meant to murder him.

Even more fascinating are the chapters about the baboons. In chapter 15, "The Baboons: The Unstable Years," Sapolsky amusingly describes the results of the alpha male Saul's having been overthrown by a junta of younger baboons but with no clear leader taking his place:

> All hell broke loose for months afterward. . . . Ranks flip-flopped daily. . . . Chaos reigned. Everyone was scheming, spending hours forming coalitional partnerships that would collapse within minutes of their first test. . . . The number of fights went through the roof, as did the rate of injuries. Nobody ate much, nobody was grooming, sex was forgotten. Public works projects were halted and mail service became unreliable.

Sapolsky's observations and dartings and blood samplings were invaluable, leading to a variety of scientific publications throughout the 1980's and 1990's:

> By the end of the years of instability in the troop's hierarchy, I had been making pretty good progress with my scientific research. It was now clear to me that if you had a choice in the matter, you didn't want to be a low-ranking male. They had elevated levels of a key stress hormone all the time, indicating that everyday life was miserable enough to activate a stress response. Their immune systems didn't seem to function as well as did those of dominant animals. They had less of the good version of cholesterol in their bloodstreams, and I had indirect evidence that they had elevated blood pressure. . . . I was finding that the hypersecretion in those baboons was due to the same constellation of changes in the brain and pituitary and adrenal glands that gave rise to the hypersecretion in depressed humans.

Sapolsky found that the key to handling stress might be cultivating friendly relations with one's troopmates. Male baboons who spent the most time grooming and being groomed, spending time with females who were not in heat, and playing with infants had the lowest levels of stress hormones. He also learned that rank did indeed matter. The top baboons in a stable dominance hierarchy—first Solomon, and later Saul—had lower stress-hormone levels than did the mid-ranking young males who thought they had a chance at leadership one day, and certainly less stress than the lowest in the pecking order, who were harassed by anybody who had come off worst in a fight or was generally having a bad day.

Sapolsky spent his summers in the Serengeti, having to return to the United States for university semesters to write his thesis and, eventually, to publish and lecture. He hired two Kenyans, Richard (brother of Samwelly) and Hudson, to collect data on the baboons whenever he had to leave. The three became lasting friends. Sapolsky recalls fondly the time when Richard decided to take revenge on the neighboring Masai, who harassed him because he was a mere farmer's boy and not a warrior. The Masai based their arrogance on their daily habit of drinking cow's blood; Richard and Sapolsky arranged a drama in which it appeared that they insouciantly drank baboons' blood. The Masai were so horrified that, afterward, they left Richard alone.

Sapolsky recounts his meeting with the lovely Lisa in the United States (they were eventually to marry) and his triumphant presentation of his Serengeti to her when she visited for the summer. To his embarrassment, she communicated more expertly with the Masai villagers than he did, and met the rigors of camping with no qualms.

Lisa was present during the tragic summer whose events conclude the book. The baboons of the neighboring troop, who were in the habit of feeding from the garbage heap of a tourist lodge, became ill with tuberculosis. Sapolsky was drawn in to investigate against his will, and after much dirty detective work discovered that a handful of corrupt men lay behind the fast-spreading disease. He describes their outrageous indifference in feeding the apes the viscera of tuberculoid cattle, his attempts to expose the scandal before his own beloved baboons could sicken, and his anger and frustration and helplessness. There was nothing he could do, he reports sadly and with lingering anger, because baboons are not endangered, and they are nobody's favorite animal.

The roll call of the dead in the final pages will bring tears to the loyal reader, but it is not the only chapter that remains after the book is finally closed. Long after, the reader will remember with pleasure Sapolsky's delight in the antics of his baboons, will share his fascination with their soap-opera lives of manipulation and struggle for dominance and first steps in parenting and displays of affection. Many funny moments will also remain in the memory: Sapolsky's research assistants wearying of his endless meals of rice, beans, and canned Taiwanese mackerel in tomato sauce; their awe of the crates of steaming dry ice and liquid nitrogen that he used to store his medicines and samples; his pride that

> nearly two decades later, darting remains in my blood. The other night, I was at the movies and watched some matron amble down the aisle past me, and my first thoughts were "85-90 kilos, .9 cc's of anesthetic. Go for her rump, lots of meat. Her husband will probably defend her when she goes down, but he has small canines." I am still delighted to be doing this for a living.

Sapolsky has been called, and with good reason, "the world's funniest neuroscientist." He told an interviewer for the online magazine *Salon* that he had received some censure from colleagues for writing a very accessible book, that a scientist is sneeringly termed "Saganized" (for media figure and famed astronomer Dr. Carl Sagan) if he writes for a popular audience, and that therefore he cannot possibly be serious about his own science anymore. Sapolsky shrugs this off. He is clearly influenced by the work of Farley Mowat, the Canadian biologist whose many popular works included *Never Cry Wolf* (1963), which was adapted in 1983 as a film; Mowat's works were very funny, very moving, and often accused of anthropomorphism. Sapolsky likewise shrugs off the charges of anthropomorphism; reading between the lines of *A Primate's Memoir*, the reader sees that he is constantly comparing baboons with humans, not only physiologically but as social animals as well, and the humans rarely come off looking superior. Sapolsky's book never slows, always charms and horrifies, and seems likely to become a classic in the field of primatology.

Fiona Kelleghan

Sources for Further Study

Atlanta Journal and Constitution, April 1, 2001, p. B5.
Booklist 97 (January 1-15, 2001): 891.
Library Journal 126 (February 15, 2001): 197.
New York 34 (February 26, 2001): 99.
The New York Times, April 19, 2001, p. F1.
The New York Times Book Review 106 (April 1, 2001): 14.
Publishers Weekly 248 (February 19, 2001): 81.
San Francisco Chronicle Book Review, February 26, 2001, p. A6.
Time 157 (March 12, 2001): 93.

PRIMETIME BLUES
African Americans on Network Television

Author: Donald Bogle
Publisher: Farrar, Straus and Giroux (New York). Illustrated. 520 pp. $30.00
Type of work: Media and sociology
Time: The 1950's to 2000
Locale: The United States

~

A comprehensive study of African Americans on network television programs in the United States that traces both the expanding presence of black performers in the medium and their impact upon it, and national culture

~

Principal personages

EDDIE "ROCHESTER" ANDERSON, comic sidekick of Jack Benny
DIAHANN CARROLL, star of series *Julia*; later appeared on *Dynasty*
BILL COSBY, multitalented performer with several hit series
REDD FOXX, stand-up comic and star of series *Sanford and Son*
SHERMAN HEMSLEY, star of *The Jeffersons*, a spin-off of *All in the Family*
SIDNEY POITIER, screen actor who played in many early television dramas
CICELY TYSON, best known for the television adaptation of *The Autobiography of Miss Jane Pittman*

Like it or not, television is the crude but accurate measure of the American character. The ultimate simplifier, it takes the puzzling questions of just who and what Americans are and gives them answers which must be true because they are large, broad, and often come complete with a laugh track. It distills the complications of public policy into ten-second sound bites; transforms political debate into Sunday morning shouting matches; forces all sports to dance to its own commercial rhythms; and, in its most impressive display of mastery, packages reality into thirty- and sixty-minute segments that achieve a finality and closure of which Sophocles and William Shakespeare could only dream, Anton Chekhov merely aspire. With television, viewers have become what they behold.

What do they behold when television shows African Americans? What are the images that filled the half century from television's rise in the early 1950's to the first days of the new millennium? Those are some of the questions Donald Bogle asked in writing *Primetime Blues: African Americans on Network Television*; the answers he uncovered are by turns fascinating, appalling, encouraging and—after all, this is television—in many ways entirely predictable. What is not predictable, and one of the many features which makes *Primetime Blues* so fascinating and valuable, is the story of how African American actors, writers, and directors have helped push the medium of television beyond easy, self-indulgent stereotypes.

In the beginning, there was *Amos 'n' Andy* (1951-1953), which premiered on the Columbia Broadcasting System (CBS) network on June 28, 1951 at 8:30 in the evening. Actually, there were earlier shows with African Americans with even more prominent roles (the legendary performer Ethel Waters appeared on an experimental broadcast as early as 1939) but *Amos 'n' Andy* was the first show that brought what might very loosely be called "the black experience" to the general American audience. *Amos 'n' Andy* had begun as a radio show (with the title characters played by white actors) and reached amazing popularity during the Great Depression—Huey Long, the near-dictatorial governor of Louisiana from 1928 to 1931, took his nickname of "The Kingfish" from one of the show's characters. For a new medium seeking to establish itself, *Amos 'n' Andy* offered what television has always sought: proven success, a built-in audience, and sponsors ready to pay top-of-the-line rates for commercials.

It also offered a view of African Americans that many found highly offensive. Avaricious but lazy, pompous yet illiterate, the characters in *Amos 'n' Andy* were completely separated from the white culture around them, trapped in a fantasy black world as imagined by white writers and viewers. These were not people to take seriously (after all, they hardly seemed to take themselves seriously); therefore, they could simply be laughed at and dismissed, since they were the latest act in the long-running minstrel show that helped white America keep black America, if not out of sight, then definitely out of mind. Responding to the popular new show, the National Association for the Advancement of Colored People (NAACP) issued a detailed list of reasons why *Amos 'n' Andy* should be taken off the air; among them

It tends to strengthen the conclusion among uninformed and prejudiced people that Negroes are inferior, lazy, dumb, and dishonest.

Every character in this one and only television show with an all-Negro cast is either a clown or a crook.

Negro doctors are shown as quacks and thieves.

Negro lawyers are shown as slippery cowards, ignorant of their profession, and without ethics.

Negro women are shown as cackling, screaming shrews, in big-mouth close-ups, using street slang, just short of vulgarity.

All Negroes are shown as dodging work of any kind.

Donald Bogle is a noted authority on African Americans in the media. He is the author of what is considered the classic study of African Americans in the movies: Toms, Coons, Mulattos, Mammies, and Bucks: An Interpretive History of Blacks in American Films *(1973). His work* Brown Sugar: Eighty Years of America's Black Female Superstars *(1980) was made into a popular Public Broadcasting System series.*

So network television welcomed African Americans to the nation's living rooms. As *Primetime Blues* chronicles, the relationship that has developed since then has echoed—and sometimes foreshadowed—the connections and conflicts between black and white America at large.

For a time, even early on, the relationship could be one of surprising equality. Bogle points out that Eddie "Rochester" Anderson and Jack Benny formed what was, in essence, America's first interracial comedy team, which began in radio and extended through the show's television run from 1950 to 1965. Although cast as Benny's manservant, the character of Rochester was anything but subservient. "There was nothing servile or submissive about him. He neither spoke in dialect nor was stooped over. Nor did he ever suck up to Benny or back off from telling him the truth." Rochester may have been a hired man and Benny was his boss, but the relationship between them was one that had strong elements of familiarity, friendship, and even affection. Equally tellingly, during much of the typical episode, Rochester was on camera solo, sometimes for as much as half of the show.

If Eddie "Rochester" Anderson can be said to have represented the African American as comedian in the early days of network television, then Sidney Poitier can be seen as the outstanding example of the "serious black actor," especially in the landmark production of *A Man Is Ten Feet Tall* in 1955. In this live presentation on the Philco Television Playhouse, Poitier starred with Don Murray in a drama of interracial friendship set on the docks of New York City. *A Man Is Ten Feet Tall* was one of the first serious recognitions of African Americans as characters who were not only fully human but even capable of serving as role models. In the drama, Poitier's character displays believable courage, humanity, and honesty, qualities which he imparts through his relationship to Don Murray's character. The success of *A Man Is Ten Feet Tall* led Poitier to film roles, including *The Defiant Ones* (1958), which established him as a major American film actor. Seldom has the power of television to effect social change, if on a limited scope, been more graphically shown.

With the 1960's came the flood tide of the Civil Rights movement and the expansion of African American presence on television. The two were linked. Indeed, how could they not be, since all of American life was by now touched, even directed, by the nearly omnipresent television screen? Yet sometimes it seemed that what television touched it could not help but trivialize. Ivan Dixon appeared as a black airman on the prisoner-of-war "comedy" *Hogan's Heroes* (1965-1971) while Bill Cosby starred in *I Spy* (1965-1968), the secret agent spoof that was the first of Cosby's many successful television series. However, few blacks actually flew bombing missions over Germany during World War II, and while *I Spy* broke a number of barriers, it also underscored how television entertainment was drifting from the events of the day: In the same year that an essentially lightweight, comedic parody of the James Bond films appeared, Malcolm X was assassinated and riots erupted throughout American cities.

Even when it sought to move its African Americans closer to reality, television still earned the censure of its critics, especially in the black community. The series *Julia* (1968-1971), starring Diahann Carroll, was exhibit number one. Set in Los Angeles, this was the story of Julia Baker, a Vietnam widow and nurse with a six-year-old son; with relatively little effort she lands an attractive job in the medical office of Astrospace Industries and settles into a modern, integrated apartment building. The criticism about the show began early and continued strong, especially from many in the African American community: The premise was unrealistic; there were no strong black male characters; racial prejudice was gingerly acknowledged but never really addressed. Still, as Bogle notes, *Julia* was essentially a situation comedy, and to ask more of it in addressing serious social questions simply because its star was African American was, in many ways, to carry the double standard of race relations in this country to yet another level. *Julia* brought people some entertainment, taught a few lessons, and made Carroll a star. Was that not enough?

If the 1960's were the decade when television tried to make the African American experience relevant, then the 1970's were the period when it made them figures of fun. Flip Wilson hosted a variety show (*The Flip Wilson Show*, 1970-1974) that introduced the concept to white America of a mainstream black comic. Sherman Hemsley, as George Jefferson on *All in the Family* (appearing on the 1971-1975 seasons) and later on *The Jeffersons* (1975-1985), updated the persona of the blowhard, self-made man, more successful certainly than the Kingfish but cut essentially from the same cloth. Redd Foxx, as Fred Sanford in *Sanford and Son* (1972-1977), seemed to invite whites to laugh approvingly at all their old prejudices as articulated in and by a black character. Even though *Sanford and Son* held consistently high ratings and was one of the most successful black-oriented series in television history, there was uneasy debate about its real meaning. Were its characters presenting a true black community, living on its own terms and in its own culture, or were they reinforcing the stereotypes the NAACP had railed against in *Amos 'n' Andy*? In the end, it is a matter of perspective, and since even highly popular shows such as *Sanford and Son* were considered "outside" the white American perspective, the answer remains problematical.

Just as puzzling are the African American television figures from the 1980's. What is to be made of Mr. T, who played B. A. Baracus on *The A-Team* (1983-1987)? Is he a menacing black man or comedic foil? Are Philip Michael Thomas (*Miami Vice*, 1984-1989), Howard Rollins (*Heat of the Night*, 1987-1994) and Robert Guillaume (*Benson*, 1979-1986) serious characters, cult figures, or convenient African American foils for their white costars? Above all, was Bill Cosby's incarnation as Dr. Heathcliff Huxtable (*The Cosby Show*, 1984-1992), whose wife was a successful attorney, truly relevant to black life in contemporary America? The fact that the series surged to become the most popular situation comedy in the nation for four straight years suggested that it spoke not only to black audiences but to all audiences who wrestled with the daily frustrations and joys of family life.

By the 1990's, Oprah Winfrey moved beyond being a talk show host and sometime actress to a cultural phenomenon. *The Fresh Prince of Bel-Air* (1990-1996) helped provide Will Smith with the opportunity to establish himself as a bankable film presence. Undernoted series such as the subtle, and subtly moving, *I'll Fly Away* (1991-1993) gave African American actors and actresses the chance to touch audiences in the most personal and profound ways. As America and American television entered a new millennium, both the society and the medium had finally—perhaps, just perhaps—reached a point where African Americans could be both themselves and part of the "mainstream" audience.

Michael Witkoski

Sources for Further Study

Booklist 97 (January 1, 2001): 896.
Kirkus Reviews 68 (December 1, 2000): 1654.
Library Journal 125 (November 1, 2000): 104.
Publishers Weekly 247 (November 13, 2000): 91.

PRIVILEGED SON
Otis Chandler and the Rise and Fall of the *L.A. Times* Dynasty

Author: Dennis McDougal (1947-   )
Publisher: Perseus Publishing (Cambridge. Mass.).
    526 pp. $35.00
Type of work: Biography, media, and history
Time: 1881-2001
Locale: Los Angeles, California

∼

Through a biography of Chandler, publisher of the Los
Angeles Times*, McDougal traces the story of the rise of
the newspaper to greatness and its ultimate sale by the
Chandler family to a media combine*

∼

Principal personages:
> OTIS CHANDLER, publisher of the *Los Angeles Times*
> DOROTHY BUFFAM "BUFF" CHANDLER, mother of Otis Chandler
> NORMAN CHANDLER, father of Otis Chandler
> MISSY CHANDLER, first wife of Otis Chandler
> BETTINA CHANDLER, second wife of Otis Chandler
> HARRISON GRAY OTIS, founder of the *Los Angeles Times*
> HARRY CHANDLER, grandfather of Otis Chandler

During the 1960's and 1970's, the *Los Angeles Times* became one of the nation's great newspapers under the leadership of its dynamic publisher, Otis Chandler. While the *Times* had long been influential in the politics and cultural life of Southern California, it had also been renowned for the bias of its news columns and its staunchly conservative editorial policy. The paper was highly profitable, but in journalistic circles was not thought of in the same respectful terms as the nation's first-rate papers, *The Washington Post* and *The New York Times*. Under Otis Chandler, the *Los Angeles Times* moved to the center politically and at the same time established a reputation as a reporter's newspaper that broke big stories and competed on an equal basis with its eastern rivals. By the 1980's, the *Los Angeles Times* had achieved journalistic stature at the top of the American media.

Unlike the families who headed *The New York Times* and *The Washington Post*, however, the Chandlers were not able to keep their newspaper empire together. Where the Sulzbergers succeeded in retaining control of *The New York Times* and the Graham family built *The Washington Post* into a media conglomerate, the Chandlers in the end could not maintain the cohesion and sense of common purpose of a true journalistic dynasty. They succumbed to the allure of the hundreds of millions of dollars that came from the *Chicago Tribune* interests when the *Los Angeles Times* was

A longtime staff writer for the Los
Angeles Times, *Dennis McDougal
has written several other books,
including award-winning mysteries
and true crime books, as well as*
The Last Mogul *(1998), a study of
the life of Hollywood insider Lew
Wasserman of the Music
Corporation of America (MCA).*

sold in the late 1990's. In a little more than a century, the Chandlers had come from obscurity to
great wealth in the newspaper business, only to
see their accomplishments taken over by others.
Their saga is, however, one of the most interesting and complex in the history of American journalism.

In this well-researched and lively book, Dennis McDougal traces the evolution of the *Los Angeles Times* and Southern California from the
1880's down to the present day. A writer for that
newspaper for a decade, McDougal brings a rich
background to his subject. His previous work on
Hollywood and other aspects of Southern California life have given him a mastery of the bright
and dark sides of the City of Angels. For this project, he also enjoyed the cooperation of Otis
Chandler and his family, who opened up to Mc-
Dougal in a series of candid weekly interviews.
Few intimate areas of Chandler's life were left
unexplored. McDougal also combed the *Los Angeles Times* archives thoroughly. The result is a
multidimensional account of a man who made a great newspaper only to see it become so profitable and attractive that it passed out of his control. In McDougal's
pages, Otis Chandler emerges as something of a gifted but flawed tragic figure in U.S.
journalism.

The *Los Angeles Times* got its start as the city was becoming an attraction for East-
erners and Midwesterners seeking a warm climate and economic opportunity during
the 1880's. Otis Chandler's ancestors, Harrison Gray Otis and Harry Chandler, made
it the local newspaper that spoke for the boom psychology and political conservatism
of the region. In a series of battles that featured violence on both sides, the *Los Angeles Times* sought to exclude labor unions and pushed the interests of the Republican
party. In 1911, a bitter labor dispute even led to the dynamiting of the newspaper's
headquarters. The trial of the men involved, the McNamara brothers, became one of
the most sensational such proceedings in the history of U.S. law.

The Chandler family grew wealthy from its newspaper and the profitable real estate ventures that opened up for political insiders. McDougal is adept at showing how
the Chandler fortune expanded thanks to their political connections and economic
clout. The *Los Angeles Times* provided limited coverage of this phase of California's
growth. The newspaper was a cash cow, but its news columns were slanted and its reporters were precluded from following stories that revealed the nexus between money
and power under the warm skies of the Pacific coast.

McDougal follows the interplay between the *Los Angeles Times* and the rise of
Southern California in the first half of the twentieth century with an impressive

amount of analytical skill. He untangles the corruption-laden process by which Los Angeles obtained that water needed to slake the thirst of its booming population. There is also very interesting material on the sordid history of the Los Angeles police department in McDougal's account. Those who have seen the films *Chinatown* (1974) and *L.A. Confidential* (1997) will find here the real-life settings for those fictional portrayals of the underside of Southern California. Norman Chandler, the grandfather of Otis, was reportedly the model for the villain in *Chinatown*.

A number of fascinating individuals crowd McDougal's pages. One of the most compelling is Dorthy Buffam "Buff" Chandler, the mother of Otis Chandler. Mrs. Chandler used her influence and the power of the *Los Angeles Times* to become one of the leading figures in philanthropic enterprises in the area. She was instrumental in saving the Hollywood Bowl from destruction, and she worked tirelessly to establish what became the Dorothy Chandler Pavilion for the performing arts. Although she chafed at the way the newspaper's music critic often dealt with the Los Angeles Philharmonic, Buff Chandler made an indelible mark on the culture of her city.

She also made friends with many of the most important politicians of the region, one of whom was Richard Milhouse Nixon. Mrs. Chandler became convinced that Nixon was crude and hypocritical in his personal life. Though the *Los Angeles Times* supported Nixon as a fellow Republican, the Chandlers never fully trusted Nixon, and were not surprised when his political career collapsed in the disgrace of the Watergate scandal in the 1970's.

The focus of McDougal's book is Otis Chandler and his rise to power as publisher of the *Los Angeles Times* in April, 1960, at the tender age of thirty-two. A graduate of Andover Academy and Stanford University, Otis Chandler was a bright, handsome young man who had been an outstanding track athlete and the author of a senior thesis at college on the Holocaust. After a stint in the Air Force, he went to work at the *Los Angeles Times* in 1953 and learned the newspaper business from the bottom up. His father, Norman Chandler, moved him around from department to department to provide him a firsthand sense of how the newspaper functioned and what a future publisher should know about the inner workings of the paper. Otis proved a quick learner, with a talent for the newspaper business and a burning desire to make his family's venture in journalism an importance force nationally.

However, Otis Chandler was more than just a publisher. He was a dedicated surfer, a hunter of big game, and a collector of antique cars and motorcycles. He seemed to court the physical danger and excitement that he could not find in the demands of the newspaper business. His first marriage dissolved in bitterness and his relations with his children were sometimes distant and strained. McDougal spends a perhaps undue number of his pages on these personal details, sometimes at the expense of a deeper understanding of the development of the newspaper under Otis Chandler's leadership.

Once Otis Chandler gave the *Los Angeles Times* in the 1960's and 1970's the firm professional leadership it had never previously had, the newspaper blossomed. Chandler recruited excellent reporters and provocative columnists. He expanded the paper's coverage of world affairs and devoted resources to investigative journalism. Like a kind of daily magazine, the *Los Angeles Times* offered its readers a well-written and fascinating look at the changing world. As a result, it became a newspaper where reporters loved to work because of the freedom and independence that Chandler accorded them. The newspaper won twenty-one Pulitzer Prizes during Chandler's twenty-year tenure at the helm. All the while Chandler made sure that a firewall existed between the news coverage and the advertising end of his newspaper.

Just as the old *Los Angeles Times* had taken its character from the personalities and foibles of his grandfather and father, Otis Chandler's newspaper in its heyday reflected the outlook of its maverick publisher. Chandler let his staff poke into productive stories, even if the resulting news accounts hurt some of his wealthy friends. He became a celebrity publisher himself, and was much in demand on the corporate lecture circuit. However, one of Chandler's mistakes was not to groom one of his sons to succeed him when it was time to step down. Instead, Chandler in 1980 gave way, after twenty years, to Tom Johnson, no relation to but a protégé of former president Lyndon B. Johnson. Thus, for the first time in almost one hundred years, the publisher of the *Los Angeles Times* was not a member of the Chandler family. Otis remained as chairman and editor in chief, posts he held for another five years before the members of the Times-Mirror corporate board eased him out of power in late 1985. None of these backstage quarrels interrupted the profitable success of the *Los Angeles Times* and its standing as one of the best newspapers in the world.

However, in the 1990's even the profitable *Los Angeles Times* faced financial difficulties. The downturn in the economy at the start of the decade depressed profits for the newspaper company. Reporters were terminated and a hiring freeze instituted. New executives came in to regain momentum, but in the process the news side of the paper lost some of its energy and skill. By the middle of the decade, a new chief executive officer, Mark Willes, who had no background in journalism but a great familiarity with breakfast food, instituted cost-cutting policies that eroded staff morale. More important, Willes made arrangements with large advertisers for projects that cast doubt on the journalistic integrity of the newspaper. Tearing down the firewall between news and advertising made sense to an executive in search of greater profits. When the change was revealed, however, it became major news across the country, and the fallout did not help the faltering reputation of the *Los Angeles Times*. By the end of the 1990's, the Times-Mirror company entered into negotiations with the Tribune Company of Chicago for the sale of the *Los Angeles Times* and that transaction occurred in June, 2000. As Otis Chandler put it, "we sold the family store."

The saga of Otis Chandler and the *Los Angeles Times* is well told in this engrossing book by Dennis McDougal. He gives the reader an excellent sense of how the newspaper business evolved and how fragile the creation of a great paper is. Although Otis Chandler was a flawed and often self-indulgent man, he had the capacity to foster a vital part of American journalism at a key moment in its history. No matter how many antique cars and big-game trophies he has collected, Otis Chandler will be remembered as one of the preeminent newspaper executives of the twentieth century in the United States.

Lewis L. Gould

Sources for Further Study

Booklist 97 (May 15, 2001): 1710.
Business Week, June 11, 2001, p. 25.
The New York Times Book Review 106 (June 17, 2001): 21.
Publishers Weekly 248 (April 30, 2001): 65.

PURIFIED BY FIRE
A History of Cremation in America

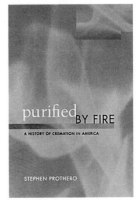

Author: Stephen Prothero (1960-   )
Publisher: University of California Press (Berkeley).
266 pp. $27.50
Type of work: Environment, religion, and sociology
Time: The mid-1800's to the late 1900's
Locale: Washington, Pennsylvania, Boston, New York,
and Salt Lake City

∿

Drawing on a daunting cache of material from a variety
of sources, Prothero traces the history of cremation in the
United States from its beginnings in 1876 to 1999

∿

Principal personages:
> COLONEL HENRY LAURENS, first Caucasian to be cremated in the United
> States
> REVEREND OCTAVIUS B. FROTHINGHAM, a procremation clergyman
> DR. FRANCIS JULIUS LEMOYNE, a procremation physician who had the
> first United States crematory erected on his estate near Washington,
> Pennsylvania
> BARON JOSEPH HENRY LOUIS CHARLES DE PALM, an Austrian baron and
> Freemason, the first person to be cremated in LeMoyne's cremato-
> rium
> HENRY STEEL OLCOTT, Baron De Palm's executor
> MRS. BENJAMIN PITMAN, the first woman to be cremated in the United
> States
> JESSICA MITFORD, a procremationist, author of *The American Way of*
> *Death* (1963)
> POPE LEO XIII, the Roman Catholic pope who in 1886 forbade Catholics
> to be cremated
> POPE PAUL VI, the Roman Catholic pope who in 1963 relaxed the
> church's ban on cremation

Subjects relating to death in the way that *Purified by Fire* does often fail to entice imaginative writers or, when they do, may result in books that border on the morbid. Fortunately, Stephen Prothero, an assistant professor of religion at Boston University, has brought to his task of detailing the history of cremation in the United States an admirable energy, wit, and writing ability. Prothero's earlier book, *The White Buddhist: The Asian Odyssey of Henry Steel Olcott* (1996), provided a logical springboard for *Purified by Fire.* Olcott, as executor of Baron De Palm's estate, made the arrangements for the cremation that De Palm requested before his death.

The story of this first cremation in the crema-
tory that Dr. Francis LeMoyne had constructed
on his estate near Washington, Pennsylvania, at
a cost of $1,500 is a complex and fascinating
one. Although De Palm died on May 20, 1876,
his remains were not cremated until December 6
of that year. His body was embalmed and held
until everything was in place legally for his cremation, the first indoor cremation in the United

*Stephen Prothero is an assistant
professor of religion at Boston
University. His first book was* The
White Buddhist: The Asian Odyssey
of Henry Steel Olcott *(1996).*

States. The cremation oven was so constructed that the body would not be consumed
by flames but rather broken down by heat into a white ash.

De Palm's cremation, although officially designated private, was attended by
some forty journalists, physicians, clergymen, and public health officials from around
the United States. The event, designed to be solemn, turned into a circus as newsmen
joked about the deceased's appearance and, in one case, went so far as the lift the
sheet covering the body to glimpse De Palm's genitals. Newspapers throughout the
country reported in detail the events surrounding the cremation.

Prothero, as a religious scholar, is particularly interested in how changing attitudes
toward cremation over a period of about 125 years reflect ways in which people and
religious organizations have revised their views about religious rituals during that
time. In 1886, for example, Pope Leo XIII specifically forbade Roman Catholics from
joining cremation societies and from having their remains cremated. Less than one
hundred years later, in 1963, Pope Paul VI lifted that ban, although the church still
urged Christian burial as opposed to cremation and forbade priests from accompanying corpses into crematoria and from conducting services in such facilities. The 1963
decree removed cremation from the list of mortal sins, where Pope Leo's edict had
placed it.

Proponents of cremation, including such notables as Mark Twain, Edward Everett
Hale, and a host of clergymen from the more liberal congregations, argued both on
environmental and religious grounds that cremation was preferable to burial in the
ground. Twain pointed out in *Life on the Mississippi* (1883) that above-ground intern-
ment, common in New Orleans, was a threat to sanitation and that every body buried
was a potential assassin to those who were exposed to its vapors as it decayed. On the
other hand, Walt Whitman came out foursquare in favor of burial in the earth.

Prothero notes the main secular reasons apologists for cremation advanced in presenting their cases. A major fear of many people, in an age when medicine was sufficiently limited that sometimes it was impossible to tell whether one was dead or in
some sort of trancelike coma, was the fear of being buried alive. As early as 1792,
Henry Laurens, president of the Continental Congress, opted for cremation on the
grounds of his estate in South Carolina.

Laurens's daughter had been declared dead after suffering from smallpox and was
on the brink of burial when she emerged from her deep sleep. This startling recovery
caused Laurens to state explicitly in his will that when he died, his remains be cremated, threatening disinheritance to anyone who disobeyed his edict. Fear of prema-

ture burial became a major factor in attracting many people to the cremationist cause.

A more significant factor, however, was that of sanitation. Many notable physicians supported this stand, and the American Medical Association (AMA) in 1882 passed by a vote of 159-106 a resolution endorsing cremation over burial in all large cities for sanitary reasons. This resolution was finally tabled and never again brought before the AMA.

The last third of the nineteenth century, commonly called the Gilded Age, was an era when Americans were obsessed with cleanliness. Native-born Americans were alarmed at the immigrant hordes that were flooding into the country. Many spread the notion that these foreigners were carriers of dangerous diseases. Immigrants were looked upon as the "great unwashed," whereas Americans were portrayed as clean and sanitary. Such prejudices led many to call for the establishment of crematoria near points of entry into the nation so that those who had died en route to America could be cremated immediately, thereby lessening the risk that they might infect the general public.

Alarmists within the procremation groups presented dire descriptions of how bodies decay and of how the noxious gases they exude can kill in minutes. They cited undocumented cases in which grave diggers exhuming bodies died on the spot as they went about their gruesome work. They told about a nunnery in which all the nuns became chronically ill after the body of a notable religious figure was interred beneath its floor.

Prothero demonstrates an enviable ability to place his subject succinctly within historical contexts. He characterizes the Gilded Age, which he places between the end of the Civil War and the 1890's, as an age of debate:

> Lincoln traded barbs with Douglas. Robert Ingersoll, America's most famous agnostic, took on clergymen of all stripes. Should women be allowed to vote? Should baseball games be played on Sundays? Was Darwin right? The Bible true? Each of these topics was vigorously debated on the rostrum and the editorial page. So, too, was whether to bury or to burn.

Despite its slight inaccuracy—the Lincoln-Douglas debates occurred in 1859, before the Civil War—Prothero, in about fifty words, captures gracefully in this passage the essence of the Gilded Age.

In the context of the Gilded Age, Prothero makes clear that the cremation movement, although steeped in concerns about sanitation, was not solely about that issue and fear of premature burial. The social reform climate of that era caused people to question many of their most deeply cherished beliefs and long-held convictions. Prothero writes that "the sanitary and social reform movements can themselves be viewed as ritual demonstrations—parts of a vast movement for the elimination of dirt evident in the cremation crusade and in contemporaneous campaigns for circumcision, hand washing, nail clipping, hair brushing, and bathing." He goes on to link this to a broader social context: "Perhaps even social reforms like temperance can fruitfully be interpreted as purity ties of a sort—key movements in a history of American ritual life that still waits to be written."

Purified by Fire demonstrates how cremation advanced from the social reforms of the preceding century to the business agenda of the twentieth century. First running counter to morticians, who saw their livelihood threatened by cremationists, the cremationists soon began to appease the undertaking business, showing how, as an alternate means of disposing of bodies in a dignified way, cremations could help morticians expand their business profitably. Whereas the two camps were initially at loggerheads, they began to work cooperatively and to each other's advantage.

Religions have grown increasingly more accepting of cremation than they were initially, although some still resist it. For many Jews, cremation evokes memories of Hitler's concentration camps with their gas chambers and crematoria, so some of them shrink from this means of disposing of bodies, although Reform Judaism accepts cremation. Some individuals shrink from the notion of not having a grave to which they can pay visits and commune with the dead.

Cremation is among the most inexpensive ways to dispose of human remains. When people are under financial pressure, it is sometimes the only means available to them. At the end of World War II in 1945, the cremation rate in the United States was 3.7 percent. The postwar years were prosperous ones for Americans, so in 1963, the cremation rate had not advanced at all but remained at 3.7 percent.

In 1963, Jessica Mitford's *The American Way of Death*, an exposé about the undertaking industry, was published. It had a profound effect on Americans. Topping *The New York Times'* best-seller list for several months, this book revealed the bloated underbelly of an industry that, according to Mitford, preyed upon grief-stricken people solely to extract from them as much money as possible.

Before Mitford's book, little public attention was focused on the economics of the funeral industry. Aesthetics and sentiment were touted as the major factors to be considered, much to the economic detriment of grieving survivors. Largely because of Mitford's book, California in 1972 took the initiative in legislating that undertakers had to provide an itemized list of their charges, to obtain the permission of the next of kin before embalming, to quote prices over the telephone if so requested, and to display the most inexpensive caskets along with all the others. Similar legislation is now in place in many states.

Mitford's book stimulated a gradual upturn in the numbers of cremations that took place. The figure rose to 4.5 percent in 1969. Then, in the 1970's, with the establishment of two large nationwide cremations societies, Neptune and Telophase, and a number of smaller ones, the figure reached 6.5 percent in 1975 and 9.4 percent in 1979. Perhaps spurred on by the cremation of an ever-increasing number of such prominent figures as Albert Einstein in 1955 and John Lennon in 1980, the United States' cremation rate reached a peak of 25 percent in 1999, the year in which the first prominent American Roman Catholic, John F. Kennedy, Jr., was cremated.

Although cremationists preferred to argue their cause on purely secular grounds, the religious objections to cremation have been fundamental in determining its future as a means of disposing of human remains efficiently and with dignity. In 1997, Roman Catholic bishops in the United States received a special dispensation from the

Vatican that gives them the power to decide whether cremated remains can be present at funeral masses in their dioceses.

Purified by Fire has well-chosen and effectively reproduced illustrations. Prothero provides a time line and a comprehensive bibliography of primary and secondary sources reflecting the impressive scope of his research. The book's index is disappointing in that it omits many names and a number of topical categories, such as "Gilded Age" and "feminism." The book's virtues, however, far outweigh this minor shortcoming.

R. Baird Shuman

Sources for Further Study

Booklist 97 (January 1, 2001): 887.
Choice 38 (June, 2001): 5637.
The Economist 356 (March 10, 2001): 6.
Library Journal 126 (January 1, 2001): 115.
Publishers Weekly 247 (November 20, 2000): S14.
The Wall Street Journal, April 27, 2001, p. W17.

RADICAL ENLIGHTENMENT
Philosophy and the Making of Modernity, 1650-1750

Author: Jonathan I. Israel (1946-   )
Publisher: Oxford University Press (New York). 809 pp.
  $45.00
Type of work: History and philosophy
Time: 1650-1750
Locale: Europe

A history of radical philosophical thinkers in Europe at the beginning of the modern period that considers their challenges to the intellectual and political establishment of their day and the responses of this establishment to them

⁓

Principal personages:
RENÉ DESCARTES, French philosopher
BENEDICT DE SPINOZA, Dutch philosopher
GIAMBATTISTA VICO, Italian philosopher of history

By the end of the European Middle Ages, a Christianized version of Aristotelian philosophy had achieved the status of the official Western interpretation of the world and of the place of human beings in the world. According to Aristotelian scholasticism, things are made up of matter and form. Form comes from an essence or soul within all things that also joins each form inseparably with its substance. The essence of each thing also determines how it develops and interacts with other things. Scientific thinking, from the late Middle Ages through the Early Modern period, generally involved classifying and explaining things according to their innate qualities. This view of the world, with its emphasis on essences, was consistent with the idea of souls in Christian theology and with the idea that the universe is purposeful, consisting of movement toward ends created by divine design. It was also consistent with the established political order, because political inequality among people was the result of placement decreed by God according to inborn essences.

By the seventeenth century, however, new trends in scientific and philosophical thinking began to pose challenges to Aristotelianism. A growing number of thinkers saw naturalistic and mechanistic explanations of events as more accurate than vague references to essences. From a mechanistic point of view, if something moves or changes, it is because something else causes it to move or change. This kind of explanation posed a problem for religious thinkers in the seventeenth century and after. God seemed to be left out of an account of the world that attributed every event to the interaction of bodies. In addition, there seemed to be no room for human

~

Jonathan I. Israel is professor in the School of Historical Studies at the Institute for Advanced Study at Princeton University. Formerly professor of Dutch history and institutions at University College, London, he is author of numerous articles and of eight previous books, as well as editor of five others. His book European Jewry in the Age of Mercantilism *(1985) was joint winner of the Wolfson Literary Prize for History in 1986. He is a Fellow of the British Academy and has held visiting professorships and research fellowships in the Netherlands, France, and at UCLA.*

~

thought or awareness in the machine of the universe.

French philosopher René Descartes (1596-1650) came up with one ingenious and influential solution to the problems posed by mechanism. By carefully reflecting on his own thoughts, Descartes found that the world seemed to be divided into himself as a thinking being and the mechanistic objects outside of himself. This managed to maintain both the supernatural and the scientific mechanisms of nature by splitting them apart. The solution offered by Descartes was frequently viewed with suspicion by leaders of church and state, but there were still some radical thinkers, such as Benedict de Spinoza (1632-1677) who went even further than Descartes and discarded the supernatural altogether.

Jonathan Israel argues, in this comprehensive and detailed volume, that the naturalistic radicals did not merely exist at the fringes of Enlightenment thinking. Although repeatedly denounced by church and state officials and frequently given only covert support even by their followers, the radicals played a central part in the creation of a modern view of the world. The radicals made substantial contributions both to the naturalistic perspective of modern science and to secular, democratizing trends in politics.

Earlier studies of the Enlightenment have frequently approached the period as a matter of national politics. Insofar as these studies have understood the Enlightenment as a European occurrence, they have portrayed it as the projection of a single nation's influence. Those who place France at the center of the events of the time have seen Europe revolving around the writings of the *philosophes* from Charles de Montesquieu (1689-1755) to Jean-Jacques Rousseau (1712-1788). Those in the English school have argued that the empiricism and materialistic philosophies of John Locke (1632-1704), Sir Isaac Newton (1642-1727), and their colleagues established the current of the era. Israel does acknowledge the importance of French thinkers, although he also maintains that the development of the French Enlightenment was hampered by the hostility of the court of King Louis XIV (ruled 1643-1715). Israel also recognizes that English thinking was widely influential, particularly during the "Anglomania," the fashion for English ideas and styles that swept through European intellectual life in the 1730's and 1740's. However, he sees the Enlightenment as a continental phenomenon, a set of challenges to received views and social hierarchies that arose in all parts of Europe and took varied forms in response to varied conditions.

Insofar as Israel gives priority to any country in setting the pace of the times, he gives it to the Netherlands. Some readers may feel that this is simply the author's professional bias. He specializes in Early Modern Dutch history and the academic tendency to see one's own field as the center of the world may have led him to emphasize the importance of things Dutch. Nevertheless, there are two reasons to accept his argument for Dutch importance. First, the Dutch Republic was one of Europe's two freest societies, along with England. Many of the books that more repressive governments attempted to censor elsewhere in Europe were produced in the Netherlands. Second, the greatest radical of the seventeenth century, the arch-heretic Spinoza, was Dutch.

Spinoza was an enormously influential figure, who corresponded with Gottfried Leibniz (1646-1716) and many of the other foremost intellectuals of the time. He was also the writer who was most widely demonized by the political and religious conservatives of his time. According to Israel's account, "Spinozism" was a term that provoked the same sorts of fears and reactions in the seventeenth century that "communism" provoked among western countries in the twentieth century. Spinoza's radicalism, as it appears in this volume, was simultaneously theological and political. Spinoza, also, according to Israel, was one of the foremost proponents of freedom of thought and expression in his age.

Israel's approach to the radical wing of Enlightenment thinkers is topical rather than chronological. He begins by looking at developments that set the stage for philosophical radicalism. He considers the rise of Cartesianism and its reception by governments in Central Europe, in Scandinavia and the Baltic, and in the Italian states. He discusses the urban social milieu and the changing social institutions that fostered both political and philosophical radicalism. He also describes the relative emancipation of women (at least privileged women) that marked the beginning of the modern period. These efforts at social history, while interesting, may be the weakest part of the book. Israel never seems to make a convincing argument about just what urbanization or women's increased participation had to do with philosophical radicalism, or to make it clear whether he sees social change as cause or consequence of new thinking. He also gives little attention to the great economic changes of the era, or to how shifts in popular mentalities may have been related to the ideas of intellectual elites. He is on much stronger ground when concentrating on more traditional concerns of intellectual history, and he gives good accounts of how the rise of diversified libraries and the circulation of learned journals assisted the spread of ideas.

In looking at the rise of philosophical radicalism, Israel makes his case for Spinoza's central position. He describes some of the outstanding political and religious figures of the time, many of whom had personal ties to Spinoza. These included Spinoza's teacher, Franciscus van den Enden (1602-1674), an ardent proponent of democratic republics who was hanged for conspiring against the French King Louis XIV; the brothers Johannes Koerbagh (1634-1672) and Adriaen Koerbagh (1632-1669), who were put on trial for expressing Spinozistic ideas in popular Dutch rather than scholarly Latin; and Lodwijk Meyer (1629-1681), who attempted to use a rationalistic philosophy to interpret Scripture. Israel looks at how Spinoza's officially banned ideas spread throughout Europe, often secretly published and circulating in books with false title-pages.

Israel places the major intellectual controversies in Europe that followed Spinoza's death in the context of the rise of naturalistic ideas, and he examines the reaction to radicalism in the early eighteenth century. Finally, he discusses how the thoughts of the Radical Enlightenment made quiet progress throughout the nations of continental Europe and England up to 1750. One of the most interesting sections of this last part of the book is in the chapter in which he looks at the radical impact in Italy. The Italian philosopher of history Giambattista Vico (1668-1744) has been something of a cult figure among those interested in cyclical theories of history. Twentieth century writer James Joyce is often said to have used Vico's ideas as the basis for *Finnegans Wake* (1939). Vico, who argued that human societies go through set phases determined by irrational human impulses, is generally seen as deeply conservative and antimodern. Israel makes a good case for seeing Vico as not only influenced by Enlightenment ideas but also as directly influenced by Spinoza's works.

Israel also manages to show the pervasive influence of Spinoza on English deism. The deists accepted the existence of God but saw little room for divine operation in the world, which they saw as functioning according to naturalistic processes of cause and effect. Although it is recognized that Spinoza corresponded with Henry Oldenburg (1620-1677), the secretary of the London Royal Society, historians often portray English and Irish intellectual life as largely isolated from continental Europe. Israel acknowledges that the English tended to be inward-looking and suspicious of foreign influences. Nevertheless, he points out that Spinoza's ideas were widely debated in England and he identifies Spinoza's impact on such English radicals as John Toland (1670-1722), Anthony Collins (1676-1729), Matthew Tindal (1657-1733), and Bernard Mandeville (1670-1730). The English chemist Robert Boyle (1627-1691) discussed Spinoza's ideas with Henry Oldenburg, and the great English philosopher John Locke had all of Spinoza's books in his library and may have met with followers of the Dutch radical.

At the end, Israel moves beyond his historical period to look at the consequences of the Radical Enlightenment, in the form of the French Revolution. Most historians would regard this event as the defining moment of the beginning of the late modern world. Israel argues that the radical ideas of the mid-seventeenth century through the mid-eighteenth century helped to make the revolution, but that the revolution, in a sense, also helped to remake those ideas. The revolutionaries and those opposed to them looked back at Spinoza and the other radicals and reinterpreted the thinking of those earlier philosophers. One of the consequences was that many of the early radicals were overshadowed by the figure of Jean-Jacques Rousseau (1712-1778), who derived many of his ideas from the earlier *philosophes*, but who came to be seen as the chief intellectual symbol of the Revolution.

While it is loosely organized and often skips abruptly from one topic to another, *Radical Enlightenment* is an impressive work of scholarship. Erudite and expansive in its scope, the book provides an outstanding survey of trends in intellectual history during early modern times. It clarifies the connection between philosophical materialism and opposition to traditional political hierarchies. It also provides support for a new perspective on Spinoza's role in the Enlightenment. In his recent biography,

Spinoza: A Life (1999), Stephen Nadler argued that the Dutch philosopher was not the social isolate that many have considered him, and that Spinoza was deeply involved in the intellectual networks of his day. Now, Jonathan Israel has convincingly maintained that Spinoza was actually at the center of those networks, not only in the area around the Netherlands, but throughout Europe.

Carl L. Bankston III

Sources for Further Study

New Statesman 130 (December 17, 2001): 79.
The Village Voice 46 (December 11, 2001): 58.

REFLECTIONS ON EXILE AND OTHER ESSAYS

Author: Edward W. Said (1936-   )
Publisher: Harvard University Press (Cambridge, Mass.).
  576 pp. $35.00
Type of work: Essays and literary criticism

❧

*A wide-ranging collection of forty-six essays, forty-five
of which were previously published in a variety of periodicals from 1967 to 1998, by a prominent Palestinian American literary and social critic*

❧

The essays in this collection are arranged chronologically by date of publication.
In the introduction to the book, Said identifies them as the result of thirty-five years of
intellectual activity. The first essay, on the French philosopher Maurice Merleau-
Ponty, appeared in 1967. The next-to-last, on the author's experience of living between the Arab and American worlds, was published in 1998. The last, a criticism of
Samuel Huntington's argument that future world history will be dominated by a clash
between Western and non-Western civilizations, is the only work to appear for the
first time in this volume. However, many readers may want to start with the title essay, published in 1984 and reproduced here as chapter 17. In this essay, Said ponders
how the experience of exile from a homeland can create a unique perspective. He cites
one of his favorite quotations, from the twelfth century monk Hugh of St. Victor, who
wrote: "The man who finds his homeland sweet is still a tender beginner; he to whom
every soil is as his native one is already strong; but he is perfect to whom the entire
world is as a foreign land." The exile's perspective, seeing all lands as foreign, is the
starting point for the thirty years of essays on literature, music, film, and politics
brought together in this book.

Said has undergone his own long, thoughtful, and thought-provoking exile. He
was born to a Palestinian family in Jerusalem before the creation of the state of Israel.
He grew up in Egypt and the United States, and he has taught at Columbia University
in New York since 1963. Early on, he made contact with the famous New York intellectuals connected to the journal *Partisan Review.* However, he grew to realize that
their concerns with Stalinism and Soviet Communism were not his own. The war in
Vietnam and the rise of the Palestinian people as a political force during the 1960's
turned his attention in a different direction. The role of literature in the relations of
colonized and colonizing countries has been one of his central interests. He has been
involved with the cause of the Palestinians both as a writer and as an activist. Said attracted wide attention with his book *Orientalism* (1978), which argued that the concept of "the Orient" and European scholarly, literary, and artistic views of the lands
east of Europe were expressions of colonial domination. He argued that many of the

assumptions of orientalism, in turn, affected how the people of the colonized lands saw themselves and their colonizers. Thus, cultures are shaped by on-going dialogues between insiders and outsiders, and the cultural creations of individuals emerge within these dialogues. Throughout his work, Said has argued that one of the goals of intellectual activity is to step outside of particular cultures in order to understand the interaction of cultures.

Joseph Conrad (1857-1924) is among Said's favorite cultural outsiders. Conrad was the subject of Said's first book, *Joseph Conrad and the Fiction of Autobiography* (1966). Two of the essays are devoted to this Polish-born wanderer, who wrote in an English that he always spoke with a heavy accent. Said also cites Conrad in a number of other essays, including "Reflections on Exile," in which he describes Conrad's story

Edward W. Said was born to a Palestinian family in Jerusalem. Shortly before the creation of Israel in 1948, Said's family moved to Cairo, Egypt. Said's family sent him to boarding school in Massachusetts, after which he attended Princeton University, taking a bachelor's degree in 1957. He was hired as an instructor at Columbia University in 1963 and earned a Ph.D. in English literature from Harvard in 1964. He has produced numerous books, including the influential Orientalism *(1978) and* Culture and Imperialism *(1993).*

"Amy Foster" as "perhaps the most uncompromising representation of exile ever written." In the chapter entitled "Conrad and Nietzsche," first published in 1976, he discusses the similarities between Conrad's narratives and Friedrich Nietzsche's (1844-1900) radical reinterpretations of the European philosophical tradition. In "Through Gringo Eyes: With Conrad in Latin America," originally published in 1988, Said presents the novel *Nostromo* (1904), Conrad's only major work set in Latin America, as an early examination of the nature of modern imperialism.

Said's interest in the cultural connections between the Arab world and Europe appears repeatedly throughout the essays. In a piece on T. E. Lawrence (1888-1935), Said considers how the writing of the British agent and author known as Lawrence of Arabia emerged from Lawrence's personal and political self-contradictions. An essay on Arabic literature after 1948 identifies the years 1948 (the year of war resulting from Israel's creation) and 1967 (the Six-day War) as critical for Arabic prose. A 1983 article on the new Egyptian wing of the Metropolitan Museum of New York ranges through the history of European Egyptology and classic films such as *Cleopatra* (1934) and *The Ten Commandments* (1956) to describe how the museum showings illustrate Western views of Egypt.

Although Edward Said is known as a literary critic, he is also a pianist, and several of the essays present his reflections on music. In these, he shows a unique ability to draw parallels between music and literature. He is also able to place music, as well as literature, in historical and political context.

The essays also display an interest in popular culture, especially in film. His chapter on Johnny Weismuller in the Tarzan films of the 1930's and 1940's recognizes the racism in these films but expresses a fascination with Weismuller's ape-man as an ecological hero. His enjoyment of the Weismuller films illustrates that Said does not reduce all cultural expressions to political statements. He does recognize that there is an aesthetic dimension to culture that always retains connections with the political but also continues to have a reality apart from politics.

The previously unpublished essay that ends the collection treats one of the latest episodes in the Western interpretation of the non-Western world. In 1993, Samuel P. Huntington published "The Coming Clash of Civilizations" in the journal *Foreign Affairs*. He expanded this article into the book *The Clash of Civilizations and the Remaking of World Order* (1996). Huntington argued that nations were entering a new phase in world political history. For much of the twentieth century, according to Huntington, ideology had been the basis of international conflict. In particular, Communism and anti-Communism had provided reasons for rivalry and alliance. Following the fall of Communism in the Soviet Union and Eastern Europe, Huntington maintained, the clash of cultural traditions of civilizations was beginning to replace the clash of opposing ideologies. The United States and other nations of the West would face challenges from Islamic and Confucian civilizations, in place of the old challenge of Communism.

Said attacks Huntington's view as based on loose reasoning, faulty generalizations, and stereotypes. It is not true, Said observes, that non-Western civilizations necessarily clash with the West. Replacing opposition to Communism with opposition to other countries may be a good way to justify military spending, but it does not offer a realistic way of seeing the world. Further, seeing non-Western cultures as necessarily hostile appeals to popular fears of the foreign and unfamiliar. This kind of thinking, according to Said, portrays civilizations as monoliths, giant blocks of sameness. In fact, there is substantial variation among Islamic societies and among societies with Confucian traditions. The West itself, Said points out, does not derive from a single, unchanging cultural tradition. He maintains that traditions are developed and invented over time, and that there is continual cultural borrowing. Many of the sources of European and American culture are Asian and African in origin. Although inaccurate, Huntington's prediction of global conflict may become a self-fulfilling one if American policy-makers and the American public accept it and treat the nations of Asia and Africa as potential enemies.

Some readers may feel that Said himself oversimplifies culture, by reducing so many of its aspects to the heritage of colonialism. Said also heaps praise on intellectuals such as Frantz Fanon and Michel Foucault, without considering the criticisms of these writers. Fanon has been accused of advocating violence by colonized people for the sake of psychological self-purification. Foucault was often nihilistic in his attacks on established order and his scholarship has been called into question. Said's essays, then, may show a tendency to take sides and give unquestioning acceptance to those he sees as intellectual allies, while employing his critical intelligence as a weapon against those he defines as the opposition. Although the book is less political in orientation than some of Said's others, his political perspectives are clear throughout the volume. These perspectives may enrage some readers, especially those who are sympathetic to the position of the Israeli government in the conflict between that government and its Palestinian opposition.

Throughout the essays, there is a tendency to toss off long lists of names of authors and composers. While this often seems like name-dropping, it may actually reflect Said's effort to divide the world of literature into sides and schools on the basis of a few chosen similarities. Readers may sometimes tire of the lists, and they often seem to be another form of oversimplification.

Said's interpretations often seem willful and based on little evidence other than his own political preferences. For example, he claims that in the film *The Ten Commandments*, Charlton Heston as Moses facing the Egyptians represents Americans defending contemporary Israel against the Arab Egypt of the 1950's. The miracles that Moses brings back with him from the desert are said to represent the technological wonders of postwar America. Perhaps Said sees these modern analogies in the film, but whether these were the conscious or unconscious messages conveyed by director Cecil B. De Mille or perceived by American audiences is open to debate.

Because the book is a collection of essays, and not a single book written at one point in time, it is somewhat repetitive. The essays vary in quality, as well as in length. Some are obviously written to meet magazine deadlines, while others show more careful consideration.

Despite the limitations and eccentricities of some of these essays, however, Edward Said's critics and supporters will find a monument to an impressive career in this book. It shows a wide range of learning, a unique intelligence, and a willingness to draw connections between the world of international politics and the world of letters. All those interested in the development of this influential intellectual's thought will want to find a place for this volume on their library shelves.

Carl L. Bankston III

Sources for Further Study

Booklist 97 (February 1, 2001): 1035.
The Nation 273 (November 26, 2001): 24.
The New York Times Book Review 106 (February 18, 2001): 28.
Publishers Weekly 248 (January 1, 2001): 75.

THE REIGN OF NAPOLEON BONAPARTE

Author: Robert B. Asprey (1923-　　)
First published: The Rise and Fall of Napoleon Bona-
parte: Volume 2, 2001, in Great Britain
Publisher: Basic Books (New York). Illustrated. 480 pp.
$35.00
Type of work: Biography
Time: 1805-1821
Locale: Europe

≈

A fast-paced and colorful account of the French em-
peror's life from the aftermath of his great victory at
Austerlitz in 1805 to his death as an exile in 1821

≈

　　　　Principal personages:
　　　　　　NAPOLEON BONAPARTE, emperor of France
　　　　　　EMPRESS JOSEPHINE, Napoleon's first wife
　　　　　　EMPRESS MARIE LOUISE, Napoleon's second wife
　　　　　　MARIE WALEWSKA, Napoleon's mistress
　　　　　　CLEMENS VON METTERNICH, Austrian statesman

　　Robert Asprey's *The Reign of Napoleon Bonaparte* is the second of a two-part biography. The first volume, *The Rise of Napoleon Bonaparte* (2000), chronicled Napoleon's improbable journey from birth in a Corsican cave to glory as emperor of
France. This second installment picks up Napoleon's story right after Austerlitz, his
most brilliantly fought battle. There Napoleon had defeated and humiliated the Austrian and Russian empires, making him the master of continental Europe. From this
high point, Asprey traces the gradual decline of Napoleon's fortunes, as his own mistakes and the implacable hatred of his enemies resulted in a series of wars that drained
the resources of France dry.

　　The saga of Napoleon Bonaparte is inherently dramatic. Emerging from obscurity,
he demonstrated military genius of the highest order in a long series of wars. His successes are legendary. His final defeat at Waterloo is proverbial. The trajectory of his
career is so aesthetically satisfying that it has offered rich material to sensationalists
and moralists alike.

　　Napoleon stands in the select company of Alexander the Great, Julius Caesar,
Genghis Khan, and Adolf Hitler as a conqueror who shaped the course of world history. Napoleon bestrode his age like a colossus. He still lives in the popular imagination, usually in the poses left to us by the great painter Jacques-Louis David. We see
him as the young general, astride his rearing horse, leading an army across the Alps;
as the self-made emperor, usurping the place of the pope and crowning himself; or, fi-

nally, as the mature, increasingly pudgy, master of Europe, staring confidently out of his portrait, his hand mysteriously tucked inside his waistcoat. Both as a historical figure and as an icon, Napoleon Bonaparte is an irresistible subject for biographers. Books about Napoleon continue to pour off the presses. Asprey's biography is a recent and useful contribution to this vast literature.

∼

Robert Asprey is a veteran of the United States Marine Corps, and he saw action in two wars. He is the author of a number of books on military history.

∼

Biographers of Napoleon have tended to fall into two broad camps. One tradition of Napoleonic scholarship has portrayed the emperor as an overweening tyrant, whose inordinate ambitions had to be foiled by a coalition of the long-suffering victims of his aggression. Another line of interpretation sees Napoleon as a heroic figure, defender of much of the best of the French Revolution, whose laudable goal of spreading enlightened law and government was ultimately frustrated by the forces of reaction, usually personified in the figure of the scheming Austrian diplomat Count Clemens von Metternich. These conflicting views of Napoleon can be traced back to the propaganda, con and pro, that was inspired by the emperor in his own time.

Now, as then, a full appreciation of Napoleon Bonaparte can not be separated from an assessment of the French Revolution, the protean social and political convulsion that gave birth to the modern Western world. For good or ill, Napoleon was the Revolution's legatee. His greatest civil achievement, the Napoleonic Code, which still forms the basis of law in France and other European nations, guaranteed once and for all such fundamental revolutionary principles as the equality of all men before the law. For those who regard the French Revolution as a bloody precursor to modern totalitarianism, with the guillotine as a fitting symbol of its brutal experiments in social engineering, Napoleon is just a military adventurer who hijacked an illegitimate government already rotting away with corruption. To those who believe that the Revolution was a noble attempt to create a just society, Napoleon is the inevitable result of a war of self-defense, a man whose troops exposed people all over Europe to the ideals of liberty, equality, and fraternity.

Hanging on the outcome of this clash of interpretations is the meaning of Napoleon's epic reign. If the first school prevails, then Napoleon is an accident, a dictator who took advantage of his opportunities and lived to write a highly conspicuous chapter in the ever-lengthening book of human oppression. If the second school prevails, Napoleon is the agent of modernity, the man who broke up the ossified *ancien régime* and became the father of the modern world. Napoleon's place in history is secure; his reputation is not.

Robert Asprey falls emphatically into the second school of interpretation. His Napoleon is a tragic hero, like a character in an ancient Greek drama who wrestles simultaneously with his own failings and malevolent forces directed against him from outside. Asprey readily acknowledges Napoleon's despotism and makes few excuses for his crimes. Instead, he defends his subject by asking the reader to recognize that his subject was formed by desperate and dangerous times. For Asprey, Napoleon was the heir to and apostle of the liberal vision of the French Revolution, but he was also a survivor of the Great Terror, and the most gifted product of a revolutionary milieu in which ruthlessness and guile were the keys to success.

Napoleon was no saint, but to Asprey he compares favorably with his opponents. Asprey finds little to respect in the aristocratic defenders of the old order who repeatedly took to the field against the French. Their program was self-serving and purblind. They dreamed of restoring a world that was irretrievably gone, a world in which the aspirations of the many would be effectively suppressed. Asprey can summon up little more sympathy for the pope and the champions of traditional religion. He exhibits a very Napoleonic disdain for faith. Thus, in Asprey's account there are no heroes in the resistance to Napoleon. None of the enemy paladins, not even the Duke of Wellington, can match his hero. Their victories are the result of catching Napoleon at a disadvantage, or won easily at the expense of his subordinates. For Asprey, it seems, Napoleon's stature is enhanced by the smallness of those surrounding him.

The Reign of Napoleon Bonaparte is not part of a definitive biography of Napoleon. Instead, Asprey has crafted a useful introduction to his subject's life. Asprey is a skilled popular historian who has specialized in military history. His style is clear and easily accessible. Asprey moves his narrative along at a rapid clip. He does not devote much time to analysis, background, or description. He keeps his focus resolutely on Napoleon and lets the flow of events carry his story along. The pace of the book captures something of the rush of Napoleon's last years in power.

Napoleon's enemies gave him little time for leisure. Following his victory at Austerlitz, he compelled the Austrians to surrender. The Russians fell back to lick their wounds. At this point, Prussia began to take the first steps toward war. This was folly on the part of the Prussian government. Had the Prussians moved more quickly and brought needed assistance to the Austrians and Russians before the battle of Austerlitz was fought in December, 1805, they might have made their weight felt. Going alone against Napoleon and his Grand Army was military madness on their part. However, seduced by memories of the glory won by Frederick the Great a half century earlier, the Prussians declared war in June, 1806. Napoleon mobilized his forces and crushed the Prussians in a campaign that culminated in the twin battles of Jena and Auerstadt. Victory here lured Napoleon into Poland and a campaign to bring the Russians to heel. Two grueling campaigns fought in the winter of 1806-1807 resulted in the bloody but indecisive battles of Pultusk and Eylau. Finally, in June, Napoleon won a decisive victory at Friedland, and the Russian Czar Alexander I sued for peace.

In the interludes between battles, Napoleon found time for romance. Empress Josephine was far away, and Napoleon was already worrying about the dynastic implications of their childlessness. In Poland, he was introduced to the Countess Marie Walewska and immediately fell in love. Countess Walewska was a twenty-year-old mother married to a man in his seventies. Friends and family, hoping that Napoleon would restore Polish independence, urged her to accept Napoleon's advances from patriotic motives. This she did, yet over time the couple grew genuinely attached to each other. Marie remained loyal to Napoleon through all the vicissitudes of the coming years, and eventually bore him a son.

Napoleon was now at the height of his power. He soon began making the mistakes that would lead to his downfall. His most implacable enemy was Great Britain, but the island nation remained invulnerable behind the shield of the British navy. Napoleon decided to strike at Britain by crippling its commerce. He ordered his allies and dependents to cease trading with the British. This Continental System never worked. It deepened the hostility of Britain and encouraged rebellion amongst the nations subject to France.

Napoleon also decided to conquer Spain. He thought that this would relieve him of the embarrassment of an unreliable ally. Instead, it embroiled him in a quagmire that swallowed up thousands of troops he could not afford to lose. Asprey points out that Napoleon, for all his military genius, was a thoroughly conventional warrior who never understood the potential and dangers of guerrilla warfare. He waited in vain for his generals to disperse the bands of civilian fighters who rose up to resist the French invasion.

Napoleon was still embroiled deeply in Spain when he was forced to turn his attention once again to central Europe. The Austrians chafed under Napoleon's domination. They rebuilt their army and began intriguing for a new coalition against the French. Before they could bring this to fruition, Napoleon moved against them. After an initial defeat, he crushed their new army at Wagram. Once again Napoleon was able to dictate terms to the Austrians, but it was becoming obvious that Europe was growing restive under his heel.

Napoleon carried off more than military laurels from Austria. Convinced that he needed a new wife to produce an heir to his empire, Napoleon divorced the Empress Josephine. He took as his new wife the Austrian princess Marie Louise. Within a year Marie Louise gave him the son he desired. Napoleon fondly believed that his dynasty was secure.

During the year 1811, his peace with the Russians began to sour. The Russians were behaving less as allies than as rivals. The Russian court became a haven for Napoleon's enemies, and English gold fostered anti-French sentiment. Napoleon then made the fateful decision to invade Russia. In 1812, he led a huge international army into Russia. He reached Moscow after winning a bloody victory at Borodino, but the Russian emperor and his army always avoided decisive defeat or capture. When Moscow burned around him, Napoleon was forced into a disastrous winter retreat from Russia that ruined his great army.

In Russia, Napoleon lost his aura of invincibility. A new coalition rose against him, composed of Britain, Russia, Austria, and Prussia. Napoleon cobbled together another army and fought heroically, but he was forced out of Germany at the Battle of Leipzig in October, 1813. In the first months of 1814, he defended France with a small force of partially trained troops. He demonstrated all his old martial brilliance, but in the end was overborne by numbers and forced to abdicate. He was exiled to the small Mediterranean island of Elba. Napoleon languished there for less than a year before gambling on a return to France. For one hundred days he ruled once again, before meeting final defeat at Waterloo.

This time, his conquerors sent him to a tiny island in the south Atlantic named St. Helena. There he was kept in close confinement, suffering from petty harassment and depression until his death of stomach cancer in 1821. Whatever his disappointments and regrets at the end of his life, Napoleon died knowing that he would be the stuff of legend for centuries to come. Robert Asprey has done his part to introduce a new generation of readers to the remarkable tale of the rise and fall of Napoleon Bonaparte.

Daniel P. Murphy

Sources for Further Study

Library Journal 126 (November 15, 2001): 74.
Publishers Weekly 248 (October 15, 2001): 56.

RETHINKING THE HOLOCAUST

Author: Yehuda Bauer (1926-   )
Publisher: Yale University Press (New Haven, Conn.)
   335 pp. $29.95
Type of work: History
Time: 1933-1945
Locale: Germany and elsewhere in Europe

~

Assessing current Holocaust debates, historian Bauer revisits key issues and continues a distinguished scholarly career by defending his important views about Nazi Germany's attempt to destroy the Jewish people

~

Born in the Czech city of Prague, Yehuda Bauer escaped the Holocaust when he and his parents immigrated to Palestine in 1939. Nevertheless, Nazi Germany's destruction of European Jewry marks his life, for after serving in Israel's 1948-1949 War of Independence and completing his doctoral studies at Hebrew University in Jerusalem, this Jewish scholar became a leading historian whose work does much to define Holocaust studies.

Bauer's book is not a history of the Holocaust but "an attempt to rethink categories and issues that arise out of the contemplation of that watershed event in human history." Rethinking the Holocaust requires what he calls "historiosophy," a term denoting investigations within the territories where philosophy and Holocaust history intersect. Focusing on how the Holocaust happened and why, Bauer identifies key implications of that dark chapter in human experience. His inquiries also shed light on his own methods and concerns. As the work unfolds, it becomes apparent that a mature scholar seeks to restake his claim to ideas and interpretations that he fears will be distorted, overridden, or eclipsed by scholarly competitors.

To support these claims, consider five themes that distinguish Bauer's outlook: The Holocaust remains unprecedented. The Holocaust is, at least in principle, explicable. If scholars probe why the Holocaust happened, a task that many of them tend to avoid, anti-Semitism looms large. The Holocaust is best understood from a Jewish perspective. Study of the Holocaust involves political aims.

First, Bauer defends the Holocaust's uniqueness, although his rethinking makes him prefer the term "unprecedentedness" instead. By switching terminology, he tries to elude a criticism, namely, that the concept of uniqueness lacks meaning because all historical events are particular and therefore unique in one way or another. Bauer contends that this criticism is neither telling nor helpful, for it overlooks the point that sound analysis entails comparison of historical events. When comparison takes place, and one event exhibits an element—especially one of immense importance—that all

~

The former director of the
International Institute for Holocaust
Research at Yad Vashem, the Israeli
Holocaust memorial and research
center in Jerusalem, Yehuda Bauer
continues to write about the
Holocaust, adding to his impressive
body of work, which includes
previous books such as The
Holocaust in Historical Perspective
(1978), American Jewry and the
Holocaust *(1981), and* Jews for
Sale? *(1994).*

~

others lack, then a claim for that event's uniqueness, far from being trivial, is appropriate and
significant. Bauer hopes to avoid misunderstanding by using "unprecedented" instead of
"unique," but the change reaffirms the Holocaust's uniqueness nonetheless.

To advance his claim about the Holocaust's
unprecedentedness, Bauer acknowledges that the
Holocaust was a genocide, but he also argues
that much more needs to be said to answer the
question, "What was the Holocaust?" As the
term "genocide" is commonly used, it refers primarily to the destruction of a national, ethnic, or
so-called racial group. Genocide, however, does
not necessarily mean that the murder of every
single member of such a group is intended, but
that was the fate that Adolf Hitler and his Nazi followers had in mind for the Jews. In
ways never seen before or since, says Bauer, Nazi ideology, a "pure fantasy" that
combined racial anti-Semitism with belief in a global Jewish conspiracy to control the
world, condemned Jews "anywhere in the world" to death "just for being born," and
murdered them in killing centers that were brought "to a totally new stage of development."

Second, if the Holocaust is unique, especially in the sense that no event before or
since has been driven by such lethal intentions, then it could be argued that the Holocaust defies explanation. The brutality involved was so senseless, the vastness of the
catastrophe so immense, the suffering of the victims so devastating that we are at a
loss to understand how the Holocaust could happen. Bauer rejects such reasoning. Far
from making the Holocaust inexplicable, the Holocaust's unprecedentedness depends
on the fact that its horror was unleashed by one group of human beings and inflicted
on another. Unless it is claimed that human beings cannot be understood, which it is
not, the Holocaust can be comprehended by historical analysis because it was a human event from start to finish.

Up to a point, Bauer realizes that his position about the Holocaust's intelligibility
involves problems. Thus, he underscores that he is not saying that anyone has fully
comprehended how the Holocaust happened and why. He stresses that historians develop interpretations and theories to explain events. Not only do these efforts involve
alternative and even competing views, but the historians' accounts do not—indeed
cannot—encompass everything. They are incomplete, subject to correction as errors
are discovered, and destined for revision as new evidence is found.

Bauer hedges his bets on the degree of explicability one can expect, but still his
analysis does not probe deeply enough. Because historical analysis is a human endeavor, one that inevitably lacks omniscience, there is no good reason to assume that
full historical comprehension of the Holocaust is possible. If full historical comprehension is impossible, then claims that the Holocaust is explicable—even "perfectly

explicable," at least in part, as Bauer sometimes says—are in more trouble than he thinks. God might possess the comprehension that is needed to make the Holocaust fully explicable, but while Bauer finds Holocaust-related theology fascinating, he concludes it is "a dead end," and thus does not turn to God for the explicability he seeks. Still, Bauer-the-historian insists, the Holocaust remains explicable in principle.

Unfortunately, Bauer's rationalism deceives him at this point, for his appeals to explicability in principle, let alone his claims about "perfectly explicable," are too problematic to be trusted completely. If no one, in fact, can finally explain the Holocaust through historical analysis—and that is where the logic of Bauer's "historiosophy" leads—then how does it make sense to say that, in principle, the Holocaust is explicable historically? At best, the reader ultimately seems to be left with hypotheses that are "likely stories"—some far better documented and more accurate than others—but probably not more than that. The point is not that the Holocaust escapes human understanding altogether, but rather than clinging to the specious reed of explicability in principle, Bauer would be on firmer ground to settle for the fact that the historical comprehension of the Holocaust, real though it is, has serious limits, partly because of the finite and fallible nature of human capacities and partly because the event raises questions and possesses implications that are more than historical analysis alone can contain. Ultimately, the question, "Why did the Holocaust happen?" is the most important question of that kind. Historical analysis always remains inadequate to respond to it sufficiently.

Third, Bauer stresses that anti-Semitism must loom large if one is to grasp why the Holocaust happened. This emphasis plays a central role in his conviction that one goal of historians should be to present "overarching pictures of the Holocaust that make sense." Scholars such as Raul Hilberg and Zygmunt Bauman have rightly emphasized that the Holocaust involved an immense bureaucracy—involving expertise from virtually every sector of German society—that was necessary to implement the Nazis' genocidal intentions. Bauer contends, however, that their accounts evade or respond inadequately to the issue of motivation. Concentrating on what activated the bureaucracy, Bauer thinks that ideology was the decisive factor—not the only one, but a condition much more salient than it is for Hilberg or Bauman. At the core of Nazi ideology, Bauer finds a racial anti-Semitism that took Jews to be so threatening and detestable, politically and cosmically, that their elimination from Nazi Germany's "superior" culture became imperative. That anti-Semitism, suggests Bauer, provides "a central explanation for the Holocaust." On this point, Bauer's analysis puts him in qualified agreement with Daniel Goldhagen, whose controversial book *Hitler's Willing Executioners* (1996) achieved best-seller status in the late 1990's.

Bauer stresses that his own views constitute just one among the interpretations that seek support from readers and listeners, but when he goes on to say that he naturally finds his own views convincing, he rarely misses an occasion to argue that the interpretations of other scholars are wanting, especially Goldhagen. Although Goldhagen does better than some scholars in emphasizing anti-Semitism, Bauer insists that Goldhagen has a simplistic, unnuanced understanding of anti-Semitism, which, among other things, fails to account adequately for ways in which political and administrative structures were also necessary to promote genocide. On the other hand, whenever Bauer finds that Goldhagen is on target, he is quick to argue that Goldhagen is a latecomer whose views are neither original nor properly credited to his scholarly predecessors—including, predictably, Bauer himself. Goldhagen receives more of Bauer's criticism than other scholars, but Bauer is prepared to trump all of his scholarly peers. Too often for its own good, *Rethinking the Holocaust* finds Bauer—his modest protests to the contrary notwithstanding—concerned with buttressing his positions so that their superiority will be acknowledged.

Fourth, Bauer thinks that the Holocaust is best understood from a Jewish perspective. Hence, he says that the core of his interpretation is found in two chapters that focus on Jewish responses, especially resistance, to the Nazi Germany's onslaught. Contrary to persistent myths, Bauer argues that Jewish resistance took diverse and widespread forms. He interprets resistance in relation to the Hebrew term *amidah*, which means "standing up against." Understood in that way, resistance could be armed or unarmed, individual or communal. It could and did involve, for instance, food smuggling to keep life going in Jewish ghettos as well as violent escape attempts at death camps such as Treblinka and Sobibor. Resistance also could and did involve what the Jewish tradition calls "sanctification of life," which in the Holocaust's context included efforts such as educating children or practicing religion to keep life meaningful on Jewish terms, in spite of the overwhelming odds that German domination inflicted.

Bauer does not contend that resistance is the whole story of Jewish responses during the Holocaust, but he thinks that the best explanations for this mixed picture require a focus on German power more than on flawed Jewish character. Specifically, in the cases where resistance was not evident or sustainable, especially in the "sanctification of life" dimensions of *amidah*, Bauer finds that minimal conditions necessary for its appearance were lacking. For example, the chances for organized resistance among ghettoized Jews were scant whenever German rule early on combined factors such as "totally ruthless exploitation, starvation, and mass murder of young men." As Bauer assesses the evidence, Jews were anything but passive, although the Holocaust conditions brought to bear against them could and did become so devastating that death prevailed.

By focusing on the Holocaust from a Jewish perspective, Bauer believes, "a lesson, possibly, a warning, possibly, or an encouragement, possibly" may be found. Thus, *Rethinking the Holocaust* makes a fifth point clear: It is Bauer's conviction that study of the Holocaust involves political aims. The book ends with a speech that Bauer gave to the Bundestag, the German house of representatives, on January 27, 1998, the German Holocaust Memorial Day. As his speech concluded, Bauer alluded to the biblical Ten Commandments, suggesting that where mass murder, genocide, or "a Holocaust-like disaster" threaten, the Decalogue should be supplemented by three additional imperatives: You shall not become a perpetrator. You shall not allow yourselves to become victims. You shall not become bystanders.

Rethinking the Holocaust shows that the Holocaust is studied because it happened, but not only for that reason. "Too many humans have been murdered," says Bauer, "and the time has come to try and stop these waves that threaten to engulf us." The Holocaust compels attention because, unprecedented though it may be, the warning that it could become—and to some extent already has been—a precedent in our time is still needed. Bauer's book has its flaws, but the moral intentions that inspire it are not among them.

John K. Roth

Sources for Further Study

Choice 38 (July/August, 2001): 2011.
The New York Times Book Review 106 (January 28, 2001): 10.
Publishers Weekly 248 (January 1, 2001): 82.
The Washington Post Book World, February 4, 2001, p. 13.

RETURN PASSAGES
Great American Travel Writing, 1780-1910

Author: Larzer Ziff (1927-   )
Publisher: Yale University Press (New Haven, Conn.).
   320 pp. $29.95
Type of work: History, biography, and literary criticism
Time: The late eighteenth through the early twentieth
   centuries
Locale: The world

~

*Critical examinations of the writings of five Americans
who pioneered distinctly American forms of travel writing*

~

Principal personages:
> JOHN LEDYARD, American sailor who wrote an account of Captain
>   James Cook's last voyage
> JOHN LLOYD STEPHENS, American travel writer and founder of Mayan
>   archaeology
> BAYARD TAYLOR, America's first pure travel writer
> MARK TWAIN (Samuel Langhorne Clemens), American novelist and
>   humorist, whose reputation was first built on his travel writing
> HENRY JAMES (1843-1916), American expatriate novelist and travel
>   writer

   The early twenty-first century is an age when many Americans take distant travel
for granted and feel themselves broadly familiar with the entire globe thanks to the
news media, television programs, and films. However, if they do want to learn more
about the world, they are not likely seek enlightenment in travel books, which constitute a distinctly minor and vaguely defined literary genre that rarely attracts attention.
   This was not always so. During the nineteenth century, travel books were among
the best-selling and most enthusiastically read books throughout the United States,
and many eminent literary figures of the time wrote them. Before the advent of modern mass communication and entertainment, Americans felt isolated from the rest of
the world and were hungry for information. The nineteenth century was, moreover,
the last great era of world exploration, when travelers might literally stumble across
undiscovered lands or the remains of lost civilizations.
   Despite the importance of travel writing in the nineteenth century, relatively little
critical attention has been paid to it. Larzer Ziff's *Return Passages: Great American
Travel Writing, 1780-1910* is a welcome contribution. A literary scholar, Ziff has
built his career around innovative explorations of American culture. In *Return Passages* he examines early American travel writing as a literary genre, focusing on its

peculiarly American traits. To this end, he has selected five travel writers whom he regards the best and most important representatives of the field and devotes a long chapter to each: John Ledyard, John Lloyd Stephens, Bayard Taylor, Mark Twain, and Henry James.

Larzer Ziff is Caroline Donovan Research Professor of English at The Johns Hopkins University. Among his books are The American 1890's *(1966),* Literary Democracy *(1981), and* Writing in the New Nation *(1991).*

Each of these writers made signal contributions to the travel writing field. Of the five, only Mark Twain and Henry James are still well known and widely read; however, they all enjoyed immense popularity during their lifetimes and left enduring legacies. While Ziff's focus is on the writers' travels and travel writings, he provides enough biographical information on each—particularly on the first three—to enable readers to see their writings in the larger contexts of the writers' lives.

Born in New England in 1752, John Ledyard published only one book during his lifetime but had what may have been the most incredible travel career of any of the five writers. In 1774, he sailed on a merchant ship to England, where he was forced into military service on the eve of the American Revolution. He managed to join Royal Navy captain James Cook's third and last great voyage of exploration, which carried him throughout the Pacific Ocean. He returned home after the colonies had won their independence and made his name by publishing his experiences as *A Journal of Captain Cook's Last Voyage to the Pacific Ocean and in Quest of a North-West Passage* (1783). This book, which Ziff calls the first American travel book, is remarkable in several ways. As the first published account of Cook's voyage, it found an eager audience and also contained the only published firsthand description of Cook's death at the hands of Hawaiian islanders. Ledyard was unusual for his time in empathizing with the Hawaiians, who had been roughly treated by Cook. Ziff sees Ledyard's empathy for non-Western peoples of primitive cultures as an outgrowth of the democratic values he imbibed as an American.

Following the success of his book, Ledyard sought support for further ambitious journeys, including a planned solo walk across North America. Since Ledyard could not sail to the point where he wanted to start his overland journey, he went to Russia, hoping to cross Siberia to the North Pacific and then find his way to the North American coast—virtually to walk around the world. He might have succeeded, had the Russian government not stopped him from completing his trek across Siberia. He did succeed, however, in becoming the first American to travel inside Siberia, and his journal of that trip was published posthumously. Ledyard's next plan was to cross Africa. However, he contracted bilious fever in Egypt and died in Cairo in 1789, barely thirty-seven years old.

John Lloyd Stephens—whom Ziff regards as possibly the greatest travel writer of them all—is better remembered than Ledyard, not so much for his writings as for his contributions to Mesoamerican archaeology. Stephens wrote four great books of travel: *Incidents of Travel in Egypt, Arabia Petraea, and the Holy Land* (1837), *Inci-*

dents of Travel in Greece, Turkey, Russia, and Poland (1838), *Incidents of Travel in Central America, Chiapas, and Yucatan* (1841), and *Incidents of Travel in Yucatan* (1843). It is for the last two works that Stephens is best known, as they established him as the founder of Mayan archaeology. What Ziff most admires about Stephens's writings is his adeptness at alternating between descriptions of his personal adventures and discussions of the broader issues of the places he describes. Moreover, Stephens, like Ledyard, was always primarily interested in the people he encountered.

The success of Stephens's first two books put him in a financial position to undertake a more ambitious journey, and he chose to go to Central America to determine whether there was any truth to rumors about "lost cities" in the jungle. He happened to undertake the trip at an extraordinary moment in the region's turbulent history. With the exception of British Honduras, all the Central American territories had only recently won their independence from Spain. They attempted to unite under a federal government, but this experiment was failing. To facilitate his travels, he arranged to be appointed American minister to the Republic of Central America. Meanwhile, he had the good fortune to engage as a member of his expedition the English artist Frederick Catherwood.

When Stephens and Catherwood reached Central America, they hoped only to find enough stone ruins to justify an illustrated book of travel. What they succeeded in doing, however, was bringing to the world's attention the previously unsuspected ancient Mayan civilization, laying the foundations for all future Mesoamerican archaeology. Equally important, their discoveries demonstrated that the New World had its own advanced ancient civilization. Stephens's book—graced by Catherwood's accurate and exquisite illustrations of ruins and inscriptions—was a best-seller, and Stephens and Catherwood soon made a second expedition, which led to more discoveries and a second book. Afterward, Stephens devoted the rest of his life to building a railway across the Isthmus of Panama—a venture that would contribute to ending his life before he reached forty-seven.

Bayard Taylor is probably the least well remembered of Ziff's five writers today, but he enjoyed great popularity during the peak of his writing career and is credited with inventing the art of pure travel writing. Indeed, Ziff regards him as the first writer who traveled for no reason other than to write about his travels.

Born in Pennsylvania in 1825, Taylor aspired to be taken seriously as a writer—preferably as a poet. However, he achieved such success in travel writing that he found himself trapped in a field that he came to loathe. That success began in 1846 with *Views A-foot*, a little book that he compiled from travel letters he had written for Horace Greeley's *New York Tribune* during a sojourn in Europe. What made that book popular was a combination of Taylor's unabashed enthusiasm for all that he saw and his practical advice on traveling on a small budget. Until that time, Americans generally assumed that only the rich could afford to go to Europe. In demonstrating what could be done on a budget, Taylor anticipated the later "Europe-on-five-dollars-a-day" school of travel writing.

Other travel books followed, but Taylor achieved his real fame after inveigling his way into the tightly closed naval expedition that U.S. commodore Matthew Perry led into Japan in 1853 and publishing an account of that trip. After 1857, Taylor fell on harder times; while writing prodigiously in all fields, he struggled to obtain a diplomatic post in Europe. In 1878, President Rutherford B. Hayes named him ambassador to Germany, but Taylor's health was failing, and he died in Berlin in December.

Although most of Mark Twain's books have stayed in print since he first published them, it may not be generally recognized that he built his reputation on his travel books. In fact, his first two major books—and two of his most successful—were travel books: *The Innocents Abroad* (1869), about Europe and the Holy Land, and *Roughing It* (1872), about his earlier years in the Far West and Hawaii. After following these books with several novels, Twain wrote two more travel books, *A Tramp Abroad* (1880) about Europe and *Life on the Mississippi* (1883), which combined an embellished memoir of his earlier years as a steamboat pilot with a description of his return to the river in 1882. All these books were successes, and *The Innocents Abroad* was probably the best-selling American travel book of the nineteenth century.

Twain fell into travel writing almost by accident; like Taylor, he wrote travel letters for newspapers. In 1867, he carried the practice to a higher level when a San Francisco newspaper hired him to write letters as a passenger on the first tourist cruise to the Mediterranean. Those letters were so widely reprinted throughout the United States that he returned home to find he was a national celebrity. Until that time he had never thought of himself as an author, but after a publisher persuaded him to turn his travel letters into the book that became *The Innocents Abroad*, his entire life changed.

Apart from the strands of humor running through Twain's travel books, they are so different from one another as to defy easy generalizations. However, what Ziff regards as important in *The Innocents Abroad* is that it is not so much about travel as it is about tourism. The book adds little aside from irreverence to what many earlier travel books had to say about the places Twain visited; what sets it apart is its satirical treatment of the travelers themselves, whose "innocence" and gullibility Twain relentlessly mocks. Moreover, the book has a strongly American central theme: Travelers to the Old World should meet it on their terms, not its.

Ziff reserves his strongest praise for Twain's last and least characteristic travel book, *Following the Equator* (1897), which recounts a round-the-world lecture tour he made to pay off debts. That tour took him through Fiji, New Zealand, Australia, Ceylon, India, and South Africa, bringing him into close contact with many nonwhite peoples. *Following the Equator* is a much more straightforward and conventional travel narrative than any of Twain's earlier books, but Ziff finds it remarkable for its evidence of Twain's success in overcoming his earlier racial prejudices in poignant anecdotes in which he confronts his past in the slave-owning South.

In contrast to Mark Twain, novelist Henry James has a name that is practically synonymous with travel writing. In addition to his half dozen popular books of travel, he wrote a string of novels about Americans in Europe. James himself became a British subject and, after returning to the United States for a visit, wrote one of his finest travel books, *The American Scene* (1907).

Whereas Ledyard and Stephens wrote books on difficult journeys of original exploration, and Taylor and Twain often "roughed it" while following well-beaten paths, James traveled as a true tourist. Enjoying genteel accommodations and conveyances, he made no pretense of breaking new ground. Indeed, for him to have done so would have been to contradict a central theme of all his writings—the need for America to come to grips with the well-established culture and history of the Old World. However, his travel writings reveal a somewhat edgier, more personal side of him than is found in his fiction, revealing that as much as he admired European culture, he was not its uncritical slave.

With subject matter as rich as these five fascinating authors, *Return Passages* is itself unfailingly fascinating. While meeting most of the requirements of scholarly writing, it remains completely accessible to all general readers.

R. Kent Rasmussen

Sources for Further Study

Choice 38 (May, 2001): 1633.
The New Republic 225 (August 6, 2001): 34.
The New York Times Book Review 106 (March 4, 2001): 34.

RICHARD WRIGHT
The Life and Times

Author: Hazel Rowley (1951-   )
Publisher: John Macrae/Henry Holt (New York). 626 pp.
  $35.00
Type of work: Literary biography
Time: 1908-1960
Locale: Natchez and Jackson, Mississippi; Chicago; New
  York; Cuernavaca, Mexico; Paris; Buenos Aires, Argen-
  tina; Gold Coast, Africa; Spain; Bandung, Indonesia

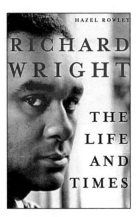

∽

*This well-written biography of the first African Ameri-
can to write best-sellers explores thoroughly a career en-
ergized by his confrontations with racism*

∽

Principal personages:
RICHARD WRIGHT, African American writer
EDWARD ASWELL, publisher at Harper & Brothers, later Wright's editor
ELLEN WRIGHT, Wright's second wife and mother of their two daughters
RALPH ELLISON, probably the closest of Wright's many literary friends
PAUL REYNOLDS, Wright's literary agent
MARGARET WALKER, briefly Wright's lover and later his biographer

Richard Wright (1908-1960) is best known for his novel *Native Son* (1940) and his autobiographical *Black Boy: A Record of Childhood and Youth* (1945). Between 1968 and 1988 four biographies of him appeared, two of them before his voluminous papers became readily available to researchers, one of them (that by Margaret Walker) soured by unhappy personal relations with her subject, and none of them approaching in thoroughness and literary grace Hazel Rowley's "life and times."

The contrast between the violent, primitive black men who predominate in Wright's fiction and their author is striking. Although Wright was as intense and angry as his most famous character, Bigger Thomas of *Native Son*, his weapon against racial oppression was always the English language, whether his literary recreations of the versions spoken by African Americans in his native Mississippi and in Chicago's South Side or the sophisticated prose of his nonfiction works. A gifted, self-taught writer, Wright found the intellectual stimulation he needed as a young man not in any college or university, but in the American Communist Party in Chicago. He always regarded his membership in the Party, which endured for twelve years and generated substantial files in the Federal Bureau of Investigation (FBI) and, later, the Central Intelligence Agency (CIA), as primarily an opportunity to meet and learn from writers who shared his conviction of the inequalities and injustices of American society. Only

~

Hazel Rowley's first book, a biography of the author Christina Stead (1993), was designated a Notable Book of 1994 by The New York Times. *She has taught at the University of Iowa and Deakin University, in Melbourne, Australia, and is a Bunting Fellow of Radcliffe College.*

~

in gatherings of Party members could he escape the racial bigotry that assailed him and associate freely with whites, including many Jews burdened with their own legacy of persecution. His fierce independence, however, produced deeply ambivalent feelings in him, prevented him from contributing the degree of activism and loyalty that the Party expected, and ultimately evoked suspicion and even hostility in fellow members.

Despite his restless and peripatetic nature, Wright apparently never threw away notes, drafts, jottings of any sort, or letters written to him, and Hazel Rowley seems to have mined all of them that are accessible. (Not all his correspondents saved his letters, while his letters to some correspondents, notably Margaret Walker, remain unavailable to the public.) Along with the works of earlier biographers and critics, Rowley has drawn on FBI files on Wright and several of his associates, which often came grudgingly and with many details blacked out. She has deftly organized the fruits of this extensive research and unfolded the life of a complex man in an unobtrusive yet vigorous style.

One of the strands of this complexity was a fierce and defiant independence which vitalized his writing but vitiated his personal and family life, especially when it tended toward selfishness and self-indulgence. His behavior following the great success of *Native Son* early in 1940 is a case in point. Reading a magazine article by an acquaintance who had settled in Cuernavaca, Mexico, filled Wright with an urge to do the same. Mexico promised an array of amenities—a large house, gardens, a swimming pool—within the budget of a man whose Book-of-the-Month Club novel had, for the first time in his life, made such a dream into a real possibility. In Cuernavaca, the recently married Wright fell out of the habit of regular writing, brooded over the absence of his Chicago friends, and proved his basic incompatibility with his wife, Dhimah Meidman. Both the Mexican sojourn and the marriage itself lasted only a matter of months.

The following year he took a more suitable bride, Ellen Poplowitz, like Dhimah a Jew, but a more intelligent woman and a fellow Party member. They stayed together for years, had two daughters, and seemed to many of their friends to be truly in love, but eventually Wright's unfaithfulness turned the union into one kept alive only for the sake of the children. Rowley passes no judgment on his conduct but leaves the reader with the impression that Ellen was an attractive and devoted wife until the later years, when Wright lived in Paris, she and their daughters in England.

Tongue and groove with Wright's independence went his restlessness. By early 1945, with World War II winding down and his latest book, *Black Boy*, another Book-of-the-Month Club choice, the thirty-six-year-old Wright began to feel the expatriate urge that has so frequently gripped serious American writers. Like many other African Americans in the 1920's, he had migrated from the Deep South to Chicago, and like a number of the more ambitious ones he made a subsequent jump to New York.

The further move to Europe proved particularly attractive to talented African Americans, who found there not only opportunity but relative freedom from racial prejudice. A review he had written of Gertrude Stein's *Wars I Have Seen* (1945) having kindled his interest in the work of that eminent expatriate, an intermediary put him in touch with her and strengthened his desire to move to France. By May, 1946 he, Ellen, and their daughter Julia were on their way.

Rowley shows the extent to which living abroad widened Wright's horizons. Although he ceased to write so well about the land he had left behind, Wright branched out with significant books on three wide-ranging topics. His visit to the African Gold Coast resulted in *Black Power: A Record of Reactions in a Land of Pathos* (1954). While Wright remained too American in his attitudes to achieve the hoped-for brotherly empathy with Gold Coast natives, he produced a book "decades ahead of its time," as Rowley puts it. Critics with traditional notions of literary genre, however, rejected his mingling of subjective and objective elements, of history, biography, social commentary, and political satire.

In *The Color Curtain: A Report on the Bandung Conference* (1956), Wright gave a more objective account of an event that excited his interest as history's first international conference of people of color. Westerner that he was, he could not appreciate what he took to be the participants' resolve to resuscitate dead and dying cultures. In his view, they should have been considering the solicitation of financial and technical assistance from the West as a bulwark against the influence of the Communist regimes which by this time Wright had come to despise. Not surprisingly, however, the independent stance of the chief organizer of the conference, Prime Minister Jawaharlal Nehru of India, impressed him favorably.

A trip to the Iberian peninsula resulted in *Pagan Spain* (1957), another of his books that in Rowley's view suffered from being ahead of its time. It was a travel book that incorporated techniques thought more appropriate to fiction, such as dialogue, provocative criticisms distasteful to American officialdom (then concerned with building a working relationship with the Franco regime), and a radical flip-flop of reportorial roles—for here was a black man abroad commenting on white "natives."

In common with many of his manuscripts, *Pagan Spain* reflected Wright's tendency to overwrite. A notoriously bad critic of his own work, he had benefitted greatly over the years from the advice of his literary agent, Paul Reynolds, and his longtime editor, Edward Aswell, but Reynolds did not like the book on Spain, and Aswell had been fired by Harper & Brothers, the book's publisher. As Rowley sees it, Wright's new editor, while recognizing the need for severe cuts in the manuscript, made the wrong ones for the most part. Nonetheless, when the book emerged, severely truncated in both American and foreign editions, it still received more favorable reviews than any of his works since *Black Boy*.

Another interesting, if unimportant, example of Wright's inability to assess his own work pertains to his poetic ventures. At one point he proposed to Aswell a series of novels expressing the theme of the conflict between individuality and society—a lifelong interest already well illustrated in his writing—and linked by passages of free verse. Some of these lines, best described as bad imitations of Walt Whitman, Rowley quotes discreetly in an endnote. On the other hand, late in Wright's life, while ill, he exercised his considerable lyrical talent (a talent often on display in his prose—even in his angry, vituperative prose) on no fewer than four thousand haikus. He seems to have undertaken this ancient Japanese form not with any intent to publish but as a form of therapy for himself in a time of fear and doubt. One of them reads:

> I am nobody:
> A red sinking autumn sun
> Took my name away.

Although Wright may have felt like a nobody at the time, he was quite a different sort of nobody from the writer of another "nobody" poem. Emily Dickinson developed into a shy, reclusive homebody, but from his earliest days in Chicago Richard Wright sought the company of fellow writers, while later he familiarized himself with all of the world's continents except Australia. As might be expected, his most extensive relationships were with other black artists, and Rowley frequently shows the clash of literary and social convictions among his friends and acquaintances. Their various reactions to Wright's books often centered on the question of how African Americans and the black community in general should be depicted in fiction.

Reviewing Wright's first published book, *Uncle Tom's Children: Four Novellas* (1938), in the *Saturday Review*, Zora Neale Hurston wrote: "Not one act of understanding and sympathy comes to pass in the entire work. . . . All the characters in the book are elemental and brutish." Wright had already accused Hurston of pandering to the tastes of white audiences in a review of her *Their Eyes Were Watching God* (1937). Hurston thought that Wright had no pride in his race; he felt that racial pride necessitated defiance of "white" expectations.

Most black writers praised *Native Son* highly when it appeared, but eventually Wright's penchant for creating violent young men with few redeeming qualities came under fire. W. E. B. DuBois found the protagonist of *Black Boy* "loathsome." Young James Baldwin identified Wright's root emotion as "rage"—for him a liberating and shared emotion. Wright, needless to say, exerted a powerful influence on Baldwin's own work. Ralph Ellison, who insisted that rage should be tempered with love, proved a good friend as well as a perceptive critic. His essay on *Black Boy*, "Richard Wright's Blues," became something of a classic in its own right.

Hazel Rowley does not attempt any sustained criticism of Wright's work—or for that matter of his character. She is content to produce a comprehensive narrative of a life that began six years before the outbreak of World War I. Her subject came of age only a few weeks before the 1929 stock market crash, spent his early manhood amidst the sociopolitical struggles of the 1930's, first impacted the American literary scene in the gathering storm of World War II, and died in 1960 while the Cold War raged. Yet this biography makes clear that for Richard Wright the most bitter and prolonged conflict of all was that between an articulate and sensitive black man and a racist society.

Robert P. Ellis

Sources for Further Study

Booklist 97 (July, 2001): 1969.
Library Journal 126 (July, 2001): 91.
The New York Review of Books 48 (November 1, 2001): 68.
The New York Times Book Review 106 (August 26, 2001): 11.
Publishers Weekly 248 (June 18, 2001): 68.

ROMANCING
The Life and Work of Henry Green

Author: Jeremy Treglown (1946-)
First published: 2000, in Great Britain
Publisher: Random House (New York). Illustrated.
  331 pp. $26.95
Type of work: Literary biography
Time: 1905-1973
Locale: Primarily Great Britain

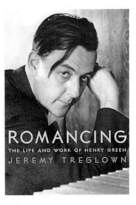

∾

This first full-length biography of Henry Vincent Yorke examines his life and work both as an upper-class British businessman and writing as the pseudonymous Henry Green, who published nine experimental novels and an autobiography

∾

Principal personages:
> HENRY VINCENT YORKE (HENRY GREEN), avant-garde novelist, businessman, and son of a wealthy upper-class family
> MAUD WYNDHAM YORKE, Green's mother
> GERALD YORKE, Green's older brother
> MARY ADELAIDE BIDDULPH YORKE, Green's wife
> SEBASTIAN YORKE, Green's son
> ANTHONY POWELL, novelist, a friend of Green at prep school and university
> TERRY SOUTHERN, novelist who became a friend of Green

Just before the outbreak of World War II, Henry Green published an "interim" autobiography, *Pack My Bag: A Self Portrait,* in which he describes himself in the opening paragraph:

> I was born a mouthbreather with a silver spoon in 1905, three years after one war and nine before another, too late for both. But not too late for the war which seems to be coming upon us now and that is the reason to put down what comes to mind before one is killed, and surely it would be asking much to pretend one had a chance to live.

Green felt keenly that in fact he would not survive the coming war and with only two novels published he obviously felt the need to get something more into print before dying. *Pack My Bag* is dated 1938-1939 and really only covers Green's early years at home, at school, and at Oxford. It is full of his thoughts on a variety of subjects, anecdotes of family life, and contains a cursory account of his love affairs, enthusiasm for movies, and the like. For an autobiography it leaves out much, and that is why Jeremy

Treglown's new book is so valuable. *Romancing* is an unauthorized biography (although Treglown recounts he was originally to write an authorized one), which examines the life and career of Henry Vincent Yorke, who was born into a noble family and spent his life working in various family firms, and who also engaged in writing, under the pseudonym of Henry Green, nine highly experimental novels, so original that according to Treglown they place him in the ranks of other such modernist authors as Virginia Woolf and James Joyce.

～

Jeremy Treglown is a professor of English and comparative literary studies at the University of Warwick, England. He has published several books and has written for The New Yorker *and* Grand Street. *A former editor of* The Times Literary Supplement, *he has been a visiting fellow at Princeton University, the California Institute of Technology, and All Souls College, Oxford.*

～

Henry Vincent Yorke was born on October 29, 1905, at the family home Forthampton Court, near Tewkesbury, Gloucestershire, during the heyday of Edwardian opulence and security before both were destroyed by World War I. His father, Vincent Wodehouse Yorke, was a landowner and rich businessman. His brother, Henry's uncle, was a general. A distant ancestor, Isabelle de Charrière, wrote satires of upper-class life under the disguises of pseudonymous narrators and letter writers, especially in *The Portrait of Zélide*, which are reminiscent of Henry's commentary on his society. Henry's mother, Maud Wyndham Yorke, came from an ancient family of note that had been prominent since the Middle Ages. Her father was Baron Leconfield, one of the richest members of the British aristocracy and owner of Petworth in Sussex, one of the most magnificent houses in England, which during his childhood became Henry's second home.

As any rich and well-connected young man of his times, Henry was first schooled locally and then in 1912 passed on to New Beacon, a prep school in Sevenoakes, Kent, where his brother Philip, who died in 1917, had preceded him and was a star pupil. Among his classmates was Anthony Powell, later himself a noted novelist, who wrote of his friendship with Henry in his multivolumed autobiography. As the war was stumbling to a close, Henry went to Eton, where he was surrounded by relatives, including his other brother Gerald, and by the sons of the rich and great who would later play prominent roles in running Britain and what was left of the empire. At Eton Henry dabbled in the arts, rejected formal religion, and halfheartedly rebelled against his family's traditions. At the beginning of 1924, his last year at school, Henry began writing the novel that would eventually be published as *Blindness*. Becoming a writer, Treglown notes, was one of Henry's fantasies.

Henry spent the summer after he left Eton in Paris and later Avignon to polish his French. In the autumn he went up to Magdalen College, Oxford, at first to study Classical Mods (Greek and Latin classics). Then he switched to the relatively new subject, for Oxford, of English language and literature, where he studied under the newly arrived Ulsterman C. S. Lewis, who was a fellow in English. Academics was never one of Henry's strong suits, and he initially began his studies for a Pass rather than an Honors degree. However, his real interests while at university, according to

Treglown, were cinema, billiards, his novel, and his society of friends, many of whom had preceded him to various Oxford colleges from Eton: Robert Byron at Merton, Anthony Powell at Balliol, Harold Acton, Brian Howard, and Bryan Guinness at Christ Church. Henry's college experience became one of friendships rather than scholarship.

On May 30, 1925, he completed his novel, and *Blindness* was published the next year by the London firm of J. M. Dent. Henry became an author at twenty, and his father had to sign his contract since he was still not of legal age. The reviews were few but respectful and the young Oxford undergraduate was taken up by the cultural maven Lady Ottoline Morrell, who had championed so many other modern writers and artists. He was invited to Garsington, her manor house outside Oxford, where he could meet such figures as Duncan Grant, L. P. Hartley, Aldous Huxley, Augustus John, D. H. Lawrence, Katherine Mansfield, Bertrand Russell, Siegfried Sassoon, Virginia Woolf, and W. B. Yeats. His parents seemed pleased by his success but were worried about Henry becoming an author, in their estimation a risky business. By the time *Blindness* came out, however, Henry had started writing his second novel, and his future seemed already fixed.

Life at Oxford was not so exhilarating nor so successful, and by his third year, with final exams looming and most of his friends now gone from the university, Henry felt lonely and depressed. He left Oxford at Christmas, 1926, without taking a degree. Unlike many young writers with his social standing and wealth, Henry did not insist on some years of travel or devoting himself to literature; instead he wanted to go to work in one of the family's businesses, and in January, 1926, he began as the storekeeper's "extra laborer" at the Farringdon Works of H. Pontifex and Sons in Birmingham. He took rooms in a big Victorian boardinghouse and walked to work. Treglown notes that in many ways, the next two years at the factory were the happiest of his life.

Days at the factory placed him among working-class people, with whom, like the servants of his youth, he felt comfortable, away from the social and intellectual competition of his previous years at school and university. Henry was always in many ways an observer of life, barred by his natural diffidence and social unease from fully participating in the world around him. He continued to frequent the cinema, enjoyed socializing at the local, pursued his romances, and did a bit of traveling. He also continued to work, if often in a rather desultory way, at his writing.

One of Treglown's main emphases is that Henry led essentially two lives: one as a member of his upper-class family and as a businessman, and the other as a writer, apparently never really feeling at home in either world. The two intersect in the perspective that writing as "Henry Green" lent to his fiction, which was not only distinctly avant-garde in style but also social comedy, a critique of British culture, including of his own class. Nonetheless, he remained throughout his life largely conventional, as his concerns over the heavy taxation of the postwar Labour government and his consistently upper-class lifestyle attest.

His second novel, *Living*, came out three years after his first, but there was a ten-year gap before he published another. In the meantime Henry continued to work for Pontifex and socialized according to the tastes of his class. In 1929, the same year that

Living came out, he married Mary Adelaide Biddulph, a woman from a distinguished family, to whom, despite his later womanizing and alcoholism, he remained married for the rest of his life. His only child, a son Sebastian, was born in 1934, and his life before the war was largely taken up with his duties as a businessman (now promoted from his early humble position in the firm to a managerial role), father, and husband. The onset of World War II changed all that.

To contribute to the war effort, Henry became active in the fire service in London, all the while continuing to serve his family's firm. His drinking and affairs also increased during these years. Despite his increased responsibilities and his more hectic personal life, Henry's fear of imminent death seemed to spur his creativity. Besides publishing his autobiography in 1939, in rather quick order Henry wrote and published short fiction and the novels *Caught* (1943), *Loving* (1945), *Back* (1946), *Concluding* (1948), *Nothing* (1950), *Party Going* (1951), and *Doting* (1952). After this flurry of activity Henry Green lapsed into silence, and although he started a number of other projects, he published little else during the rest of his life.

Although he worked for the family for most of his career and even achieved a few minor accomplishments, Henry was never much of a success as a businessman, a failure he largely blamed on his overbearing father, who, he claimed, never really gave him a chance to prove himself in the firm. In his career as a writer he also never received the recognition he probably deserved. In addition, his marriage, which on the surface appeared tranquil enough, apparently did not provide him with much contentment. All of this may help to explain why in his later years, Henry's life was so miserable. The drinking and romancing which in his youth placed him among the post-World War I generation of bright young things, by middle age had become excessive and unattractive.

Henry's last years were sad. No longer actively publishing, he did appear occasionally on various BBC talks about writing, and he was befriended by a few younger authors, most notably Terry Southern and Eudora Welty, who had discovered in his fiction the marks of a modernist master.

For the most part, however, his life declined into alcoholism, womanizing, and increasingly eccentric behavior. The remainder of his life Henry spent as a virtual recluse, confined to his house, unkempt and paranoid. His friends either passed away or had been long abandoned, and Henry Vincent Yorke died in London on December 13, 1973.

In an interview for *The Paris Review* in 1958, Terry Southern said about Henry Green that he was not only a writer's writer but a writer's writer's writer, placing him among the few genuine innovators of prose in the twentieth century. Jeremy Treglown agrees. Green's prose is truly original, some might say eccentric, but nevertheless writing that has attracted the admiration of other writers if not the public at large. Katherine Mansfield praised his humanity; W. H. Auden called him once the finest living English novelist; and John Updike in his introduction to a collection of *Loving*, *Living*, and *Party Going* paid homage to Green by extolling his liberating, ingenious voice and his matchless dialogue that retained the softness of groping, of sensation, of living.

Jeremy Treglown has written a comprehensive study which manages to provide an overview of Green's fiction as well, so that the reader comes away with a fuller portrait of the author and man than is usual in literary biographies. Treglown also makes his case for Henry's divided life which was nevertheless graced by periods of friendship and love despite his sordid end. *Romancing* proves an engaging and valuable book, one that will hopefully encourage a reevaluation of Henry Green's writing.

Charles L. P. Silet

Sources for Further Study

Booklist 97 (February 15, 2001): 1110.
Library Journal 126 (March 1, 2001): 88.
The New York Review of Books 48 (October 18, 2001): 18.
The New York Times Book Review 106 (March 25, 2001): 11.
Publishers Weekly 248 (February 26, 2001): 75.

SAILING ALONE AROUND THE ROOM
New and Selected Poems

Author: Billy Collins (1941-   )
Publisher: Random House (New York). 172 pp. $21.95
Type of work: Poetry

∾

This volume brings together some of the poems which have established Collins's reputation as a poet who blends humor and accessibility with surprise; the collection also contains twenty new poems

∾

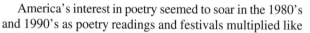

America's interest in poetry seemed to soar in the 1980's and 1990's as poetry readings and festivals multiplied like coffee houses. In the great welter of poetic voices and styles that emerged during the period, Billy Collins especially seemed to capture public attention. *Sailing Alone Around the Room* arrives after a very public conflict between two of Collins's publishers delayed the volume's publication for over a year. The book selects poems from Collins's last four books—*The Apple That Astonished Paris* (1988), *Questions About Angels* (1991), *The Art of Drowning* (1995), and *Picnic, Lightning* (1998); the collection also contains twenty new poems. Named Poet Laureate of the United States for 2001-2002, Collins offers in *Sailing Alone* many poems which readers will recognize from his previous volumes, as well as from his appearances on National Public Radio shows such as *Fresh Air* and *Prairie Home Companion*. The collection documents Collins's thoroughly American voice in his choice of subjects as well as in his approach to them, surely a major reason for his popularity.

Collins's fondness for homely subjects and settings accounts in part for his accessibility. Those settings are well represented in this volume, beginning with the first poem, "Another Reason Why I Don't Keep a Gun in the House." Here the hapless speaker is victim of a neighbor's dog; its relentless barking has driven him nearly mad. At last he closes the windows and puts a Beethoven symphony on, "full blast," but the dog continues to bark and in fact acts as if Beethoven had written "a part for barking dog" including a solo, "that endless coda that first established/ Beethoven as an innovative genius." This poem illustrates a technique which Collins uses often— the poem which starts in the mundane and spins out into fantasy.

Barking dogs aside, Collins's poems frequently celebrate the joys of the mundane—the pleasures of the garden, a cup of tea, sun falling across a familiar desk. That is the theme of "Tuesday, June 4, 1991" in which Collins imagines himself to be "the secretary to the morning whose only/ responsibility is to take down its bright, airy dictation . . . ." He compares himself to a court stenographer or to Samuel Pepys, the seventeenth century English diarist who faithfully recorded all the events of his

∽

Billy Collins has published many collections of poetry. He is a distinguished professor of English at Lehman College of the City University of New York, and he was named Poet Laureate of the United States for 2001-2002.

∽

life, from quarrels with his wife to the great fire which leveled central London. Here Collins notes the arrival of the painter, the antics of the kitten, the state of the garden's flowers; he concludes that this record will be even better if it begins at dawn tomorrow, when the dawn goddess Aurora will greet him with "a handful of birdsong and a small cup of light." This is the basic material of our lives, Collins implies, and it is worth recording. Like the good dinner which makes the subject of "Osso Buco," the pleasures of ordinary life are "something you don't hear about much in poetry," which more usually deals with suffering. The final image of "Osso Buco" pictures the speaker slipping in sleep down into the very marrow of the earth, the only world we know. In the fantasy "Shoveling Snow With Buddha," the speaker shovels the driveway and chatters about the delights of the experience while Buddha, his helper, maintains a contemplative silence until near the end, when he requests a game of cards when the job is done, and the speaker imagines them drinking hot chocolate and playing cards while their snowy boots drip on the mat.

An important part of Collins's celebration focuses on music and especially on jazz and its performers. "Questions About Angels" opens with a series of whimsical questions which Collins suggests never get asked about angels—their diet, what they think about, the fabric of their clothes. Instead, he says, people insist on asking how many angels can dance on the head of a pin; the answer, he says, is one—a single female angel whom he pictures as a "dancing alone in her stocking feet " to the music of a jazz combo.

As heavenly music, jazz naturally has the power to move its human listeners. In "I Chop Some Parsley While Listening to Art Blakey's Version of 'Three Blind Mice,'" the speaker begins with some questions about the likelihood of three mice burdened with the same disability; "was it a common accident?" he wonders, and how did they happen to find each other, let alone the farmer's wife? The picture of the three hapless mice, sightless and tailless, may bring tears to the speaker's eyes, although the onion he is now chopping may have caused the tears or—and now the reader recognizes the poem's serious theme—the tears may rise from Blakey's music, or perhaps from Frankie Hubbard's mournful trumpet on the next cut.

The reason for the power of jazz to move the listener is examined in "Nightclub," in which Collins speculates, first humorously and then seriously, about the possible variants for the lyrics of the standard café singer's song; "I have never heard anyone sing/ I am so beautiful/ and you are a fool to be in love with me." He similarly rejects other possible but unlikely variations. The inspiration for this speculation is a recording by Johnny Hartman. Collins's meditation suggests that the music (like poetry) has the power to transform ordinary human foolishness into beauty.

Much about Collins's poetry seems to cultivate a tone that is intentionally nonpoetic, at least in the popular sense. A reader whose idea of poetry stems from a high school exposure to the nineteenth century English poet William Wordsworth will find

Collins a great contrast. Collins's diction is simple; his syntax is direct; many of his subjects are familiar territory to most readers. These qualities go far to account for his popularity, but another of Collins's favorite subjects is poetry itself along with other literary subjects such as books and reading.

"Introduction to Poetry" expresses Collins's desire that readers not treat his poems as puzzles to be solved but as friendly communications from poet to reader. Instead, he says, some readers (who sound a little like college freshmen) want to "tie the poem to a chair with rope/ and torture a confession out of it." In "Workshop," the would-be poets of the writers' workshop make a sort of opposite number to the readers in "Introduction," and Collins takes a friendly jab at their clichés. "Maybe it's just me. . ." the workshopper begins, and goes on to critique a poem that gives him "a very powerful sense of something," although he never manages to name what that something is.

Collins spends part of his days teaching literature and often praises books, as in the poem "Books" in which he begins by describing a university library at night and goes on to trace his own history of reading. At last the poem offers a metaphor from "Hansel and Gretel"; their breadcrumbs become the words which lead the readers into the story to hear the voices of the lost children. In "First Reader," however, Collins reminds readers that as children learn to interpret the words under the cheery pictures of Dick and Jane in the elementary readers, they are also learning to let books substitute for their own observations in interpreting the world.

Collins's humor is one of his most appealing features, and this collection offers a full sampling. Often his humor rises from the contrast between the ordinary world and a fantastic vision it can inspire. A typical example is "Insomnia," where to fall asleep the speaker counts "all the sheep in the world"; then he goes on to count every other type of animal, from snail to wildebeest. The resulting sleep brings on a dream about Noah's ark and that dream leaves the dreamer afloat on waves where colorful fish are leaping fences.

Irony is often an element in Collins's humor. In "To a Stranger Born in Some Distant Country Hundreds of Years from Now," disparity occurs between what the reader might logically expect from the ponderous title and the poem's actual message to those far-off readers—that wet dogs will be no more welcome in the pubs of the future than they are today. "Nostalgia" pokes gentle fun at the present age's willingness to romanticize the past, its fashions and dances. "Where has the summer of 1572 gone?" the speaker asks, and the 1790's and even 1901. Always the past looks better than now, and he concludes that even the unknown future may outshine the present moment .

"Forgetfulness" illustrates Collins's skill with metaphors which, though simple and often funny, also capture the subject at hand. In this poem Collins is talking about the sort of memory lapses associated with middle age; dozens of ordinary facts (authors, titles, even plots) escape the boundaries of memory as if they had "decided to retire to . . . a little fishing village where there are no phones." The sufferer struggles to remember something that has "floated away down a dark mythological river," leaving the forgetful one detached even from the moon in love poems he once had memorized.

Among the twenty new poems in this collection, Collins's fans will recognize some of their favorite Collins modes. "Dharma" celebrates the attitudes of the family dog; "Snow Day" and "Pavilion" celebrate household scenes. Jazz is here along with fantasy and folk tales (with an additional meditation on the peasant who receives three wishes). Several poems address the problems of writing poetry. The last two poems offer a new sort of surprise. In "The Iron Bridge" Collins creates a brief memoir of his mother, born the year before the bridge in question was built. Collins thinks of her infancy and then of her death in 1997, using the dive and underwater flight of the cormorant as a metaphor for her departure into "some boundless province." Despite the poems filled with books and jazz and family pets and tea, Collins typically keeps a measure of distance between himself and his reader. Indeed, he has expressed distrust of highly personal poetry on the grounds that it substitutes events from the poet's life for the more universal understandings which should be the poet's goal. "Iron Bridge" closes that distance in a way that is perhaps the more moving because it is so rare. A similar, though more playful, expression is in the last poem of the collection, "The Flight of the Reader," in which Collins speculates on what keeps his readers with him and what he will do without them on the day they depart, finally suggesting first that he will not mind being alone again and then, ironically, admitting that he will mind indeed.

Billy Collins's critics have sometimes implied that his accessibility makes him a lightweight, as if to be worthy poems must also be dense. Critics have also accused him of repeating himself by repeating his techniques. Both charges have a degree of justice. Collins's poems do not usually address extremely complex subjects, and he approaches them from a limited number of directions. (He refers to both of these issues in "The Flight of the Reader.") Collins, however, can never be accused of securing his popularity by pandering to public fondness for cliché and sentimentality. Instead, he has given American readers a poetry written in their own language, a poetry which lets them, as he requested in "Introduction to Poetry," "walk inside the poem's room/ and feel the wall for a light switch." In Collins's poetry, as this volume shows, the light switch is always available and the room always welcomes its visitors.

Ann D. Garbett

Sources for Further Study

Booklist 97 (August, 2001): 2078.
Library Journal 126 (September 1, 2001): 184.
The New York Times, October 8, 2001, p. E7.
The New York Times Book Review 106 (September 23, 2001): 10.
Publishers Weekly 248 (June 18, 2001): 78.

SAINT-SIMON AND THE COURT OF LOUIS XIV

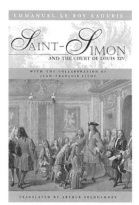

Author: Emmanuel Le Roy Ladurie (1929-   ), with
    Jean-François Fitou
First published: Saint-Simon, ou le système de la Cour,
    1997, in France
Translated from the French by Arthur Goldhammer
Publisher: The University of Chicago Press (Chicago).
    Illustrated. 432 pp. $35.00
Type of work: Biography and history
Time: 1690-1723
Locale: Versailles and Paris

≈

*A learned, witty account of the scandals, gossip, and in-
trigues of the French court, drawn largely from the voluminous* Memoirs *(numbering thousands of pages) of the duc
de Saint-Simon*

≈

Principal personages:
> LOUIS DE ROUVROY (1675-1755), duc de Saint-Simon and eager chroni-
> cler of the personalities and events of the French court between 1691
> and 1723
> LOUIS XIV (1638-1715), "the Sun King," king of France from 1643 to
> 1715
> LOUIS, LE GRAND DAUPHIN (1661-1711), son of Louis XIV, known as
> "Monseigneur"
> PHILIPPE (1640-1701), brother of Louis XIV, duc d'Orléans, known as
> "Monsieur"
> PHILIPPE II (1674-1723), son of Monsieur, duc d'Orléans, and regent
> after the death of Louis XIV in 1715
> LOUIS XV (1710-1774), king of France from 1715 to 1774
> GUILLAUME DUBOIS (1656-1723), abbé, later cardinal, and a powerful
> influence during the Regency
> JOHN LAW (1671-1729), Scottish-born comptroller general of finances
> during the Regency

    Louis de Rouvroy, the future duc de Saint-Simon, was born to Claude, the first duc
de Saint-Simon, in 1675 and in 1693 inherited a decent fortune with the title. He
served in the army with no distinction from 1691 till 1697, in 1694 marrying Mlle de
Lorges, with whom he would have three children. His *Memoirs* were composed during the reign of Louis XV, but his early writings around 1691 announced one of his
most obsessive themes, bastards in general and, in particular, their "mixed marriages"
to persons of legitimate birth. Saint-Simon became a friend of Philippe II, the son of

*Emmanuel Le Roy Ladurie is a
professor at the Collège de France
and he has written several books on
French history, including*
Montaillou: The Promised Land of
Error *(1978). In the present
instance, he drafted the whole work
and Jean-François Fitou, the deputy
prefect of Langon, France, wrote
the footnotes and revised the text.*

Monsieur, the king's brother, and when Philippe became a duke upon his father's death in 1701, Saint-Simon could claim powerful allies at the court. By 1704, Saint-Simon had maneuvered himself into a tiny apartment at Versailles, moving in 1710 to luxury quarters that provided the perfect vantage point for observing the foibles and follies of the court.

Philippe became regent in 1715 and in 1719 allowed Saint-Simon to live in the castle of Meudon. In 1721, Saint-Simon was appointed ambassador extraordinary to Spain, where he negotiated the marriage of the regent's daughter to the prince of Asturias before coming home in 1722. Upon Louis XV's attaining the age of majority in 1723, the Upper Council replaced the Regency Council, and Saint-Simon retired to private life after being evicted from Meudon. During his retirement from court life, Saint-Simon wrote several lesser works before composing the *Memoirs* between 1739 and 1749, concluding his account with the death of the regent in December, 1723. When Saint-Simon died in 1755, he had become identified with support for social hierarchies and what Ladurie calls "a purer, more Jansenist religion."

Ladurie divides his narrative into six chapters on the court system from 1690 till the death of Louis XIV in 1715, and a chapter each on the "liberal" Regency (1715-1718) and the "authoritarian" Regency (1718-1723). The first chapter treats hierarchy and rank at Versailles, from 1690 to 1715, and borrows a table taken from Henri Brocher, *À la cour de Louis XIV: Le Rang et l'étiquette sous l'Ancien Régime* (1934; at the court of Louis XIV: rank and etiquette under the *ancien régime*), to illustrate the elaborate system of seating that prevailed at the court. In order of rank, the king and queen were followed by the dauphin and the dauphine and other sons and daughters of France; then came the grandsons and granddaughters of France, princesses of the blood, princes of the blood, and cardinals; next came duchesses, foreign princesses, Spanish grandees (female), followed by dukes, foreign princes, Spanish grandees (male), and finally Women of Quality preceding only Men of Quality. For each there was an appropriate seating arrangement. A princess of the blood in the presence of the king or queen, for instance, was entitled to a stool, whereas a prince of the blood had to stand. Cardinals were expected to stand before the king but could use a stool before the queen. Princesses of the blood were allowed a chair with back before grandsons and granddaughters of France, but Men of Quality had to stand. Armchairs were ordinarily the privilege of only the ranking personage. Saint-Simon applauded this emphasis on hierarchy that existed throughout Europe, and he recognized merit as well as rank and birth.

In matters of the sacred and the profane, the sacred took precedence. In observing Communion, the king knelt on the floor, and Ladurie remarks, "Before the obscure sanctuary of Christianity's central mystery, the Eucharist, knelt the monarchy, the central mystery of the state." At the top of the secular hierarchy, the king was thus a link between the clergy and the nobility. The intricacies of protocol shine in Ladurie's description of a mass in the Spanish royal chapel, with the king kneeling before the cardinal but making up for playing second fiddle by occupying a gorgeously upholstered armchair while the cardinal made do with one of plain wood.

Ladurie's chapter on "The Pure and the Impure" reveals dramatically the French court's obsession with cleansing their insides with emetics, enemas, and bloodletting. Saint-Simon's *Memoirs* betrays an astonishing interest in royal commodes, disclosing, for example, that Louis XIV scheduled monthly *jours de médecine* (medicine days) on which he was purged. Ladurie relates, "After the king was purged, a mass was said and the royal family visited the sovereign in his bed." For Saint-Simon, the most monstrous impurity was bastardy in the royal family, a blemish associated in his mind with offenses against Christianity. Ladurie points out that Saint-Simon's metaphors for sexual impurities are excremental ("foul muck," *boue infecte*) and those for low birth are "dregs" (*lie*) or "mire" (*bourbe*). Homosexuality appeared to Saint-Simon, says Ladurie, as an "aggravating circumstance, magnifying impurity to the utmost degree." In the *Memoirs*, there are suggestions that Saint-Simon's disgust at illicit sex had roots in his lifelong inclination toward the Augustinian teachings of Jansenism.

Saint-Simon's own analyses provide the substance for a chapter on "Cabals, Linkages, and Power." The cabals encompass three generations: the Maintenon cabal, named after Louis XIV's wife; the Monseigneur cabal, named after Louis XIV's son; and the third-generation cabal named after the duc and duchesse de Bourgogne. Ladurie's diagram of the relationships between and among these cabal leaders and the extensive casts of bit players will exhaust all but the most determined readers of gossip columns. ("It is all too easy to lose track," notes Ladurie.) The cabals of Maintenon and Monseigneur, united with the faction of the duc du Maine, bastard of Louis XIV, formed "a flexible, decentralized, yet supreme power structure" that dominated the court and the entire bureaucracy of government. At the top remained "that supreme patrimonialist summit, the royal house."

The various editions of the *Memoirs* include dates of birth and death for 1,834 men and 782 women of the approximately 10,000 individuals Saint-Simon names, and these figures provide Ladurie some revealing statistics on demography and marriage patterns. For instance, of the three groups of military officers—high-ranking, middle-ranking, and low-ranking—the life expectancies were 69.8, 61.2, and 50.9 years, respectively. Officers of lower rank obviously could be expected to face greater danger (what Ladurie calls a "manifest" inequality), but there was also a "latent" inequality in that a man's chances of achieving high rank were directly correlated to his rank in the aristocracy. On another subject, Saint-Simon's notes on marriages yield figures for endogamy (marrying within one's own class), female hypergamy (marrying up) and female hypogamy (marrying down). Of 1,366 marriages, 740 were endogamous, 378 hypergamous, 133 hypogamous, and 115 unclassifiable. Not surprisingly, old men frequently sought out young women, sometimes with embarrassing results, as Saint-Simon relates of the eighty-one-year-old duc de Gesvres: "He was punished for it, and his young bride was punished even more: he fouled the bed so badly that both of them had to be scrubbed down and all the linen changed." Saint-Simon's preoccupation with rank made him sensitive to all nonendogamous marriages, and he probably meant the verb "punished" seriously.

Ladurie's chapter on "Renouncers and Jesuits" illuminates the theological enmities of the day, "renouncers" being a term he borrows from the historian Louis Dumont to describe individuals avoiding social constraints. Saint-Simon had strong sympathies for the renouncers, men such as Abbé de Rancé, the superior of a Trappist monastery, and was most influenced by the Jansenist theologian Father Pasquier Quesnel, whose study of the New Testament, *Nouveau Testament en français avec des réflexions morales* (1692; New Testament in French with thoughts on morality) was read by many and admired by Saint-Simon. The *Réflexiones* prompted the *Unigenitus*, Clement XI's Constitution of 1713 condemning 101 Jansenist-tainted propositions discovered by the authorities. Another renouncer whom Saint-Simon appreciated was Jacques-Joseph Duguet, whose *Institution d'un prince* (1729; education of a prince) considered the role of renunciation in the affairs of sovereign princes. On the question of Saint-Simon's attitude toward Jansenism, Ladurie places him in the so-called Catholic third party, those of a "middle way" between "the Augustinian fanatics of grace and the Jesuit apologists of personal merit."

The "liberal" Regency prevailed from the autumn of 1715 until the summer of 1718, with Saint-Simon on the sidelines as the government moved from Versailles to Paris. Ladurie's account of this period summarizes the "machinations of cabals." The cabal around the duc de Bourgogne had withered away, the faction headed by Monseigneur collapsed with the death of the Grand Dauphin, and the powerful group dominated by Mme de Maintenon and the duc du Maine was dependent on the strong ministers. Ladurie concludes that despite the shuffling of power after the king's death, the period from 1715 to 1723 became the "only fully successful royal succession in the whole period from 1559 to 1789." One of the main conflicts of these years centered on three groups: the *parlementaires* and princes of the blood joined forces as favorites of the regent; the legitimized bastards struggled to find allies among the nonducal nobility; and the dukes and peers had their own grudges with Parlement. In the end, the dukes lost out, but the bastards benefited from the Edict of Marly (1714) that gave them all the prerogatives of princes of the blood in perpetuity, a blessing that enraged many, including Saint-Simon, who predicted the collapse of civilization. During his first three years, the regent created a government by "polysynody," or a series of councils, France's first experiment in representative government. In 1718, however, Orléans abandoned the councils and delegated considerable authority to the shrewd Guillaume Dubois, abbé and later cardinal, who was to mastermind the "authoritarian" regency of 1718-1723.

Dubois's only rival in government was John Law, the regent's Scottish-born guide in financial policies whose creation of money led to an inflation that gave ordinary citizens debt relief and eased unemployment. Despite the howls of the creditors, Law built a foundation for a sound currency—or so Ladurie thinks—and did more good than harm. When Law went out of favor in December, 1720, Dubois had a clear space to operate in and promptly finagled a cardinal's red hat while walking a tightrope between the Jansenists on his "left" and the ultramontane Romans on his "right." The wily Cardinal Dubois quickly sought more power for men of the cloth, sacked the deadbeats lingering from the old court, destroyed Law's system, and finagled a prominent role for himself in the Regency Council. Dubois was a relentless schemer who manipulated the system for remarkable personal wealth, but Ladurie's estimate of his accomplishments is high.

The ghost of the German sociologist Norbert Elias hovers over Ladurie's reflections on the court, a ghost that Ladurie swipes at impatiently *en passant* and finally tries to banish for good in an appendix. Ladurie rejects Elias's thesis that French court society of the seventeenth century derived its manners from the Middle Ages and evolved into modern courtesy. Thus, "Saint-Simon is not the foundation or underpinning of any later edifice; he is a ruin, ripe for excavation." However, this is a matter best left to the professional students of Ladurie's absorbing account of a man and his age.

Frank Day

Sources for Further Study

Journal of World History 72 (March, 2000): 212.
The New York Review of Books 48 (November 15, 2001): 50.

SAVAGE BEAUTY
The Life of Edna St. Vincent Millay

Author: Nancy Milford (1938-   )
Publisher: Random House (New York). 552 pp. $29.95
Type of work: Literary biography
Time: 1892-1950
Locale: Maine, New York, and France

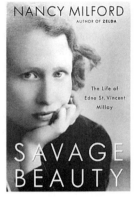

≈

A detailed biography of Millay that makes use of newly available papers of the flamboyant, once adulated American poet

≈

Principal personages:

EDNA ST. VINCENT MILLAY, American poet
CORA BUZZELL MILLAY, her mother
NORMA MILLAY ELLIS, the poet's sister
KATHLEEN KALLOCH MILLAY, the poet's sister
HENRY TOLMAN MILLAY, the poet's father
FERDINAND EARLE, editor, Millay's early champion
CAROLINE B. DOW, Millay's wealthy benefactor
ELAINE RALLI, wealthy Vassar classmate of Millay
EUGEN JAN BOISSEVAIN, Millay's husband
FLOYD DELL, radical playwright and editor
EDMUND WILSON, critic and editor
JOHN PEALE BISHOP, poet
ARTHUR D. FICKE, poet and lawyer
WITTER BYNNER, poet
GEORGE DILLON, poet and editor
ELINOR WYLIE, poet

No star in the American literary firmament during the first half of the twentieth century shined as brightly and plummeted as precipitously as did Edna St. Vincent Millay. A female Byron, she was a passionate poet who aroused the passions of many others, male and female. Millay was as seductive in person as in print, and no one, not even Robert Frost, was as popular and provocative on the reading circuit. The first woman to win the Pulitzer Prize in poetry (in 1923), Millay, voted one of the ten most famous women in America in 1938, was as famous for her flamboyant, unconventional life as for her plangent if conventional verse. Thomas Hardy quipped that, along with skyscrapers, Edna St. Vincent Millay was one of two great things in America. As late as 1939, Harvard president James Conant was introducing her on the radio as "the greatest woman poet since Sappho." Yet the revolution in style and sensibility led by Ezra Pound, T. S. Eliot, and William Carlos Williams bypassed Millay, and well before her death in 1950, her metrical, rhymed poetry had come to seem quaint, an epigone's echo of nineteenth century Romanticism. To contemporary poets and the readers of contemporary poetry, Millay is less scorned than ignored.

Millay's eventful but relatively brief life was sensational, even lurid. Yet there would seem no need to supersede three existing biographies—Vincent Sheean's *The Indigo Bunting* (1951), Miriam Gurko's *Restless Spirit* (1962), and Norman A. Brittin's *Edna St. Vincent Millay* (1982)—except to provide new information and to revive Millay's reputation. Nancy Milford, whose bestselling 1970 biography *Zelda* drew F. Scott Fitzgerald's wife out from the shadow of her famous husband, attempts to do both. She was granted exclusive access to Millay's papers by her surviving sister, Norma Millay Ellis, and she was sufficiently convinced of the poet's enduring merits to have edited *The Selected Poetry of Edna St. Vincent Millay*, which was published by Random House in a Modern Library edition simultaneously with Milford's biography. While eager to counter the neglect of Millay's life and

Nancy Milford achieved both popular and critical success with Zelda *(1970), her biography of F. Scott Fitzgerald's wife. Granted exclusive access to the Millay papers in 1972, Milford worked on the poet's biography for almost thirty years. She was an Annenberg Fellow at Brown University in 1995 and a Fulbright Scholar in Turkey in 1999 and has taught at the University of Michigan and Vassar College.*

work, Milford, who worked on *Savage Beauty: The Life of Edna St. Vincent Millay* for almost thirty years, cannot have been especially pleased by the simultaneous publication of a rival biography—Daniel Mark Epstein's *What Lips My Lips Have Kissed: The Loves and Love Poems of Edna St. Vincent Millay*. Readers curious about Millay's poetry might best turn to Epstein, himself a poet. Those intent on immersing themselves in the sometimes sordid details of her life will find Milford an able and assiduous guide.

Milford interrupts her narrative periodically to interpolate conversations she had with an aging Norma Millay Ellis, the poet's executor and only heir. Otherwise, *Savage Beauty* is a chronological account, documented with quotations from letters, notebooks, diaries, poems, and drafts, of a phenomenal career. It begins as a kind of fairy tale, the story of three pretty little sisters—blonde, brunette, and redhead—growing up poor in Camden, Maine. Edna St. Vincent, called "Vincent" by Milford as she was by those who knew her and named for the New York hospital in which her uncle was saved from death, was the eldest, born in 1892. She was followed by Norma in 1893 and Kathleen in 1896. Cora, their fiercely devoted mother, was remarkably independent and outspoken, and in 1900 she dismissed her feckless husband, Henry, whom Vincent never saw again. In order to provide for her three girls, Cora, whom Milford contends remained, despite everything, the love of Vincent's life, took distant nursing jobs. In her absence, the oldest daughter functioned as head of the household.

Millay manifested precocious literary abilities, assembling a chapbook she titled *Poetical Works of Vincent Millay* by age sixteen. At twenty, she submitted a long poem, "Renascence," to a contest conducted by a literary magazine called *The Lyric Year*, whose married editor, Ferdinand Earle, began a torrid correspondence with the coy young author. Though it received only honorable mention, "Renascence" created a commotion and prompted affluent Caroline B. Dow to pay the poet's way through Vassar College. Despite her meager academic background and her humble pedigree, Millay became the darling of the campus and particularly of Elaine Ralli, a wealthy classmate whom she conquered and abandoned.

After graduation, Millay moved to Greenwich Village, then America's bohemia, where she gained increasing recognition as a poet, playwright, and social rebel. She also performed in several productions of the Provincetown Players, an innovative theater company, and ended up living with Floyd Dell, one of its leading members. While arranging for her sister Kathleen to attend Vassar, she brought her mother and her sister Norma to live with her, and the plucky Millay women dazzled New York, making of their lives, writes Milford, "a family romance. It was their story of triumph over adversity, one of the best women's stories there is in America: hopeful, enduring, centered in family, and fraudulent—not especially because it was deceitful but because it was built on so much unadmitted pain that it was impossible to sustain."

The romance with Dell, who was prosecuted for dissident activities, was not sustained very long, and Millay took to bed a bewildering array of others, male and female, married and unmarried, younger and older. Five foot one and barely one hundred pounds, Millay was a sexually voracious charmer, and among the prominent literary figures whom she conquered and discarded were two best friends, critic Edmund Wilson and poet John Peale Bishop. Two other friends also competed for her favors, Arthur D. Ficke and Witter Bynner, though the latter was homosexual. Her relationship with George Dillon, a poet fourteen years her junior with whom she translated the French poet Charles-Pierre Baudelaire (1821-1867), endured longer than most others. She shared a particularly close friendship with her fellow poet Elinor Wylie. In 1923, Millay married Eugen Jan Boissevain, a prosperous Dutch businessman who, until his death in 1949, a year before Millay broke her neck falling down a flight of stairs, made a career of sheltering and waiting on his famous wife. The couple established a base of operations at Steepletop, their 435-acre Berkshire farm in Austerlitz, New York. Boissevain tolerated and even facilitated Millay's numerous adulteries.

Much of Milford's book is a catalogue of a literary celebrity's romantic exploits. She traces the repeated cycles of infatuation and disenchantment through letters and journals written by Millay and others and reproduces, often in their entirety, poems that respond explicitly to the poet's current passions. Milford chronicles Millay's two-year sojourn in Paris, from 1921-1923, as well as other foreign adventures, including a romp through isolated Albania on horseback in the company of a smitten young diplomat. She recounts the publication and reception of each of Millay's books, her resounding success as a touring public speaker, the premiere of her plays and of an opera, *The King's Henchman* (pr. 1927), whose libretto she wrote. She also reviews the final decade, when the jaunty author's exuberance succumbed to illness, pain, alcohol, morphine, and death at the age of fifty-eight.

During an era when American women were first allowed to vote, Millay heralded a new, irreverent sensibility. As much as Fitzgerald, she was the coy voice of the Jazz Age, flippant even about its own flippancy, and her most frequently quoted poem, "First Fig," became the anthem of the generation that came of age in the boom following World War I:

> My candle burns at both ends;
> It will not last the night;
> But ah, my foes, and oh, my friends—
> It gives a lovely light!

In light of such splendid nonchalance, Millay is sometimes dismissed as froth, a hedonist for whom poetry is frippery. During times of crisis, the Great Depression and World War II, when her own powers were deteriorating, she was already beginning to seem an anachronism. Yet Milford notes Millay's active engagement in political causes, from defending the condemned anarchists Nicola Sacco and Bartolomeo Vanzetti to opposing European fascism and American isolationism. However, Millay's polemical verse has not aged as well as the sprightly work that defies age and urges its readers to seize the day. "I want to write," she wrote in 1923, "so that those who read me will say . . . 'Life can be exciting and free and intense.' I really mean it!"

Milford reads Millay as a force of nature not especially susceptible to analysis. Rarely does the biographer attempt to generalize or theorize, preferring instead to allow the poet to speak for herself, through letters, diaries, poems, and actions. What emerges after more than five hundred pages with Millay is a familiar portrait of the artist as a Roman candle, a self-destructive dynamo burning at both ends and yielding not only lovely light but also acrid smoke. Like Percy Bysshe Shelley, whom she adored, and Sylvia Plath, whom she anticipated, Millay was another phase in the dynasty of brilliant, precocious poets who distinguished themselves in the act of extinguishing themselves.

Attempting to describe Millay, Arthur D. Ficke, one of her many lovers, resorted to paradoxes: "She is the oddest mixture of genius and childish vanity, open mindedness and blind self-worship, that I have ever known." Preoccupied with restoring her subject to life, Milford resists the temptation to explain her. She certainly does not idealize her. *Savage Beauty* is another among many recent examples of biography written as pathography, the examination of an afflicted life, though a complete diagnosis is left to the reader. Millay was a woman adept at dramatizing herself, but the biographer refrains from analyzing a performance that combined elements of comedy, farce, and tragedy.

In 1931, Millay's book *Fatal Interview* sold 33,000 copies within ten weeks, an astonishing accomplishment for a sonnet sequence in the midst of the Depression. Milford quotes an anonymous journalist who, impressed by the poet's enormous popularity, confidently predicted that Millay's work ". . . throughout the years will be a bookseller's staple, like Shakespeare and ink and two-cent stamps." Shakespeare abides, but, seventy years later, though she wrote a few of the finest Shakespearean sonnets of the twentieth century, a quaint distinction, Millay's works have, like ink and two-cent stamps, vanished from contemporary bookstores. Though it reacquaints the reader with an extraordinary woman, *Savage Beauty* is not likely to revive the popularity of her poetry.

Steven G. Kellman

Sources for Further Study

The Atlantic Monthly 288 (October, 2001): 112.
Los Angeles Times Book Review, September 16, 2001, p. 1.
Newsweek 138 (September 10, 2001): 62.
The New York Times, September 11, 2001, p. E9.
The New York Times Book Review 106 (September 16, 2001): 12.
The New Yorker 77 (September 3, 2001): 86.
Publishers Weekly 248 (June 18, 2001): 67.
USA Today, September 4, 2001, p. D01.
The Wall Street Journal, September 6, 2001, p. A20.
The Washington Post Book World, September 23, 2001, p. 11.

THE SCARLET PROFESSOR
Newton Arvin—A Literary Life Shattered by Scandal

Author: Barry Werth (1952-   )
Publisher: Nan A. Talese/Doubleday (New York). Illustrated. 326 pages, $26.00; paperback, $14.00
Type of work: Literary biography
Time: 1924-1963
Locale: Northampton, Massachusetts; Valparaiso, Indiana; Nantucket, Massachusetts; Saratoga Springs, White Plains, and New York City, New York

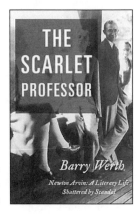

≈

More than merely a literary biography, this consideration of literary critic Newton Arvin's rise and fall provides an incisive assessment of the unwarranted inroads made by governmental interference in the lives of individuals during and immediately following the witch hunts of Senator Joseph McCarthy in the 1950's

≈

Principal personages:
> (FREDERICK) NEWTON ARVIN, a major literary critic and distinguished professor of English at Smith College
> TRUMAN CAPOTE, American novelist, Arvin's lover for two years
> DAVID LILIENTHAL, Arvin's lifelong friend, chair of the Tennessee Valley Authority, later head of the Atomic Energy Commission
> VAN WYCK BROOKS, noted critic of American literature
> WENDELL STACY JOHNSON, hired on Arvin's recommendation to teach English at Smith College
> NED STOFFORD, among Arvin's closest friends, hired on his recommendation to teach classics at Smith College
> JOEL DORIUS, instructor in Smith's English Department
> MARY GARRISON ARVIN, Arvin's wife from 1932 to 1940
> THOMAS MENDENHALL, president of Smith College during Arvin's difficulties
> HELEN H. BACON, chair of Smith's English Department
> JOHN REGAN, a politically ambitious member of the Massachusetts State Police

Newton Arvin's fragile world tumbled around him on September 2, 1960, when five policemen in two unmarked Ford automobiles arrived in front of his modest apartment at 45 Prospect Street in Northampton, Massachusetts. They entered the building that stood only a short walk from Smith College, a prestigious women's college, where Arvin had taught for thirty-seven years and was Mary Augusta Jordan

~

Barry Werth, author of The Billion Dollar Molecule *(1994) and* Damage *(1998), lives in Northampton, Massachusetts, maintaining his office in the four-room, cruciform apartment occupied by Newton Arvin during his final years.*

~

Professor of English, the most distinguished professorship in his department. The police officers ascended two narrow, winding flights of stairs and pounded aggressively on Arvin's door. It was eleven A.M.

Leading the group were John Regan of the Massachusetts State Police and his partner, Gerald Crowley. Regan, an imposing figure, stood six feet tall and weighed 220 pounds. When the diminutive Arvin opened the door, he saw only Regan and Crowley, but soon all five officers forced their way into his small foyer. Regan informed the timid professor that his name had been linked to organized traffic in pornography.

He and Crowley asked to search Arvin's apartment and quickly, despite the lack of a search warrant, turned his residence inside out. The police unearthed pictures of nude or seminude males, some in compromising situations, as well as various muscle builder and physical fitness magazines, copies of *One* (the publication of the homosexually oriented Mattachine Society), and, most damaging as it turned out, stacks of Arvin's journals and diaries dating to 1940.

Newton Arvin grew up a sickly child in Valparaiso, Indiana, small, frail, and unsuited to play sports or engage in "manly" pursuits, which never attracted him. His interests were intellectual. He read incessantly. He resented his mother's domineering tendencies and never felt close to his father. Upon finishing four painful years of secondary school, he enrolled in Harvard University, where he entered a milieu that suited him better than any he had previously known.

Arvin's happiest memories of Valparaiso were connected with his only close childhood friend, David Lilienthal, who eventually chaired the Tennessee Valley Authority during the administrations of Franklin Delano Roosevelt and Harry S. Truman and was appointed head of the Atomic Energy Commission by President Dwight D. Eisenhower. Although Lilienthal, thoroughly heterosexual, failed to understand Arvin's sexual orientation when he became aware of it belatedly, he remained a supportive friend throughout Arvin's lifetime.

Completing his bachelor's degree at Harvard in three and one-half years, Arvin began teaching at Detroit Country Day School in Michigan. Close to nervous collapse, he resigned from the job before the Christmas break. Arvin's fondest wish was to become a literary critic focusing on a rapidly developing new academic field, American literature.

Arvin had no enthusiasm for teaching and, largely because of his shy and retiring personality, was never the riveting or even memorable teacher that some of his close friends were, particularly Ned Stofford and Wendell Stacy Johnson. He developed a friendship with Van Wyck Brooks, who, in the early 1920's, was being lionized for *America's Coming of Age* (1915) and *The Ordeal of Mark Twain* (1920). Brooks encouraged Arvin to produce a book-length study in American literature, which culminated in Arvin's *Hawthorne* (1929), a book that established him as a critic to be reckoned with. This book, followed by *Whitman* (1938) and *Herman Melville* (1950), unequivocally placed him shoulder-to-shoulder with the most revered critics of American literature.

Barry Werth demonstrates how Arvin's need to live a life of secrecy and, at times, deception is reflected in his critical writing, which deals with the inner, secret lives of his subjects and with the effects of secrecy upon their writing. This approach, which distinguished him as a scholar, followed naturally from the element in his life that tormented him most. He was forever oppressed by the need to be more circumspect than his heterosexual colleagues.

In 1932, in a somewhat hysterical attempt to create a smoke screen, Arvin married an ex-Smith student, Mary Garrison. Although he was genuinely fond of Mary, he felt smothered and constrained by her presence in his house, where he had previously enjoyed the solitude he required to work. Although he was married to Mary Garrison until 1940, they lived apart for all but several months during their eight-year marriage.

When Arvin's legal problems came to light, Smith College's board of trustees insisted on dismissing him from his teaching position, quite contrary to the advice of the English department in which he taught and of Smith's president, David Mendenhall. Because of his conviction for possessing pornography, he was, at age sixty, forced out of his department, clearly reflecting the unequal treatment homosexuals received in such situations. Shortly after Arvin was forced out, Smith blinked at a sexual liaison between a senior faculty member (a friend of Arvin) and one of his female students, giving this established professor only a reprimand.

Werth demonstrates here and elsewhere the pervasiveness of the double standard that even Smith, a notably liberal institution, applied to homosexuals in the 1960's. Following his conviction, the college permitted Arvin, certainly its most renowned professor, to keep his office and use the library. It acknowledged that his thirty-seven years of teaching, which finally brought him an annual salary of $10,800, should qualify him for half salary during his forced early retirement. This pittance was not enough to sustain him, forcing him in the final three years of his life to accept loans from friends and supporters such as David Lilienthal and Truman Capote.

Werth points out the irony that Arvin, a worthwhile person who was not threatening to the welfare of his students, suffered ruination because a burly policeman, John Regan, had political ambitions and realized that the raid on Arvin's apartment would receive considerable publicity that would help him advance politically. Sadly, confronted with the evidence that Regan and his strike force illegally unearthed, Arvin offered little resistance and named other people who had viewed his pornographic materials with him, including his close friends and colleagues, Ned Stofford and Joel Dorius.

Wendell Stacy Johnson, who like Dorius had a sexual relationship with Arvin, was not prosecuted because he was away when the raid occurred and returned to Northampton in time to destroy materials he possessed that would have placed him under the same threat as the others had they been uncovered. The chair of Smith's Department of English, Helen H. Bacon, supportive of her colleagues who were arrested, put up bail for both Stofford and Dorius. Later she cashed in her war bonds to pay their fines. Although Smith granted her tenure shortly after the unfortunate witch hunt, she left voluntarily at the end of the year to accept a teaching position at Barnard College in New York City. Wendell Johnson, an outspoken supporter of Arvin, Stofford, and Dorius, left Smith for the City College of New York.

Fortunately, Barry Werth resists the temptation to engage in amateur psychologizing in his consideration of Arvin. He deals briefly with Arvin's early life and avoids discussing in any depth his relationships with his family. The focus of his book is clear: How did a scholar of Arvin's reputation manage to lead a double life, the revelation of which destroyed him and ultimately ended his career? Werth forces himself to remain within the confines he has set as he unravels his fascinating story of the bleak post-McCarthy days. Part 1 provides all the background material readers need to understand how Arvin's downfall occurred. Part 2, with all the tension and forward thrust of a well-wrought adventure story, deals with the precipitating event and its aftermath. Werth's writing is lucid, direct, and engaging.

Refusing to make value judgments about Arvin's involvement of his friends in his statements to the police, Werth succinctly presents his subject's state of mind during and immediately after the shattering raid on his residence. He writes,

> The sudden seizure of his secret history completed the shattering of Arvin's world. When he saw police returning with the slender volumes [diaries and journals], opening them and flipping through their lined pages—beginning to decipher the penciled hieroglyphics that unlocked his inmost life—it was as if there was nothing left of him to take or preserve. He was in utter panic, shaking, his face fallen.

In this frame of mind, Arvin told the police the names of those who had come to his apartment to view his pornography with him. Because they were named in his journals anyway, he apparently saw no way to protect them by refusing to cooperate with the police, despite their high-handed, unconstitutional tactics. His friends from Yaddo, the writers' colony in Saratoga Springs, New York, where Arvin spent most of his summers and to which he had been appointed a director, generally were forgiving "about his giving the police names . . . [viewing his doing so] as an unfortunate but understandable reaction by a sensitive, scared man to brutal, repressive, and ultimately overwhelming government force." Arvin was, nevertheless, forced to resign his directorship at Yaddo. He was essentially banned from returning because of the public relations implications of Yaddo's ignoring what had happened to him. Being *persona non grata* at Yaddo, which had become virtually a surrogate family for Arvin, was one of the cruelest blows to which his fall from grace subjected him.

During his emotional upheavals through the years, Arvin had committed himself to psychiatric hospitals. Unable to bear returning to his apartment, with its lingering memories, and unwilling to face people in Northampton, which, because of his suspended sentence, he was not able to leave without permission from his parole officer, he again turned to the state mental hospital in Northampton for help. Gradually, his mental state improved, and he could return to his office to work on his forthcoming study of Henry Wadsworth Longfellow.

In late 1962 and early 1963, Arvin's health deteriorated. He underwent prostate surgery and finally, in February, 1963, exploratory surgery that revealed pancreatic cancer that his physician considered incurable. On March 21, 1963, Newton Arvin died at Northampton's Cooley Dickinson Hospital, having hung on just long enough to see his Longfellow study in print.

R. Baird Shuman

Sources for Further Study

The Advocate, June 19, 2001, p. 100.
Booklist 97 (April 1, 2001): 1443.
Library Journal 126 (April 1, 2001): 102.
The Nation 273 (July 23, 2001): 33.
The New York Times Book Review 106 (August 5, 2001): 26.
Publishers Weekly 248 (April 30, 2001): 71.
The Washington Post Book World, April 15, 2001, p. 2.

SCHNITZLER'S CENTURY
The Making of Middle-Class Culture, 1815-1914

Author: Peter Gay (1923-   )
Publisher: W. W. Norton (New York). Illustrated.
  334 pp. $27.50
Type of work: History
Time: 1815-1914
Locale: Western Europe, the United States, and Russia

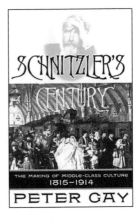

~

Gay's study provides a fundamental reworking of the current understanding of nineteenth century sexuality, as well as a revisionist explanation of other significant expressions of the middle-class mind, such as its preoccupation with decorum, its sympathy with modernist art, its approach to religion and Darwinism, and its obsession with privacy

~

Principal personage:
 ARTHUR SCHNITZLER, Viennese Jewish writer whom Gay takes as the
   archetype of nineteenth century bourgeois culture

Over the past fifteen years, Peter Gay has published a magisterial five-volume study of the Victorian world which he has called *The Bourgeois Experience: Victoria to Freud* (1984-1998). Intending to correct misperceptions about nineteenth century middle-class life, he has been at some pains to provide evidence that our ancestors were not as prudish, materialistic, or conventional as had formerly been thought. His task has been monumental, and in pursuing this collective historical enterprise, he has unearthed a library of original source material only scantily examined before. As a result, Gay has more than made his point. In his works the Victorian middle class—and within this category he includes the middle class in North America and throughout western Europe, not just in Great Britain—comes off as much more delightfully human, enjoyable, and accessible.

In *Schnitzler's Century: The Making of Middle-Class Culture, 1815-1914*, Gay provides a synthesis of his findings previously published in those five separate volumes. Although the author is careful to explain that this present work is not just a compilation of his previous findings, the book is in many ways just that and will provide those unfamiliar with his other volumes with an excellent and condensed version of them. For this present work, Gay has chosen to focus on the life and work of the Austrian writer Arthur Schnitzler (1862-1931) as a kind of palimpsest through which to revisit his earlier findings.

Schnitzler proves an excellent choice for such a task. The son of a well-to-do Viennese Jewish physician, he grew up in the same environment and with the same background as Sigmund Freud, one of the central figures Gay refers to throughout his work. He even wrote a biography of the psychoanalyst along the way. Schnitzler himself was often described as the Freud of fiction, since much of his literary output deals with the same psychocultural world that Freud examined and which formed the basis for his extraordinary breakthrough in the field of psychiatry. In fact, as Gay points out, Freud even wrote to Schnitzler about the far-reaching agreement between his own studies and Schnitzler's fiction, especially on erotic questions. Gay quotes Freud, never very generous with his praise, who enviously wondered how Schnitzler had arrived at the secret knowledge through the artist's intuition without having to do the laborious research imposed on the psychoanalyst.

∼

Peter Gay is Sterling Professor of History emeritus at Yale University and, since 1997, director of the Center for Scholars and Writers at the New York Public Library. Among his many publications is the monumental five-volume study The Bourgeois Experience: Victoria to Freud. *His* Freud: A Life for Our Times *(1988) has been translated into nine languages, and he won the National Book Award for the first volume of* The Enlightenment: An Interpretation *(1966-1969).*

∼

Schnitzler is probably best known for his plays, novellas, and other short fiction, in which he examined the erotic relationships between men and women in turn-of-the-century Vienna; relationships, Gay points out, that often mirrored Schnitzler's own. His fiction frequently involves a male philanderer and his emotional and erotic exploits with a series of more of less compliant female partners. Although Schnitzler was primarily focused on his male characters, in many of his works he presented women sympathetically, particularly in their erotic experiences, and he did so with some complexity. His emphasis on female sexuality was one of the primary reasons that his work attracted Freud's attention.

Gay admits that Schnitzler was hardly a typical bourgeois but, as he confesses, in the course of his research he discovered that Schnitzler had the qualities that made him a credible and resourceful witness to the world of the middle class that Gay had been depicting in his previous books, and so the historian decided to make him the center of his current one. Schnitzler was a man who bridged two centuries—a man of the nineteenth century, he lived well into the twentieth—and he provides an example of how indebted the present world is to the Victorians. A writer who helped to revolutionize modern drama, Schnitzler was one of the avant-garde artists who contributed to the fashioning of modernism, the primary artistic movement of the last century. Widely read, open to high culture, and sympathetic to new movements in the arts, he was still a solid bourgeois in his own, highly individual way, and therefore he can be a useful touchstone for Gay's own theories about the Victorian middle class.

Gay begins his examination of the middle classes by recounting a brief, but highly suggestive, entry in Schnitzler's youthful diary, which his father, Arthur, discovered in his son's locked desk. In his schoolboy enthusiasm, Schnitzler recounted his erotic exploits to what he believed was the sacrosanct privacy of his personal diary. This episode, the breach of the son's trust by his father, and its aftermath, a heated lecture by his father on the dangers of sexually transmitted diseases, apparently left an indelible impression on the author, as he remarked years later in his autobiography. Gay sees this as a central moment in shaping Schnitzler's outlook on his life and the world. It also provides one of the central themes for Gay's book. Safety is nowhere, Schnitzler would remark later, and Gay responds that this sentiment served as his motto throughout his life, a motto that could also serve that of his class.

Gay uses such forays into Schnitzler's biography and work throughout his book to introduce themes concerned with middle-class life. *Schnitzler's Century* is divided into three main parts. Part 1, "Fundamentals," is subdivided into two sections. The first is a brief study of middle-class life in general, "Bourgeoisie(s)," in which Gay explains that, in spite of the general historical consensus, there were many different middle classes in the nineteenth century, reflecting a wide variety of characteristics, from the comfortable, pleasure-loving Dickensian caricature to the sincere idealist who deliberately rejected such comfort and security. For every self-confident philistine there was one who rebelled from such complacency and narrow-mindedness. In religion there were doubters as well as the supremely assured. There were middle-class families on the way up and on the way down. Gay makes the point that the nineteenth century middle class never felt itself very secure.

The second section in part 1 is titled "Home, Bittersweet Home," and in it Gay wrestles with the ways in which the members of the nineteenth century middle class thought of their domestic world. As he does with each of the other categories with which he explores middle-class life, Gay presents a wide spectrum of attitudes, overturning, as he announces in his introductory remarks, the conventional and stereotypical views of that life currently in use among both professional historians and the general public.

In part 2, "Drives and Defenses," Gay pursues most aggressively the psychoanalysis that informs his cultural history. "Eros: Rapture and Symptom" is concerned with middle-class attitudes toward sex and sexuality. While there is plenty of reason, superficially at least, for maintaining the view that Victorians were prudish and fearful of their sexuality, Gay presents enough convincing data to the contrary to modify this picture. While not denying that Victorians were reticent, certainly in public, about their sex lives, he has discovered enough private material to suggest that there were more options for middle-class Victorian sexuality than previously thought. "Alibis for Aggression" confronts Victorian attitudes toward war, as well as, among other things, its relationship with Darwinian ideas about the survival of the fittest. This section also covers Victorian anti-semitism and attitudes toward slavery. The third section of part 2 is titled "Grounds for Anxiety," and anxiety might well be the single most consistent and important of middle-class attitudes. Gay calls the Victorians "happy pessimists." It seems that the Victorian middle class was anxious about practically everything, including religion, social and economic change, masturbation, the rules of conduct, and success.

Part 3, "The Victorian Mind," deals with the more public side of Victorian life: art, religion and work. The opening section, "Obituaries and Revivals," evaluates the onslaught on Christianity by rationalism, romanticism, and various forms of socialism and communism, which produced a variety of alternative faiths and a pervasive skepticism about religious matters. The forces of modernity, especially the rise of science and technology, but also politics, philosophy, and scholarship, undermined the complacent beliefs of the previous century. Such a mix of competing forces gave rise to spiritualism, theosophy, and a host of otherworldly systems of beliefs. "The Problematic Gospel of Work," as its title suggests, deals with the issue not only of work but also of idleness. If the Victorians idealized employment, they also demonized sloth. Not surprisingly, such concerns lent to an examination of issues of class, domestic division of labor, and the place of the poor in nineteenth century society.

Gay's survey of Victorian culture is wide-ranging, and in the last two sections of the book, "Matters of Taste" and "A Room of One's Own," he explores the place of art and privacy in the forming of middle-class life. Gay points out that the conventional summary of Victorian taste is between the consumers of the conventional and the mutinous moderns who championed the unconventional. The eventual success of modernism has led those who live in the present day to side with the mutinous Victorians, making the previously unconventional conventional. However, as with all things Victorian, Gay's reading presents conflict in this stereotyped view. The lines between the two camps are porous. Rich, middle-class merchants supported avant-garde artists of all stripes, the middle-class public attended the opera, concerts, and plays of a stunning variety, and they read the critics in an attempt at self-education about the arts. The bourgeois founded and stocked museums, supported symphony orchestras, established publishing houses, and in general lent their considerable financial clout to cultural enterprises of all sorts. Gay also notes, in "A Room of One's Own," that privacy is a modern ideology. In this section he discusses architecture, the private letter, diaries, and the notion of individualism.

Gay concludes *Schnitzler's Century* with a coda, quoting Lytton Strachey, that eminent biographer of Victorian society, to the effect that the history of the Victorian age will never be written because so much is known about it. Gay feels that this is dead wrong, and that only now have historians begun to acquire the information to judge the age fairly. Strachey's *Eminent Victorians* (1918) and books like it have stood in the way of a fair assessment. Although he has no desire to idealize the Victorians, Gay believes too much credit has been given to what he calls the "bourgeoisophobes" who, in the later decades of the nineteenth century, carried out an unsparing assault on middle-class culture, the results of which branded it as vicious, vulgar, and frigid or at least unheroic and dull, and that view is still with us. All Gay attempts to do is to balance the record and to offer a corrective view.

Peter Gay's *Schnitzler's Century* is a fascinating work, and for those readers unfamiliar with his larger-scale *The Bourgeois Experience: Victoria to Freud*, this book will also be an enlightening one. The range of his scholarly reading is truly amazing, as it crosses national boundaries and languages, academic disciplines, and cultural frontiers. His style is accessible, which in an age of increasingly sectarian prose is a welcome relief. For any reader interested in knowing something about our immediate ancestors in the Western tradition, *Schnitzler's Century* is a perfect place to begin.

Charles L. P. Silet

Sources for Further Study

Booklist 98 (October 15, 2001): 379.
Library Journal 126 (November 1, 2001): 108.
The New York Times Book Review 106 (November 11, 2001): 17.
Publishers Weekly 248 (September 10, 2001): 69.

SEABISCUIT
An American Legend

Author: Laura Hillenbrand (1967-   )
Publisher: Random House (New York). Illustrated.
    404 pp. $24.95
Type of work: Biography and history
Time: 1933-1940
Locale: Racetracks around the United States, and
    Tijuana, Mexico

≈

A well-documented and engaging story of how three un-
likely men combined to turn an equally unlikely horse into
one of thoroughbred racing's greatest champions and na-
tional heroes

≈

Principal personages:

SEABISCUIT (1933-1947), a thoroughbred race horse
CHARLES S. HOWARD (1877-1950), a pioneer automobile dealer and
    race-horse owner
JOHNNY "RED" POLLARD (1909-1981), a failed prizefighter and failing
    jockey
TOM SMITH (1879-1957), old-time cowboy and later a horse trainer

To those not old enough to remember the Great Depression firsthand, "Seabiscuit" is likely just the name of yet another old-time race horse. He was not just another great horse, though. He was an anomaly, trained by another anomaly, and ridden by yet a third anomaly. It was only the combination of these people and this horse that created this legendary racing career. Racing writer Laura Hillenbrand tells the tale of Seabiscuit and the unusual people around him, but along the way she also gives readers a window into the harsh world of racing in the 1930's and the national popularity of the sport's heroes.

In today's multimedia era, it can be hard to imagine daily life without live coverage of baseball, football, basketball, hockey, soccer, racing, and numerous other sports. When Seabiscuit was born, newsreels in the movie theaters were the only way most people would ever get to see their heroes. The only medium for live coverage was radio, and it was not until the 1930's that radios became something most people could afford to own. When Seabiscuit began racing in 1935, two-thirds of U.S. homes were newly equipped with radios. The excited narration of horse racing was a natural attraction, and people flocked to it. In 1938, some forty million people listened to the call as Seabiscuit and War Admiral raced one-on-one at the racetrack in Pimlico, Maryland. Even President Franklin D. Roosevelt kept a room-

Laura Hillenbrand has been writing about thoroughbred horse racing since 1988. She has been a contributing editor to Equus *magazine since 1989 and has also appeared in* Talk *magazine,* The Blood-Horse, Thoroughbred Times, The Backstretch, Turf and Sport Digest, *and other publications. Her* American Heritage *article on Seabiscuit won the Eclipse Award, the highest award in thoroughbred journalism.*

ful of advisers waiting while he listened to the race.

Bicycle racer and mechanic Charles Howard, later to become Seabiscuit's owner, was twenty-four when he traveled from New York to California, arriving with twenty-one cents in his pocket. The horseless carriage was also a newcomer in 1903 San Francisco, without much success. Nevertheless, Howard saw opportunity and figured out how to repair the primitive cars. Soon he was driving in auto races. Audaciously, he took a train back to Detroit and talked Will Durant, chief of Buick Automobiles, into giving him the sales franchise for his new home town. When the 1906 earthquake hit San Francisco, Howard used his Buicks as rescue vehicles, proving their worth and paving his way toward sole distributorship of all General Motors cars throughout the western United States. The new millionaire bought a seventeen-thousand-acre ranch in Northern California.

Gambling had been banned in the United States during Prohibition, but California made race betting legal again in 1933. Howard, Bing Crosby, and others financed construction of the three-million-dollar Santa Anita Park outside Los Angeles. At a time when $50,000 was a rare purse for a race anywhere in the United States, the new Santa Anita Handicap offered more than $100,000. Howard wanted to win it. By 1935, he had bought a stable of modestly talented horses.

Tom Smith came from the prairies. The Indians called him "the lone plainsman," and white men called him Silent Tom. "In the company of men," Hillenbrand writes, "Smith was clipped and bristling. With horses, he was gracefully at ease." Although Smith had little to say to men, he listened carefully to horses. Sometimes he would just squat quietly for hours, watching a horse, drawing understanding out of the smallest of motions. "It's easy to talk to a horse if you understand its language," he once said. "Horses stay the same from the day they are born until the day they die. . . . They are only changed by the way people treat them."

As the Old West retreated, it left Smith behind. He gravitated to horse racing, first as a farrier, then as a trainer. When one employer retired, he gave Smith a lame, well-traveled horse. Smith worked with the horse for a while, then brought him back to the track, sound and fit. He kept winning higher and higher classes of races. One day in 1934, a friend of Charles Howard recognized in this man, living in a Tijuana stable, a brilliant horseman being wasted. Howard did too, and hired Smith to be his trainer. Smith devised new and different ways to teach his horses how to break from the gate. Howard's stable became the runaway leader in wins.

Seabiscuit first raced in January, 1935, finishing fourth at seventeen-to-one odds. That year, Seabiscuit started an amazing thirty-five times. His trainer, the legendary Sunny Jim Fitzsimmons, had seen what he was capable of. However, the colt was "dead lazy," so they raced him every five days on average, triple the usual workload. He ran at eleven different tracks that season, traveling some 6,000 miles. His first win was in his seventeenth race, and he had only four more wins that year. His owners had more promising horses to spend Fitzsimmons' time on, so they tried the whole time to sell Seabiscuit, without success.

In June, 1936, Howard had sent Smith to the East to look for a bargain horse with potential. In Boston, Smith sized up a weedy three-year-old bay. "His stunted build reflected none of the beauty and breadth of his forebears," says Hillenbrand. "The colt's body, built low to the ground, had all the properties of a cinder block." He had "baseball glove" knees that did not quite straighten all the way, and he ran with an "eggbeater gait, making a spastic sideways flailing motion with his left foreleg as he swung it forward, as if he were swatting at flies." Nonetheless, he triggered Smith's horse sense.

In Saratoga Springs, New York, that August, Howard called Smith to come and take a look at the homely colt that had caught his eye. Smith recognized Seabiscuit immediately. Howard bought the animal for a mere eight thousand dollars. Before retiring to stud in 1940, he had earned $437,740.

The horse's name was a synonym for that of his sire, Hard Tack, who was a son of the famous Man o' War. Although both of those were famously obstreperous, Seabiscuit was just the opposite. He was about as relaxed as they came. Most horses tend to catch little spurts of sleep throughout the day and night and rarely sleep long on the ground, but Seabiscuit would keel over and sleep for hours.

Johnny "Red" Pollard, who had tried and failed to emulate his prizefighting brother, was sixteen when he left his Edmonton, Canada, family to become a jockey. After a couple of years, he began to look like he was going to make it. In the early 1930's, in a race he only rode as a favor for a friend, a stray rock flew up from another horse's hoof and struck Pollard's head, instantly blinding his right eye. If he told anyone, he would probably never get another ride, so he kept his blindness a secret. Remarkably, he generally managed to cope with the loss of depth perception. His career started going downhill soon after that, however. In August, 1936, he straggled into Detroit, looking for a ride. Introduced to Tom Smith and then to Seabiscuit, he found friends.

Seabiscuit was two hundred pounds underweight, refused to eat, and would not behave. Smith figured out how to stop his rebelliousness. Smith told a beleaguered exercise rider to give him his head. When the horse figured out he was not going to be fought anymore, he let himself be guided. Then Pollard climbed aboard Seabiscuit for the first time, came back, and told Smith to put the whip away with this horse.

The team of Smith, Pollard, and Seabiscuit went about accumulating one of the best racing records ever. Most of this was on the West Coast, while on the East Coast, a high-strung cousin named War Admiral was making an equally impressive name for himself. The two thoroughbreds were polar opposites. Where Seabiscuit was as genial as a big dog, War Admiral was a wired hellion, requiring walk-up starts. Howard tried numerous ways to arrange a two-horse race between the two, and eventually got a match arranged for Belmont Park, New York, on Memorial Day, 1938. Six days before, with thirty thousand dollars spent to promote the race and public anticipation at a fever pitch, Seabiscuit developed a sore knee, which forced Howard to cancel the race.

Months later, against all odds, another match-up was arranged for Pimlico, in Maryland, November 1. On race day, Pimlico was stuffed with forty thousand people, two and one-half times capacity. Forty million more, including President Roosevelt, were glued to their radios. It was a tense and exciting race between two well-matched opponents, but at the finish line, it was Seabiscuit who won by lengths.

Hillenbrand tells the story in a comfortable style that makes the book hard to put down. She weaves the lives of all the involved people and horses into a tapestry of adventure, conveying the emotions along with the factual series of events. Along the way, she describes the horrible conditions of jockey's lives in that period, including the draconian means they used to stay under their allowed weights and the carelessness with which many horse owners treated them when they got hurt. She avoids lacing her narrative with jargon—which abounds in the racing world—but explains those terms that are necessary to the telling, such as "bug boys" and "imposts."

At the end of the book are seven pages of acknowledgments and thirty-five pages of endnotes that document the interviews and other research that went into the production of this book.

In April, 2001, Hillenbrand told a radio interviewer that she felt some camaraderie with the horse who did not fit the usual mold.

> I have chronic fatigue syndrome and for me that is manifested in quite severe exhaustion and chronic vertigo, which ironically makes reading and writing very difficult. I put myself through a lot of punishment to do it, because the more I read and write the worse my vertigo is, and there are few symptoms in the world that are worse than chronic severe dizziness. But on the other hand, this is the kind of story that you want to escape into when you're in a physical condition like mine. It was a wonderful thing to wake up in the morning and be able to step out of this broken body of mine and into this world, into 1938 and into the life of these vigorous individuals.

She said that as she researched the book, she learned something from Seabiscuit.

> The main theme that runs through this story and through each of these very different lives that I'm talking about is overwhelming hardship, and the struggle of will to overcome it. And this is a main theme in my life because of my health. They were a daily lesson to me in how to get up with dignity and go on with your life when devastating things happen to you. And I look at all of them as models for my own life.

A Web site, http://www.seabiscuitonline.com/book.htm, contains all the photographs from the book, along with review comments, and information about the author.

J. Edmund Rush

Sources for Further Study

Business Week, March 26, 2001, p. 27.
The Economist 356 (February 24, 2001): 87.
The New York Times Book Review 106 (March 11, 2001): 12.
Sports Illustrated, May 14, 2001, p. 30.

THE SEVEN AGES

Author: Louise Glück (1943-   )
Publisher: Ecco Press/HarperCollins (New York). 68 pp.
    $23.00
Type of work: Poetry

❧

A powerful poetry collection with an emphasis on the mythic and the metaphysical

❧

Louise Glück is one of the best-known American poets writing today; her work has received numerous awards, and she has also received several honorary degrees, has been selected as judge for numerous national and international contests, and is a member of the American Academy of Arts and Letters and PEN. She is an essayist as well as a poet and has written a provocative series of essays on the nature of poetry, *Proofs and Theories: Essays on Poetry* (1994).

A native New Yorker, Glück was educated at Columbia University and Sarah Lawrence College and has held a number of prestigious teaching posts at Williams College, the University of California at Berkeley, Harvard, Brandeis, and elsewhere. She has been an important voice in American poetry since her first book, *Firstborn*, was published in 1968. Her style is a distinctive mingling of the personal and the mythic, presented in free verse or experimental patterns. Her spare language and careful attention to sound, combined with her falling rhythms, provide a sense of closure and give weight to her words.

Glück's poetry resists easy analysis but rewards careful reading, and her latest book, *The Seven Ages*, is no exception. A poet who has resisted the current vogue of metrically exact formalism as well as the postmodern flatness of effect and difficult wordplay, Glück is not classifiable—her work is not like anyone else's, not even enough for critics to assign her tentatively to a shelf. Her work is based on her life, but her newer work is not confessional or even, in a sense, personal. Rather, it is myth-haunted and even abstract. Her style is sparse, though not quite minimalist; rather, its distant feminine voice is archaic and oracular. As her work has developed over the decades, her voice has become more disembodied and impersonal. Her first poems (in *Firstborn*) were criticized by some for being confessional in the manner of Sylvia Plath and Anne Sexton, but even these had a reserve that has become more and more distinct. Glück's poetry from the onset makes a claim for the visionary as an essential element of poetic statement, and therefore, the personal tends to dissolve into the mythic. No one would be likely to suggest that the poems of *The Seven Ages* are confessional; they hide as they reveal.

The Seven Ages, Glück's eleventh book of poems, is filled with summer poems, but they are not light reading. Earlier books were more self-consciously mythic, taking subjects and figures from Greek mythology and from the Bible and grafting elements of contemporary life onto them. These poems use the old stories, particularly the family myth, more indirectly. They have an intense stillness, are deep rather than broad, and take the reader on a spiritual search at the height of summer. Although they focus on women at various ages, they give the perspective of a woman of fifty looking at her life from middle age, remembering earlier experiences and interpreting them in the light of what she now knows. They are an analysis of her history and a coming to terms with what inevitably follows. In many ways they may remind the reader of Wallace Stevens's work, not only for their reimagining of the seasonal imagery but also for the intensity of their concentration and for their tone that combines celebration and elegy.

Louise Glück's poetry has received top awards, including a Pulitzer Prize, the National Book Critics Circle Award, the Melville Cane Award, the William Carlos Williams award, a Guggenheim Fellowship, and three grants and fellowships from the National Endowment for the Arts.

The seasons have always been a major commanding presence in Glück's work, as have times of day; her collection *The Wild Iris*, which won the Pulitzer prize, uses morning and evening as its organizing principle but is filled with seasonal imagery. *The Seven Ages* is inhabited by two main figures, the speaker and her sister, whom she watches grow up. The summer of the book has all the suggestions of the season, ripening, progress toward decay, idleness, sensuousness, heat, stillness, and a sense of summer vision. The center of summer, fully aware of itself, prepares for the coming, less hospitable seasons. "The Sensual World" begins

> I call to you across a monstrous river or chasm
> to caution you, to prepare you.
>
> Earth will seduce you, slowly, imperceptibly,
> subtly, not to say with connivance.
>
> I was not prepared: I stood in my grandmother's kitchen,
> holding out my glass. Stewed plums, stewed apricots—
>
> the juice poured off into the glass of ice.
> And the water added, patiently, in small increments,
>
> the various cousins discriminating, tasting
> with each addition—
>
> aroma of summer fruit, intensity of concentration:
> the colored liquid turning gradually lighter, more radiant,
>
> more light passing through it.
> Delight, then solace. . . .

The speaker warns an unnamed addressee of the illusion of the sensual world, its addictive power and its ultimate abandonment. The world, the lover, nourishes and feeds on the beloved, and ultimately ". . . it will feed you, it will ravish you/ it will not keep you alive." The indeterminate "you" that dominates some of these poems adds authority—you the reader, you the figure in the speaker's life, you who are all of us.

> I caution you as I was never cautioned:
>
> you will never let go, you will never be satiated.
> You will be damaged and scarred, you will continue to hunger.

The child of the poem, tasting the distilled essence of summer, grows to the older woman who remembers it, without losing the desire for the physical world. This is a secular sacrament, the tasting of the fruit, and the longing it engenders is never to be surpassed or lost, despite the limits life imposes. In fact, these poems are filled with secular sacraments, ritual ways of marking a harmony or unity with the physical world. Often these attempts to bridge the abyss between body and soul show only the impenetrability of that boundary and the intensity of the longing to cross it. They also show the earth as the grounding of the sacred: Whatever there is of deity must be read and understood through the earth.

The Seven Ages is filled with fruit—peach, quince, apricot, plum—suggesting the delights of the senses and their inevitable decline. Flowers fulfill a similar function, and Glück is known for her lush floral imagery; the garden image is predominant in many of her most frequently anthologized poems. (Characteristically, she uses well-known fruit but lesser-known plants and flowers with many-syllabled, redolent names: lisanthus, mertensia, chionodoxa, penstemon.) The flowers take such life in the poems that the reader wants to research them. Again, the work of Wallace Stevens comes to mind, particularly in the poems of *Harmonium* (1923) in which the physical world is both mourned and celebrated, and in which the fruit and flowers are evoked as a kind of compensation for death.

Glück's metaphysics are always read through the physical world, in this book and others, but God ghosts the poems. The situations in the narratives are open-endedly allegorical, so that their meanings are arguable but nevertheless suggestive of immanence. The language often suggests the sacred, though it is applied to the natural. "Quince Tree" begins

> We had, in the end, only the weather for a subject.
> Luckily, we lived in a world with seasons—
> we felt, still, access to variety:
> darkness, euphoria, various kinds of waiting.

The speaker ponders the separation of the past, "lost to us as referent,/ lost as image, as narrative." She asks what the past was, what it contained, then continues

> In the end, we didn't need to ask. Because
> we felt the past; it was, somehow,
> in these things, the front lawn and the back lawn,

suffusing them, giving the little quince tree
a weight and meaning almost beyond enduring.

Utterly lost and yet strangely alive, the whole of our human existence—

The past revitalizing the presence, and the invisible, unnameable force by which this occurs, are celebrated: "In its grandeur and splendor, the world/ was finally present." It is the constant awareness of death that brings the world's beauty close.

This collection more than any of Glück's others seems to be about desire, about longing. The desire is physical and metaphysical; the speaker looks to the natural world for truths that will be satisfying. If she never finds true closure, if she only finds temporary satisfactions that contain in them the stimulus for deeper longings, these lesser epiphanies are persuasive and point toward greater ones. In "Screened Porch" the speaker looks to the natural world for enlightenment, and in a sense she finds it:

> We sat on our terraces, our screened porches,
> as though we expected to gather, even now,
> fresh information or sympathy. The stars
> glittered a bit above the landscape, the hills
> suffused still with a faint retroactive light.
> Darkness. Luminous earth. We stared out, starved for knowledge,
> and we felt, in its place, a substitute:
> indifference that appeared benign.

The watchers merely projected "onto the glowing hills/ qualities we needed" but the results were the same as if the gift had come from God:

> And our intense need was absorbed by the night
> and returned as sustenance.

Glück's work does not answer the question of where longing and its satisfaction ultimately come from, but simply describes this very human desire, expressed as experienced by a middle-aged woman, and shows her attempts to find her world sufficient. However, the metaphysical is present, evasive but luminous, throughout the poem. Indeed the last dreamlike, open poem suggests its mystery. "Fable" is the shortest poem in the book, and it does not explain itself.

> Then I looked down and saw
> the world I was entering, that would be my home.
> And I turned to my companion, and I said *Where are we?*
> And he replied *Nirvana.*
> And I said again *But the light will give us no peace.*

Nirvana is the other world, the opposite of the sensual one—but its offerings are obscure and perhaps frightening. This book is full of opposites which the poet longs to reconcile: mind and body, summer and winter, youth and age, life and death. Since the opposites can never be reconciled, the poet seems to be looking for some larger container in which they may coexist. This search sets fire to the poet's life and gives a metaphysical edge to poems steeped in the natural world.

Glück's poetry is unusual in contemporary work for her consistent voice, visionary, mythic, and personal at once, and for the layers which allow even the casual reader a glimpse of her world, but repay rereading and study. She presents a feminine world, yet much of its content is relevant to men also—the femininity is in the angle of her vision, the kinds of nature images that convey her experience. She uses the myths partly as Jungian archetypes and partly as an idiosyncratic binary symbol system that evokes a wide spectrum of responses. The authority of the clear, distinctive voice commands attention as it speaks for the importance of the life journey it chronicles as well as for the significance of poetry itself as guide and balm.

Janet McCann

Sources for Further Study

The American Poetry Review 30 (January/February, 2001): 28.
The Christian Science Monitor, April 26, 2001, p. 17.
The New York Times Book Review 106 (May 13 2001): 24.

SHEBA
Through the Desert in Search of the Legendary Queen

Author: Nicholas Clapp (1936-   )
Publisher: Houghton Mifflin (Boston). Illustrated.
   372 pp. $26.00
Type of work: Travel and history
Time: Ancient times
Locale: Arabia, Ethiopia, Israel, and Syria

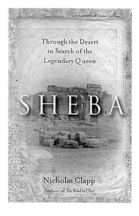

~

An amateur archaeologist tells the story of the Queen of Sheba and looks for material remains datable to her time and place

~

Principal personages:
>   QUEEN OF SHEBA (also known as Bilqis or Balkis in Arabic and Malkath in Hebrew), who traveled from her kingdom to visit King Solomon and brought him gold
>   SOLOMON, son of David, ancient king of a united Israel and traditional builder of the first Jewish Temple in Jerusalem

Nicholas Clapp spent more than twenty years in his search for the Queen of Sheba. His topic crosses at least four continents and spans three millennia. *Sheba* begins with Clapp's personal encounter with the Queen of Sheba legend in the very city where she met King Solomon. While in Jerusalem in 1982 to film ancient sites for a documentary, Clapp visited the chapel of the Ethiopian Copts in the Church of the Holy Sepulchre. There he discovered a modern painting of the queen's arrival before Solomon. The regal dignity of the queen in this painting led Clapp on an adventurous search for the woman behind this image. This journey took him to the stacks of the New York Public Library, a scholarly seminar in Los Angeles, a winery in Dijon, France, a psychiatric ward in Jerusalem, a nearly shipwrecked dhow en route from Djibouti to Yemen, and into the hands of a potential Yemeni kidnapper. Along the way there were hints of his queen in unusual and unexpected places, such as the lyrics of a 1920 Tin Pan Ally song about a "queen-o' Pal-es-teen-na," in the title of a paperback novel read by an elderly Frenchwoman, and in the intense eyes of an Ethiopian woman on a train from Addis Ababa to Djibouti.

In *Sheba*, Clapp offers more than an adventurous and personal travelogue. He surveys scholarly and archaeological materials in a careful and thoughtful manner and offers the reader photographs of some less-known but historically significant places in Arabia and in Africa. Clapp begins his quest with the brief but memorable biblical tale told in I Kings 10:1-13, where the queen came laden with gold and gems to test the fabled wisdom of the Israelite king, and Solomon in turn gave the queen all she de-

An award-winning producer of documentary films, lecturer, and author, Nicholas Clapp also pursued his interest in archaeology in The Road to Ubar: Finding the Atlantis of the Sands *(1998).*

sired before she returned home. Sheba is also mentioned occasionally in other books of the Old Testament, but her appearance in the Koran takes on a stronger religious and moral tone, as the queen agrees to abandon polytheism and to submit herself to Solomon's god. Clapp, however, cautiously acknowledges the frustrating attempts of biblical scholars and ancient historians to find any historical basis for the story.

The relationship between the Jewish king and his royal visitor becomes even more complicated if Solomon and Sheba are understood to be the lovers in the biblical Song of Songs (also called the Song of Solomon). In support of this reading, Clapp cites authorities such as St. Thomas Aquinas, who died with references to this biblical book on his lips, but Clapp nevertheless admits that the Song of Songs offers little in the way of solid clues about the historical queen.

Unfortunately, the queen's existence is corroborated by no independent ancient documents. Old Testament references are even uncertain about the location of Sheba's eponymous kingdom, which could have been in Arabia, Ethiopia, or somewhere else. Clapp's journey reflects many of these possibilities, as he considers whether the queen was actually the human equivalent of the Near Eastern goddess Astarte, a powerful ruler of a tribe in northern Arabia, the mother of the first emperor of Ethiopia, or (the theory Clapp clearly prefers) a queen of Saba in southern Yemen.

Solomon is in an equally uncertain historical position. Traditionalists accept the Biblical texts as essentially historical and date Solomon's reign to the tenth century B.C.E. Other scholars, sometimes known as Minimalists, suggest that many aspects of Solomon's life are more myth than fact. They question the historicity of his birth, under a cloud of adultery and murder, to King David and Bathsheba, the claim that he united the twelve tribes of Israel into a single nation and, especially, descriptions of his magnificent temple in Jerusalem. Noting that solid archaeological evidence or contemporary written references have yet to be discovered for either the king or any of his buildings in Jerusalem, the Minimalists call into question the very existence of Solomon and his temple.

Clapp is not only interested in the historical queen but also in the legends which have grown around her throughout the centuries. From the Koran, Clapp follows the transformations of Sheba in Arab legend, especially as told by Mohammed ibn 'Abd Allah Kisa'i in his eleventh century *Qisas al-Anabiya'* (*Tales of the Prophets of Al-Kisa'i*, 1978). Here the queen, named Bilqis, kills a tyrannical king and becomes ruler of Sheba. Solomon learns of the queen's success from a talking bird and invites her to Jerusalem, where Solomon steals her magnificent throne and through trickery uncovers the queen's hairy legs and ass's foot. They then produce a son named Rehoboam.

In Ethiopian legends, the queen of Sheba returns home bearing Solomon's son, Menelik, the first emperor of Ethiopia. In their fourteenth century national epic, the *Kebra Nagast* (the glory of kings; *Magda, Queen of Sheba*, 1907), Ethiopians state that Menelik even stole the Ark of the Covenant from his father's temple and brought it to his capital of Aksum. According to this legend, Menelik's dynasty continued to rule Ethiopia until the death of Haile Selassie in 1975.

Sheba's tradition found its way into Europe, where a goose- (rather than ass-) footed queen was carved on the cathedral in Dijon, France. In the *Legenda Aurea* (*The Golden Legend*, 1483), a thirteenth century religious discourse by Jacobus de Voragine, the Queen of Sheba played a significant role in the history of human salvation. On her way to visit Solomon, the queen had a vision that the tree trunk used to cross over a pond would someday become the cross on which the savior of humankind would hang. When Sheba waded through the pond rather than desecrate the tree by walking upon it, her web foot became human. The queen was thus identified as the first human to acknowledge Jesus' role as redeemer of the sin of Adam, over whose grave this same tree was said to have grown.

Clapp traces the legend into more recent secular literature, music, and image. The queen receives attention in Giovanni Boccaccio's *De Mulieribus claris* (c. 1361-1375; *Concerning Famous Women*, 1943), Gustave Flaubert's *La Tentation de Saint Antoine* (1874; *The Temptation of Saint Anthony*, 1895), and Rudyard Kipling's poetry. Solomon's paramour is also the subject of musical compositions such as George Frideric Handel's oratorio *Solomon* (1749) and Karl Goldmark's *Die Königin von Saba* (pr. 1875), very popular in its day. Less familiar appearances of the queen are found in *The Queen of Sheba*, a popular 1877 novel by Thomas B. Aldrich, and in Charles Gounod's opera *La Reine de Saba* (pr. 1862). Clapp also describes how the queen's legend has been used in popular culture, such as American circus shows, a California silver mine, and a 1921 film production starring Betty Blythe. His black-and-white plates include photographs of Blythe as Sheba, a 1590 Persian miniature of the queen, an Ethiopian animal-skin painting, an illumination from a medieval German manuscript, a stained-glass window from Canterbury Cathedral, and Piero della Francesca's 1452 fresco in Arezzo, Italy.

Finding no evidence of Solomon or Sheba in Jerusalem, Clapp traveled to the traditionally Solomonic six-chambered gates at Gezer and at Megiddo, neither of which can be dated with any certainty earlier than a century later than Solomon. Clapp therefore turned his attention from the queen's encounter with Solomon to the queen's route back to her mysterious home. His first stop was the ancient kingdom of Midian in the Negev desert, with its tradition of the dynastic queens Zabibi and Samsi, mentioned by the Assyrians in the eighth century B.C.E. While these rulers lived too late to be the fabled queen of Sheba, Clapp admits the possibility his queen was their ancestor.

Clapp sought another suspect for the queen of Sheba at the archaeological site of Palmyra in Syria, where the caliph 'Abd al-Malik (646/647-705 C.E.) is said to have built a magnificent tomb for the queen. The most likely location for this tomb was a mosque built into an ancient temple of the god Bel. Here Clapp found the fragment of a relief depicting a winged female, identifiable perhaps as either the Greek deity Nike (Victory) or the fertility goddess Astarte, whom Solomon is said (in I Kings 11:5) to have worshiped. Some scholars suggest that the queen of Sheba is therefore the embodiment of the goddess, that the story of Solomon and Sheba is actually intended as an endorsement of Solomon's rule by a powerful neighboring deity.

The next stop on Clapp's itinerary was the incense road through southern Arabia in present-day Yemen. Here he visited a series of archaeological remains, including a palace at Shabwa, tombs in Qataban, and a large tell at Hajar bin Humeid. Especially impressive was the walled city of Ma'rib in the ancient kingdom of Saba, with its sophisticated dam and irrigation systems, begun c. 1500 B.C.E., and a Temple of the Moon also known as the Mahram Bilqis ("the sacred precinct of Bilqis," that is, of Sheba). This site yielded a large number of inscriptions recorded and deciphered by Albert Jamme (*Sabaean Inscriptions from Mahram Bilqis*, 1962). From these inscriptions, Jamme and other scholars worked out a list of rulers of Saba, one of whom, Karibil Watar I, seems to be the "Karibilu" mentioned in Assyrian texts datable to 685 B.C.E. Coordinating Karibil's reign with the list of Sabean rulers, scholars have pushed back the beginning of Sabean civilization to the thirteenth century B.C.E. The resulting chronology of Sabean rulers from c. 1200 B.C.E. to 577 C.E. allows for the possibility that a Sabean queen ruled in the time of Solomon. While no queens actually appear in the list, an unnamed widowed queen may have served as regent for her son. Any further evidence for such a queen at Saba lies in the essentially unexcavated remains of the Mahram Bilqis.

From Ma'rib, Clapp hoped to travel to Sirwah, traditionally Saba's early capital. Unfortunately, in 1997 the site was the center of a Yemeni civil war and Clapp had to postpone his visit for safety reasons and to travel instead to Ethiopia. Here Clapp's attention was drawn to a number of ancient churches and temples in and around the ancient and holy city of Aksum, where Menelik, the son of Solomon and the queen of Sheba, is said to have founded his long-lasting dynasty. Noting striking similarities in architecture, sculpture, and written scripts between Ethiopia and its neighbor Saba across the Red Sea, Clapp wondered whether the tenth century B.C.E. rulers of Saba may have had control over this portion of Ethiopia. If so, then traditions associating the queen of Sheba with both southern Arabia and Ethiopia may reflect historical reality.

From Ethiopia, Clapp tried once more to visit Sirwah. He traveled on the now-defunct Franco-Ethiopian railroad from Addis Ababa to Djibouti and from there by dhow to Mokha, Yemen. This time Clapp was able to reach the impressive site of Sirwah, on a mesa called al-Kharibeh ("Place of Ruins"). Traditionally the burial site for the Queen of Sheba's treasure, Sirwah's complex temple of 'Ilumqah has yet to be excavated. Clapp hopes that the site may also yield a royal archive and even a throne belonging to the Queen of Sheba.

Clapp concludes his quest with a hypothetical history of ancient Saba from the migrations from the Fertile Crescent c. 6000 B.C.E., to the introduction of artificial irrigation at Ma' rib c. 3200, the development of a written language c. 1450, and the domestication of the camel c. 1200. Saba soon became the center of the incense and spice trade. It is in this context, Clapp suggests, that a Sabean queen may have traveled north to work out long-range trade agreements with Israel and her neighbors. Despite the biblical version of the encounter, Clapp argues that the Sabean queen was more powerful than her Israelite host and that their relationship was based less on sex and religion than on economics and trade.

A fuller historical picture of the Queen of Sheba must await further archaeological work, especially in southern Arabia. Until then Clapp's quest is as close as one gets to that illusive and enigmatic queen.

Thomas J. Sienkewicz

Sources for Further Study

Booklist 97 (April 15, 2001): 1529.
Library Journal 126 (May 15, 2001): 140.
Publishers Weekly 248 (April 2, 2001): 53.

THE SITUATION AND THE STORY
The Art of Personal Narrative

Author: Vivian Gornick (1935-   )
Publisher: Farrar, Straus and Giroux (New York).
  165 pp. $21.00
Type of work: Memoirs, literary criticism, and literary
  theory
Time: The nineteenth and twentieth centuries
Locale: Europe, North America, and Africa

≈

*Finding a true voice by fashioning a credible persona is
essential in locating the story, the argument at the core of
any successful memoir, because it is the instrument of illumination*

≈

This engrossing little book is part memoir, part literary analysis, and part instruc-
tional text. In a clear and evocative style, Vivian Gornick reveals the secret of successfully turning the situation, her term for the raw material of a memoir or an essay,
into the "story," the argument of a narrative that is focused by a coherent, created persona who has the authority to make the argument. Such a persona is, she writes, vital;
it is the "instrument of . . . illumination." No persona, no story. To achieve it, the
writer must discover not only the occasion of one's speaking but exactly who is
speaking, that is, the "who" that is either discovered or created by the writer. With that
discovery or creation, the writer may be reasonably assured of reaching and holding
the audience without boredom and confusion.

Gornick's strategy is to divide personal narrative into two different sets of materials that, although similar in requiring a foregrounded first-person narrator (a "truth
speaker") are different in their perspectives and their purposes. First she examines the
personal essay, a form written by writers who believe they "know who they are *at the
moment of writing*." Failure to be clear about this intersection of purpose and personal
voice leads to confusion and failure. As an example, Gornick analyzes the false and
limited voice of D. H. Lawrence's essay "Do Women Change?" noting that while it
is "[o]stensibly a meditation on the cyclical recurrence throughout history of the
modern, the piece in actuality is a denunciation of 1920's feminists." Gornick argues
that it fails because Lawrence "does not know what he is about," and that he lacks the
sort of sympathy with his subject that renders his novels powerful and true.

In contrast, she offers William Hazlitt who, while he certainly could have written a
similar denunciation of feminists, always "owns his anger" and lets one see the fear
behind the anger. That self-knowledge and that courage make all the difference. The
struggle to make sense of his feelings is always apparent in Hazlitt, Gornick as-

serts, and the struggle makes his subject vital. To achieve this quality, the writer must have and demonstrate sympathy for the subject, a "level of empathic understanding that endows the subject with dimension," by implicating the writer with it in an effort to clarify it. Gornick's acuity of analysis and clarity of writing make her discussion of personal essays by Harry Crews, Joan Didion, and Edward Hoagland not only delightful to read but truly clarifying of the distinction

Vivian Gornick was born and raised in the West Farms section of the Bronx in a working-class neighborhood. Teaching writing for fifteen years in M.F.A. programs provided the background for this book.

she seeks to make not only between personal essay and memoir but of the qualities of voice and discernment that make one essay ring true while another one seems false.

Her chapter on the personal essay identifies other important qualities of this genre of personal narrative that distinguish it from the memoir. For instance, she argues that the personal narrative explores a subject other than the writer's self. That is, the subject is outside the writer: the nature of marriage, for instance, rather than a narrative of the writer's own marriage. Essays by Lynn Darling and Natalia Ginzburg reveal under Gornick's analysis just how this intersection of purpose and perspective works. Each writer's strategies and styles are radically different, yet both are intent upon discovering the mysterious in the familiar of their marriages while also discovering that they are complicitous in the widening rift within their marriages. Each uses her personal experience to explain and reveal the nature of modern marriage rather than to tell the story of her own marriage. Gornick also argues that readers have an obligation to accumulate a wide experience and knowledge of other writers' personal essays because doing so will make the reading experience much richer than reading in isolation. In much the same way that one's experience of novels and poems is made richer with the echoes and images of other novels and poems in one's mind, so too with the personal essay.

Gornick's third chapter takes account of the increasing popularity of the memoir as the form to which people turn when they think they have a story that needs telling. The tale taken directly from life rather than invented out of bits and pieces of experience and fashioned by the imagination has overtaken the novel because, she argues, modernism has stripped us of the pleasures of narrative: Novels "have been all voice: a voice speaking to us from inside its own emotional space, anchored neither in plot nor in circumstance," and readers are tired of it. They long for authenticity in the storytelling experience and find increasingly that memoir will "tell a tale rich in context, alive to situation, shot through with event and perspective." Furthermore, "the age is characterized by the need to testify" to our role in the great issues of civil rights and emancipation of all sorts. A life no matter how "ordinary" or "terrible" may best "signify" if presented in a "work of sustained narrative prose controlled by an idea of the self under obligation to lift from the raw material of life a tale that will shape experience, transform event, deliver wisdom." This definition of memoir argues that its central quality derives from the writer's attempting to make sense of his or her experience, to engage "what happened" in writing that is powerful when it is "artful," shaped always by a growing clarification of the answer to the question, "Who am I?" and made significant by a narrative voice that is credible, believable, and always reliable.

Gornick marshals a series of memoirs in sets of two or three, each member of the set having in common a theme, a circumstance, a situation. Her analysis of each of these works is useful because it is penetrating and insightful, helpful to reader and writer alike for its clarity and insights into the methods, processes, and substance of memoirs. In making her analysis, Gornick provides a personal but useful survey of memoirists, mostly of the nineteenth and twentieth centuries, whose works, in her judgment, have the most to teach about writing memoir. Her survey of the long history of the nonfiction persona reveals how adaptable it has been to cultural change and how it has continued to reinvent itself. Writers seem in most instances to achieve this sense of authorial reliability, even if the cultural idea of the emergent self is steadily changing, through a flash of insight that illuminates their struggle to understand and clarify a formative experience and focus their efforts to get to the bottom of it. This pursuit, Gornick says, provides the writer's organizing principle, and becomes the "story," the "argument" of the memoir.

Even in the work of two of "the most neurotic narrators in the annals of memoir writing," Oscar Wilde and Thomas De Quincey, the reader may easily trace their sufferings "to a will permanently divided against itself." The single-mindedness of each writer's persona lets the reader see what the author cannot and yet speaks truth, indirectly perhaps but truth nevertheless. Both writers have a kind of confiding style that invites the reader. Gornick argues that Wilde's *De Profundis* (1905) is "remarkable for the speed and efficiency with which [he] states the case and establishes a believable atmosphere of introspection," confessing his weaknesses and his struggles and his insights. Then he repeats his material three times, in writing that always dazzles even as its structure falls apart—"rightly so," says Gornick, because we are in the presence of a man "in a trance of self-analysis" who will never act on his insights. His writing reveals himself to be a writer totally enslaved.

De Quincey's speaking voice is even more confiding than Wilde's as he describes and explains his lifelong addiction to opium. In his account, he is totally alone. No other human being is brought to life—no family, no friends, no characters of any sort. He is clear on the consequences of his addiction, its destructiveness to any semblance of a normal life, the physical and mental exhaustion of it, the totality of the life that he dedicated to it. He could make no connection with any other human being, no human soul, and thus was solitary even for another thirty years after he finished *Confessions of an English Opium Eater* (1821).

In the twentieth century, a number of memoirs were written that likewise explored the theme of the true nature of loneliness. Loren Eiseley was for forty years an anthropologist studying bones, animals, and oceans. As a writer, Gornick points out, Eiseley intended that his memoir, *All the Strange Hours*, completed in 1977 shortly before his death, present himself as he had presented any other "specimen" in his long professional life. The son of a deaf mother and a ruined father, Eiseley left home at nineteen and wandered the roads with other desperate men and women cast adrift by the Great

Depression. He returned to school in his late twenties and became an anthropologist and an excellent author of essays and poetry in which he "excavated his life" as he excavated his specimens. His memoir is, Gornick asserts, "some of the best Depression writing you will ever read;" in it he evokes "a kind of starved, murderous haze that keeps drifting up from the middle of the socialized world." Like De Quincey in his lifelong isolation but unlike him in his answer to it, he got up every morning, went to his desk, and worked. *All the Strange Hours*, reveals a preoccupation with human isolation that seems, according to Gornick, to have grown steadily over the past hundred years. The problem for the narrator of such a memoir is how to present that isolation.

Gornick concludes by analyzing three memoirs of the last fifty years that present practical solutions to the problem of human isolation. Beryl Markham's *West with the Night* (1942), Marguerite Duras's *L'Amant* (1984; *The Lover* 1985), and W. G. Sebald's *The Rings of Saturn* (1995) rely not on a confiding narrator but rather on maintaining a tone, an "apprehension of human solitariness expressed so richly and so peculiarly that *it* becomes the persona through which the memoirist speaks." If postmodern fiction is indeed a bankrupt form, Gornick argues, memoirs such as these have the power still to make us feel acutely this life, our one life. When written by nonfiction truth speakers, memoir reveals our common situation, and we are grateful.

Theodore C. Humphrey

Sources for Further Study

Library Journal 126 (July 1, 2001): 103.
Publishers Weekly 248 (June 18, 2001): 67.

THE SONG OF THE EARTH

Author: Hugh Nissenson (1933-   )
Publisher: Algonquin Books/Workman (Chapel Hill,
N.C.). Illustrated. 244 pp., $24.95
Type of work: Novel
Time: The twenty-first century
Locale: Nebraska, Japan, Washington D.C., New York
City

≈

The biography of a fictional twenty-first century artist

≈

Principal characters:
> JOHN FIRTH BAKER, the protagonist, a genetically engineered visual
> artist
> JEANETTE BAKER, his mother
> SRI BILLY LEE MOOKERJEE (SRIMAANJI), the male-female guru of an
> Earth Mother cult
> YUKIO TANAKA, Baker's roommate, also a genetically engineered visual
> artist

A tale about the near future, *The Song of the Earth* poses as the chronologically arranged biography of its protagonist, John Firth Baker, "the first genetically engineered visual artist." It is presented as a compilation, mostly of diary entries, interviews, and World Wide Web downloads, amassed by Katherine K. Jackson, a scholar of twenty-first century manual arts, and illustrated by Baker's artwork.

The first part of the novel focuses on Jeanette Baker, a Ph.D. candidate and lesbian who lives in Lincoln, Nebraska, in a domed community called Cather Keep. For those who can afford living in them, such communities are a necessity due to a rise in global temperatures which not only has raised the sea level to such an extent that New York has become a city of canals but also has turned Nebraska into a dust desert. Jeanette hears of the work of John Rust Plowman, a geneticist who has invented a process to implant arsogenes ("genes that govern the development of artistic talents") into a "humin" egg (the words "human," "woman" and "women" end in "-in" in this novel). Jeanette realizes that the metamorph produced by this process is exactly the kind of child she wants for herself. She secretly undergoes the illegal procedure in Japan, where Plowman, who provides the sperm to impregnate her egg, directs the Ozaki Metamorphic Institute of Kyoto.

Thus begins the life of John Firth Baker. A primary complication in Baker's character comes to light when he is twelve years old. He becomes infatuated with a high school student, Theodore (Teddy) Petrakis, with whom he has his first sexual experience. Perhaps because both of his parents are gay, this proclivity dominates his sex life from then on and is connected to his artistic life in one way or another. For example, an early lover, to whom he later returns, is Anselmo Diaz, who serves Baker as an extreme example of the entrepreneurship critical to an artist's development. Diaz, having been sold to a "dogfight promoter" as a boy-slave, manages to escape and make something of himself both as a hair stylist and as a trombone player in the local of the Hair-stylists' Union.

The most influential object of Baker's sexual desire, and eventually his lover or "sheila," is Sri Billy Lee Mookerjee. He is initially an accountant, but he is advised by a guru, Srimaati Brianna Andrews, to worship Gaia, or Mother Earth. This leads him to realize that "every humin, myself included, is a synergistic cell in Gaia's evolving composite brain and reproductive system." He joins Andrews's harem of "bearded, big-titted she-hes," first quitting his job at the

Hugh Nissenson's books include A Pile of Stones *(1965),* The Tree of Life *(1985), and* The Elephant and My Jewish Problem, *(1988). He has been a finalist for a National Book Award and a PEN/Faulkner Award.*

Phoenix branch of the Bank of China and undergoing a genetic procedure that makes him grow breasts. Having presented himself to Andrews and listened to her sing a Gaian song to him, he gains "Gaian Consciousness" and falls to the sidewalk.

When Baker encounters Mookerjee, he has already been taught at least one Gaian principle by his mentor Arturo, a robot, who tells him, "Death is the mother of evolution." He has also demonstrated an intense need to be loved. He brings this need to a Halloween party hosted by Mookerjee, where he falls in love with the guru. He is fifteen at the time. Fascinated by the mask that Mookerjee, disguised as a tree, is wearing, he gets Emma Torchlight, the lesbian artist who carved it, to help him draw it. Mookerjee takes an interest in him, but destroys the mask in order to illustrate that art is not immortal, only Gaia, and he declines to accept Baker as his sheila.

Emma Torchlight and Jeanette Baker become lovers, while John Baker is encouraged when Mookerjee's current sheila, Alfred Howe, takes a job on the Moon. However, Mookerjee still will not have John, telling him this time that he should not pursue him, but his art. Baker joins the Young Gynarchist League at his high school. He also sells himself as a sex slave for the summer in order to pay for "a no-frills transgenic mastogenesis," hoping Mookerjee will take him as his sheila, but Mookerjee still rejects him.

Baker becomes a street artist in Washington, D.C., but failing to make enough money, he advertizes himself online as "a 17-year-old she-he," including a scratchboard drawing of his blossoming breasts. He is delighted by the response and by his success but yet again sees Mookerjee at a party, and yet again he is spurned. This time Mookerjee urges Baker to pretend he is a child and to draw as if he were. Baker agrees, but it is not until he gives up everything, including art, that Mookerjee announces on his home page, "I'm pleased to have taken John Firth Baker, 17, as my sheila. Johnny has dropped out of high school and abandoned a promising career as a manual artist to devote himself to my service in her pursuit of Gaian consciousness."

Mookerjee runs a shelter in Washington, D.C., and Baker goes to work there. Also while in Mookerjee's service, Baker nurses on the guru's breasts in his effort to become a baby again and is initiated by his master into the cult of Mamagon Gaia, or "monster mother," who embodies both the creation and the destruction that define the "Motherworld." Forbidding Baker to draw, Mookerjee instructs him to simply look at things, which ties in with the "lust of the eye" his mother had taught him to assume of his arsogenic talent when he really was a baby.

Baker accompanies Mookerjee to a "planetary reproduction" conference in Japan, and then the two go to Kyoto, where Baker meets his father. Plowman, now known as Fritz, is in mourning over the death of his parrot. When Baker tells him he wants to gain Gaian Consciousness to conquer his fear of death, Plowman responds, "The fear of death is the beginning of wisdom"—the one piece of spiritual insight he ever gives his son.

Baker also meets Yukio Tanaka, the other survivor among the original arsogenic metamorphs in the Ozaki Project. With John severed from making art because of Mookerjee's prohibition, and Yukio unable to make art out of fear of his father's ghost, Plowman's project seems to have been a failure after all. Hope for Baker returning to art vanishes when he realizes that Mookerjee "is Gaia in humin form" and makes love with him, believing, as he renounces his talent to his distraught mother and to Plowman, that he is on the verge of the Gaian Consciousness he craves. In the meantime, he is attracted to Tanaka because his teeth are beautiful, though the object of his desire is not gay. Both young men admit to each other that they miss drawing, but Yukio can do nothing about it, saying that his father told him in a dream, "I forbid you to draw or paint again on pain of death."

After Baker returns to his life in Mookerjee's shelter in Washington, his mother kills herself. Afflicted by a nightmare of her dead face pushing up from the ground, and remembering her telling him when he was a child that the only way to rid himself of a nightmare was to draw it, he decides to take up art again. When Mookerjee tells him he must chose between art and himself, Baker leaves him and moves in with ninety-two-year-old Clorene Wells, a famous poet, in New York. Later he rents a room in the studio of Nat Glowgo, a nonmanual artist "interested in integrating words and images" like Baker, who is accustomed to incorporating words in his drawings. With paints his mother once gave him and he never used, Baker begins to put "color, texture, and sculpted relief" into his art. The items he makes in this format begin with the nightmare image of his mother's face and, twelve works later, end with a sculpture of his own skull and breasts titled *Mother Earth*—the series named "Baker's Dozen" by Mookerjee, the designation it becomes known by thereafter.

During this surge in his art, Baker invites Yukio Tanaka to stay with him in New York. While he continues to attempt to seduce Tanaka, Baker allows Emma Torchlight to be artificially inseminated with his sperm, since she wants a daughter in memory of Baker's mother. Finally, after threatening to send him back to Japan, Baker gets

Tanaka to become his reluctant lover. Tanaka's allegiance lies with heterosexual males in the worldwide gender conflict, and he ardently supports the male-dominated "Japanese Imperial past, when Japan ruled Asia."

Violence is the inheritance of the future from the ideological violence of the present, and it is part of Baker's life. He may see hope in the consequence of destruction it implies, mainly because he sees mortality as the prime creative element in Gaia, but he is, at the same time, well acquainted with violence as an evil. When he is working in the shelter, for example, he saves a seven-year-old black child from a customary beating by her mother's boyfriend, Bud Claypool, whose genes the Capitol Hags, "a local Gynarchist underground action squad," tamper with until he has an overwhelming urge to care for children; he is subsequently murdered by Lee McKibben, another abuser, when he tries to prevent McKibben from beating his daughter with a wire hanger. In the end, Baker himself, at the age of nineteen, is stabbed to death by Yukio Tanaka, who, after gouging out Baker's eyes with the scissors used as the murder weapon, jumps out the window to his own death, enraged at having been, in his mind, emasculated by Baker, and convinced that only a profound act of violence will earn him the forgiveness of his dead father. According to Mookerjee, Baker has become "the first Gaian artist guru," and having achieved the union of his spiritual life and his art, his death, undignified as it is, becomes the denouement of the story.

The Song of the Earth is so full of examples that encourage laughter that it is hard to tell if the novel is a comic satire on the antics of art and gender politics or not. John's first lover, Teddy Petrakis, for instance, says of him, "He often . . . undressed and danced *en point* for me in . . . pink ballet slippers." Of John Rust Plowman's parrot Sozoshii, his lover Wakinoya Yoshiharu comments that "Fritz and that bird were crazy about each other. . . . Then, without warning . . . she keeled over from a mutated form of avian TB. . . . There were no last words." Yoshiharu also relates that, when Baker's mother came to Japan to be impregnated, "After Fritz talked with Jeanette in the garden, he rushed me into the IVF lab, where I jerked him off into a test tube." Furthermore, the art that brings Baker his fame—from the pleasantly silly drawings of his infancy to the simple drawings and caricatures and the more complex artworks of his young adulthood—is difficult to credit as the work of an extraordinary talent, suggesting that it is not intended to be taken seriously. If this is so, as the oversimplified way in which the characters express their concerns might be as well, then Hugh Nissenson's view of the future is comic indeed.

Mark McCloskey

Sources for Further Study

Booklist 97 (April 15, 2001): 1542.
Publishers Weekly 248 (April 30, 2001): 56.

THE SOUTHERN WOMAN
New and Selected Fiction

Author: Elizabeth Spencer (1921-   )
Publisher: Modern Library/Random House (New York).
   462 pp. $23.95
Type of work: Short fiction
Time: The twentieth century
Locale: The American South, Italy, New York, and
   Montreal

~

*A collection of Spencer's finest short works, stories old
and new, as well as the novella* The Light in the Piazza

~

Principal character:

MARILEE SUMMERALL, the only recurring character, a nice Southern girl
with a mind of her own

Elizabeth Spencer's short fiction is luminous in its depiction of time and place. This collection of her stories and the novella *The Light in the Piazza* is categorized according to these qualities. It is divided into four sections: The South, Italy, Up North, and New Stories. Although the Italian novella is perhaps her most widely read short fiction, the stories set in the southern United States stand out as the strongest of her works. It is clear that she knows this landscape intimately and instinctively, in the way that one can only know the world of one's childhood years.

The southeastern United States of Elizabeth Spencer's early years was a land of racial complexity, and in describing this she shines. For example, the first story of the collection, "The Little Brown Girl," describes black/white relationships from the point of view of a young woman named Maybeth, who becomes intrigued by the description of his daughter by Jim Williams, a black employee of her father. Set in the days when the polite appellation for African Americans was Negro, this story gives a clear-eyed picture of the gap between the races, yet also describes their symbiosis.

In her portrayal of race in the South, Spencer reveals its workings as only an insider, black or white, can. She steers clear of the stereotypical depiction of the Southern racist as either a stupid "redneck" member of the Ku Klux Klan or an aristocrat with nothing but disdain for "those people." She focuses instead on members of the middle or lower classes, black and white, who because of circumstances must interact in the world they inhabit, but do not always have to like it. Often her racists are obviously responding to something which has been bred in the bone and are unaware of the implications of their behavior; these are clear to the reader but not the character.

Also, Spencer reveals that even those who are least racist cannot escape an awareness of race and the sense of the "Other."

This is clearly displayed in one of her most anthologized stories, "Sharon," which is one of those featuring Marilee, an intelligent and sensitive child who is the first-person narrator. "Sharon" tells the story of Uncle Hernan, whose full name was Hernando de Soto Wirth, and his relationship with Melissa, a young African American woman who had come to his home, called Sharon, with his young bride and had stayed on after she died. As is typical of the story narrated by a young person, the reader realizes before the narrator who the father of Melissa's children is and why Marilee's mother cannot stand her. Although it is clear that the main offense of this couple is their interracial bonding, a certain attempt at middle-class civility is maintained.

Elizabeth Spencer has been a distinguished writer of fiction throughout the second half of the twentieth century. Recipient of several O. Henry Awards, the Rosenthal Award from the American Academy of Arts and Letter, and the Award of Merit Medal, she has published many novels and short-story collections.

As is bound to occur for any Southern woman writer, comparisons have been made between Spencer and Eudora Welty, Carson McCullers, and Katherine Anne Porter, but many of Spencer's stories have more in common with William Faulkner and Edith Wharton, two writers not often mentioned in the same sentence. Certainly one of the finest of the stories in this collection, "First Dark," not only has Faulknerian overtones, but seems in some way a response to that author's "A Rose for Emily," the classic story of Southern gentility degraded into Southern grotesque.

In "First Dark," a woman in her thirties is courted by a man who has moved from Richton, their small hometown, to Jackson, Mississippi, but has started returning to get back in touch with his roots. Tom Beavers has had the experience of seeing a ghost at "first dark," an old, light-skinned African American man who signals to cars to stop. Frances Harvey, a woman from a family laden with history, who has remained in Richton to care for her aging mother in their large old home, had also witnessed this phenomenon, a fact that draws the couple together. They begin to care for each other deeply, but it is clear that Frances will not marry until her mother passes on, although her mother herself seems delighted with the relationship between the two despite Tom's lower-class background.

Her mother dies, but Frances is paralyzed, unable to decide what to do with her mother's things in the house. She once again sees the ghost—but does not recognize it as such—when he speaks to her in the graveyard, asking that she move her car so he can carry a sick woman to the hospital in his cart. Frances does so, but then spends a restless night, feeling she should have done more for the man. She goes to look for sleeping pills that had been prescribed for her mother, and so discovers that they are gone, that her mother had deliberately taken herself out of the way. At first light, she goes back to the road where she had seen the man and again speaks with him; he tells her that all is well. Frances returns home and tells Tom about this when he comes to visit. He knows that this is the ghost, for it fits another story he has been told; he suggests they leave for good. Frances, who has been unable even to agree to go out with him to a movie so soon after her mother's death, considers this proposal, gets her coat, and leaves with him, thus saving herself from the fate of Faulkner's Miss Emily, of moldering loneliness. So it is that only the house itself enters "the land of mourning and shadows and memory."

Not only does this story give a twist to the Southern gothic tale, releasing a woman into a productive future instead of showing her trapped in a horrifying nostalgic past, it also is a showcase for the perfect descriptions, the phrases that Spencer quietly includes, which capture moments, ways of being, that are purely American Southern. For example, Tom Beavers, when he wishes not to let on what he is thinking, is described as sitting with "his eyes looking up over his coffee cup, as though he sat behind a hand of cards." Describing Mrs. Harvey, Frances's mother and a well-to-do Southern lady of the old school, Spencer notes that "she vexed you with no ideas, she tried to protect you from even a moment of silence." Finally, most deliciously, Tom Beavers is both complimented and condemned by being described as "smart;" "By 'smart,' Southerners mean intellectual, and they say it in an almost condescending way, smart being what you are when you can't be anything else, but it is better, at least, than being nothing."

The Italian stories included in this collections also have that sense of the underplayed climax, where a small gesture, a moment of sanity, encompasses a whole world of action. For example, in "The White Azalea" Miss Theresa Stubblefield, a genteel Southern lady of a certain age, has finally achieved Europe after years of nursing her aunt, her mother, and her father through lengthy illnesses. Then, while in Rome, she receives letters from home indicating another crisis, another elderly relative needing her care. Having read her way through the greats of European fiction (Honoré de Balzac, Charles Dickens, Stendhal) while caring for her relatives, she realizes in Rome that although the Stubblefields are of utmost importance back home, they mean nothing there. She tears up the letters that hint that she really should come home to take up the burden they have assigned her and buries them in the dirt around the white azalea of the title, recognizing as she does so that in the bloody history of Europe, her act is a considerate one. Thus, in one small gesture, we see the liberation of a soul.

Perhaps the best-known of Spencer's works is *The Light in the Piazza*; this novella has been translated and reprinted around the world, sold over two million copies, and was made into a film in 1962. Set in Italy, it is the story of Margaret Johnson and her daughter Clara, a beautiful twenty-six-year-old woman who, due to an unfortunate accident when she was a child, has the mental age of a child of eleven. This handicap is glaringly obvious to her compatriots back home, but a facility for language and the differing customs of Europe, especially with regard to women, make her seem normal to an Italian family, whose favorite son falls in love with her. *The Light in the Piazza* might have been written by Edith Wharton; the attitudes and ambience bear a striking resemblance to that author's "Roman Fever." There is the same exquisite detail, the sensitive depiction of the agonies of a wife and mother who wants the best for her daughter and is willing to compromise her strong sense of honor and loyalty to achieve it, and the delightful feeling at the end that through perhaps less than straight-forward means, the right thing has occurred.

The weakest stories in the collection are those which are set "Up North." Although "I, Maureen" is a powerful depiction of a woman going through a nervous break-down, the main character is so unappealing that it is hard to appreciate the sufferings she endures in her quest for sanity, autonomy, even survival. Although the situation is one with which the reader can sympathize—that of a woman who has married into a different class and is being stifled by the expectations and restrictions placed upon her—her self-absorption becomes stifling. "Jack of Diamonds" explores a young girl's loss of innocence when she realizes that her father had been cheating on her mother before she died. Although the characters in these stories will survive their dis-illusionments, they do not do so with the same strong sense of independence and certain hint of humor as those in the Southern stories.

The final selection includes six new stories, which again display Spencer's ability to strike just the right note, to find just the right detail to characterize a person or indicate a stupendous denouement with just a line or a gesture. Of these, perhaps the finest is "The Runaways," which tells the story of Joclyn and Edward, who meet in a Mexican retreat where they have each resorted for their own reasons. As they grow closer, they tell each other their stories; his is that he is a fugitive for killing his wife, hers that she is dying. In the end, they speak the truth to each other; his is that he was lying, hers is that she was not. The darkest of these stories is "The Weekend Travelers," which is perhaps a little too Northern gothic, a New England version of the deadly pastoral.

Overall, this is a wonderful collection. There can be no doubt that Elizabeth Spencer is a master of short fiction, nor that she deserves wider recognition than she has received. One hopes to see more of her work printed and reprinted, and more taught, studied, and most of all enjoyed.

Mary LeDonne Cassidy

Sources for Further Study

Library Journal 126 (August, 2001): 168.
The New York Times Book Review 106 (August 26, 2001): 7.
Publishers Weekly 248 (July 23, 2001): 49.

STRANGER SHORES
Literary Essays, 1986-1999

Author: J. M. Coetzee (1940-   )
Publisher: Viking (New York). 295 pp. $24.95
Type of work: Literary criticism and literary history

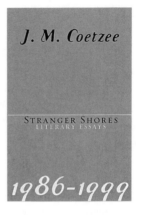

≈

Essays covering a diverse group of international authors organized so as to present and develop a conception of literary and cultural accomplishment

≈

It is not too strong a description to call the opening essay of J. M. Coetzee's *Stranger Shores* a declaration of intellectual intention. In accepting the challenge proposed by the essay's title—"What Is a Classic?"—Coetzee begins his provocative and enlightening examination of literary achievement with an assertion of standards and values, presented with a confident, authoritative tone suggested by the essay's subtitle, "A Lecture." While this appellation is informative, since the essay was developed from a lecture Coetzee delivered in Austria in 1991, its implications convey the sense of education in an ancient and venerable institution, a key to the approach that Coetzee takes here and in the other essays in the volume.

At the core of Coetzee's argument is a direct assault on a once very powerful arbiter of cultural status, the poet T. S. Eliot (1888-1965), who is still regarded as an influential figure in academic circles. Coetzee intends to subvert the aura of cultural sovereignty that Eliot projected in the Western world and, by extension, to establish some alternate strategies for measuring and assessing the enduring significance of the artists Coetzee admires and whose work he wants to discuss with a discerning audience.

While recognizing his capabilities as a poet and critic, Coetzee does not hold Eliot in the kind of veneration that elevated his intellectual expressions in the mid-twentieth century into canonical pronouncements. Insisting on a consideration of the social context in which Eliot operated, Coetzee calls Eliot's "decades-long program" to "redefine and resituate nationality" an effort to avoid being "sidelined as an eager American cultural arriviste" and a way to a escape from "the reality of his not-so-grand position as a man whose narrowly academic, Eurocentric education had prepared him for little else but life as a mandarin in one of the New England ivory towers." Coetzee's own experiences as a "provincial" or "young colonial" in South Africa endow him with both a degree of sympathetic understanding and a wary suspicion of Eliot's motives, and lead toward his own decades-long journey away to the "stranger shores"—beyond the bounds of the British Isles—of an international community of artistic achievement. Whereas Eliot defined a classic as a part of a line from Vergil and Dante through Anglican England, Coetzee, in essays written over the last fifteen years of the twentieth century, charts a course that touches parts of the globe that Eliot and his epigones regarded as barbaric and beyond consideration.

Coetzee's critique of Eliot's efforts to establish cultural dominion forms the aesthetic foundation for his own criteria for a classic. His suggestion that Eliot denied an inherent element of identity while fabricating a more advantageous personal construct is at the crux of his insistence that individual experience is crucial in responding to a work of art. In developing his own definition, Coetzee relies on his first exposure to Johann Sebastian Bach's *Well-Tempered Clavier* (1722) when his response to "classical music" was "somewhat suspicious and even hostile in a teenage manner," as a means of illustrating how appreciation and judgement are intricately connected to social and personal circumstance. As he puts it, he and Eliot were "trying to match their inherited culture to their daily experience." The concept of a "classic" that Coetzee moved toward depends on the Horatian dictum of persistence over time ("long-lasting"), but insists

J. M. Coetzee's novels Life & Times of Michael K *(1984) and* Disgrace *(2000) won the prestigious Booker Prize. His essays and translations have been similarly acclaimed. He has taught in the United States and in South Africa, where he is a professor of general literature at the University of Capetown.*

that its "timelessness" is undermined by day-to-day testing, so that a work is revitalized by its contact with succeeding eras, operating as a form of allegory for any age. In summation to his searching and elaborate argument, Coetzee says that "the interrogation of the classic, no matter how hostile" is "inevitable and to be welcomed" for "as along as the classic needs to be protected from attack, it can never prove itself classic." Thus, Eliot's acts of reverence must be self-defeating and criticism functions as "one of the instruments of the cunning of history." The essays that follow are Coetzee's method for charting a historical galaxy unlike any previously conceived.

Coetzee makes high demands of his readers, but the body of *Stranger Shores* is composed of essays that engage the work of writers whose life conditions are an intricate aspect of their endeavor. The focus on intriguing human beings tends to balance the intellectual demands that Coetzee's imaginative and often unconventional positions produce. The twenty-six separate essays that make up the contents of *Stranger Shores* are effective as solitary insights, but the density of detail, exciting erudition, and strong opinion that Coetzee brings to each essay requires such close attention from the reader that it is somewhat exhausting to try to read more than a few on any occasion. Nonetheless, their arrangement clearly indicates that Coetzee had some patterns of coherence in mind over the course of their composition. In addition to operating as evidentiary exhibits of his thesis about what constitutes a "classic," Coetzee has other structural connections in action throughout the book.

The essays which immediately follow "What Is a Classic?" are devoted to Daniel Defoe's *Robinson Crusoe* (1719) and Samuel Richardson's *Clarissa* (1748), books which Eliot would have accepted as a part of the tradition which he supported, and books which have retained a readership across time. As Coetzee examines these texts, however, he expands the English orientation that the books convey. Coetzee's Crusoe is a transoceanic traveler lost in a strange land—forecasting the patterns of migration that Coetzee regards as one of the primary themes of the literature that interests him— as well as a kind of Everyman whose disobedience to authority is mixed with an uneasy paternalism (toward Friday), his legacy from the British Empire. Coetzee's interpretation of *Clarissa* resists both feminist claims for Clarissa's status as victim and Eliot's attempt to support a Pauline version of Christianity in Richardson's treatment of virginity, while supporting Clarissa's actions in turning toward death and Lovelace's unravelling in the face of "soul-harrowing beauty." The last paragraph of both of these essays is more of an invitation to further pursue the ideas introduced than any type of conclusion.

Following these two bracing discussions about books regarded as "classics," which are designed to demonstrate the efficacy of Coetzee's approach, he turns toward a group of authors who share several characteristics that especially interest him. They are writers who have lived in more than one country, written in more than one language, suffered through social and political turmoil, and whose work is marked by a kind of quest for an elusive "homeland." The thirteenth essay, positioned in the middle of the collection, is devoted to the life and work of Jorge Luis Borges (1899-1986), who epitomizes this situation. As Coetzee introduces him, he

> was born in 1899 into a prosperous middle-class family in a Buenos Aires where Spanish—to say nothing of Italian—descent was not deemed a social asset. One of his grandmothers was from England; the family chose to stress their English affiliations and to bring up the children speaking English as well as Spanish. Borges remained a lifelong Anglophile.

Borges brought this blend of languages to his work, which was affected significantly by an interrogative relationship to modernism and Magical Realism, and by his disputatious connection to the shifting political situation in Argentina. For Coetzee, who has the linguistic capability to assess the merits of various translations of the authors he considers, Borges's greatness resides in the ways in which he combined imaginative fiction with a recognizable Argentinian social reality, and by the manner in which, in "the finest of the stories of *The Garden of Forking Paths*—'Tlon, Uqbar, Orbis Tertius' and 'The Library of Babel' . . . the philosophical argument folds discreetly into the narrative." These qualities, emphasized in terms of the specific circumstances of the writer's histories, are also present in various forms in the other writers Coetzee considers.

The people he has chosen permit Coetzee to concentrate on the part of their writing lives that is relevant to the evolving sense of what he thinks matters in literature. The fact that they are not that well known in the transoceanic literary world that Coetzee regards as his audience is an important feature in his essays on the Dutch writers

Marcellus Emants (1848-1943), Harry Mulisch (born 1927), and Cees Nooteboom (born 1933), as are the Dutch roots of the Afrikaner background of Coetzee himself. The next essay, on Rainer Maria Rilke (1875-1926)—one of only three entries on poets—is a turn toward European writers whose work was introduced to an English-speaking readership by a well-known translator, whose initial presentation has been augmented (or replaced) by a more recent attempt. Coetzee's linguistic ability is obvi-ous—his own translations have impressed scholars—and his examinations of the problems and possibilities that a translator faces with Rilke, Franz Kafka (1883-1924), Robert Musil (1880-1942), Josef Skvorecky (born 1924), and Fyodor Dos-toevsky (1821-1881) constitute one of the strongest and most compelling sections of *Stranger Shores*.

The essay "Translating Kafka" begins with the pioneering work of Edwin and Willa Muir, Scots who introduced Kafka to the United Kingdom and the United States. Coetzee traces the Muir's cultural experiences and shows how their interest in Kafka was shaped by their political and philosophical beliefs. Then, he examines some of the basic differences between English and German, moving from there to specific passages to "cite instances to give an idea of the range of the Muir's inade-quacies." The context deepens as Coetzee covers the ways in which Kafka's friend and champion Max Brod rescued Kafka's manuscripts and directed both translations and intertrepetations for several decades, and then widens as Coetzee discusses a translation of *The Castle* (1998) by Mark Harmon, which he calls "a task richly worthwhile." Neither this praise nor his evaluation that "for the general reader as for the student, it will be the translation of preference for some time to come," deter Coetzee from noting "lapses" in Harmon's work. "I list a few," he says, before giving seven examples of passages where alternative versions might be preferable. During the entire essay, his own insights and ideas about Kafka inform the text, and his ac-knowledgement that in some places the problems posed by Kafka's vocabulary and syntax are "finally intractable" is a concession to the difficulties a translator con-fronts, as well as a statement by implacation of the traceable roots that the translator must consider. Coetzee's sensitivity to the nuances of language operate in his assess-ments of all the authors who come to readers of English through the work of their translators.

The last group of essays deals with writers from South Africa, Coetzee's place of origin and his home ground. Like Nadine Gordimer (born 1923), the Nobel laureate he discusses in an essay that compares her work to the Russian Ivan Turgenev (1818-1883), Coetzee has had to struggle with the convergent forces of a land that is marked by appealing and appalling charateristics. His admiration for Gordimer's (and Doris Lessing's) efforts "to manage a double discourse" is clear, but the South African writer he seems closest to is Breyten Breytenbach (born 1939?), a man who served seven years in a South African prison and an Afrikaner who defied the ruling Afri-kaner culture with his ringing declaration, "We are a bastard people with a bastard language" in an assault on the system of apartheid. In some ways, Breytenbach is like a secret sharer, with Coetzee, of a maverick sensibility that requires a resistance to al-most any ruling dogma. Breytenbach's insistence that his role in the future will be, as in the past, "against the norm, orthodoxy, the canon, hegemony, politics, the State, power" has touched a responsive chord in Coetzee, a man of a more taciturn temperament but of equal intensity about his deepest convictions. In discussing Breytenbach's *Dog Heart* (1999), Coetzee sees a hopeful direction in the memoir's framing of a "countercurrent" in which "fragments of groups in disarray" find a new way of cohering, not "around a political philosophy but around a shared language larger and wiser than the sum of its speakers, and a shared history, bitter and divided through that history may be." From this flux, the kind of literature Coetzee calls classic might be made.

Leon Lewis

Sources for Further Study

Booklist 97 (August, 2001): 2075.
Library Journal 126 (July, 2001): 89.
The New York Times Book Review 106 (September 16, 2001): 29.

THE TALE OF GENJI

Author: Murasaki Shikibu (973-1014?)
First published: Genji monogatari, eleventh century, in
 Japan
Translated from the Japanese, with introduction and
 notes, by Royall Tyler
Publisher: Viking (New York). Illustrated. 2 volumes.
 1,200 pp. $60.00
Type of work: Novel
Time: The tenth century
Locale: The imperial Japanese capital of Kyoto, and sur-
 roundings

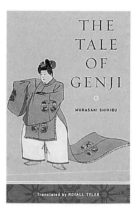

∾

*In a time of imperial pomp and circumstance, where courtly love and dalliance
must be conducted in stealth and with circumspection to avoid the wrath of the court
and the glaring eyes of others, Genji, the playboy hero, impressively courts, loves,
mourns, and lives in the splendor of an extraordinary age and ultimately ensures the
survival of his lineage*

∾

Principal characters:
 GENJI, son of Emperor Kiritsubo no Mikado and his "intimate"
  Kiritsubo no Koi, removed from the imperial family so that he can
  serve as a commoner and a senior government official
 KOKIDEN CONSORT, one of Emperor Kiritsubo's consorts, powerful and
  evil tempered, the mother of his firstborn son, Suzaku, who is heir
  apparent and future emperor
 AOI, first wife of Genji, who bears him a son, Yugiri
 FUJITSUBO, the wife of Emperor Kiritsubo, who loves Genji
 REIZEI, secret son of Genji and Fujitsubo, who will be emperor after
  Suzaku because everyone believes that he is the son of Genji's father
  and Fujitsubo
 MURASAKI, niece of Fujitsubo, Genji's greatest love because she looks
  just like her aunt
 AKASHI NO KIMI, daughter of the Akashi novice; she gives birth to
  Genji's daughter Akashi no Himegimi, who will be a future
  empress
 ONNA SAN NO MIYA, third daughter of Emperor Suzaku, Genji's wife at
  the emperor's request; she has a son, Kaoru, with a young courtier
  while Genji is away, and the son is assumed to be Genji's
 NIOU, son of Akashi no Himegimi (now empress), Genji's grandson
 OIGIMI, NAKA NO KIMI, and UKIFUNE, three daughters of a certain
  prince, pursued by the rivals Kaoru and Niou

Murasaki Shikibu was born into the midlevel aristocracy in Japan. Known for her talents in writing Japanese fiction, which was considered the domain of women in her society, she was requested to serve the Empress Akiko in 1006.

Written a thousand years ago in Japan by Lady Murasaki Shikibu, *The Tale of Genji* takes place in Japan's imperial city of Kyoto. It is a time of aristocracy, strict social hierarchy, and imperial wealth and ceremony, and court intrigues and powerful alliances are endemic. Social order and imperial protocol frown upon superficial gallantry, gossips, and scandals, yet these very predilections prevail under the guise of good manners, social etiquette, and propriety, and flourish among lords and ladies of gentility.

Incredibly popular in Japan, and considered one of its enduring classics, *The Tale of Genji* has only been fully translated into English in the twentieth century. Royall Tyler's authoritative, comprehensive, and unexpurgated new translation finally gives an English speaker the chance to enjoy Japan's favorite medieval romance to the fullest. Presented in a beautiful, two-volume slipcase, Tyler's translation offers an elegant prose which captures the spirit and flair of the original and reads as beautifully as some of the spectacular sights of its narrative, which are also captured in appealing illustrations.

Into this realm of Murasaki Shikibu's rich imagination, which is drawn in part from her real-life observations but set almost a century earlier than the author's life, Genji, a son of the emperor and his intimate Kiritsubo, is born. Since she is only the emperor's intimate, which ranks below the consorts and even lower than his single empress, Kiritsubo's only livelihood is Genji and the emperor's affection. The emperor gives up his desire to make Genji heir apparent over his firstborn son because the court would not allow such an unprecedented move. Thus, his favorite son is made a commoner and given the surname Genji (or Minamoto), freeing him to a life of wide-ranging romantic action and experience.

While Genji clearly occupies the central place and is the most colorfully drawn character and hero of the novel, *The Tale of Genji* does not lack at all in other characters, plots and subplots, episodic occurrences, and confusing relationships and interrelationships among the lords and ladies of the imperial realm. However, it is Genji who binds the often-fragmentary novel together. In essence, he is what gives life to the book, and Tyler's translation effectively captures the richness of his character without detracting from the many others populating Shikibu's masterfully spun narrative.

When Genji is twelve years old, he is married to Aoi, a sixteen-year-old daughter of an influential courtier. He is too young for the marriage to affect him much. Though officially married, he still lives in the imperial palace near the emperor and his future empress, Fujitsubo, while his wife lives at her father's residence. This was not out of the ordinary for the upper classes in medieval Japan. Despite their distant behavior and her indifference toward him, Genji and Aoi eventually have a son, Yugiri, who resembles Genji closely.

During his early years, Genji is often near Fujitsubo. Even though the required curtains, blinds, or screens separate them physically, as was mandatory between a man and a women of respectability, Genji develops a special devotion toward Fujitsubo because she resembles his late mother closely. In a culture which strongly believes in reincarnation and rebirth, this motivation is not as repellent as it may be for a contemporary Western reader. Tyler's informative footnotes help to fill in cultural gaps, and the illustrations give a nice visual sense of the culture which gave rise to Genji's adventures.

As Genji matures, his father does not let him be so close to Fujitsubo any longer, with good reason. Yet Genji defies the older man and succeeds in secretly making love to Fujitsubo. The result is a son, the future Emperor Reizei, whom the cuckolded Emperor believes is his own. He even deems it natural that the boy should look just like his other son, Genji.

Despite this momentous transgression, Fujitsubo is still beyond Genji's reach. He can truly communicate with her only by writing poems and brief letters, which are delivered by messengers. These poems are what helped distinguish *The Tale of Genji* in its time, since medieval Japanese society considered poetry the highest and most genteel art. All early Japanese literature placed poetry above prose. Thus, it is not unusual that Genji's messages to all his women are carefully written and crafted with poetic allusions and penned on types of paper selected according to the recipient's rank and the occasion of the lines.

To make up for his desire to have someone entirely his own, Genji insists on taking a little girl into his care and virtually kidnaps her from her nurse when her mother is dead. Again, he is attracted because the girl is Fujitsubo's niece and looks just like her aunt, the woman Genji can never possess. In time, the little girl will grow up to be Lady Murasaki, and become his true and greatest love. She will have the sole privilege of daily interaction with Genji. Ironically, the real first name of the *Tale*'s author remains unknown; she was given the name of Murasaki by her enchanted readers, who came to identify her with one of her most endearing creations.

Tyler's translation captures well the spirit of adolescent male bonding in the classic early chapter when the teenage Genji joins three other young men to discuss the follies and virtues of women on one rainy night. Each man rates women according to their class, family support, and other backings, but mainly on their feminine charms. This amusing discussion turns out to be almost an education to the adolescent Genji, and ironically points at his ubiquitous devotion to romance.

Shikibu's text continues in a gently ironic vein, as the many women whom Genji comes to love all seem deadly afraid of Genji because of his devastating good looks and stature. Often his lovers recoil in awe, though secretly they yearn for him. By this token resistance, they only heighten and affirm his suave and seductive ways, which has given his character the reputation of a playboy, or, more negatively, that of a sexual predator. Yet in the world of the *Tale*, Genji is forgiven by virtue of his perfect good looks, masculinity, charms, and elegance. He is a character who possesses the noble grace and talents in music and musical instruments, poetry, and calligraphy that Shikibu's court culture valued above all else. Whether this makes him a literary paragon or subtle satire on that society is left for the reader to decide. What Tyler offers the English-speaking reader is a rendition of Genji's adventures that tries to stay as close to the original as possible, and he succeeds amazingly well.

At times, even Genji cannot escape disasters and utterly comical mishaps. Finally, Genji is punished for making love to the Kokiden consort's younger sister after her father catches him. The consort uses this excuse to have him ostracized from court, one of the worst punishments in Shikibu's genteel society. Yet even in exile, Genji remains a romantic hero. Urged by her father, he accepts Akashi no Kimi into his heart and bed. When Genji's punishment is rescinded by Emperor Suzaku, he returns to the imperial city. His fortune continues to rise as Akashi bears him his last child, a daughter who will later become an empress.

As the novel unfolds, Genji gains in dignity, grace, looks, and wisdom. He essentially marries the retired emperor Suzaku's favorite daughter, Onna San no Miya, at the former's request. Yet his heart belongs to Lady Murasaki, whose only flaw is that she gives him no children, reflecting again the values of the medieval author's society. While Genji is away, Kashiwagi, a young courtier, becomes besotted with Onna San, and manages to make love to her. Their son, Kaoru, is naturally believed to be Genji's son. Love- and shame-stricken, Kashiwagi dies while Genji maintains Onna San's reputation, despite his fury at being given a dose of his own medicine.

The last third of the novel concentrates on Kaoru and Niou, who is a son of Genji's only daughter, now empress. The two men are best friends and enjoy many adventures. Yet the innocent days of Genji's time are less so in this new generation. Shikibu conveys that loss and is slightly critical of the time Kaoru and Niou live in because it is somewhat darker, and the human spirit sparkles less lively. The translation captures this sense of loss very well, giving the reader a sense of nostalgia for Genji's own days.

Though both are handsome, Kaoru is always more respectable, devout, and serious, whereas Niou is the ever-gallant playboy, with a proclivity for fleeting dalliance and love affairs. In their rivalry for love, their character traits display who they are. Here Shikibu suggests that human qualities, in essence, bind them to this world—the human condition—making them real and fallible, albeit less beautiful and ideal than Genji. Kaoru and Niou get involved in a multilayered love triangle involving three daughters of an unnamed prince. Oigimi, the oldest, is the most respectable, moving Niou to court the middle sister, Naka no Kimi. Eventually both men compete for the youngest, Ukifune, and their rivalry rises to new, slightly overheated heights.

In all its leisurely length, Murasaki Shikibu's fascinating epic tale about an idealized time and world where the hero Genji is almost godlike but still fallible has enchanted readers for centuries, and its ending echoes the human condition at its best and worst. Tyler's eloquent and well-researched translation finally makes this classic available in an English which beautifully captures the literary craft and timeless splendor of *The Tale of Genji*.

R. C. Lutz

Sources for Further Study

Kirkus Review 69 (September 15, 2001): 1320.
Library Journal 126 (September 15, 2001): 81.
Publishers Weekly 248 (August 20, 2001): 49.

TAPS

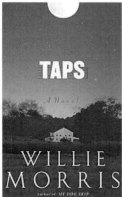

Author: Willie Morris (1935-1999)
Publisher: Houghton Mifflin (Boston). 340 pp. $26.
Type of work: Novel
Time: 1951
Locale: Fisk's Landing, Mississippi

≈

Morris's posthumously published autobiographical novel is an elegiac story about coming-of-age in the South during the Korean War

≈

Principal characters:

SWAYZE BARKSDALE, the narrator
GEORGIA APPLEWHITE, Swayze's girlfriend
ELLA BARKSDALE, Swayze's widowed alcoholic mother, a tap-dance teacher
ARCH KIDD, Swayze's classmate and fellow trumpeter
LUKE CARTWRIGHT, World War II veteran, Swayze's mentor
POTTER RICKS, the local mortician
AMANDA PETTIBONE, Luke's clandestine lover
DURLEY GODBOLD, Amanda's arrogant, rich husband

In *The Reivers*, a short, rambunctious novel published weeks before his death in 1962, William Faulkner offered a bittersweet story about coming-of-age in his fictional slice of the South, Yoknapatawpha County, half a century earlier. *Taps*, the late Willie Morris's final testament, also looks back fifty years to ponder the mysteries of growing up in the Mississippi Delta at mid-century during the Korean War.

In 1951, the young men of Fisk's Landing, a Dixie cotton town so close to the soil that none of its buildings exceeds four stories, begin to return from Asia in caskets. The area's entire National Guard unit had been mobilized in response to hostilities in Korea. For the increasingly common graveside ceremonies, two high school trumpeters, Arch Kidd and Swayze Barksdale, are recruited by the local American Legion chapter to play "Taps." Although he is not quite old enough for military service, Swayze bears vigilant witness to the dismal fate of local boys who were. Lank Hemphill returns without an arm, but many others come back to Fisk's Landing only as corpses. For each burial, the flip of a coin determines who—either Swayze or Arch—performs beside the coffin and who stands at a distance repeating on his own horn every mournful phrase. Those notes in turn resound throughout the county, and, later, in the memories of a grown-up trumpeter. Swayze, the fictional narrator whose recollections of his seventeenth year constitute *Taps*, can still summon up "the wonderful thrill of hearing the echo to one's *own* echo as it dissolves tenderly, reluctantly almost, into the distance, palpitating into the faraway hush."

In North Toward Home *(1967),*
Willie Morris recounted growing up
in Yazoo City, Mississippi, studying
at the University of Texas, and
editing The Texas Observer. *In New*
York, he became the precocious,
flamboyant editor of Harper's *before*
returning to Yazoo City. Other
Morris books include New York
Days *(1993),* My Dog Skip *(1995),*
and My Cat Spit McGee *(1999).*

If writing is an echo of experience, it also generates its own resonances. In writing the novel *Taps*, Morris, who inscribes the book "For the people of Yazoo," drew on his own childhood in the Mississippi Delta, a time and place evoked exquisitely in the first section of his first book, *North Toward Home* (1967). "The past is never dead," declared Faulkner in a statement that Morris appropriated as his memoir's epigraph. "It's not even past." Reviving things past, Morris in *Taps* again revisits Yazoo City, renaming it Fisk's Landing, a rural metropolis with a population of 10,184, and he calls himself Swayze. *Taps* is in effect a gloss on the seventh chapter of the "Mississippi" section in *North Toward Home*, a ten-page stretch in which Morris recalls his adolescent experience playing trumpet at the funerals of Korean fatalities. (Chapter 5 is the germ of a 1995 novel, *My Dog Skip*). "Is it not true that the past is the only thing we truly possess?" asks Swayze, acutely aware that the answer is no, that everything is always slipping away. Precisely because the past is never dead, it is elusive. Invoking memory and invention, *Taps* returns one last time to scenes that can be glimpsed but not fixed.

In 1952, Morris left Mississippi for Austin, Texas, to attend the University of Texas and edit *The Daily Texan*. At age twenty-five, he returned to the Texas capital, after four years in Oxford—England, not Mississippi—as a Rhodes Scholar, to edit *The Texas Observer*. At thirty-two, he became editor of *Harper's* magazine and an influential figure in American literary culture. He conquered New York, but even after Gotham deposed its conqueror and Morris headed south toward home for his final years, he never lost the aura of the wunderkind. If, as George Orwell noted, "at fifty, everyone has the face he deserves," Morris's famous babyface revealed a man who never outgrew youthful wonder. Perhaps because they so often cultivate green memories, even his seasoned efforts seem precocious.

At the time of his early death at age sixty-four in 1999, *Taps*, which Morris worked on throughout his adult life, was still in manuscript, and its author was denied the thrill of hearing an echo to his own echo. In a seamless job of editing and a labor of love, his widow, JoAnne Prichard Morris, has brought the book into posthumous print. *Taps* is a fitting valediction to a man whose work deserves to echo. Its title refers not only to the lament that teenage Swayze plays in memoriam to his fallen townsmen, or to the fact that his widowed, alcoholic mother, a frustrated ballerina, gives lessons to local children in tap dancing. It also recalls the lesson that an adolescent learns about the place of death in human life. Like Walt Whitman's poem "Out of the Cradle Endlessly Rocking," *Taps* is both an epiphany about mortality and an exploration of the sources for the author's mature art, a portrait of the artist as a young man with a horn.

Swayze presents himself as "a solitary brotherless and fatherless boy growing up in a house full of tap dancers and a crazed mother." Ella Barksdale, a neurotic nag who regards herself as a fallen patrician and "led an anxious life riven with gloom," might have been a mother of Tennessee Williams's invention. Though he is the high school spelling champ, Swayze is plagued by a sense of his own unworthiness. He is devastated when pretty, wealthy Georgia Applewhite, his sweetheart since childhood, dumps him for a football star. Swayze's trumpet duties throw him together with his classmate Arch Kidd, a lazy, surly, scowling misanthrope whose only redeeming virtue is the consummate grace with which he plays high F. Swayze is a lonely only child whose father died when he was ten. His closest bonds are to his golden retriever, Dusty, and to a couple of older men. Luke Cartwright is a veteran of World War II who teaches Swayze poker and much else and recruits him to play "Taps" for the casualties of the current war. Potter Ricks is the gentle, courtly undertaker who buries them. It is through these local sages, and through sexual initiation and rejection, that Swayze comes of age, which is to say that he learns to accept the inexorable expense of aging, "the terrible fluidity of life on this planet."

If there is a single moment of transcendent revelation, it comes toward the end of the book, when, after agreeing to Potter Ricks's request that he drive a hearse carrying a dreadful cargo, Swayze wanders into the mortuary. He comes upon the hideously mangled, decomposed corpse of a soldier killed in Korea. The young trumpeter is profoundly affected by the sight, though the judgment that Swayze renders as an adult narrator is uncharacteristically sententious and nihilistic. About his fifty-year-old memory of the "putrescent sunken mass" he gazed at in a coffin, the narrator notes: "And it was in that moment, oddly, that I believe I saw life as it truly was for the first time." The novel's affectionate solicitude toward details of Swayze's experience seems at odds with a view that life can be reduced to rotting flesh. If what Swayze beholds in that coffin is what life truly is, it is truly not very much, but the narrator's wistful, tender, compassionate tone belies that bleak conclusion.

Taps is attentive to the sociology of its time and place, where the local Sears is beginning to sell the first television sets that the town has ever seen, and when a Southern boy still can follow the distant World Series only through the radio. It is an insular world on the verge of momentous, irreversible change. The novel opens by noting the local caste system that distinguishes the privileged flatland residents from the rustic folk who inhabit the hills surrounding Fisk's Landing: "We were flatland people, each of us in this little long-ago tale: Luke and Amanda and Durley, Georgia and Arch and myself, Potter and Godbold and all the others." Though he mingles with the flatland aristocracy, Swayze grows up shabby genteel, with a lingering sense of inferiority yet with a tacit understanding that his privileges exceed those of the blacks clustered in the boisterous neighborhood called "the Quarters." Fisk's Landing in 1951 is a segregated society, though the cosmos mocks the community's racial categories: "We lived and died by nature, Anglos and Africans bound together in the whims of the timeless clouds." Presided over by a Jew, three-term Mayor Isaac J. Fink, the town is an ethnic amalgam that includes Italians, Greeks, Poles, Germans, and Lebanese but apparently no Latinos. (The term "Anglo," meaning non-Hispanic, seems a misnomer appropriated from Texas and a later era.) As recalled by a white man many decades later, racial bigotry in midcentury Fisk's Landing is casual and cruel.

The story of how "our people played seven-card stud against God," *Taps* reveals its hand slowly, through leisurely recollections of basketball games, drinking binges, spelling bees, and English classes. The novel lingers over striking minor figures, including Swayze's English teacher, Mrs. Idella King, and his basketball coach, Asphalt Thomas. What binds it all together are the dire occasions spread throughout the year when Swayze is called upon to go to the cemetery and play his trumpet. What gives it all drama is the unstable romantic triangle formed by Luke Cartwright, a veteran infantry sergeant who owns a hardware store, beautiful, talented Amanda Pettibone, and Durley Godbold, her rich, arrogant, and violent husband. Durley is the heir to an imperious patriarch and is himself a grown-up bully who is presumed lost in battle in Korea. Swayze becomes go-between, witness, and chorus in a tragedy he is powerless to avert. Morris, the God of Fisk's Landing, if not Yazoo City, has stacked his poker deck.

He writes in gorgeously redolent sentences that seem to grow directly out of the lush Delta landscape that they evoke. The author's manifest zest in telling his story denies its grimness. Morris is enamored of the sumptuous options of the English language, reveling both in the vernacular and in more recondite usage; Swayze notes that Arch calls his greasy hair lotion "stinkum," but he also explains Arch's prank of putting a cow in the high school auditorium by noting that "he distracted himself from lassitude in those days with flamboyant gambits and divertissements." Sometimes, as when he describes the ecstasy of first sex ("the glowing, pillowy rapture of joy"), Morris's prose is colored purple, but it never lacks the same awe over the power and pathos of words that Swayze, listening to the funereal weeping as to "the murmur of mourning doves at dusk, or the breathless flow of water in a summer's stream," brings to the music he releases from his trumpet. Like his narrator, Morris is occasionally unsteady at high F, but *Taps*, the elegy he was rehearsing throughout his writing life, proves he knew how to sing.

Steven G. Kellman

Sources for Further Study

Atlanta Journal and Constitution, April 8, 2001, p. C1.
Chicago Tribune, May 3, 2001, p. 11.
The Christian Science Monitor, April 5, 2001, p. 21.
Los Angeles Times Book Review, June 10, 2001, p. 22.
The New York Times Book Review 106 (April 22, 2001): 23.
Publishers Weekly 248 (April 2, 2001): 19.
USA Today, April 9, 2001, p. D04.
The Washington Post Book World, April 8, 2001, p. 15.

THEODORE REX

Author: Edmund Morris (1940-   )
Publisher: Random House (New York). Illustrated.
   772 pp. $35.00
Type of work: Biography and history
Time: 1901-1909
Locale: Washington, D.C., Oyster Bay, New York, other
   parts of the United States, and Panama

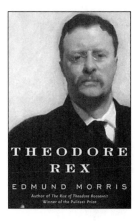

≈

*The second volume of Morris's projected three-volume
biography of Theodore Roosevelt, covering Roosevelt's
presidential years, 1901 to 1909, wherein the author discusses both the subject's public career as well as his private life*

≈

Principal personages:
   THEODORE ROOSEVELT, president of the United States, 1901-1909
   EDITH KERMIT ROOSEVELT, Roosevelt's second wife
   ALICE,
   THEODORE, JR.,
   KERMIT,
   ETHEL,
   ARCHIBALD, and
   QUENTIN ROOSEVELT, Roosevelt's six children
   HENRY ADAMS, historian and scion of the presidential Adams family
   NELSON W. ALDRICH, Republican senator from Rhode Island
   JOSEPH G. CANNON, congressman from Illinois and speaker of the House
      of Representatives
   GEORGE BRUCE CORTELYOU, secretary of commerce and Republican
      National Committee chairman
   JOSEPH BENSON FORAKER, senator from Ohio
   MARCUS ALONZO HANNA, senator from Ohio
   JOHN HAY, secretary to Abraham Lincoln, and secretary of state under
      William McKinley and Roosevelt
   JEAN JULES JUSSERAND, French ambassador to the United States
   PHILANDER CHASE KNOX, Roosevelt's attorney general and later senator
      from Pennsylvania
   HENRY CABOT LODGE, senator from Massachusetts
   JOHN PIERPONT MORGAN, banker and financier
   ELIHU ROOT, secretary of war and secretary of state
   WILLIAM HOWARD TAFT, governor of the Philippines, secretary of war,
      and Roosevelt's successor as president
   BOOKER T. WASHINGTON, African American educator

∽

*Edmund Morris was awarded the
Pulitzer Prize and the American
Book Award for* The Rise of
Theodore Roosevelt *(1979), the
preceding volume in his biography
of Roosevelt. He is also the author
of* Dutch: A Memoir of Ronald
Reagan *(1999), controversial
because of its seminovelization of
Reagan's biography.*

∽

Theodore Roosevelt is one of the United States' most beloved presidents thanks to the Teddy Bear as well as his grand enthusiasm for life, which he often expressed in the terms of an adolescent (or even younger: a friend once noted that Roosevelt sometimes acted as if he were about six years old). Many of his statements or expressions have become common lore, such as using the presidency as a "bully pulpit" and to "speak softly but carry a big stick." A many-sided individual, he was a rancher and cowboy, war hero, moral reformer, astute politician, brilliant diplomat, recipient of both the Nobel Peace Prize and the Congressional Medal of Honor, and a notable author—no U.S. president wrote more books and articles than Roosevelt. The nation's youngest president, he and his family (which included six children) captivated the country during the first decade of the twentieth century. His presidency in many ways was the paradigm for the twentieth century in his use of executive power, and he was a powerful influence on his cousin, Franklin Delano Roosevelt. Along with George Washington, Thomas Jefferson, and Abraham Lincoln, he is immortalized in granite at South Dakota's Mount Rushmore.

Roosevelt's presidential reputation has varied over time. When he died in 1919 at the age of sixty, his approval rating was at its apogee, and if he had lived he likely would have been the Republican presidential nominee in 1920. In the reaction to the destruction of World War I and in the years of the Great Depression, his energetic personality and enthusiastic optimism seemed, in restrospect, misguided by some, and his reputation was overshadowed by the other Roosevelt. However, by the end of the twentieth century, most historians ranked him among the top four presidents, behind only Washington, Lincoln, and his cousin Franklin. Theodore Roosevelt's high standing is due in part to several biographical works which have appeared in recent decades, not least Edmund Morris's *The Rise of Theodore Roosevelt* (1979), which related Roosevelt's youth and pre-presidential years. The work was awarded the Pulitzer Prize and Morris's sequel was widely anticipated.

It would be more than twenty years before *Theodore Rex* appeared. In the interval, Morris had become the official biographer of Ronald Reagan. The result was *Dutch: A Memoir of Ronald Reagan*, published with great controversy in 1999. Apparently unable to fathom the depth—or lack of it—in Reagan's intellect, Morris invented scenes and added characters which made *Dutch* appear to be more novel than historical biography, a result which incensed many reviewers. What was successful in *Dutch*, however, was Morris's very readable narrative style. *Theodore Rex* is also eminently readable, and its publication just two years after Morris's work on Reagan indicates that Morris had continued to work on the Roosevelt biography even as he attempted to come to grips with the often opaque Reagan.

There was little that was opaque with Roosevelt, as is indicated in his own extensive writings, including the 100,000 letters that he wrote over the years. One does not have to invent or fictionally create a Roosevelt persona. If *Dutch* might be called the first deconstructionist presidential biography, *Theodore Rex* is utterly orthodox in its historical approach, as is indicated in the extensive sources cited in the 165 pages of notes accompanying the narrative. The biography begins dramatically in September, 1901, with Roosevelt madly racing through the night from Mount Marcy in New York's Adirondacks to Buffalo, where President William McKinley lay dying, the victim of an assassin's bullet. Morris argues, correctly, that few persons in the history of the United States were better qualified to be president than Theodore Roosevelt in spite of his relatively young age of forty-two years (John F. Kennedy was forty-three when he was elected). He had served in the New York legislature and as that state's governor after his heroic and well-publicized actions in the Spanish-American War. He had been a federal civil service commissioner and the assistant secretary of the Navy in Washington, D.C. A member of one of New York's old Dutch families, Roosevelt was partly driven to excel and to serve because of a class sense of noblesse oblige and partly perhaps to compensate for the physical weaknesses he had experienced as a child. Always ambitious, he tested himself in the political arena as well as in the wilderness, and victory was the goal, whether it be over foreign foes, political rivals, or grizzly bears.

The early twentieth century was an era of bitter rivalry between the nation's political parties. A Republican by inheritance—his father was a friend of Abraham Lincoln—Roosevelt had little use for Democrats, but he also had little respect for many of the conservative leaders of his own party. Roosevelt, who supplemented some inherited wealth by publishing books and articles, was often suspicious of the nouveau riche industrialists and bankers, the so-called captains of industry and finance, such as J. Pierpont Morgan and John D. Rockefeller. His animosities against his opponents, political and industrial, were tempered by an acute political sensitivity that belies Roosevelt's reputation as an impetuous adolescent or a simple moralistic bully. A moralist Roosevelt most definitely was, but he also understood the nuances of politics. When he succeeded McKinley, he promised to not swerve from McKinley's policies, and he kept that promise long enough to reassure not only the country but also its economic and political elite. Mark Hanna was his chief rival for the 1904 presidential nomination, but Roosevelt quickly and cleverly outmaneuvered the Ohio senator.

Roosevelt's initial campaign against the power of the economic elite and their business monopolies focused upon the Northern Securities Company, created by J. Pierpont Morgan, James J. Hill, and Edward H. Harriman, and which controlled the railway network of the nation's northwest. The government's suit was successful and Roosevelt picked up the nickname as the "trust-buster." However, sheer size was never his primary concern, and other presidents "broke" more trusts. For Roosevelt, business behavior was more important than size itself.

Among the many issues and events related by Morris which occupied Roosevelt's crowded hours, two in particular might be singled out for their relevance to a later era. Roosevelt was a product of his own time and place, and his attitudes on race would not seem particularly enlightened to a different generation. However, in comparison with the other progressive president of the early twentieth century, Woodrow Wilson, Roosevelt's actions and attitudes deserve praise. He was very much a social Darwinist, but when Roosevelt discussed superior races he really meant superior cultures. He was not a believer in the virtues of multiculturalism. For him, American society, largely but not exclusively based upon European civilization, was superior to any other, but he believed that any biological race, be it African, Asian, or whatever, could and would eventually achieve equality and parity in the United States. One of the most controversial acts of his presidency, for which he was much vilified, was his invitation to Booker T. Washington, the prominent African American educator, to dine at the White House. Roosevelt was apparently shocked at the negative reaction, and Roosevelt the politician did not invite Washington back. On another occasion he vociferously condemned a lynching of an African American in Wilmington, Delaware, a response that most politicians of his era would not have made. On the other hand, when African American troops were accused of rioting in Brownsville, Texas, Roosevelt had them all discharged from the Army when none of the soldiers would identify any of the supposed rioters. Would Roosevelt have done the same if it had been a white regiment? Probably not, but he might have, as he invariably made decisions based on morality and honor as defined by himself.

Conservation was the other domestic issue which continues to reverberate through the generations. More than any president before or since, Roosevelt was a conservationist. An outdoorsman from an early age, Roosevelt was an avid hunter of big and small game, something for which he would be criticized in a later and different America. His scientific knowledge of birds and animals was extensive, and he had an aesthetic appreciation for the natural world. He camped in Yosemite with the radical naturalist John Muir, and he established national monuments and bird sanctuaries, supported reclamation projects, and set aside millions of acres of forest land for the public's use. In May, 1908, to give publicity to the issue of conservation and to plan for the future, he sponsored the nation's first national conservation conference, which was attended by the nation's governors and other luminaries. Few of his successors have been so enlightened and so committed to the preservation of the nation's natural resources.

Morris devotes much of *Theodore Rex* to the foreign policy events of Roosevelt's almost eight years as president. No philosophical pacifist, Roosevelt had personally experienced the triumph and tragedy of war in Cuba in 1898. A practitioner of realpolitik, he had an appreciation for the uses of power, for good and ill, in international affairs. In spite of his popular image, Roosevelt was a consummate diplomat, achieving his aims and ends more often than not by stealth and secrecy. A threat by Germany to occupy Venezuela saw Roosevelt use an iron fist in a velvet glove, allowing Germany to back down without loss of face. He labored subtly and successfully to end the Russo-Japanese War, for which he was awarded the Nobel Peace Prize. Japan's rise to world power status found Roosevelt attempting to meliorate the friction caused by Japanese immigration to the United States, particularly to California, the citizens of which had responded with various acts of discrimination against Japanese immigrants. Roosevelt tolerated if not encouraged the secession of Panama from Columbia in order to facilitate the long-sought canal across Central America, an act for which he was both praised and excoriated. The final act of his presidency was to send an American naval fleet around the world, and he witnessed its safe return just before the end of his term in March, 1909.

Theodore Rex holds the reader's attention, in part because of Morris's writing skills, in part because Roosevelt himself was such a formidable figure. The work is largely a study of Roosevelt the public man. Roosevelt the husband and father is portrayed, but not with particular depth or revelation, possibly because Edith Kermit Roosevelt destroyed the correspondence between herself and her husband after his death. Morris generally succeeds in this work, but by closely focusing upon Roosevelt and using a relatively rigid chronological approach, a lack of context and analysis is occasionally apparent. Nevertheless, when completed, Morris's life of Roosevelt will remain the standard biography for some considerable time.

Eugene Larson

Sources for Further Study

Booklist 98 (October 1, 2001): 268.
The New York Times Book Review 106 (December 9, 2001): 10.
The New Yorker 77 (November 19, 2001): 81.
Publishers Weekly 248 (October 15, 2001): 55.

THINKS . . .

Author: David Lodge (1935-   )
Publisher: Viking (New York). 342 pp. $24.95
Type of work: Novel
Time: The late 1990's
Locale: Gloucestershire, England

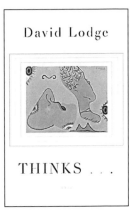

⁓

A novel set in a fictional English university where an eminent but philandering cognitive scientist, whose chief interest is exploring the nature of human consciousness, sets his lustful sights on an attractive, widowed novelist

⁓

Principal characters:
> RALPH MESSENGER, professor of cognitive science at Gloucester University
> CARRIE MESSENGER, his wife, an American
> HELEN REED, a novelist who is teaching a course in creative writing at Gloucester University
> MARIANNE RICHMOND, a married woman who has a flirtation with Messenger
> DOUGLAS C. DOUGLAS, professor of cognitive science at Gloucester University
> SANDRA PICKERING, a student in Helen Reed's class
> LUDMILA LISK, a student from the Czech Republic who has a brief affair with Messenger

David Lodge has long been a writer of engaging, literate, witty, entertaining novels, many of them taking place in an academic setting. Reading him is always a pleasure because his irony is never savage; while poking gentle fun at his characters, such as the famous Morris Zapp in *Changing Places* (1975) and *Small World* (1984), he never dislikes them. His is a tolerant, wryly amused voice, one that always has empathy for the small vanities and hypocrisies, the tangle of imperfect relationships and thwarted desires that seem to go with the human condition. *Thinks . . .* is no exception. As in *Nice Work* (1988), in which Lodge juxtaposed a trendy female left-wing academic with her direct, opposite, a down-to-earth, practical businessman, so in *Thinks . . .* he sets up his two main characters as typifying opposing approaches to the nature of human consciousness, the topic he wishes to explore. Lest the reader find such a topic too daunting, Lodge makes sure that he does not lose his comic touch, and his gift for presenting real characters in believable interactions is as apparent as ever. The ideas do not overwhelm the story, which is skillfully plotted and contains many twists and surprises along the way.

The two protagonists in *Thinks . . .* are Ralph Messenger, professor of cognitive science at Gloucester University, and Helen Reed, an established novelist who is taking on a temporary assignment as a creative writing instructor at the university. The story alternates between their points of view and also has chapters told by a narrator in the third person. There are also some fine literary parodies which occur when Reed's students, in a literary exercise, imitate the styles of some well-known writers.

Messenger (that is what his wife calls him) is a fine creation. He is a charismatic, highly suc-

~

David Lodge is the author of several novels and a novella, including Changing Places *(1975),* Small World *(1984, shortlisted for the Booker Prize),* Nice Work *(1988, also shortlisted for the Booker),* Paradise News *(1991), and* Therapy *(1995). He is also the author of several works of literary criticism, including* The Art of Fiction *(1992).*

~

cessful academic and media star, the sort who is always popping up on radio and television explaining new scientific discoveries, hot psychological issues, and the like. As a popularizer, he is regarded with some suspicion by other academics, particularly his dour, uptight colleague Douglas C. Douglas, who has the brains but lacks Messenger's powerful presence and so misses out on the trappings of success. Messenger's intellectual interests lie in the field of consciousness, the systematic study of the human mind, which, he says, was once the domain of just a few philosophers but is now the biggest game in town, attracting the interest of physicists, biologists, zoologists, mathematicians, and neurologists. Messenger heads the prestigious Holt Belling Center for Cognitive Science and spends a lot of time thinking about topics such as artificial intelligence, or AI, as it is known in the profession. He and his graduate students are all involved in projects that attempt to duplicate in robots or computers the workings of human consciousness. This includes something called "affective modeling," which is computer simulation of the way emotions affect human behavior.

Messenger is an argumentative fellow, not given to self-doubt. He is confident that his way of seeing the world is the correct one, and he has little patience with views that run counter to his own. He recognizes the validity only of things that can be objectively measured. He does not believe in such abstractions as the soul or spirit, which for him are simply ways of speaking of certain kinds of brain activity. In his view, when the brain ceases to function, consciousness ceases also. He has no time for what cognitive scientists call "pan psychism," the idea that consciousness is the fundamental component of the universe, which he associates with a vague transcendentalism or oriental religion. He believes that everything that processes information (including a human being), is a machine, and can be explained in purely physical terms.

When Messenger is not thinking about issues surrounding the study of consciousness, he is thinking about sex (or perhaps it should be the other way round). He has had many extramarital affairs, and has developed an unspoken agreement with his American wife Carrie that he can continue to do this just as long as his affairs take place well away from their own neighborhood. For the most part, this arrangement works well for him, since he travels extensively to academic conferences, although at the beginning of the novel he is developing a risky flirtation with Marianne Richmond, the wife of the head of the English department.

What really upsets the smooth running of Messenger's intellectual, professional, and marital life is the arrival on campus of novelist Helen Reed. They meet at a dinner party, and Helen is rather fascinated by his movie star presence. When they meet again by chance and have lunch together, it becomes apparent that their attitudes and worldviews are decidedly different. Helen was brought up as a Catholic, and she cannot entirely relinquish the remnants of her faith, especially as she is still recovering from the recent death of her husband. She does not believe that the universe is entirely random or without purpose, and clings to the belief that there must be some kind of afterlife, an idea that to Messenger seems pointless.

However, Helen is sufficiently interested in Messenger's theories to encourage him to tell her more about his pet subject. He tells her that the human brain functions like a computer, "running lots of programs simultaneously. What we call 'attention' is a particular interaction between various parts of the total system. The subsystems and possible connections and combinations between them are so multitudinous and complex that it's very difficult to simulate the whole process." The ultimate goal, as Helen deduces, is to design a computer that thinks like a human being. Helen has her doubts. "A computer that has hangovers and falls in love and suffers bereavement?" she pointedly inquires. Or a robot that laughs at another robot's jokes?

Helen is extremely skeptical that any computer program could even come close to replicating the mechanics of human consciousness. For Helen, the experts in the study of consciousness are not Messenger and his friends in cognitive science but the great novelists, especially Henry James. It is they who are able to penetrate what goes on in someone's head—their emotions, feelings, and memories. In the jargon of cognitive science, these elements of consciousness are known as *qualia*. But Messenger, who loves a good argument and is attracted to Helen partly because she is able to give as good as she gets, claims that all a reader can discover from a novel is what the writer thought, which in his opinion is not real knowledge. Messenger is only prepared to accept scientific knowledge, so his quest is to find a way, so far impossible, to give an objective, verifiable account of the subjective phenomenon of consciousness.

One experiment Messenger is trying is dictating his thoughts into a tape recorder, just as they come to him, without censoring or editing, to see whether this could reveal anything about the structure of thought. He soon finds out the difficulties involved in such an enterprise. Not only does the knowledge that he is conducting an experiment alter the direction and content of his thoughts, but when the thoughts are articulated, he is already at one remove from the phenomenon of consciousness itself. He realizes that every phrase he speaks is like a "bulletin, an agreed text hammered out behind closed doors after a nanosecond's intense editorial debate, and then released to the speech centers of the brain for outward transmission . . . And that editing process is impossible to record or observe, except as a pattern of electro-chemical activity between millions of neurons."

The transcribed text of Messenger's thoughts makes interesting reading. It is a disconnected stream-of-consciousness narrative that jumps back and forth from philosophical ideas to mundane thoughts to explicit details of Messenger's sexual desires and exploits, both in the past and in the anticipated future. One object of his desire, spelled out in some detail, is Helen Reed, and it does not take him long to make a pass at her. She firmly rejects this, but they do become friends. When Messenger discovers that Helen keeps a journal, he is extremely curious as to what her private thoughts are, and he proposes a very risky experiment—that they make an exchange. He presents this idea to her as an opportunity to discover what it is normally impossible to know— what is going on in the mind of another. Fortunately for Messenger, Helen refuses.

The plot now moves into high gear. Helen has for a while been disconcerted after she discovered eerie similarities between a character in the work-in-progress of her student, Sandra Pickering, and Helen's dead husband, Martin. At first Helen assumed that Sandra was merely borrowing from one of Helen's own novels, but the similarities go even further than would have been possible through literary plagiarism. When she challenges Sandra, the truth comes out: Sandra had an affair with Martin when she worked at the BBC, where he was a radio producer. Helen is devastated, even more so when she discovers that Sandra was not the first young woman to be seduced by Martin, whom she had thought to be the perfect husband. Helen is thrown into further confusion when she discovers that Carrie, Messenger's wife, is having an affair with an art professor from the university. Faced with such evidence of betrayal all around her, Helen reverses her previous attitude regarding Messenger, and they embark on a passionate affair.

The events that so disturb Helen are confirmation of the central idea of *Thinks . . . ,* that one cannot know what is going on in someone's else's head. This is also clear from the journals of Messenger and Helen, since they sometimes offer divergent views of events in which they both participated, or misconstrue the motives and intentions of the other. Needless to say, things do not turn out too well for the secret lovers, who go through—as lovers do—numerous subtle shifts in their emotions and end up with a relationship that neither of them wants. No robots could match them.

Bryan Aubrey

Sources for Further Study

America 185 (September 24, 2001): 29.
The Atlantic Monthly 287 (June, 2001): 104.
Booklist 97 (April 1, 2001): 1428.
Commonweal 128 (August 17, 2001): 24.
Library Journal 126 (June 1, 2001): 217.
The Nation 273 (July 23, 2001): 42.
The New York Review of Books 48 (August 9, 2001): 27.
The New York Times, June 5, 2001, p. B7.
The New York Times Book Review 106 (June 10, 2001): 8.
Publishers Weekly 248 (June 4, 2001): 58.
The Times Literary Supplement, February 23, 2001, p. 21.

THIS IS NOT A NOVEL

Author: David Markson (1927-   )
Publisher: Counterpoint (Washington, D.C.). 190 pp.
   $15.00
Type of work: Novel

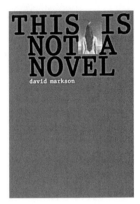

~

A highly experimental work presenting itself as an anti-novel without plot, characters, or setting, yet interspersing the musings of a central authorial voice with a wry collage of historical facts, wide-ranging quotations, and literary anecdotes, all focusing on the rigors of the creative life in the face of aging, neglect, and inevitable death

~

   Principal character:
         WRITER, the protagonist and central focus of self-reflexive commentary
            about the genre of this book and its relationship to the life of its aging
            author

   This Is Not a Novel has the feel of a valediction. "Farewell and be kind," the book concludes, appropriating the last words of Robert Burton's singular treatise, *The Anatomy of Melancholy* (1628). David Markson, in his mid-seventies and evidently in poor health, appears to bid adieu not only to the reader of this slender book but also to the craft that has been his life's passion and heartache for nearly half a century. Notwithstanding this long career as a novelist, Markson's published works of fiction are comparatively few. Following the appearance of three "entertainments," *The Ballad of Dingus Magee* (1965) was his most commercially successful novel, adapted into a Western film starring Frank Sinatra. Markson's career took a different turn in his next two works, *Going Down* (1970) and *Springer's Progress* (1977), ambitious novels that did not attract a large readership. The latter in particular appealed chiefly to a select but remarkably enthusiastic audience who appreciated its Joycean play with language and its bawdy comedy. Clearly the apex in Markson's critical reputation was reached, however, with *Wittgenstein's Mistress* (1988), a highly experimental narrative featuring a complex female protagonist, a painter convinced that she is the last human on earth. Nearly a decade passed before the appearance of another novel, *Reader's Block* (1997) which, like *This Is Not a Novel*, offers an idiosyncratic collage of anecdotes, quotations, gossip, obituary notes, and self-reflexive musings on the writing life.
   Despite the acclaim earned by these works, especially *Wittgenstein's Mistress*—called by critic David Foster Wallace "pretty much the high point of experimental fiction in this country"—Markson has perhaps been as well known by some for his literary friendships, which include those with Malcolm Lowry (his one-time mentor),

Conrad Aiken, Dylan Thomas, and Jack Kerouac. Fully aware of the relative obscurity of his own artistic efforts, Markson has arrived at a propitious point from which to take stock of his life and career. In effect, *This Is Not a Novel* responds to this need, though in a rather quirky way.

One of the work's refrains is "*Timor mortis conturbat me/* The fear of death distresses me." That the book is haunted by death is undeniable. Indeed, the deaths of almost five hundred prominent artists, philosophers, statesmen, actors, athletes—their precise causes and attendant circumstances—are ruefully enumerated throughout *This Is Not a Novel*. Thus James McNeill Whistler, Benjamin Britten, and William Butler Yeats all died of heart failure. Vergil, Ludovico Ariosto, Stephen Crane, and pitcher Rube Waddell succumbed to tuberculosis. Strokes claimed Ben Jonson, Jean-Jacques Rousseau, Miguel de Unamuno y Jugo, and Theolonius Monk. Julius Caesar, Jean-Paul Marat, and John F. Kennedy were assassinated. Dante Alighieri died from malaria, Geoffrey Chaucer from plague, Isaac Newton from complications caused by a kidney stone, Ludwig von Beethoven from dropsy,

A lifelong New Yorker, David Markson is the author of many novels, including the highly regarded Wittgenstein's Mistress (1988); several "entertainments"; a volume of Collected Poems (1993); and Malcolm Lowry's "Volcano": Myth, Symbol, Meaning (1978), a seminal critical study devoted to the masterpiece of his close friend and one-time mentor.

Charles Baudelaire from syphilis. Victims of that modern scourge, cancer, include Ty Cobb, Gertrude Stein, Ludwig Wittgenstein, Rachel Carlson, and James Baldwin. Joseph Stalin and Sergei Prokofiev died on the same day, as did President Kennedy and Aldous Huxley. F. Scott Fitzgerald and Nathaniel West died on successive days, having dined together a week before. Swallowing a toothpick led to Sherwood Anderson's death from peritonitis. Eighty-eight-year-old Hilaire Belloc set his clothes on fire when he spilled coal from a grate. Tennessee Williams "choked to death on a plastic cap of a nasal spray."

These obituary notices are profusely scattered throughout the book, several appearing on most pages. The cumulative effect of this necrological incantation is something like that of viewing the names listed on the black marble wall of the Vietnam Veterans Memorial. Death is inexorable, capricious, and always decisive even when its precise means are unclear (for instance, the cause of Antonio Vivaldi's death was uncertain but was listed in the 1741 Vienna church registry as brought on by "internal fire"). It claims the mighty and the mild impartially. Nevertheless, death's ubiquity only underscores the artist's dream of arresting or transcending time through the alchemy of imagination. For his part, Markson notes "the mistake of thinking that one may pluck a single leaf from the laurel tree without paying for it with his life." Yet he also quotes Pindar on the permanence of art: "When the city I extol shall have perished, when the men to whom I sing shall have faded into oblivion, my words shall remain."

Despite this bravado, much of *This Is Not a Novel* is devoted to a kind of lamentation over the sad neglect of serious artists, particularly in America. He records such shameful facts as Herman Melville's earnings from nearly a half century of fiction, just above $10,000; and F. Scott Fitzgerald's final royalty statement, disclosing that just seven copies of *The Great Gatsby* were sold during the six months preceding his death. The fact that writers now considered among the most important could be so overlooked or forgotten in their own lifetimes gives added piquancy to Markson's own valediction.

Some of the allusions to eminent writers, painters, composers, and thinkers are decidedly more lighthearted. Predictably, given the ongoing concern with neglected artists, critics draw fire. "Dear Sir," begins an imaginary letter to one reviewer, "I am sitting in the smallest room of my house. Your review is before me. Shortly it will be behind me." Sjøren Kierkegaard's apt analogy for reading reviews of his work is cited: "The long martyrdom of being trampled to death by geese." A small sample of such a trampling is Alfred Noyes's verdict on James Joyce's monumental novel *Ulysses:* "There is no foulness conceivable to the mind of man that has not been poured forth into its imbecile pages." As Jean J. Sibelius noted with justice, "No one ever put up a statue of a critic." To these quotations Markson adds a generous sample of amusing anecdotes about writers and artists through the ages. Henry James once took cover behind a tree to avoid a meeting with Ford Madox Ford. Salvadore Dali wore a diving helmet while giving a lecture in London, and almost suffocated. W. H. Auden was arrested in Barcelona for urinating in a public park; in later life, he was known to attend the opera wearing a stained tuxedo and bedroom slippers. George Orwell once described Auden, known for his leftist politics during the 1930's, as "the kind of person who is always somewhere else when the trigger is pulled." Not to be outdone in the arena of invective, Auden once described Rainer Maria Rilke (who was male) as "the greatest lesbian poet since Sappho." The Mexican muralist Diego Rivera, a notorious womanizer, rarely bathed. For his part, Auguste Renoir found Leonardo da Vinci to be a bore, while Michelangelo concluded that his countryman was "as ignorant as a maidservant."

While these tidbits have the undeniable interest of highbrow celebrity gossip, Markson leavens the mix by adding a number of anomalous "factoids" and queries. For instance, he notes that there is no mention of writing in either *The Iliad* or the New Testament; that the particulars of Helen's beauty are never actually described in *The Iliad*; that Abraham Lincoln never visited Europe; that the tail gunner on the *Enola Gay* wore a Brooklyn Dodgers cap. Among the questions raised: What was the black substance spilling out of the dead heroine's mouth in *Madame Bovary*? Was Shane the hero's first or last name, in the famous film of that title? What was the cause of Addie Bundren's death in William Faulkner's *As I Lay Dying*? If the Nazis had won World War II, what would be known of the Holocaust? References to baseball further diversify the range of anecdotes. At five feet, four inches, Wee Willie Keeler was more than three inches taller than John Keats. Pitcher Hugh Casey once out-boxed Ernest Hemingway, until the latter kicked him in the groin. Poet Marianne Moore read a book by Christy Mathewson about the art of pitching. Joe DiMaggio died on the birthday of Al Gionfriddo, whose famous play in a World Series had once robbed the Yankees star of a home run, and so on.

Given such a curious mixture of elements, what can be said about the kind of work this is? Reviewers have described it variously as a literary Chinese box, a collage of aphorisms and artsy gossip, a commonplace book (that is, an anthology of miscellaneous quotations with commentary), or a sort of confession in the form of a list. While there is some merit in each of these descriptions, the question of genre is raised most saliently in the book itself, first of all by its very title. A character referred to throughout simply as Writer announces at the outset that he is "weary unto death of making up stories . . . [and] of inventing characters." He wishes instead to contrive a plotless, characterless novel which "seduc[es] the reader into turning pages nonetheless." Though this work would contain "no *sequence of events*" and "no indicated *passage of time*," and would have no setting—no description of place, no portrayal of society or manners—it would still "get somewhere." If not a novel, what would this work be? Writer considers several possible analogues from other artistic or discursive forms: an autobiography, a heap of riddles, a sort of mural, a treatise on human nature, an epic poem, a polyphonic opera, a prose alternative to T. S. Eliot's poem *The Waste Land*. He attempts still another definition in terms of structure: "Nonlinear. Discontinuous. Collage-like. An assemblage. . . . Obstinately cross-referenced and of cryptic interconnective syntax."

It is the last point that bears special scrutiny. Do the various elements assembled in *This Is Not a Novel* ultimately connect? Is there a significant intensification or coming together, despite the avoidance of familiar narrative conventions? If the book's fuguelike arrangement seems to move in different directions, sooner or later it returns to the same issue of the artist's struggle to create while facing a death sentence. In the end, the vast network of intertextual references serves as a sort of backdrop against which the existence of Writer as a character takes on added definition. In a book that eschews inventing characters, he asks early on, "does Writer even exist?" Writer, "not being a character but the author, here," describes himself sitting as he writes, talking to himself, reacting to the passages quoted, suffering from backaches and even a "silent heart attack;" all of this, along with the gathering strands of the book, serves to verify Writer's existence and validate his destiny: "Writer is *writing*, is all. Still." If "life consists in what a man is thinking all day," as Ralph Waldo Emerson believed, then Writer's reflections on sundry figures, from Homer to Dizzy Dean, constitute a life of the mind—and this is the substance of the novel regarded as what D. H. Lawrence termed "a thought-adventure."

Markson withholds his climactic disclosure until the book's final page: "Writer's cancer." This line has considerable impact, precisely because of the jettisoning of most traditional narrative devices. Freed from customary attention to causality and temporal change, the reader is tacitly invited to participate in the realization of Writer's fate and to appreciate its cost. One reviewer, Sven Birkerts, has gone so far as to claim that by means of the book's nonlinear arrangement "we are released into history in a new achronological way. Suddenly . . . we are all brothers under the skin." Writer, for his part, returns once more to the question of classification: "Or was it possibly nothing more than a fundamentally recognizable genre all the while, no matter what Writer averred?/ Nothing more or less than a *read*?/ Simply an unconventional, generally melancholy though sometimes even playful now-ending read?" This is surely a rhetorical question, for in the words of Dizzy Dean (who died of a heart attack), "If you can do it, it ain't bragging."

Ronald G. Walker

Sources for Further Study

Booklist 97 (April 15, 2001): 1535.
The Boston Globe, May 2, 2001, p. F10.
Newsday, March 25, 2001, p. B14.
Publishers Weekly, 248 (March 19, 2001): 74.
Review of Contemporary Fiction 21 (Summer, 2001): 158.
The Washington Post Book World, April 8, 2001, p. 15.

TIP O'NEILL AND THE DEMOCRATIC CENTURY

Author: John A. Farrell (1953-   )
Publisher: Little, Brown (Boston). 776 pp. $29.95
Type of work: Biography and history
Time: 1912-1994
Locale: The United States

~

Based largely on some three hundred interviews, this is a prodigious and elegant journalistic account of an immensely engaging and sometimes ruthless New Deal Democrat who served as Speaker of the House of Representatives during the presidencies of Jimmy Carter and Ronald Reagan

~

Principal personages:
> THOMAS P. "TIP" O'NEILL, speaker of the U.S. House of Representatives, 1977-1987
> JIMMY CARTER, thirty-ninth president of the United States
> RONALD REAGAN, fortieth president of the United States
> KIRK O'DONNELL, Speaker O'Neill's staff counsel
> JAMES (JIM) WRIGHT, speaker of the U.S. House of Representatives, 1987-1090

Shortly before his death in January, 1994, at the age of eighty-one, Tip O'Neill, proud Massachusetts son of a North Cambridge ward heeler, put together an acute political primer entitled *All Politics Is Local—And Other Rules* (with Gary Hymel, 1994). Born in a rented third-floor apartment, he never lost sight of his roots and wanted the worth of his half-century career as a public servant measured in terms of opportunities provided for working-class people. With his towering bulk, back-room mannerisms, and faith that government could ameliorate, if not cure, society's ills, he personified to his admirers an old-fashioned concept of politics as service to constituents. To conservatives he exemplified the flatulence of tax-and-spend liberalism. To its great credit, *Tip O'Neill and the Democratic Century* examines both the strengths and weaknesses of its subject's political creed and character. Readers learn about O'Neill's ingratiating qualities but also his flaws. Like former U.S. president Warren G. Harding, he could not say "no" to cronies and was an inveterate gambler. After witnessing a hydrogen bomb explosion at Yucca Flats, Nevada, he discovered bruises around his belly. He feared radiation poisoning, but the discoloration turned out to be from leaning against Las Vegas craps tables. Though some thought the nickname "Tip" was short for "tipsy," alcoholism was not one of his vices. The nickname derived from a St. Louis Browns namesake who mastered the art of fouling off pitches

John A. Farrell is the Washington editor of The Boston Globe, *where he has reported on national politics since 1987. He has won the George Polk Award, the Gerald Ford Prize and White House Correspondents Association award for White House coverage, and a Dirksen Congressional Center grant.*

until he got a fat one to hit. It was once common for O'Neills to be called Tip, much like Rhodes boys were called Dusty.

Irish American Bostonians, writes Farrell, viewed politics "through a prism of ethnic resentment." While a Harvard lawn boy, O'Neill received a reprimand for clipping around trees seated rather than from a kneeling position. The children of Boston Brahmins snubbed his sister at Boston Latin School. O'Neill's friend Jeremiah Sullivan could not get in the door of blueblood law firms despite a Harvard law degree. Rarely did "town and gown" come together as equals although, according to family lore, O'Neill's great-great-grandmother, Catherine Quinlan O'Connell, swapped stories with poet Henry Wadsworth Longfellow in a Harvard Square grocery store. Mummy Kate, as she was called, returned to Ireland at age one hundred with a seventy-nine-year-old son and lived three more years.

Thomas P. O'Neill, Jr., inherited a love for politics from his father, an immigrant's son with an eye toward social mobility. At fourteen, he and other Barry's Corner gang members passed out leaflets for State Representative Charles Cavanaugh. A year later, they campaigned for Al Smith, grandson of an Irishman and the United States' first Catholic major-party candidate for president. In 1935, O'Neill made a bid for Cambridge City Council while attending Boston College. The following year, on the coattails of Franklin D. Roosevelt's reelection landslide, he won a seat to the Massachusetts General Court. Because a poker-playing buddy was the brother of presidential intimate Missy LeHand, he got to meet FDR. O'Neill later claimed to have been dumbfounded to find his hero in a wheelchair.

O'Neill served sixteen years in the Commonwealth's Lower House. During his freshman term, he earned the wrath of the Cambridge American Legion for opposing a bill requiring educators to take a loyalty oath. He believed it demeaned his sister, who taught parochial school. In 1949, the wily lawmaker became the first Democrat to serve as Massachusetts house speaker. Looking for broader horizons, he eyed John F. Kennedy's congressional seat. The two were never particularly close, but O'Neill appreciated Kennedy's tipping him off in advance about his intent to run against incumbent senator Henry Cabot Lodge in 1952, thus giving him a head start on rival Michael LoPresti. Farrell compares the LoPresti-O'Neill fight to a tribal war. O'Neill won under questionable circumstances. An adversary noted, "The gravestones voted."

Initially, O'Neill disliked being a U.S. Representative. Leaving his wife Millie and five children back home, he roomed with fellow freshman Eddie Boland in sparse quarters and joined the Tuesday-Thursday delegation that went home for long week-ends. He curried favor with constituents, badgering judges, prison wardens, or immigration officials for favors and letting lobbyists make phone calls from his office or trade on his good name. His biggest headache was keeping the obsolete Boston Naval Shipyard afloat (it remained open until 1973). A protégé of party leader John McCormick (whose poker games were too rich for his blood), O'Neill secured a spot on the powerful House Rules Committee. Soon he gained entry to the "Board of Education," Speaker Rayburn's smoke-filled hideaway inner sanctum. There "Mr. Sam's" closest buddies relaxed and drank hard liquor, occasionally relieving themselves in a small sink. O'Neill entertained them with stories about Boston rogue politicians such as James Michael Curley.

In 1960, O'Neill flirted with running for governor of Massachusetts. His wife Millie realized he would be a disaster as an administrator and convinced him to stay put. Months later, he helped John F. Kennedy obtain the presidential nomination and was a conduit in negotiations to get Lyndon B. Johnson on the ticket. Kennedy needed the Texan in order to be competitive in the South but did not want to tender the offer only to have it refused. In turn, Kennedy learned that if offered the second spot, Johnson would feel honor-bound to accept. To appease angry liberals, Farrell concludes, Bobby Kennedy concocted the canard that his brother had expected that Johnson would turn the deal down.

The politicians who engineered U.S. involvement in Vietnam, regarded O'Neill as a parochial embarrassment and denied him meaningful White House access, especially after he, in lockstep with Catholic prelates, opposed Kennedy's federal aid to education bill. In foreign policy, he supported containment in South Vietnam. In 1966, he told an antiwar delegation that they were a bunch of Communist sympathizers, then shifted positions the following year under pressure from family and constituents. Enraged at the betrayal, Lyndon B. Johnson called him an "S.O.B." at an emotional Oval Office meeting.

Upon John W. McCormack's retirement in 1970, the diminutive Oklahoman Carl Albert became Speaker of the House, the charismatic Louisianan Hale Boggs moved up to Majority Leader, and the position of Whip opened up. The job might have gone to Hugh Carey, another Catholic Northerner, but fellow New Yorkers James Delaney and John Rooney blackballed him. "It was a case of the pig-shit Irish being jealous of the lace-curtain Irish," an informant told Farrell. Two years later, Boggs was killed in a plane crash in Alaska, and O'Neill became majority leader. Four years later, Albert stepped down, and O'Neill's ascension was complete.

Watergate temporarily reversed the trend toward an imperial presidency. The House transformed itself, in Farrell's words, "from a sleepy feudal" domain into a body "that distributed its reclaimed powers among a host of youthful, more ideological, and determinedly independent representatives." Initially, O'Neill had supported President Richard Nixon's bailout of Lockheed Aircraft and his revenue sharing legislation. In turn, Nixon signed Democrat-sponsored bills establishing the Environmental Protection Agency and hiking Social Security benefits through cost-of-living adjustments. When Vice President Spiro Agnew resigned in disgrace, O'Neill pressed Nixon to replace him with House Minority Leader Gerald Ford. He was following the advice of Carl Albert, who in Farrell's opinion was more sagacious than his impish persona suggested. Many liberals wanted to stall Ford's confirmation and push for impeachment, since Albert was next in line of presidential succession. Such a coup would have backfired, O'Neill realized. Unlike Republican House leaders during the Monica Lewinsky scandal of President Bill Clinton's administration, O'Neill insisted the impeachment process unfold in a visibly nonpartisan and judicious manner. O'Neill winced when a fellow congressman asked how it felt to bring down a president.

Speaker O'Neill practiced policies of inclusion that gave colleagues a role in the process and a stake in the outcome. Farrell writes, "Soon every major issue had a task force, and a bright young member to chair it, willing to trade his or her independence for the power and celebrity of serving the leadership." Freshman Congressman Richard Gephardt, age thirty-six, chaired a Social Security task force which recommended the largest ever increase in payroll taxes. On the other hand, O'Neill's close relationship with Korean businessman (and Korean CIA agent) Tongsun Park came under scrutiny in the reform-minded post-Watergate atmosphere, as did his participation in a nursing home sweetheart deal. Common Causes's Fred Wertheimer put these sleazy items in perspective:

> He may have done favors for his friends. He may have cut corners. But he didn't leave here with TV stations, a bank account, or a large stock portfolio. He wasn't in this for personal financial gain.

The latter 1970's were years of retrenchment and retreat for liberals compared to the salad days of the 1960's. O'Neill swam against the tide, jousting frequently with President Jimmy Carter, whose arrogant staff did not pay him proper deference. After a series of misunderstandings, O'Neill nicknamed chief-of-staff Hamilton Jordan "Hannibal Jerkin." The squabbling reached a fever pitch in 1978 with the firing of O'Neill crony Bob Griffin as deputy administrator of the General Services Administration. At a White House breakfast, tears streamed down O'Neill's face as he lashed out at such shabby treatment. Carter retreated and appointed Griffin a U.S. trade representative.

In 1980, Republicans viewed the florid, cigar-smoking Speaker with a penchant for blarney as "the perfect caricature of old-time politics" and ran commercials of him in an obsolete gas-guzzling car. To their delight, Ronald Reagan's landslide victory combined with their capture of the Senate left O'Neill as opposition leader. Refurbishing his image, O'Neill proved, as Farrell concludes, that an old dog could learn new tricks. The resulting face-off between the two canny Irishmen for America's soul is what gives his book its high drama. Writes Farrell: "Theirs was no sophistic debate: these were worldviews clashing, hot lava meeting thundering surf."

At their first face-to-face meeting, O'Neill promised the president-elect a six-month honeymoon and welcomed him to "the big leagues" (he was an avid Red Sox fan, his adversary a former baseball announcer who had once played the role of pitcher Grover Cleveland Alexander). Reagan won a stunning tax-cut victory, but

O'Neill made a successful stand when presidential advisers took aim at Social Security. In 1982, a severe recession helped Democrats pick up twenty-six House seats. O'Neill took particular delight in the defeat of Long Islander John LeBoutillier, who had labeled him "big, fat, and out of control—just like the federal government," and Pennsylvanian Gene Atkinson, who had switched parties and earned from O'Neill the nickname "Gyppo," after the turncoat played by Victor McLaglen in John Ford's movie *The Informer* (1935). In 1984, O'Neill pushed hard for Geraldine Ferraro's inclusion on his party's national ticket. Despite Reagan's easy reelection victory, many credited O'Neill with having prevented the loss of the House. After serving one more term, O'Neill helped Bobby Kennedy's son Joseph P. Kennedy II secure his House seat.

O'Neill's mark on history, Farrell concludes, was limiting the impact of the so-called Reagan revolution. Yet even if the core of the welfare state survived, the Reagan revolution succeeded attitudinally. By easing the path of white ethnics into the middle class, Democrats paid a price for their success. Independent-minded white-collar Catholics joined the Republican opposition in droves in disgruntlement over the spiraling cost of Great Society entitlement programs and the party's stance on social and racial issues. Eight years after O'Neill's retirement and eleven months following his fatal heart attack, Democrats lost control of the House to Newt Gingrich's supporters. Two years later, "New Democrat" Bill Clinton announced that "the era of big government is over." Even so, at the end of "the Democratic Century," countless workers and contractors in the Boston metropolitan area were still benefiting from a fifteen-year-old multibillion-dollar prime-the-pump project, the Central Artery/Third Harbor Tunnel known as the Big Dig. O'Neill had feared it would be known as "Tip's Folly," but it was his legacy, proof, as he himself put it, that "the squeaky wheel gets the grease in Washington."

James B. Lane

Sources for Further Study

The Atlantic Monthly 287 (March, 2001): 90.
The Christian Science Monitor, March 13, 2001, p. 11.
Library Journal 126 (November 9, 2001): 121.
The New York Times Book Review 106 (March 11, 2001): 8.

TO THE HERMITAGE

Author: Malcolm Bradbury (1932-2000)
Publisher: Overlook Press (Woodstock, N.Y.). 498 pp.
  $27.95
Type of work: Novel
Time: 1773-1993
Locale: Stockholm, St. Petersburg, and Paris

～

*Bradbury deftly compares and contrasts the Enlighten-
ment and the Postmodern Age in this comic novel of two
cities, ages, and temperaments, published shortly before
his death*

～

Principal characters:
  DENIS DIDEROT, the great eighteenth century French philosopher and
    novelist
  CATHERINE THE GREAT, the tsarina who buys Diderot's library and his
    services
  THE WRITER, an unnamed British novelist and academic who travels to
    St. Petersburg as part of the Diderot Project
  BO LUNEBERG, Swedish academic who organizes the Diderot Project
  JACK-PAUL VERSO, trendy American professor of critical thinking
  MADAME GALINA SOLANGE-STAVARONOVA, Russian librarian

Long before he died in November, 2000, at age sixty-eight, Malcolm Bradbury
had turned the heart condition that had forced, or rather allowed, him to spend his
youth reading into one of the most prolific, varied, and influential literary careers in
postwar Britain. He wrote fiction, plays, literary criticism, screenplays, and teleplays,
and edited volumes of fiction and criticism. Long associated and even confused with
his friend, former colleague, and fellow academic-writer-critic David Lodge, he was
half of a mythical creature called Brodge, sometimes said to dwell at an equally mythical writer's retreat called Bradbury Lodge, where he, or they, perfected that peculiarly English invention, the campus novel. Yet Bradbury did more than wake the English novel out of its sleepy postwar provincialism. He helped introduce American
literature and American Studies into the British university system and in 1970 co-
founded Britain's first (and still premier) American-style university writing program
at the University of East Anglia, whose graduates include novelists Ian McEwan and
Kazuo Ishiguro. As chair of the 1981 Booker Prize committee, he was instrumental in
bringing postcolonial fiction into the contemporary British mainstream with the selection of Salman Rushdie's *Midnight's Children.*

Skeptical inquiry and intelligent play are typical of Bradbury's work, along with a
moral questioning that never degenerates into mere earnestness. *To the Hermitage,*

Bradbury's last, longest, and most leisurely novel, exists, as does much of Bradbury's fiction, at the point where John Barth and Saul Bellow intersect. It is a shaggy dog story of sorts, as well as "an intellectual sitcom," a "joyful feast of reason and whimsy," "a virtual adventure in the history of ideas," "a love letter to the life of the mind" that deals with "great political ideas and our own human mortality." It is also Bradbury's most Lodge-like novel, in its twin, alternating-narrative structure, each story set in a different time and having its own narrator, style, and cast of characters.

Malcolm Bradbury's novel Rates of Exchange *(1983) was shortlisted for the prestigious Booker Prize, and he received the Royal Society of Literature Heinemann Award for* The History Man *(1975) and a Monte Carlo award for his television series* The Gravy Train. *He was awarded a CBE in 1991 and a knighthood in 1999 for his contributions to British letters and cultural life.*

"Now" takes place in October, 1993, and starts out in Stockholm, "liberal, simple, decent, and without irony," where Bo Luneberg, grammarian and member of the Nobel Prize committee, has gathered a "mixed salad" of participants for his Diderot Project. (The real Bo—Goranzon, not Luneberg—organized an actual Diderot Project which included the real Bradbury.) The ostensible purpose of this grant-sponsored academic junket along the "Enlightenment trail" is "to track down what has happened to all our friend's books and papers after they went to the Hermitage. You know that story, of course," Bo tells the nameless, Bradbury-like narrator who, of course, does not know the story, though he does know more about Diderot than most of the other "pilgrims." These are Bo and his wife Alma, a carpenter, a diva, a diplomat, a dramaturge, a trade unionist (all Swedes), the unnamed (British) writer, and an American professor of contemporary thinking at Cornell, hilariously named Jack-Paul Verso, who is as trendy in his dress as he is in his thinking, or rather his theory. They are the kind of caricatures one generally finds in Bradbury's wonderfully comic novels and the narrator just the latest (and lamentably last), as well as oldest, in a long-line of semiautobiographical naïfs who play the part of hapless protagonist. Once out of his very English element, he is at a loss. At a bank, for example, he manages to exchange one hundred British pounds for just forty U.S. dollars. Cut off from the familiar, he finds himself aboard a ferry named for Lenin headed for a postcommunist Russia he may not be able to enter, for just as the pilgrims leave Stockholm, history in the form of Boris Yeltsin decides to complicate Bo's project and Bradbury's narrative. Yeltsin has chosen this moment to decide that the only way to save parliamentary democracy in post-Soviet Russia is to act as despotically as any tsar and dissolve the Russian parliament, the Duma.

Worse, and funnier, once arrived in St. Petersburg the narrator is the only one of the project's participants interested in actually seeing that obscure and ostensible object of the pilgrims' desire, Diderot's library, purchased by Catherine the Great. Thanks to Madame Galina Solange-Stavaronova, see it he does, or rather, see what she has managed to salvage from the Hermitage's vast and uncatalogued holdings. Anything that has not yet been stolen or sold and that looks like it may date from the eighteenth century she has placed in a damp room with a leaking ceiling. It is a strange act of salvage and preservation, including both more and less than the 2,904 volumes in the original collection that Diderot sold in part to help pay for his daughter's wedding. Galina gives the narrator two of the books—volumes 5 and 6 of Laurence Sterne's *The Life and Opinions of Tristram Shandy, Gent.* (1759-1767). Diderot loved Sterne's novel and went on to write fiction in a similar vein. The volumes Galina gives the narrator may be the very ones Sterne sent Diderot, and the handwriting on the endpapers may be Diderot's as he began a work inspired by *Tristram Shandy*. Whether they are or are not, whether it is or is not, one truth remains: "Books breed books, writing breeds writing."

"Then" takes place two centuries earlier, mainly during the time Diderot was in St. (or Sankt) Petersburg, 1773-1774. Diderot may be a great philosopher (and fiction writer), but he is also another of Bradbury's naïve protagonists, well-intentioned but also well out of his element. He arrives to find his room occupied, his baggage confiscated, the disease that would eventually kill him already started, and a pupil who is also his patron and master. There is another reason that Diderot, author of the *Encyclopédie: Ou, Dictionnaire raisonné des sciences, des arts, et des métiers* (1751-1772, 17 vols. of text, 11 vols. of plates; *Encyclopedia*, 1965) is an especially logical choice for protagonist. All of Bradbury's fiction, and much of his criticism, takes the form of an inquiry about what it means to be human in the modern world, and Diderot is a central figure in the making of that world—not just its philosophy but its art. In *Rameau and His Nephew*, the philosopher G. W. F Hegel said Diderot created the first modern character and one of the first modern novels as well. As a result, Bradbury depicts Diderot as a similarly modern figure, as comical as he is complex, and nowhere more complex than in his motivation for finally accepting the tsarina's invitation.

This part of the novel is similarly complex in its playful inquiry into the effects of both the sale of Diderot's library and his philosophical conversations with Catherine. "Then" ideas still mattered; "Now" they do not. "Then" they could be dangerous; "Now," at best, they can only be sold, one (more) commodity among many. Diderot sells not only his library but his prestige, his name, to Catherine, who is not just a monarch with an inquiring mind but a wealthy person with a few hours to spare each afternoon. She is also the precursor of former Philippine First Lady Imelda Marcos, an obsessive collector not of shoes (Imelda's specialty) but art, books, and as much of the rest of high culture (philosophers included) as she can cram into her cart as she drains the nation's coffers to pay for "her great Enlightenment shopping spree," a colossal act of conspicuous consumption that is also an attempt to make Russia a more civilized place, which is to say more like Europe, in whose image St. Petersburg was built. This is not to say that Diderot's philosophizing does not have a positive effect on Catherine, both great (stimulating her to be a better and more democratic ruler) or small (as one courtier says, the hours she spends with Diderot each afternoon are hours she does not spend oppressing her people). Still, one has the feeling that Diderot is just one more (replaceable) jewel in Catherine's imposing crown of cultural acquisitions.

Late in the novel, late too in Diderot's life, long after he has returned from St. Petersburg to Paris, Benjamin Franklin pays a visit and gives Diderot reason to regret having made the trip on which he continues to pin his financial and philosophical hopes. "You went for the right reason," Franklin tells him, "but to the wrong place," the right place being America. Later still, the American Revolution now over and the far bloodier French one that will signal the end of the Age of Reason just five years in the future, Thomas Jefferson comes to pay homage. He tells Diderot about the *Notes on the State of Virginia* that Diderot's *Encyclopédie* inspired, and about his plans for his university and his country, plans very much like what Diderot himself has written about in the sixty-six notebooks he had planned to send to Catherine, who, all those afternoon conversations notwithstanding, has turned to the east to the darkness of Russian nationalism. After his guest departs, Diderot picks up one of the American apricots that Jefferson gave him. He bites, coughs, and dies; either America is the deadly forbidden fruit that kills Diderot or Diderot is the Moses who is only allowed to see the Promised Land, not enter it.

Diderot's death is both funny and sad, like the larger novel in which the intellectual and narrative comedy is undercut by or made to coexist with an elegaic quality that has largely gone unremarked in Bradbury's novels. It is not surprising that a novel written when Bradbury was in his sixties should be as elegaic in its way as so much of his beloved Saul Bellow's has been at least since *Mr. Sammler's Planet* (1970). The elegaic quality here, and in Bellow, has as much to do with the passing of certain values as it does with the two writers' sense of their own approaching mortality. In Bradbury's case, this is the loss of those neo-Arnoldian liberal humanist values in which he, as the son of a railway employee and beneficiary not of Catherine's largess but of a state-funded education he otherwise would have been denied, believed so strongly. These were the values critic F. R. Leavis extolled, but the dilemma for Bradbury was trying to be a Leavisite in a postliberal humanist, postmodern age. The dream of an enlightened, rational, liberal, humanistic and democratic America that is on Diderot's mind as he bites into that apricot has transmogrified itself into the America in whose hyperconsumerist image the rest of the world is rapidly remaking itself. As the bemused and saddened narrator puts it, "Ours is no longer a time of ideology; in fact it's the Age of Shopping. Politics have turned into lifestyle, Star Wars to Nintendo, history into retro."

To his credit, Malcolm Bradbury did not merely extol liberal humanism or lament its demise, and with it the demise of what Diderot reprsents, thinking man at his very best. Rather, he tested both liberal humanism and the modern/postmodern world against each other, wishing the one more relevant, the other less dehumanizing. Like Diderot at the moment of his death, Bradbury seemed forever poised between hope and regret, half Candide, half Voltaire.

Robert A. Morace

Sources for Further Study

The Atlantic Monthly 287 (April, 2001): 107.
Contemporary Review 278 (March, 2001): 159.
The New York Times, November 29, 2000, p. A33.
The New York Times Book Review 106 (April 1, 2001): 11.

TREASON BY THE BOOK

Author: Jonathan D. Spence (1936-   )
Publisher: Viking (New York). 300 pp. $24.95
Type of work: Novel
Time: 1728-1736
Locale: China

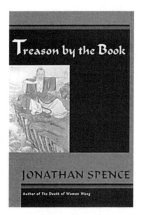

~

Historian Jonathan Spence tells the tale of the political
conspiracy to overthrow the Manchu dynasty at the court
of the enlightened eighteenth century Chinese emperor
Yongzheng

~

Principal characters:

EMPEROR YONGZHENG, early eighteenth century emperor of China
YUE ZHONGQI, the governor general of Shaanxi and Sichuan provinces
ZHANG XI, a mysterious messenger who sets the action in motion
ZENG JING, a wandering dissident scholar and plotter against the emperor
LU LIULIANG, Confucian scholar whose teachings fuel the plot to over-
    throw the emperor
QUINLONG, Emperor Yongzheng's son and heir

Renowned Yale University historian Jonathan D. Spence, one of the greatest contemporary sinologists, uses the form of the novel to tell this riveting true story. In
characteristic spy novel structure, Spence discloses bit by bit what at first seems an insignificant story. Although somewhat interesting, at the onset the reader wonders why
he has bothered to construct a whole book out of such a paltry incident. It takes a
while to catch on to the fact that there is a lot more going on in the scrupulously researched *Treason by the Book* than initially meets the eye. It is not until about halfway through the book that Spence's brilliant narrative structure, the circuitous pattern
of plots within plots, emerges. Just when it seems that the consequences can be
glimpsed, another complication arises. Indeed, it is not until the last chapter, the last
page, in fact, that the reader brings together the true significance of what seems to be,
at first glance, such an unimportant event.

The event in question concerns a large envelope passed, on an October day in
1728, into the hands of Yue Zhongqi, the commanding forty-two-year-old governor
general of Shaanxi and Sichuan provinces. The far-reaching consequences of this single act make up Spence's book. The envelope, which is delivered by Zhang Xi, a mysterious messenger, contains a letter detailing a secret, treacherous plot to overthrow
the Manchu (or Qing) dynasty, which ruled China from 1644 to 1911. Scholarly non-
conformists, it seems, are deeply embittered against the rule of Emperor Yongzheng,
the third Manchu emperor, who ruled China from 1723 to 1735. In particular, the dissidents cry out against his callous absolutism and centralization of power, and call for

his removal. The non-Han-speaking Manchus, who eighty years earlier had ousted the Chinese Ming dynasty, are barbarians in the plotters' estimation. Governor Yue Zhongqi, they hope, will head up their proposed rebellion, because his eponymous ancestor had attempted six centuries earlier, in the time of the Song dynasty, to rally the Chinese to reclaim the northern lands they had lost to the Manchu conquerors. However, Governor Yue, intent on climbing up the political and social ladder and realizing full well his undisputed dependency upon the emperor, wants no part of their nefarious scheme. He imprisons Zhang Xi and immediately informs Emperor Yongzheng of these rebellious stirrings against him.

Jonathan D. Spence is Sterling Professor of History at Yale University and has won many awards, among them Guggenheim and MacArthur Fellowships. A remarkable storyteller, he has written many books on Chinese history and culture, including The Search for Modern China *(1999),* The Gate of Heavenly Peace *(1981), and* The Death of Woman Wang *(1978).*

After rereading the hostile letter, however, Governor Yue pretends to join the revolutionary's attempt to regain for China her "mountains and rivers" in an attempt to trick Zhang into naming his cohorts. Governor Yue's plan works, and Zhang soon names his coconspirator and mentor, Zeng Jing, a Hunanese peasant schoolteacher whose misconceptions about the Manchu dynasty are based on rumors and lies, and whose seditious ideas are far-reaching. Upon learning about the conspiracy, Emperor Yongzheng, who rules a people who literally do not speak his language, embarks on a systematic, painstaking investigation to unearth those involved. Officials are dispatched to arrest the family members and colleagues of Zeng Jing, and the emperor closely scrutinizes their investigations by constantly dispatching extensive written directives. In a short time, corpses are dug up, suspects are beheaded, mothers and children are enslaved, all in an effort by a ruler to root out dissent.

Treason by the Book offers a dramatic picture of life as it was lived in the outlying provinces of eighteenth century China. It offers fascinating insights into imperial China's political, legal, and communication systems, in which much of the investigation takes place. It examines the backbiting world of Chinese scholars and government officials, and ultimately the workings of the emperor's absolute power, its efficient machinations, its cold precision, and the violence of a single ruler's extraordinary ability to administer and monitor such a vast geographical area. As the investigation speeds up, Emperor Yongzheng emerges as a very complex, introspective, and some would argue, enlightened scholar-ruler. Indeed, rather than summarily pronouncing death sentences on both plotters, the emperor utilizes the situation as a learning opportunity and becomes intent on attempting to understand the influences behind Zeng Jing's rebellious actions. This sets in the motion the multilayered, impossible attempt to find the original sources of such far-reaching, mutinous rumors. The lengthy investigation, which encompasses several high-ranking investigators and the ransacking of several libraries, results in dozens of arrests. Among the additional characters that come under investigation are a Buddhist monk, a cluster of court eunuchs, a group of convicts being transported to prison, and a scholar wearing a purple jacket who impersonated an imperial official.

Ultimately, the Emperor's relentless investigation leads to apprehension of the dissidents who had dared impugn the imperial system. In the end, the roots of the rebellion lie with a deceased, formerly venerated Confucian scholar named Lu Liuliang, whose transgression lies merely in a form of nostalgia for the fallen Ming dynasty. Again, rather than calling for the heads of the conspirators, Emperor Yongzheng attempts to persuade Zeng Jing, through a detailed correspondence, of the many virtues of Manchu rule. Zeng Jing is ultimately convinced by his teachings, realizes that he has badly misjudged the emperor, sees the errors of his ways, writes a detailed confession renouncing Lu Liuliang's ideas, and begs the emperor's forgiveness. All these communications between prisoner and emperor are ultimately published with the title *Awakening from Delusion* (*Dayi juemi lu*). The book contains Zeng Jing's original treasonous letter, a summary of his radical ideas, his recantation, and, it would seem, his deep apologies. It also contains the emperor's attempts to address Zeng Jing's beliefs, along with his own extensive imperial commentary.

The verdict in the Zeng Jing case was pronounced in 1736 and was nothing less than stunning. Indeed, despite the unanimous findings of his officials that Zeng Jing should be put to death by the slicing away of his flesh, Emperor Yongsheng surprisingly set him free, along with the original messenger Zhang Xi, in an unprecedented act of clemency. In the emperor's estimation, it is the deceased scholar Lu Liuliang who is at fault and who was the true conspirator, not Zeng Jing. It remains the emperor's hope that, because of his generosity, his capacity for understanding, and his enlightened attitude, posterity will revere his name. No doubt the impetus behind the emperor's forgiveness of Zeng Jing and the publishing of *Awakening from Delusion* is to assuage the rumors of his ineffectiveness and to assure his place in history as a compassionate and wise ruler.

Before long, the multivolume tome *Awakening from Delusion* is mass-produced and distributed throughout China, not just to officials' offices and libraries but circulated to everyone in China and made mandatory reading in all educational institutions. The mass publication of the many ideas that the emperor finds offensive does seem modernistic in a reverse-psychology sense. However, the idea of Emperor Yongsheng as representative of eighteenth century Enlightenment thinking goes out the window when it becomes clear that punishment for the revered scholar's treason entails the "harshest possible" punishments, the execution of Lu Liuliang's surviving children and grandchildren. In addition, when an official, Tang Sungao, proclaims the greatness of Lu Liuliang, whose teaching harkens back longingly to the Ming dynasty, Emperor Yongzheng summarily orders his execution. On the one hand, therefore, through the mass distribution of *Awakening from Delusion*, Emperor Yongsheng attempts to portray himself as a perceptive, beneficent ruler, but he remains, on the other hand, and in hard fact, an absolute tyrant.

Although the plotter Zeng Jing receives a pardon and a generous stipend from the emperor, he is placed under constant scrutiny, given a nominal government job, and spends his days looking for something to occupy his time. The messenger Zhang Xi is allowed to return to his village. It is unclear whether both men ever met again. The reaction to the emperor's leniency among scholars is unforgiving. They remain irate that Zeng Jing went free, while the distinguished scholar Lu Liuliang's corpse was disinterred and disgraced. Consequently, it is hardly surprising that shortly after Emperor Yongzheng's death in 1735, the new twenty-four-year-old emperor, Qianlong, reevaluates the infamous case and declares that Zeng Jing be executed by being sliced to death.

Treason by the Book is a scrupulously researched, fascinating tale of political discontent and absolute imperial action. Spence's chronicle of historical events, which draws on original manuscripts from the Emperor Yongzheng's era (1728-1735) stored in the Beijing and Taipei archives, flows gracefully despite the often troublesomely unfamiliar Chinese names. While a broad knowledge of Chinese history and culture would no doubt be useful, it is not necessary to deeply appreciate the book. The author gently guides the reader through the oftentimes complex times gone by and interjects interesting cultural tidbits. For instance, only the emperor was allowed to use red ink (vermilion), and he answered his officials' letters by writing comments in red between the lines of the black Chinese characters.

Partly a study of the intellectual background of the early Manchu dynasty and partly an examination of a culture and the political and legal systems of eighteenth century China, Spence's novel vividly combines history and mystery, casting light upon the world of eighteenth century Chinese scholarship, which was severely limited by bureaucratic examinations. In short, Spence explores the unstable boundaries between fact, rumor, and truth. Although now almost three hundred years old, Zeng Jing's story of high political intrigue strongly resonates in China today, inspiring television documentaries and academic studies. Spence no doubt prefigures the culture of repression in today's China, where any dissent is considered a threat to the state and continues to be brutally crushed.

In addition, by painstakingly deconstructing a thwarted uprising in 1728 China, Spence reveals the role that words and books have played in Chinese history. Accompanying the history of this particular era in China is a continual reflection on the power of the written word, in particular as it is used to express hostility, control, and subtle yet persistent persuasion. What also becomes apparent is the importance and the lasting magic of the written word, not just during the Manchu dynasty, but during any historical era. *Treason by the Book* is an entrancing chronicle of a seemingly obscure, but deeply significant, episode in Chinese history. This book is not a fast read, for it demands the reader's total engagement—but the effort pays off.

M. Casey Diana

Sources for Further Study

Booklist 97 (March 1, 2001): 1224.
Library Journal 126 (February 15, 2001): 184.
The New York Review of Books 48 (May 17, 2001): 38.
The New York Times Book Review 106 (March 18, 2001): 7.
Publishers Weekly 248 (January 8, 2001): 55.

TRUE HISTORY OF THE KELLY GANG

Author: Peter Carey (1943-   )
First published: 2000, in Australia
Publisher: Alfred A. Knopf (New York). 352 pp. $25.00
Type of work: Novel
Time: 1855-1880
Locale: Australia

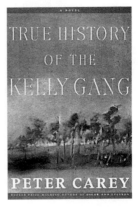

≈

The story of the legendary nineteenth century Australian outlaw Ned Kelly and his notorious gang in the guise of his confession to a daughter whom he has never met

≈

Principal characters:
NED KELLY, the narrator and legendary outlaw
ELLEN KELLY, his mother
JOHN KELLY, his father
DAN KELLY, his younger brother and a member of the Kelly gang
JOE BYRNE, a member of the Kelly gang
STEVE HART, a member of the Kelly gang
HARRY POWER, a bushranger and one of Ellen Kelly's lovers
MARY HEARN, Kelly's sweetheart and the mother of his child

Although Peter Carey resettled in New York in the 1980's, he has not lost his connection with the land of his birth. He has established through his fiction a bold and penetrating examination of what it means to be an Australian. Carey burst upon the literary landscape in 1974 with the publication of his collection of stories *The Fat Man in History*. He published his first novel, *Bliss*, in 1981. It was in his second novel, *Illywhacker*, that Carey boldly demonstrated that he could be a provocative and inventive novelist of the first order. The novel spanned more than one hundred years of colonial life in Australia. Mixing myth and history, Carey created a startling fictional world that verged on science fiction. His 1988 novel *Oscar and Lucinda* truly established him as a major author. It tells the story of an eccentric nineteenth century Australian couple who attempt to transport a glass church through the outback with heartbreaking consequences. The novel was widely acclaimed and won the prestigious Booker Prize. Carey was fast becoming a master at juggling the whimsical with the serious, the mythic with the cold hard facts. In his 1998 novel *Jack Maggs*, he created a nineteenth century world that owed its inspiration to Charles Dickens's novel *Great Expectations* (1860-1861). The protagonist of *Jack Maggs* is a criminal who, after being exiled to Australia, makes his way back to England. While Carey is supremely adept at recreating the nineteenth century, he is first and foremost a postmodern novelist.

For *True History of the Kelly Gang*, Carey took on the challenge of telling the story of a legendary Australian outlaw. Ned Kelly is well-known to all Australians, and every Australian has made up his or her mind whether they see him as a mere scoundrel or as a folk hero. For many, Kelly is one of the downtrodden who was brutalized by the British and, therefore, forced by circumstances to take up arms against his exploiters, while for others Kelly is no more than a common murderer. Carey, who has made it quite clear in his earlier novels that he has little sympathy with the British establishment, has found in Kelly a perfect whetstone on which to grind his particular postmodern axe. While Carey clearly understood the pitfalls of choosing to write about a legendary figure, he knew that he could not shy away from the challenge. He has done a thorough job of researching the all-too-brief and violent life of Kelly, yet Carey—as author—does not hesitate to manipulate the facts in order to fit his overall scheme. Carey made the decision to have Kelly tell his own story.

Peter Carey has established himself as one of the leading Australian novelists of his generation. He has won such awards as the Ditmar Award for Best Australian Science Fiction Novel for Illywhacker *(1985); the Miles Franklin Award for* Bliss *(1981) and* Oscar and Lucinda *(1988); the Age Book of the Year Award for* Illywhacker, The Unusual Life of Tristan Smith *(1994), and* Jack Maggs *(1997); and the Booker Prize for* Oscar and Lucinda *and* True History of the Kelly Gang.

The novel is divided into thirteen parcels or chapters and is supposedly the autobiography that Kelly wrote toward the end of his short life for an infant daughter that he has not seen. Before each parcel there is a detailed bibliographic description of the document. Carey examined the one surviving document that Kelly wrote and used it as a guide for this novel. The document is known as the "Jerilderie Letter" and was written by Kelly a year before he was executed. In the letter, he did his best to justify his life. Carey found the letter to be written in an "amazing, breathless, Irish language." He went so far as to type "out all 8,000 words" of the letter and carry "it around with me for years." For Carey, this project was inevitable. He also realized that it would be imperative for him to exploit the power and authenticity of "colloquial speech" for the novel. Since Kelly was not an educated man, Carey had to adopt a rough narrative where punctuation and sentence structure would be awkward at best.

This approach to the retelling of the legend of the Kelly gang and, through them, what it was like to live in nineteenth century Australia works marvelously in *True History of the Kelly Gang*. What grows out of Carey's approach is a narrative style that comes close to folk poetry. Kelly expresses himself with such images as "In a settler's hut the smallest flutter of a mother's eyelids are like a thin sheet rattling in the wind," and "I lost my own father from a secret he might as well been snatched by a roiling river fallen from a ravine I lost him from my heart so long I cannot even now properly make the place for him that he deserves." In addition to the awkward, yet colorful, syntax is the avoidance of spelling out any profane word by either leaving only the first and last letter of a vulgar word or by using alternative words to take their place together. The word "adjectival" is used for the slang word "bloody." Carey wished to stay true to the nineteenth century sensibility and the novel is all the more extraordinary for his ability to walk such a perilous tightrope.

Kelly was born in 1855 of Irish stock. His father was sent to Australia in 1842 as a convict. Kelly's father died in 1866 and left a widow and several children living in poverty. The family had a difficult time trying to make ends meet. Because they were Irish and branded by a father who had been a convict, the Kelly family had to exist as outcasts in British-controlled Australia. During the nineteenth century, there were many so-called bushrangers or gangs that terrorized the Australian countryside by stealing livestock and robbing banks. Ned Kelly and his gang were merely another irritant to the British establishment until they killed three policemen. The gang—which included his younger brother Dan, Joe Byrne, and Steve Hart—was then hunted down relentlessly for two years. Kelly eventually was captured and was hanged in 1880. The territory of North Eastern Victoria is presented as a harsh environment and a place where it was extremely difficult for anyone to eke out an honest living. For those who by birth or misdeed were not members of the British establishment, life was more times than not extremely brutal.

Kelly was devoted to his mother. After her husband died, Ellen Kelly had numerous male callers and her son could not always fathom why her attention would be focused on them and not on her loving son. At one point Kelly confesses that "I would much prefer that she invited no new husbands to her bed but seeing as I couldn't have this wish I preferred old Harry Power." Power is one of her lovers and also a bushranger. Kelly's mother eventually sells her son to this man. It is under the tutelage of Power that Kelly learns the ways of a bushranger. They become partners and Kelly's fate seems to be sealed. His mother rails that she also should receive some of their ill-gotten rewards. She is saddened to learn from her son that robbing is not bringing a vast sum of money. He has to break the news to her that "The bushranging aint as profitable as you'd expect."

No matter what demands his mother makes of him, Kelly's love for her never waivers. His mother is unjustly sent to prison after a policeman is wounded at the Kelly home. Enraged by how the system has once again mistreated his family, Kelly becomes even more bitter and unable to see any other course for him but bushranging. He attempts to make a deal with the authorities in order to free his mother from a three-year sentence in prison by turning himself over to them in exchange for her release, but this deal is not accepted. As other writers successfully have done before, Carey takes liberties with the historical record in the name of artistic license. Mary Hearn, Kelly's sweetheart and the mother of his child, is a creation of the author. She is a prostitute with a "heart of gold" and is loyal to her man. Through the efforts of Kelly, she is able to sail for San Francisco, where she gives birth to a daughter. Upon hearing the news of the birth, Kelly makes time to write down his story for the child he will never meet. The thirteen parcels are his way of justifying his life to his daughter. In addition to the parcels, Carey has written a prologue and two final chapters. It is in these concluding chapters that Kelly's actual capture and execution by hanging are described.

Carey has fashioned another amazing Australian story. The novel is full of bombast, tall tales, mythic figures, social injustice, and rebellion against towering odds. Through the vessel of the doomed Ned Kelly, Carey has written what he has called "the book I've waited my whole life to write." According to Carey, Kelly is part Jesse James, part Billy the Kid, part Huck Finn, and part Robin Hood. He is an Australian folk hero of national importance. Carey also is adept at rendering the Australian outback. The beauty, the harshness, and all of the oddities that make Australia unique are described by the sensitive outlaw on the run. While no one can truly excuse the criminal activity of Kelly and his gang, Carey has found a way to make Kelly a sympathetic character.

In an interview, Carey stated that the life that Kelly led was "the ultimate Australian story." Since Australia began as a British dumping ground for criminals and renegades, it becomes not too much of a stretch to see Kelly as someone who represents one of the countless "underdogs." As Carey sees it, Kelly is the "convict stain." A product of British imperialism, he fought against tyranny in the only way he knew how. While Carey understands that not all Australians can find much to admire in what Kelly did, the author wholeheartedly believes that this bushranger is due a fair hearing. The author had a need "to do something historians aren't allowed to do. How can you understand an important story without knowing the emotional state of the characters?" Carey has written a novel that is not only a vibrant adventure story, but one that is emotionally convincing. For *True History of the Kelly Gang*, Carey was awarded a second Booker Prize.

Jeffry Jensen

Sources for Further Study

The Christian Science Monitor, January 18, 2001, p. 20.
The Lancet 357 (February 3, 2001): 401.
Library Journal 125 (December, 2000): 186.
Los Angeles Times Book Review, January 28, 2001, p. 2.
Maclean's 114 (March 26, 2001): 48.
Meanjin 60, no. 3 (2001): 214.
The New York Review of Books 48 (March 29, 2001): 15.
The New York Times, January 4, 2001, p. E10.
The New York Times Book Review 106 (January 7, 2001): 7.
The New Yorker 76 (January 22, 2001): 80.
Publishers Weekly 247 (November 13, 2000): 84.
The Spectator 286 (January 13, 2001): 35.
The Village Voice 46 (February 13, 2001): 79.
World and I 16 (June, 2001): 251.
World Literature Today 75 (Spring, 2001): 314.

ULTIMATE JOURNEY
Retracing the Path of an Ancient Buddhist Monk Who Crossed Asia in Search of Enlightenment

Author: Richard Bernstein (1944-   )
Publisher: Alfred A. Knopf (New York). 352 pp. $26.00
Type of work: Memoirs, history, and travel
Time: 1999
Locale: China, Pakistan, and India

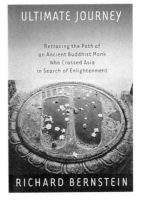

∼

A twentieth century journalist follows the path of a seventh century Chinese Buddhist monk from China to India and back again

∼

Richard Bernstein, an accomplished journalist and author, was a student of Chinese language and history at Harvard. In 1980, he opened *Time* magazine's Beijing bureau, the journal's first in China since the Communist revolution of 1949. By the late 1990's, he was a book critic for the *New York Times.* In his fifties and unmarried, he had been in a romantic relationship with a Chinese classical dancer named Zhongmei Li, but there was no permanent commitment because of Bernstein's indecisiveness. He states that in the desire to get away from the ordinary and the predictable, he debated whether to construct Shaker furniture or embark on a last adventure before the desire for stability and the onset of middle age restricted his vistas and opportunities. He decided to travel.

Bernstein's ultimate journey was something he had been considering for some time. In the 600's C.E., a Chinese Buddhist monk named Hsuan Tsang had traveled from his homeland to India and back again, a trip which took seventeen years and covered 10,000 miles, encountering different peoples and cultures, crossing blistering deserts and traversing frozen mountains. A legend in Communist China as well as in India, Hsuan Tsang is largely unknown in the West. Bernstein compares him to Marco Polo, but where Polo was seeking riches, Hsuan Tsang was searching for enlightenment, for himself and for humanity. Although he is not a Buddhist, but a secular Westerner from a Jewish background, Bernstein also describes himself as a romantic, drawn to the persons of the past whose contributions changed history. Hsuan Tsang did that, helping to transmit Buddhism from India, where it died out, to China and ultimately to Japan, where it still thrives in the twenty-first century.

Still, midlife romantic quests into the past face present-day realities. Bernstein, with Ross H. Munro, had recently written *The Coming Conflict with China*, a controversial work which was not well received by the Chinese government. Getting permission to even begin his journey presented obstacles, but he was able to obtain a no-questions-asked visa in Hong Kong. He flew to Xian, noted for its terracotta soldiers from the first Chinese emperor's tomb, where Zhongmei was waiting both to assist him with the bureaucracy and to accompany him on the first part of his pilgrimage.

If Bernstein's entrance into China was fraught with difficulties, Hsuan Tsang's exit from the Middle Kingdom had been more so. The seventh century was a contentious era in China, politically in terms of the end of the Sui dynasty and the rise of the T'ang, and religiously in terms of Buddhism, in which there were conflicts over interpretation and understanding occasioned in part by the vast cultural gulf between Buddhism's native India and Hsuan Tsang's China. The monk's motive for his long journey was to study Bud-

Richard Bernstein served as Time *magazine's first Beijing bureau chief. He has been* The New York Times *bureau chief at the United Nations and in Paris and also that newspaper's national cultural correspondent. His other books include* Dictatorship of Virtue: Multiculturalism and the Battle for America's Future *(1994) and* From the Center of the Earth: The Search for the Truth About China *(1982).*

dhism at its great university, Nalanda, in northern India, and bring manuscripts back to China. However, the T'ang emperor, Tai Tusung, had forbidden Chinese to travel to the west. Just as Bernstein escaped the possible clutches of the Communist party bureaucracy, Hsuan Tsang managed to escape the emperor's edict. There were political and military reasons for the emperor's decision, but Bernstein also notes a sociological cause: The Chinese never developed what he calls an anthropological spirit and had no true interest in, and thus little knowledge of, the world beyond China. Hsuan Tsang was unique.

Bernstein aimed to follow Hsuan Tsang's route closely, using the monk's own reports, ancient biographies, and modern writings, recognizing that modern roads, international borders, and political restrictions would necessitate some compromise. The monk traveled by foot, horse, camel, and elephant. In the late twentieth century, thanks to Zhongmei's fame as a dancer, Bernstein was given a tour of Xian in a luxury automobile. They then left for the west by train, in what passed for a first class compartment, or "soft sleeper." Western China was the eastern end of the fabulous Silk Road, the other end of which lay in the Mediterranean world, down which passed not only Chinese Buddhist monks but also Marco Polo and his uncles, Mongol raiders and other armies, and merchants of numerous cultures. In 1999, western China was a politically sensitive region because the population is mostly Muslim, and Communist authorities were fearful of any religiously inspired separatist tendencies. Bernstein's presence in Xinjiang Province was thus potentially fraught with difficulties, and on one occasion a restaurant owner accused him of being an American spy.

In *Ultimate Journey*, Bernstein discusses Hsuan Tsang's trek at considerable length, reciting the monk's difficulties in eluding Chinese authorities, including being shot at by archers, and the dangers he encountered in the deserts through which the Silk Road passed—the heat, the lack of water, sandstorms, and outlaws. Nonetheless, however closely he followed in the footsteps of the monk, Bernstein could not escape the present. In a small village in Xinjiang, after learning that Bernstein was from America, a local inhabitant wrote in the dust on the fender of the author's jeep,

MONIKA and MIKELJORDAN. On a later occasion, in Kyrgyzstan, he came across "John's Café—Your Home Away from Home on the Silk Road," which, he noted, served good Chinese and bad Western food. One can run but one cannot hide from the modern world.

Bernstein was not merely a single-minded devotee of the monk. The author's own life was at something of a crossroads. "I have lived in my undramatic way on the edge between loneliness on one side and the horror of home on the other," he says, always choosing to travel alone, to be single rather than to be encumbered with responsibilities other than to himself. When Zhongmei left him as planned to return to Beijing, Bernstein reflected on his solitary life, and although he denies it was an epiphany, perhaps it was.

He breathed a sigh of relief when he crossed the Chinese border into the Kyrgyz Republic, a part of the former Soviet Union, knowing that he would not be deported for his previous writings about China. He noted, however, that circumstances had changed since his first experience in China in 1980. In 1999, many Chinese felt free to criticize the party officials and their actions, although admittedly only in private. Bernstein's fear of China's bureaucrats was replaced by a different fear in one of the old Soviet states, when his young driver refused to accept the agreed-upon payment. Bernstein, anticipating violence, paid more; at least he was not robbed of his computer, luggage, and the rest of his money, and he notes that the same thing could happen in Johannesburg or Amsterdam.

On his path to India, Hsuan Tsang journeyed through modern Afghanistan, a nation off-limits to non-Muslim Westerners. Bernstein wanted to get as close as possible, and that was the bridge over the Amu-Darya River, which connected Afghanistan with Uzbekistan. After a discussion with two young Russian-speaking soldiers, he was able to see across into Afghanistan but no further, and he traveled on to Muslim Pakistan by air. Unlike China, which the author says is in the process of becoming a variant of the West, "Pakistan comes at you like something detonated, a plentitude of color and mass, weirdness and catastrophe." In Hsuan Tsang's time, Pakistan was largely Buddhist.

Throughout *Ultimate Journey*, Bernstein debates and discusses the beliefs of Buddhism with Buddhists he meets along the way, with himself, and with the reader. A secular Westerner and one admittedly without the temperament or receptiveness associated with Hsuan Tsang's religious quest for enlightenment, the author nevertheless wrestles with Buddhism's often difficult concepts, asking "If all is illusion, then isn't the very belief that all is illusion an illusion as well?" He worries about a religion that, unlike his native Judaism, seemingly cannot be understood by the logical mind, and he wonders if underneath the verbiage, most Buddhist concepts are ultimately untenable.

Peshawar, in Pakistan, was a great Buddhist center which had been destroyed by the Huns before Hsuan Tsang's arrival. Bernstein comments that he and the monk both arrived, hundreds of years apart, at the site of a once-vibrant civilization, with only ruins and sellers of artifacts, real and fake, to mark its passing. After brief stops in Rawalpindi and in the Lahore of Rudyard Kipling's novel *Kim* (1901), Bernstein crossed into India. Pakistan and India have been at war or near war ever since the partition of the subcontinent in 1947 when the British raj surrendered its control. In the not-so-distant past, thousands of people had crossed the border each day, but Bernstein noted he was only number eighteen that day, and it was near closing time.

In Amritsar he visited an orphanage and fantasized about adopting the child he never had, a reference to his personal situation rather than an interest in Hsuan Tsang's quest. In India, the Hindu majority filled the Hindu temples; Buddhist pilgrims went to ruins and museums. In Lumbini, the Buddha's birthplace, Bernstein was suffering from a lingering intestinal upset and was unimpressed and unaffected by what should have been a spiritual place. By the time he got to India he had experienced much, not all of it exhilarating, and was perhaps less enthusiastic in following the footsteps of Hsuan Tsang than he had been when he had started out. At Varanasi (formerly Benares) on the River Ganges, one of the holiest cities in Hinduism, Bernstein was more impressed by the river's pollution than its religious significance, and after a somewhat disconcerting interview with the maharaja of Varanasi, the author compared the dilapidated state of the maharaja's palace with the run-down river. Bernstein himself was beginning to run down.

His visits to other Buddhist holy places, including the ruins of Nalanda, failed to increase his spiritual receptiveness, and he admitted that he had the same lack of response at Confucius's birthplace, at the Church of the Holy Sepulchre, and at the Western Wall in Jerusalem, being more affected by their historical associations than with their spiritual qualities. The secular frequently overshadowed the religious. In Bodhgaya, the place where the Buddha had received enlightenment, Bernstein saw a banner which read "Coca-Cola Welcomes His Holiness the Dalai Lama." In Bombay, he tracked down a high Hindu official, who when asked by Bernstein what was the most essential principle of Hinduism, told the author it was simple living and high thinking, an answer which would have pleased America's nineteenth century transcendentalists.

Back in New Delhi, after visiting the Hindu and Buddhist caves at Ellora and Ajanta in southern India, Bernstein was joined by Zhongmei, who accompanied him for the remainder of the trip. They backtracked to Pakistan and then on to China by jeep and bus, the quality of one ride captured in the chapter's title, "The Nightmare Bus to Khotan." As he returned to China, Bernstein expressed anxiety about ending his journey, possibly his last great adventure, and again being forced to confront his sense of unbelonging and of his difficulty with the idea of home, plaintively writing, "On the other side of the mountains was the home that I missed and where I didn't want to go."

Excellently written and deeply perceptive, like the best travel books *Ultimate Journey* looks both inward and outward, an examination of the self as well as the other, not only into the past but also into the present. Bernstein's decision to follow the route of the seventh century Buddhist monk was also a personal quest, for his own past and perhaps his future, and if he did not achieve the Buddhist nirvana, he did achieve a certain enlightenment—an end note states that Bernstein and Zhongmei Li were married in September, 2000.

Eugene Larson

Sources for Further Study

Los Angeles Times, March 24, 2001, p. B2.
The New York Review of Books 48 (May 17, 2001): 32.
The New York Times, March 21, 2001, p. B8.
The New York Times Book Review 106 (March 25, 2001): 6.

UNDERGROUND
The Tokyo Gas Attack and the Japanese Psyche

Author: Haruki Murakami (1949-   )
First published: Andāguraundo, 1997, and
  Yakusokusareta basho de, 1998, in Japan
Translated from the Japanese by Alfred Birnbaum and
  Philip Gabriel
Publisher: Vintage International (New York). 366 pp.
  Paperback $14.00
Type of work: Current affairs, religion, and psychology
Time: The 1990's
Locale: Japan

~

Novelist Murakami interviews both victims of the sarin
gas attack in Tokyo's subway system on March 20, 1995,
and members of the Aum Shinrikyo cult that perpetrated
the attack in an attempt to understand the effects and
causes of this act of urban terrorism

~

On March 20, 1995, the Japanese cult Aum Shinrikyo shocked Japan and the world. Under orders from the cult's leader, five of its members carried plastic bags of a liquid form of deadly sarin gas onto the Tokyo subway. At five stations, as they had carefully rehearsed, the perpetrators systematically punctured the bags with sharpened umbrella tips, resulting in the deaths of eleven commuters and subway employees and the injury of up to five thousand others, some of whom have never completely recovered.

While the event received immediate massive media coverage in Japan and worldwide, scholars, journalists, and others have struggled for years afterward to uncover the path that led to an event that came within a hairbreadth of achieving its immediate aim, mass murder. How such an act could have been conceived and justified has been the subject of books such as Yale University psychiatrist Robert Jay Lifton's *Destroying the World to Save It* (2000), which explored the psychology and belief systems of the Aum Shinrikyo. Haruki Murakami's *Underground: The Tokyo Gas Attack and the Japanese Psyche* takes a different tack in seeking primarily to enter the world of the victims and to record and preserve their experience as well as to give an account of how postwar Japanese society spawned the cult and allowed its madness to go unchecked.

Murakami is a well-known Japanese novelist, the author of eight previous books. At the time of the subway attack he had recently returned to his homeland after an extensive period abroad, during which he attempted to see Japan through a more de-

∽

Haruki Murakami is one of Japan's best-known novelists. His books include A Wild Sheep Chase *(1989),* Hardboiled Wonderland and the End of the World *(1991),* Dance Dance Dance *(1994), and* The Wind-up Bird Chronicle *(1997).*

∽

tached lens in an attempt to understand this complex society at a deeper level. Like his compatriots, he experienced overwhelming dismay at this horrendous, seemingly meaningless act of urban terrorism.

Seeking a means to understand an event he takes to be of enormous significance, Murakami hit upon the interview method: He would create verbal snapshots of individual experiences of the attack. Once assembled, the snapshots would give readers a series of eyewitness glimpses of what victims endured, without the writer's intrusion. The result would not be a "nonfiction novel" like Truman Capote's *In Cold Blood* (1965), written in the novelist's words with the collaboration of the responsible criminals, but rather a work that would allow the victims to speak for themselves without the potential distortion of authorial interpretation.

To this end, Murakami sought interviews with as many gassing victims as he could locate and who would consent to an interview. Many who agreed to speak did so on condition of anonymity. In the interviews, Murakami himself tends to keep a low profile, allowing each individual to speak his or her mind. When the interview nears conclusion, most of those interviewed express their feelings toward the insane cult's criminal actions. Interestingly, a number expressed no anger toward Aum Shrinrikyo. In some instances, the victims say they are "beyond anger," either in the sense that they have transcended it or that their outrage is beyond ordinary expression.

The experience of the gassing victims, while varying in detail, becomes depressingly familiar with each retelling. All at once people begin coughing uncontrollably; someone slumps over, as if dead. Passersby keep passing by, ignoring the macabre scene they sidestep. Once the victim comes in contact with the noxious liquid or breathes its fumes, all becomes dark. Breathing becomes difficult. In the worst cases, taking a breath seems impossible.

Most of the injured have fully recovered from their contact with sarin—most, but not all. Murakami carefully sought survivors with unresolved medical problems. One poignant personal story concludes with an account of terrible physical duress, of gutwrenching headaches that recur frequently, without warning. Another is "Shizuko Akashi" (a pseudonym), who has lost her memory of everything prior to being gassed and has moved little from the vegetative state to which the attack reduced her. Recovery appears remote.

The title *Underground*—culled from the author's long-standing interest in exploring the depths of the human soul—brings to mind Fyodor Dostoyevsky's famous nineteenth century novella *Notes from Underground*, a profound meditation on the subterranean psychic cauldrons in which resentment ferments. Similarly, Murakami's title obvious plays on the "subways" of the human unconscious.

In the English-language version of the book, Murakami constructs a further section that adds considerable interest to the volume. He interviews members of the cult, though none of them directly involved in the 1995 attack. Through the many strikingly similar characteristics of these self-descriptions, a composite portrait emerges of the cult's membership. The most salient of these traits is alienation from society at large, though some were not alienated from their families.

In joining Aum, most members attempted to undergo a sort of rebirth. Feeling abandoned in a hostile world of ceaseless, meaningless effort, they were attracted by the cult's message of spiritual regeneration through ascetic discipline. They easily, uncritically, imbibed reigning guru Asahara's message that he alone could lead them to a higher state of being.

When, after the early 1990's, the cult's evolving doctrines turned dark and Asahara began to justify violence, including apocalyptic violence, many (though not all) of those interviewed claimed not to have noticed it. They were insulated from the approaching moral twilight by the deeply hierarchical character into which Aum Shinrikyo had grown as it grew in numbers, wealth, and material resources. Only those at the organization's apex and those in its scientific unit knew of the cult's growing capacity to lay waste to Japan's sense of security by terrorizing the innocent. This included Nazi-like human experiments, giant spraying devices to spread poison gas through cities, attempts to buy Russian nuclear warheads and to attack enemies with anthrax, the murder of apostates, and research on nuclear weapons in the Australian desert.

This was the work of the well-financed science unit—Aum Shinrikyo is estimated to have been worth $100 million by the mid-1990's—ominously called the "Ministry of Science and Technology," as if it were a government department. Indeed, for the guru and his lieutenants, Aum Shinrikyo was a government in the making, for after Armageddon, a final battle in which spiritually corrupt humanity would die, only the cult would be left and would rule what remained as an earthly paradise. While other religions, notably Christianity, taught that humanity must wait for the final battle between good and evil to approach, Aum Shinrikyo maintained that it is possible to hasten the birth (if not ease the birth pangs) of the new order—to "force the end," as it was put. The Tokyo gas attack was to be the opening of this final apocalyptic battle.

The heart of Murakami's book is the brief section he devotes to discovering what he set out to find in his investigations. What did the attack reveal about the character of contemporary Japan? Murakami doggedly pursues this line of inquiry because he fears that the Japanese will pass the attack off as merely the work of lunacy—though he is aware that it was just that. However, he is determined that the Japanese not dismiss the sarin attack, which he argues is (with the catastrophic Kobe earthquake only three month previously, on January 17, 1995) one of two seminal events of the nation's postwar history, as an event wholly external to themselves. Such dismissal, he argues, is just too easy.

The truth, Murakami suggests, lies deeper beneath the surface of ordinary consciousness—lies "underground," just as the subway gassing and the earthquake lay under the feet of those populating the arteries of Japan's teeming conurbations. Beneath the surface of the social hive is an underlying cause that Murakami deplores. It is the lack of an ethic of responsibility in Japan, of the perpetual effort to "save face," the refusal to own up to one's role in any and all of society's negative affairs. Thus, Murakami recalls his revulsion years earlier at seeing the absurdity of Aum's political tactics in attempting to elect its guru-leader to the national legislature. Murakami imagines his turning away from this cancer on Japanese society to be like the Germans of the Weimar Republic ignoring Hitler's rise, turning their back on their responsibility to deal with them. Murakami insists that Aum be considered an integral part of Japanese social reality for which citizens must take responsibility. This is the author's powerful moral lesson. It is a universal lesson, as applicable to Americans and to every mature people as it is to the Japanese.

Why was Aum such a magnet for the dissatisfied? In truth, Japan lacks a pervasive traditional religion capable of effectively assisting the individual through the travails of modern life. Thus new religions began sweeping over the nation in the 1930's. The dismantling of the cult of the emperor during the U.S. occupation after World War II only deepened the need for religious satisfaction. Aum Shrinyko was successful partly because it met a need by social misfits for a life outside the frenetic pace of postwar society.

Murakami examines the form of escape from ordinary life through which the cult met the needs of so many of its adherents. The cult was so successful in meeting their needs that many are reluctant to damn the group outright, even after realizing its role in the sarin attack. Vast numbers of citizens give over their conscience to their government during wartime and undertake killing on a massive scale, so also, those responsible for the sarin attack surrendered their faculty for moral choice to the Leader. Only in such a psychological state could the otherwise sane, humane, brilliant heart surgeon who led Aum's "Ministry of Science and Technology" have consented to direct mass murder.

As Murakami reveals it, the psychology of Aum's denizen was a variant of the twin poles of modern human psychology: a struggle between dependency needs and striving for autonomy. In an extreme, twisted form, desire for individual autonomy becomes a struggle for total independence. Such a struggle is a pervasive theme in the literature and philosophy of the past two centuries, found, for example in the acclaimed treatment by Johann Wolfgang von Goethe (1749-1832) of the Faust legend and in the philosophies of G. W. F. Hegel (1770-1831) and Jean-Paul Sartre (1905-1980), to name just a few.

Murakami shows that many of the alienated Japanese who found emotional refuge in the Aum cult sought fulfillment by complete submission of the self to the guru-leader, who seemed to embody the complete self-mastery and individual autonomy they so craved. Through identification with the guru, they vicariously lived out their wish for autonomy, even as they laid their freedom and their moral judgment at his feet. In a perverse way, they found liberty in enslavement—found freedom from the responsibilities and strivings of ordinary life, freedom from the responsibility of choosing.

Thus it is hardly accidental that a striking characteristic of Aum was the nearly complete absence of a sense of responsibility of its members. Large, complex tasks costing considerable sums might be so poorly accomplished that, in the case of construction, completed buildings had to be pulled down and rebuilt, with no recrimination or sense of failing by anyone. Nor is it surprising that former members complain that no one looked after them—few showed any sense of responsibility for fellow members. Without moral responsibility, the path lay open to violence, to imprisoning, torturing, and killing those who attempted to escape the cult, and to murderous attacks on society at large.

Murakami's *Underground* presents a disturbing but salutary message to every reader open to moral suasion. The stories of hell set loose on the Tokyo subway related by those the author interviewed are only too real. Distant, even unreal, as it may seem, the event is not fiction; it actually happened. Though it occurred in Japan, criminally insane cults exist throughout the world, many of them in the United States. The tragedy laid bare in *Underground* should provoke meditation on the meaning of reason and unreason, and on the central problem of faith: that faith can be fastened upon absolutely anything. Today in Europe and America as never before, untold numbers of academic humanists denigrate reason and rationality. The attacks proceeding on the legacy of the Enlightenment's belief in rationality are deeply wrong. The forces that denigrate rationality are the forces of destruction.

Charles F. Bahmueller

Sources for Further Study

Library Journal 126 (April 1, 2001): 117.
The New York Review of Books 48 (July 5, 2001): 39.
The New York Times Book Review 106 (June 10, 2001): 13.
Publishers Weekly 248 (April 9, 2001): 58.

THE UNIVERSE IN A NUTSHELL

Author: Stephen Hawking (1942-   )
Publisher: Bantam Books (New York). Illustrated.
216 pp. $35.00
Type of work: Science

≈

In this sequel to A Brief History of Time, *Hawking brings readers up to date on cosmological theory, explaining M-theory and the possibilities of time travel, multiple universes, and improved human beings*

≈

In 1988, Stephen Hawking, Lucasian Professor of Mathematics at the University of Cambridge, published *A Brief History of Time*. It was among the most successful popular books about science ever written. *The Universe in a Nutshell* is its sequel. Unlike the first book, the sequel comes with stunning graphics and photographs to illustrate the concepts in the text, and each has an extended caption to clarify its relevance. The text itself, however, is much more cursory in presenting the intellectual and scientific background of current cosmology, and so readers who recall the first book are best prepared to appreciate the second.

Always charming, frequently funny, and at times bewildering, *The Universe in a Nutshell* describes a universe that sounds like a carnival fun house: Nothing is really as it seems; mysteries and perils lie hidden because of humans' confined, specialized point of view; and at the end of the book, readers, thoroughly entertained, may yet wonder what exactly has gone on. Hawking wrote the seven chapters so that each could be read more or less independently of the rest, with the exception of the first two, which explain the foundation of modern cosmological theories. Accordingly, there is some repetition among the chapters, but it is never tedious—often, indeed, it is helpful, given the complexity of the concepts involved. The narrative is intended for a general readership, and so Hawking faces the dilemma confronting all popularizers of physics. He must explain theories that are mathematical in nature to readers who do not have a background in the abstruse mathematics. Although he includes equations now and then, he relies for the most part on descriptions and analogy. He is brilliant at it, too. The graphics help, but even those readers who can imagine, for instance, eleven-dimension space-time or recognize it in the two dimensions of an illustration must accept a fair amount simply on faith—faith in such baffling entities as supersymmetry, string theory, superstrings, and M-theory, which have emerged from the theorists' equations like Proteus rising from the sea.

The first chapter, "A Brief History of Relativity," is familiar territory for the armchair scientist. It recounts how Albert Einstein's special (1905) and general (1915) theories of relativity permanently changed the way scientists conceive of time and space. The special theory demonstrated that matter and energy are forms of one another and that the speed of light is the fastest velocity possible. These findings led to conceptual revolutions. Specifically, Einstein demolished the idea of a fixed medium in the universe ("ether") and with it the possibility of a single, absolute perspective on motion; also, the interchangeability of mass and energy led to development of atomic weapons and energy. The general theory was even more radical. It showed that gravity and acceleration are the same thing and that mass curves space near it. From the general theory grew modern cosmology and the exotica of astrophysics: black holes, gravitational lensing, the "big bang" origin of space-time, and the expansion of the universe.

Stephen Hawking is Lucasian Professor of Mathematics at the University of Cambridge, a position once held by Sir Isaac Newton. Born in 1942, he is recognized as one of the most brilliant theoretical physicists of his generation, legendary for his work on black holes and cosmology.

The second chapter, "The Shape of Time," extends the discussion of Einstein's general theory of relativity. Hawking considers how the theory prescribes the character of time. In the extreme curvature of space near a black hole, time actually stands still, and here Hawking's own pioneering contributions to theoretical physics come into play. He explains his theorem, derived with Roger Penrose, establishing that general relativity requires the universe to have originated from a single event and that when large stars eventually collapse upon themselves and form bodies so dense that not even light can escape, time comes to an end for that mass.

The greatest problem in modern cosmology, Hawking continues, is that general relativity does not accord with the other great physical theory of the twentieth century, quantum theory, which Einstein also helped develop. General relativity appears to break down at the infinitesimal scales at which quantum mechanical effects apply. It is therefore the goal of theoreticians in the twenty-first century to create a theory that weds quantum mechanics and relativity. There have been many attempts. The leading contenders, Hawking believes, are supersymmetric supergravity theories and string theories, which were published mostly during the 1980's and 1990's. Both, he further contends, are probably aspects of a master explanation of the cosmos, or "theory of everything" (TOE) to scientists, called M-theory.

It is this second chapter, "The Shape of Time," where the reader begins to feel his imagination stretched, folded, and twisted dizzyingly. String theories imply that the universe does not run on three dimensions of space and one of time but on ten or eleven dimensions. Where are these extra six or seven dimensions? They are out of sight in the fabric of the four that humans experience. How they are hidden is the crux of the theoretical problem, and Hawking uses geometric analogies to clarify the parameters of the problem. In particular, he borrows from the mathematical objects known as "p-branes." These are membranes that can be intersected to form lines or curled into tubes whose ends can join to form donuts, among other shapes. Add to these another remarkable mathematical construct—imaginary time—and Hawking reveals a very complex space-time fabric indeed: The known universe may be considered to be a four-dimensional image on the boundary of a higher-dimensional medium, much as a hologram is a two-dimensional record of a three-dimensional image.

It is all heady stuff, but just when readers might feel perplexed beyond endurance, Hawking's humor and tone of utter reasonableness are sure to propel them onward. For example, he introduces an influential mathematician as the "genius of p-branes." Are p-branes and imaginary time real? Hawking disarmingly acknowledges that they sound like the props of particularly fanciful science fiction. He himself had difficulty accepting them, but he is a scientific positivist, he tells readers. For positivists what is important in a mathematical theory is that it describe known phenomena coherently and be testable. Whether something implied by a theory seems real does not matter. It is a good point for readers to keep in mind as, in the following five chapters, Hawking extends the ideas of M-theory to their potential cosmological consequences.

Chapter 3, "The Universe in a Nutshell," concerns the history, or histories, of the universe. Edwin Hubble discovered in the 1920's that the universe was expanding. Others proposed that it was expanding away from an initial explosion, the big bang. Why has it grown to be just the way we find it and not some other way? To help answer this question, Hawking applies the anthropic principle. Among the more slippery proposals of science, it stands for a range of related teleological assertions. Most commonly, it stands for the belief that the universe is constructed in just such a way as to produce intelligent life. Hawking uses the principle as a way to weed out histories of the universe that, although possible given the initial conditions of the big bang, could not produce life on Earth or human intelligence. The anthropic principle may strike readers as a tautology; nevertheless, it allow scientists to adjust critical values of various constants during the early history of the universe. If Planck's constant were larger or smaller than it is, for instance, the universe would have evolved too fast or in the wrong way for intelligence to develop. Current evidence also helps define the parameters of the big bang, Hawking points out, especially the cosmic background radiation.

Chapter 4, "Predicting the Future," ponders a puzzle for theorists. If matter falls into a black hole, does it ever come out again? At stake is a basic law in physics, the conservation of mass and energy, as well as the scientist's disinclination to believe that anything lies beyond study. Again, Hawking brings to bear his own work in applying quantum mechanics to relativity. His answer—probably not, because black holes are not completely black—means that the future can be, in theory at least, predicted and so is safe. However, he admits darkly, the issue is not settled. It could be that wormholes exist, passages behind black holes that suck away matter irretrievably into other places, other times, or even other universes.

The past appears to be in even greater peril, depending upon what M-theory finally uncovers. Chapter 5, "Protecting the Past," considers time travel. One of the most famous thought problems of cosmology concerns this question: If someone traveled into the past and caused the death of his or her grandfather as a boy, what would happen? Would the course of history change in some way? Would, for instance, the time traveler softly and silently vanish away, like Lewis Carroll's snark? Current theory appears to allow time travel through time loops that are a byproduct of the universe's rotation. Hawking expresses doubt. He subscribes to the Chronology Protection Conjecture, which holds that the laws of physics conspire to prevent large masses from going back in time, something like a feedback mechanism. Again, though, the issue is not settled. In fact, he has a bet with another leading cosmologist, Kip Thorne, who thinks time travel is possible. To readers who suspect that Hawking's conclusions are part of a government cover-up on time travel, he says, well, that might be right. This quick grab into the bottom of the barrel of antigovernment paranoia is playful.

The next chapter, "Our Future? Star Trek or Not," is likely to be provocative to any but the most liberal-minded science buff. One possibility is that, as the television and film series *Star Trek* depicts, humans will be basically the same centuries from now, only with much better technology. That vision is unlikely, says Hawking, because it is static, and life is never static. Conditions on Earth constantly change (witness the present population explosion, for example), and like all species, humans evolve with the changes. Hawking discusses the nature of genetics and evolution to ponder what humans may be like in the future. He contemplates the benefits of bioengineering to improve intelligence and other traits and the possibility of human-machine hybrids. Some change is inevitable, he insists, as humanity outgrows Earth and must find and adapt to other environments.

In the final chapter, "Brane New World," he returns to M-theory and meditates upon the shape it may take, how scientists may test its conclusions, and whether it allows for only one or many universes, which may or may not be alike. As the book ends, Hawking leaves his audience actually entertaining a vision of the universe floating like one nutshell among uncountable others, universes that can collide, burst, or create new universes. It is a great achievement to bring readers in so short a flight of prose to such great contemplations and make it all seem reasonable. The excitement among cosmologists that a great breakthrough is just around the corner comes through clearly. *The Universe in a Nutshell* is a thrilling, uplifting, intellectually strenuous book.

Roger Smith

Sources for Further Study

Booklist 97 (August, 2001): 2054.
The Spectator 287 (November 10, 2001): 80.
Time 158 (November 11, 2001): 106.
The Times, November 12, 2001, p. 2.

VICTORIAN SENSATION
The Extraordinary Publication, Reception, and Secret Authorship of
Vestiges of the Natural History of Creation

Author: James A. Secord (1953-   )
Publisher: University of Chicago Press (Chicago).
   624 pp. $35.00
Type of work: History of science
Time: 1800-1850
Locale: England and Scotland

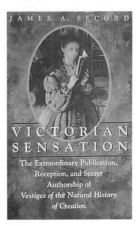

∼

Secord explores the reactions of the first readers of Robert Chambers's Vestiges of the Natural History of Cre-ation, *providing a panoramic review of the cultural, social, and intellectual background of Victorian Britain's indus-trial society, a fertile ground for breeding the controversy created by the publication of this scientific study*

∼

Principal personages:
>   ROBERT CHAMBERS, publisher, and author of *Vestiges of the Natural
>   History of Creation*
>   JOHN CHURCHILL, publisher of medical books who agreed to publish
>   *Vestiges*
>   THOMAS A. HIRST, Scottish engineer who left extensive notes of his
>   reading of *Vestiges*
>   ALEXANDER IRELAND, Chambers's close friend who help the author
>   remain anonymous
>   HUGH MILLER, author of a lengthy response refuting Chambers's book
>   ADAM SEDGWICK, Cambridge professor who led the attack on *Vestiges*
>   WILLIAM WHEWELL, respected scientist who wrote a lengthy treatise
>   attacking *Vestiges*

   Anyone familiar with the history of science knows that the appearance of Charles Darwin's *On the Origin of Species* in 1859 was not the first study to challenge the lit-eral truth of the biblical story of creation. The scandal caused by Darwin's theory of natural selection was but the latest bombshell dropped on a reading public that was still reeling from the shock of previous revelations in geology and biology that under-mined religious beliefs. If *On the Origin of Species* toppled the edifice of divine reve-lation for Victorian readers, however, it was because the foundations of received dogma had been weakened by a series of studies that began appearing in the eigh-teenth century, continuing with some regularity into the early decades of the nine-teenth. With hindsight, it is easy to see also that no precursor to Darwin's work had more impact on the British reading public than the anonymously published

Vestiges of the Natural History of Creation in 1844.

That *Vestiges* caused a stir throughout Britain when it appeared is a historical commonplace. Any work positing that men may have been descended from apes, or that the world was millions of years old, would have been met with swift condemnation by both the general public and by the intellectual community as well. Readers' reaction in 1835 to the appearance of Charles

∾

James A. Secord is reader in history and philosophy of science at the University of Cambridge. He is the author of Controversy in Victorian Geology *(1986) and editor of an edition of* Vestiges of the Natural History of Creation.

∾

Lyell's *Principles of Geology* had already demonstrated how sensational the publication of such theories could be. Despite the almost universally negative reaction to *Vestiges*, the book stayed in print for decades, was reissued in a series of editions that updated the author's findings and conclusions for a public continually tantalized and tormented by the challenges of science to theological doctrine. By their own admission, such diverse figures as the politician William Gladstone, the novelist Mary Ann Evans (George Eliot), the poet Alfred, Lord Tennyson, the humanitarian Florence Nightingale, and even Queen Victoria herself felt the impact of *Vestiges*.

In *Victorian Sensation*, James Secord, a distinguished scholar and recognized expert on the history of science, explores the reasons why *Vestiges* elicited such dynamic, and often diametrically opposite, reactions among the British reading public. Drawing from a wide variety of sources, Secord examines not only the history of this book's reception, but ways that industrial advancements, changes in taste, attitudes toward religion, the practice of politics, and university life made possible the sensational impact *Vestiges* had in England and Scotland. In doing so, he unravels the complex reasons why the Scottish publisher and editor Robert Chambers chose to maintain his anonymity as the author of such a widely read and influential study. Secord's aim, hinted at in the introductory chapters but expressed most succinctly near the end, is to explore "the introduction of an evolutionary account of nature into public debate in order to see what happens when a major historical episode is approached from the perspective of reading." *Victorian Sensation* is nothing less, he asserts, than a prolegomenon to a new form of cultural study becoming prevalent at the end of the twentieth century, the history of communication. In this respect, Secord sets for himself a daunting task, but manages to handle it masterfully.

Among the interesting threads woven throughout his study, Secord's analysis of the reasons for Chambers's choosing to keep his authorship of *Vestiges* a secret from all but a very small circle of family and friends is particularly intriguing. To Secord's readers, looking back from a world where notoriety through authorship is a much-sought-after commodity, Chambers's decision might seem curious—unless one assumes that he was simply afraid of the negative personal attacks that might be launched at him. Secord admits that such fear was partially responsible for Chambers's hesitancy in being openly associated with his controversial work, but he points out that the penchant for anonymity was more common among writers of Chambers's day than in the decades that followed. Gentlemen and businessmen, sometimes for different reasons, avoided identifying themselves as authors of even commonplace works; big-city societies found it an amusing parlor game to speculate about the authors of various works that had caught the fancy of a growing reading public.

Though Chambers did not put his name on the book, he nevertheless took great pains to establish what Secord describes as a close relationship with his readers. In fact, Secord claims, Chambers displays a constant concern for his audience that in some ways parallel those of a writer of a work of fiction. This should not be surprising, since one of the men Chambers most admired was Sir Walter Scott, author of the immensely popular *Waverly* novels. Like Scott, Chambers wanted to make history interesting for his readers—but the kind of history the publisher-turned-science-writer produced was more controversial than any novel his idol ever wrote.

From Scott, too, Chambers may have developed the idea that anonymity had important advantages. Referred to for decades as "The Great Unknown," Scott took pleasure in watching his friends and the general public guess at the authorship of the novels he turned out with regularity. Chambers sought anonymity for several reasons, Secord surmises. First, it provided him a certain degree of authority that he would have foregone had he attached his name to *Vestiges*. Chambers was not a scientist, not even by Victorian standards. Even in an age when gentlemen of means or a handful of members of the faculties at the universities dominated the practice of science, Chambers could present no significant credentials to give credence to the conclusions he put forward in his work. He had to let the work speak for itself. Nevertheless, the significant changes he introduced in subsequent editions after initial publication indicate clearly that he took the practice of science seriously and believed deeply that he was helping to advance the cause of knowledge.

Whether Chambers was simply a "brilliant amateur," as Samuel Chew and Richard Altick dubbed him in their mid-twentieth century history of nineteenth century literature, or a major contributor to scientific discovery is not fully resolved in *Victorian Sensation*. Secord's decision to pay more attention to the sensation *Vestiges* created among readers than to the bold arguments Chambers puts forth in the book leaves him open to criticism on this point. *New York Times* reviewer Arianne Chernock laments the fact that "another book on *Vestiges* itself rather than this intelligent analysis of its production and reception is needed to determine whether Secord's argument here is well founded."

This is not to suggest, however, that Secord has missed his mark in his thorough and at times brilliant analysis. Rather than analyze the question of the book's scientific accuracy, Secord instead is interested in its impact on its first readers, Chambers's contemporaries. *Vestiges* appeared at a time when Victorian England was abuzz with talk about the question of human origins. Even at the end of the twentieth century, Secord says, "books about evolution are our devils and angels." For most men and women of the early nineteenth century, the possibility that the biblical record of creation might not square with the physical evidence had even greater impact.

One might expect Secord to investigate with some care the reactions of intellectual and spiritual leaders of the period. Certainly, *Victorian Sensations* does not disappoint readers in this respect. The assessment of responses by leading men of the universities such as William Whewell and Adam Sedgwick is thorough. Secord dissects Sedgwick's damning review of *Vestiges* to show how much the establishment felt threatened by the book. Also included are extensive discussions of the reaction to the book by respected scientists such as Richard Owen and Charles Darwin. Another significant contribution Secord makes to modern readers' understanding of the ways a single book might affect the people who first read it is his careful analysis of the reaction to *Vestiges* among the populace in various cities throughout the British Isles. In separate chapters, he investigates the way the citizens of London, Liverpool, and Edinburgh responded to the work. He also illuminates the varying reactions of the professoriate at Oxford and Cambridge.

What makes *Victorian Sensation* of even greater value is Secord's ability to uncover and present the reactions of ordinary men and women, thousands of whom were able to obtain the book in cheap editions and read it for themselves. A chapter of *Victorian Sensation* is devoted to exploring the impact *Vestiges* had on Thomas Archer Hirst. Hirst was a teenager when *Vestiges* appeared in 1844. A self-taught Englishman who went on later in life to become a noted mathematician, the young Hirst read *Vestiges* carefully, comparing it to other texts and drawing his own conclusions about the validity of Chambers's argument. According to Secord, hundreds, perhaps thousands, of young men and women dealt with the book as Hirst did; their willingness to grapple with the revolutionary ideas Chambers expresses made them a receptive audience for that even more provocative successor to *Vestiges*, Darwin's *On the Origin of Species*.

Certainly, as Secord notes, it was Darwin's book and not Chambers's that became one of "the most pervasive remnants of the Victorian world" in modern culture, but regular reference to *On the Origin of Species* as "the single work that transformed manners, the novel, the periodical press, [and] the practice of the sciences" is simply implausible. What Darwin read frequently found its way into what he wrote; hence, knowing how he understood *Vestiges* tells subsequent generations something about his own scientific and creative processes.

Able to make the language of science and business easily understandable to the general reader, Secord is adept at bringing to life the period in which *Vestiges* was published. Dozens of photographs, illustrations, and memorabilia are not simply placed within the book, but are often used to vivify key points in the author's argument. The result is that *Victorian Sensation* is a genuine scholarly achievement.

Laurence W. Mazzeno

Sources for Further Study

The Chronicle of Higher Education 47 (March 2, 2001): A19.
Library Journal 125 (November 15, 2000): 82.
Nature 409 (January, 2001): 285.
The New York Times Book Review 106 (May 20, 2001): 7.
Science 291 (February 2, 2001): 833.
The Spectator 286 (March 10, 2001): 37.

WALKING THE BIBLE
A Journey by Land Through the Five Books of Moses

Author: Bruce Feiler (1964-   )
Publisher: William Morrow/HarperCollins (New York).
   451 pp. $26.00
Type of work: Travel, archaeology, history, literary criticism, and religion
Time: 2000-1200 B.C.E. and 1998-1999
Locale: The Middle East (Turkey, Israel, Palestinian territories, Jordan, Egypt)

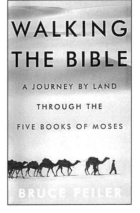

∼

This travelogue traces the author's journeys with Avner Goren, respected Israeli archaeologist, as together they retrace the steps first of the patriarchs then of the ancient Israelites, as recounted through the Pentateuch, or the Five Books of Moses

∼

Principal personages:
> BRUCE FEILER, the author and narrator, also author of several other books based on his own life experiences
> AVNER GOREN, chief Israeli archaeologist of the Sinai from 1967 to 1982

Bruce Feiler has taken an amazing journey, and he has written a rather long book describing it. In a project conceived on a visit to Jerusalem, the author wanted somehow to enter into the world of the Bible by traversing the itineraries of its first five books—the books of Moses, or the Pentateuch.

Feiler realized at the beginning of his planning that he was not up to the task. Even with extensive background reading, he knows too little about the history and archaeology of the ancient world of the Bible to find his way on his own. Perhaps more important, he knows too little about the modern world corresponding to that ancient world to make his way on his own. So he did the smart thing: He found a first-class guide. Feiler managed to get Avner Goren, a well-known Israeli archaeologist, to go with him.

What follows is an account of "a perilous, ten-thousand-mile journey, retracing the Five Books of Moses through the desert . . . through three continents, five countries, and four war zones . . ." It is alternately an informative travelogue and a stirring personal journey of faith. At times, it may also be somewhat tedious and repetitive, depending on the reader's familiarity with and interest in the subject matter.

Feiler has a few interrelated themes that run throughout the book. One of these themes is making a visceral connection with the land of the Bible. Another is the way

826

the Bible is related to that land beyond purely historical events. At the beginning of his trip, visiting Mount Ararat where Noah's ark is purported to have landed, Feiler states that "the Bible may or may not be true, it may or may not be historical, but it is undoubtedly still alive." There in Turkey, as well as in various other places throughout the journey, Feiler has an almost mystical experience with the land which in the end leaves him changed, one could even say converted.

Feiler also carries on a running theological discussion with Goren about many things: the historicity of the Bible, the nature of God, and the possibility of inclusion in the context of the diverse interests of the Middle East. Feiler moves slowly from wanting to prove or disprove the Bible on the basis of archaeology to a more sophisticated notion of what the Bible is about and how it was put together. He comes not only to tolerate but to appreciate how oral tradition and an ancient concern for putting history in the service of theology, or the transmission of values, combine

Bruce Feiler is a well-known author of numerous award-winning books and articles. In addition to his best-selling Walking the Bible, *Feiler has written* Learning to Bow *(1991),* Looking for Class *(1993),* Under the Big Top *(1995), and* Dreaming Out Loud *(1998).*

to produce texts which are, to modern sensibilities, a strange mix of the historical and the mythical. Feiler obviously struggles with this throughout his journey, and in the end he defends the Bible as having what scholars sometimes call verisimilitude, or a likeness to what might be expected from a given historical period. As Feiler says, "This doesn't mean the stories are true, but it does mean they are true to their era."

From Turkey, the travelers make their way first to Israel, then to Egypt, then to the Sinai and Negev deserts, and finally to Jordan, again on the edge of the Promised Land of the Bible. In so doing they follow the path (or part of it) of the wanderings first of the patriarchs, then of the people of Israel as recounted in Genesis. Feiler retells the stories of the Bible, or more precisely, he summarizes them. This both directly connects his travels with the Bible (one of his objectives), but also helps the reader unfamiliar with the Bible to follow the reasoning behind the itinerary. Unfortunately for those already familiar with these stories, the summaries are not as interesting as are the texts themselves, and it is easy to get details wrong. Feiler relates that Jacob worked for a second seven years for his trickster uncle Laban before he could marry Rachel, but the text states (Genesis 29:27-30) that although Jacob did indeed have to work another seven years for his favorite wife, he was able to marry her after only a week of marriage to Leah, the older daughter Laban had substituted in place of Rachel for the first seven years of service.

The more interesting journey is Feiler's own. He cannot always decide whether it is the land, the people, the Bible, or God with which he is trying to connect. It is all of the above, and these ideas and things are interconnected as well, but Feiler is on a journey of faith, as he slowly comes to realize over the course of his pilgrimage. One of the recurring tensions Feiler grapples with during his travels is the old theological paradox known as faith versus reason, or as Feiler usually puts it, the intellectual versus the feeling approach to the God of the Bible.

At various points and in various ways, Feiler uses the geography of the land to explore his own emotional, psychological, and even spiritual being. "It's as if the act of mapping the land was forcing me to remap my own internal geography. . ." He comes to the point where he no longer looks only for the connection between the land and the Bible, but also for the connection between the people he meets on the way and the Bible. Finally, he finds connections between himself and the God of the Bible, mediated by the land and the people he encounters.

The land continues to exert a strong pull on Feiler throughout his narrative. He feels that strange at-homeness in Turkey. He compares the pyramids to the Bible: "The genius of their creation is that their meaning is subtle enough to change over time." Over and over again, Feiler tries to understand the special attraction of the desert, for the people he meets, and ultimately, for him as well. In the end, his trip truly does become a pilgrimage.

Though at times the reader may wish to hurry the journey along (perhaps Feiler wanted to get across just how long such an undertaking can last, and how exhausting it can be), Feiler writes some of his best prose describing the travails on such a quest. He describes the cooking and eating of pita bread in a fire pit out in the Negev desert as follows: "At this point it was impossible to distinguish the ashes from the bread. . . . [The cook] took a stick and began beating the loaf like a dirty rug. Dust flew everywhere . . . he pulled off a piece, breathing steam . . . There was a small coating of sand around the crust, but I no longer cared. . . ."

The people Feiler and Goren meet on their way almost universally seem to be both somewhat dismissive of the factual and historical details of the Bible and reverent in their appreciation of its truth. Thus a monk a St. Catherine's monastery, when asked whether living close to the purported holy site of Mount Sinai helps his faith, replies: "It doesn't matter where you live. It matters how you feel." Basan, an Egyptian guide, asked what he thinks about the historicity of the stories of Genesis in light of the present-day commercialization of the many "authentic" biblical sites associated with the story of Joseph says, "I think religion is more powerful than history. I think Joseph existed."

Feiler comes to appreciate the Bible in a new way—not as a historical record of the events it portrays, but as an interpretation of the experience of a people with their surroundings and their God. "At this point, I was less inclined to accept a sterile, naturalistic explanation for every event, particularly when it threatened to undermine the meaning of the story. I was more interested in how the writers took possibly factual occurrences and shaped them with spiritual objectives." Feiler comes to the conclusion that while not always to be taken literally, the Bible "is forever applicable. It's always now."

Feiler has his own crisis (or crises) of faith as well. He is confronted with so many differing pictures of God during his travels and corresponding encounters with the Bible that he is forced to reflect on the subject. He ponders: "'Do you believe in God?' Must be followed immediately by 'Which version of God?' . . . the journey . . . showed me there is no single place, no such thing as an accepted notion of God." In particular, Feiler is disturbed, as many believers and unbelievers alike are as well, with the Bible's portrayal of God as at times seemingly despotic and cruel. Feiler is apparently able to put such thoughts aside, as all believers must eventually do, in order to attempt to access the mystery directly. "To me, the most fascinating thing about encountering that mystery was what [Saint] Augustine himself had described: the feeling that I was *re*covering it, not *dis*covering it . . . All I had to do was *remember* . . ."

Feiler has not just one, but a series of conversionlike experiences. At one point he realizes that the Bible is not so much about history as it is about God. A major element of this epiphany is when he begins to accept that land-people-Bible-God are like concentric circles (though he does not put it this way) which lead one inward on a journey to find oneself in connection with the God of the Bible. At the end of the journey and the end of the book, at the top of Mount Nebo, Feiler has the following revelation, ostensibly about Moses, but obviously about Feiler himself, and about all who care to listen to him: "Moses may not get the land, but he gets the promise . . . The land alone is not the destination; the destination is the place where human beings live in consort with the divine."

Robert Bascom

Sources for Further Study

Booklist 97 (February 15, 2001): 1111.
Library Journal 126 (February 1, 2001): 101.
New York 34 (April 16, 2001): 71.
Publishers Weekly 248 (February 12, 2001): 200.

THE WAR AGAINST CLICHÉ
Essays and Reviews, 1971-2000

Author: Martin Amis (1949-   )
Publisher: Talk Miramax/Hyperion (New York). 506 pp.
$35.00
Type of work: Literary criticism

≈

Seeking to expose clichés in all forms, Amis's collection of literary nonfiction celebrates and skewers figures of high and low culture

≈

With the assured voice of a best-selling author who was born with a literary pedigree, Martin Amis feels no need to pander to any school of criticism or theory in his collected essays. Principally a stylist, Amis evaluates other authors based on the originality of their prose and the number of clichés they will allow. Like John Updike in his collection of essays *Picked Up Pieces* (1975), Amis has a pleasantly informal style of analysis that moves from the skewering of writers that he scorns to the more appreciative studies of his literary heroes. Even though he claims that literary criticism has died in this age of democratized sensibility, where everyone has an equally valid claim to judge literature as they please and talent is irrelevant, Amis continues to practice his critique anyway, exposing the fraudulent and the overpraised, and shoring up his sense of what has lasting value in the literary arts. As he puts it in *The Moronic Inferno* (1986), an earlier collection of essays: "The thousand-word book review seems to me far more clearly an art form (however minor) than any of the excursions of the New Journalism, some of which are as long as *Middlemarch*."

Amis has taken pains to choose works that best suit him and reflect his erudition and interests. In *The Moronic Inferno*, Amis specifically focused on the cultural excesses and vulgarity of the United States, and again in *The War Against Cliché* he enjoys debunking iconographic figures such as rock star Elvis Presley and artist Andy Warhol. For instance, he finds that *Elvis, We Love You Tender* (1980), a book by witnesses of Elvis's debaucheries, inadvertently damns the man for his banality and the conventionality of his notions of success. Regarding Warhol's diaries, Amis finds that Warhol unconsciously lampoons himself with the flat, affectless tone of his prose, his obsession with celebrity and money, and his seeming inability to discuss art intelligently. Amis likes to sniff out the various ways that writers try to hide under pretension or sell out while affecting literary poses. Writers who attempt to complete the half-formed leftover scraps of authors such as Jane Austen and Raymond Chandler end up giving way to the current era's lack of constraint, turning classic voices into chatty bores. Amis reserves his most extreme vituperation for Thomas Harris and

his novel *Hannibal* (1999), in part because Harris clearly showed he could write accomplished
genre fiction with earlier works such as *Silence
of the Lambs* (1991), and because his new emphasis in Hannibal's cultural snobbery led to a
betrayal of his talent. As Amis phrases it, "Only
by turning his back on the vulgar could Thomas
Harris write a novel of such profound and virtu-
oso vulgarity." Hannibal's arrogance amidst all
of Harris's potboiler clichés makes the novel
doubly despicable.

*The son of British author Kingsley
Amis, Martin Amis was born in
Oxford in 1949. While he was
working as an editorial assistant
for* The Times Literary
Supplement, *Amis's first novel* The
Rachel Papers *(1973) won the 1974
Somerset Maugham Award. He has
since become the best-selling author
of* Money *(1984),* London Fields
(1989), and The Information
(1995). His memoir Experience
was published in 2000.

When it comes to reviewing British authors,
Amis can sound constrained, perhaps because
most of these pieces were originally written for
The Observer and *The Guardian* in his youth
(the collection goes back to 1971), and perhaps,
also, because his barbs could land on targets too
close to his own literary milieu or that of his father. While his discussion of J. G. Ballard offers
up a cautious admiration, Amis becomes oddly
muted when it comes to reviewing Iris Murdoch.
While his summarizing of each novel suggests
an increasing weariness with Murdoch's plot
contrivances, Amis tends to conclude his comments with a positive note, as if seeking to acknowledge her reputation even in the face of this
current weak novel. Curiously, Amis completely dismisses John Fowles for his mid-
dlebrow talent, which makes one wonder if Fowles ever panned one of Amis's novels. Generally, however, Amis's assessment of recent British writers is mainly lauda-
tory, if sometimes coolly restrained.

Amis writes best when he has a personal stake in a writer who is under attack, as in
his defense of Philip Larkin entitled "The Ending: Don Juan in Hull" written for *The
New Yorker*. A well-favored and respected poet for years, Larkin's reputation fell
abruptly after his death when politically correct critics leaped upon his passion for
pornography, the racist comments in his letters, and the Nazi elements in his upbringing. Andrew Motion's biography *Philip Larkin: A Writer's Life* (1993) pillories
Larkin for his refusal to address these habitual weaknesses in his work. Amis defends
Larkin on multiple levels, first by invoking his fond memory of the poet as a friend of
the family in the Kingsley Amis household, and then by placing Larkin's weaknesses
in historical context, and by simply acknowledging his lapses as he celebrates his poetry. Amis points out that none of the critics were as hard on Larkin as Larkin could be
on himself in his confessional poetry, and he argues that Larkin possesses an inner
complexity that critics rendered as two-dimensional. In the process of defending
Larkin, Amis exposes the intolerance and hypocrisies of critics looking to gain notori-

ety for their attacks. Repeatedly, Amis runs across critics who would like to confuse the writer's life with his or her work, and Amis insists that there is no clear correspondence between the two: The very idea of a critical biography invites a continual fallacy. One never knows entirely how a writer produces a lasting work of art, according to Amis, but to look into that life in terms of the writing can distract the critic from seeing the work on its own terms.

With postmodernist writers, Amis can be both generous and sensitive to the general reader's impatience with obscure literary experimentation. He characterizes the "failure-rate" of experimental fiction as "alarmingly high—approaching . . . 100 percent." In the midst of assessing Don DeLillo's *Mao II* (1992), Amis acknowledges postmodernism's "potential for huge boredom," but also its "tremendous predictive power" due to the prevalence of "image-management" in people's lives and its distortive power. Amis finds that DeLillo can fall into the bad habit of turning into the novelist of ideas. In the desire to get across his ideas, DeLillo ends up flattening out the differences in the voices between characters and thereby diminishing the novel's descriptive details. In the case of the postmodern cityscapes of J. G. Ballard, Amis admits that critics first greeted *Crash* (1973) with a "flurry of nervous dismay." He also claims that the novel is the "most extreme example of how beautifully and lovingly someone can write 70,000 words of vicious nonsense." Later, in an adjoining essay that considers the movie version of the novel, Amis comes around to acknowledging its cult classic status. Amis's essays about experimental novels show up his struggle to accept works that are genuinely new, demanding a shift in his critical perspective.

Amis devotes several worshipful essays to Vladimir Nabokov, one of his major mentors, along with Saul Bellow. Both writers share an extreme concern for style and blend together postmodern experimentation with a conservative interest in narrative fundamentals such as characterization, detail, and point of view. For instance, Amis's use of a scurrilous first person narrator in his novel *Money* owes much to Nabokov's *Lolita* (1955). When Amis included a figure named after himself in *Money*, his father Kingsley Amis blamed it all on Nabokov, who would often include cameo appearances of himself in novels such as *King, Queen, Knave* (1968), much in the same way that Hitchcock provided brief cameos of himself in his movies. Amis begins with an assessment of Nabokov's negligible dramatic work *The Man from the USSR* (1984), then moves on to discuss his letters and his *Lectures on Literature* (1980), but he reserves his best work for his appreciation of *Lolita*. Amis notes that readers would like to think that Nabokov just got "carried away" in his depiction of a nymphet, but he notes that "Great writers . . . never get carried away." In fact, a succession of Nabokov's Russian novels point to a clear line of succession that leads logically and inevitably to the "three-hundred-page blue streak" that constitutes *Lolita*. *Lolita* provides Amis with a kind of ideal template for his own fiction, what he calls Nabokov's "Grand Slam," a genre combining popular interest with erudition and outrageous style, blending together pulp, kitsch, and perversity. Even James Joyce's *Ulysses* (1922) falls short of attaining this ideal because of the way it appeals more to puzzle-solving critics than to a popular audience.

Sometimes Amis's treatment of other authors showcases the subtle differences in his critical aesthetics. John Updike's critical essays share much with Amis's collections in their urbanity, casual style, and erudition, but Updike has a Protestant moral sense that Amis finds distasteful, an all-inclusiveness when it comes to detail that can seem excessive, and a prediliction for reviewing obscure works in translation that Amis clearly does not want to emulate (when Amis takes on world literary authors in the chapter entitled "Ultramundane," he sticks to writers such as Shiva and V. S. Naipaul, whom he knew personally, or old standbys such as Franz Kafka). Humorously, Amis criticizes Updike's collection of essays *Picked-Up Pieces* for a sin that he also commits in *The War Against Cliché*—the occasional tendency to pick up pieces that he should have left out. In Amis's case, his inclusion of an article about British soccer players and coaches is too particular in its loyalties to one time and place to be of much general interest. An essay about the eighteenth edition of *The Guinness Book of World Records* allows Amis to discuss grotesque dwarfs, but it also does not really fit his criteria for battling cliché. Much of the time, however, even the weaker essays and reviews that Amis includes from his youth display interesting aspects of his character. When he unduly criticizes William Empson for his lapses in a book about Milton, and then gets roundly trounced in print for being wrong about the book's contents, Amis admits in a footnote that he had sold the book before reviewing it and apologizes for his error. It humanizes Amis to see him admit to making a mistake.

In the end, Amis's ability to enthusiastically enjoy and celebrate authors comes as the biggest surprise of the volume. One can see his literary consciousness develop and form biases as one reads through the collection, moving from ridicule for some to mature criticism, and even, ultimately, admiration for others. Favorites such as Saul Bellow bring out scarcely qualified praise. He flatly describes *The Adventures of Augie March* (1953) as "the Great American Novel" and then limits himself to a guided tour of the novel's plot, representative quotations, and a detailed analysis of its style. With *Ulysses*, Amis assesses that Joyce's genius makes "Beckett look pedestrian, Lawrence look laconic, Nabokov look guileless." The romantic reconciliation of Elizabeth Bennet and Mr. Darcy in Jane Austen's *Pride and Prejudice* (1813) brings out Amis's "gratitude and relief: an undiminished catharsis" even after repeated readings. Given his otherwise nihilistic world view that is reflected in his novels, such as *Time's Arrow* (1991), and his essays about nuclear weapons proliferation, Amis still finds solace in art and artists who carry on a tradition in the face of a climate of cultural banality that he believes threatens to overwhelm the literary arts. Against the prevalence of hackneyed artifice, Amis asserts the "opposed qualities of freshness, energy, and reverberation of voice."

Roy C. Flannagan

Sources for Further Study

Library Journal 126 (October 1, 2001): 96.
New Statesman 130 (April 23, 2001): 50.
The Times Literary Supplement, April 27, 2001, p. 26.

WAR IN A TIME OF PEACE
Bush, Clinton, and the Generals

Author: David Halberstam (1934-   )
Publisher: Charles Scribner's Sons (New York). 543 pp.
  $28.00
Type of work: History
Time: 1991-2000
Locale: Washington, D.C.; Dayton, Ohio; Vietnam; Somalia; the Persian Gulf; Yugoslavia (Bosnia, Serbia, Croatia, and Slovenia, including key cities Sarajevo, Kosovo, and others); Rwanda; and Haiti

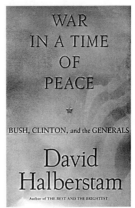

∼

Halberstam chronicles what he calls the "largely unseen tug-of-war" between the Bush and Clinton administrations and the Pentagon's senior officers in the wake of the Gulf War (1991) and extending through the U.S. disaster in Somalia (1993) and the naggingly complex American involvement in the Balkans (1993-1999) leading to the capitulation of the Serbs and Slobodan Milošević

∼

Principal personages:
  BILL CLINTON, forty-second president of the United States (1993-2001)
  GEORGE H. W. BUSH, forty-first president of the United States (1989-1993)
  WARREN CHRISTOPHER, secretary of state during Clinton's first term (1993-1996)
  MADELEINE ALBRIGHT, secretary of state during Clinton's second term (1996-2001)
  ANTHONY LAKE, national security advisor to Clinton
  RICHARD C. HOLBROOKE, assistant secretary of state under presidents Jimmy Carter and Bill Clinton
  VERNON JORDAN, adviser to Bill Clinton
  GENERAL COLIN POWELL, chairman of the Joint Chiefs of Staff (1989-1993)
  GENERAL WESLEY K. CLARK, commander of North Atlantic Treaty Organization (NATO) European forces during the United States' involvement in the Balkans
  GENERAL JOHN SHALIKASHVILI, chairman of the Joint Chiefs of Staff (1993-1997)
  ROY GUTMAN, *Newsday* reporter who covered the early signs of genocide in Bosnia

Writing about John "Shali" Shalikashvili, who succeeded Colin Powell as chairman of the Joint Chiefs of Staff in the fall of 1993 when U.S. involvement in Bosnia was fast becoming unmanageable, David Halberstam devotes a full chapter to the unlikely story of the four-star general who arrived in the United States from Warsaw in 1952, at the age of sixteen, and rose in the military to the point where, after the Gulf War, he

~

David Halberstam won a Pulitzer Prize in 1964 for his war reporting in Vietnam and has written numerous books on American politics, sports, and society.

~

was assigned the tough job of heading up Provide Comfort, a Kurdish rescue operation that may have saved as many as 600,000 lives. Halberstam's unqualified adulation—rare for him—knows no bounds. "Good novels have been written about odysseys less tortuous . . . ," he concludes.

War in a Time of Peace can only have been written by a veteran reporter on whom nothing is lost; by a writer whose voice, tuned to the expectation of dissonance from all sides, remains clear. The book is not another *War and Peace*, as Les Gelb, former *New York Times* foreign policy correspondent, proclaims on the back cover. Its pedigree is more interesting.

Thirty years before, in *The Best and the Brightest* (1972), Halberstam deconstructed another foreign-policy braintrust. A *New York Times* correspondent in South Vietnam in 1962, he encountered an official policy of reporting the war optimistically. The misrepresentation of disasters such as the 1963 Battle of Ap Bac as victories led Halberstam to write frankly about what he observed in Southeast Asia and, a decade later, to his critically acclaimed exposé of the domestic origins of the Vietnam War, the men who made the decisions to go to war, and the men who conducted it.

New York Times diplomatic correspondent Jane Perlez calls *War in a Time of Peace* "a sprawling tapestry of exquisite bottom-up reporting and powerful vignettes . . . a bookend of that earlier volume." The forbear of these two books is *Patriotic Gore* (1962), Edmund Wilson's classic study of the literature spawned by the Civil War, published in the year Halberstam went to South Vietnam. Wilson's method was to convey the history of the era largely through word portraits of persons, famous and obscure alike, who were deeply affected by the Civil War—President Abraham Lincoln, Generals Ulysses S. Grant and William Tecumseh Sherman, Justice Oliver Wendell Holmes, writers Harriet Beecher Stowe and Ambrose Bierce, and southern women such as Kate Stone, Sarah Morgan, and Mary Chesnut.

If that terrifying war loomed center stage for Wilson, the dark memory of Vietnam dominates Halberstam's study of a supposed unified America confronted by the horrors of genocide in little-known locales from Somalia and Rwanda to Kosovo. Many of the 1990's best and brightest were in some way touched by Vietnam. Under Halberstam's relentless scrutiny, the reader is privy to a Bill Clinton who ducked the draft, and to two of his chief foreign policy advisers, Anthony (Tony) Lake and Richard Holbrooke, who were young diplomats in Saigon. Others, such as Colin Powell and Wesley Clark, had significant duty tours there.

Halberstam opens his chronicle with the end of the United States' only declared war of the decade. He demonstrates that George H. W. Bush's seeming triumph in the Persian Gulf was a "virtual" one, analogous, as a Republican pollster warned, to the "Churchill Factor," in which the prime minister was voted out of office within months of his rescue of Britain in World War II. As Jane Perlez puts it: "President Bush got little electoral bounce from that first high-tech, low-casualty victory, and that was a lesson [his successor] never forgot."

In less than two short chapters, Halberstam is finished with the vulnerable Bush's weak 1992 election campaign and predictable defeat (the Clinton forces made the case for a stronger domestic economy—Bush's unaddressed short suit—that was necessary to make the United States the world leader) and moving on to Bosnia, which Al Gore early on referred to as "the issue from hell."

One of Halberstam's major concerns is to document beyond doubt that not even the leader of the free world can avoid being graded on—and often scarred by—foreign policy issues. He was witness to the undoing of the four earlier presidents on his watch—Lyndon Johnson and Vietnam, Jimmy Carter on the hostages in Iran, Ronald Reagan and the Iran-Contra scandal, and Bush on the Gulf War. Still, his coverage of Clinton's (and the Pentagon's) slow response to Serbian genocidal murders and rapes and his acquired knowledge of the Balkans which he amassed during his research for this book may well be his finest achievements.

Although Washington was lethargic in recognizing any responsibility to intervene in Bosnia, history will not overlook U.S. awareness of the Serbs' resort to ethnic cleansing, although it may well do so about the country's awareness of the death camps. The summer before the 1992 election, Richard Holbrooke, who would become a kingpin of the Democratic Party's foreign policy team, made a trip to Yugolavia and, crucially, to Bosnia. One afternoon over drinks in his hotel in Banka Luka, Bosnia, he heard a Serb woman joke that Muslims made good lampshades. The next morning, Holbrooke witnessed the already standard Serb practice of forcing Muslims who were natives of the town to sign away their property in exchange for the unlikely guarantee of safe passage to Croatia. Those who refused were abducted or killed. Holbrooke not only wrote widely of the atrocities but got the message to Clinton to no avail, leading Holbrooke to comment that the inevitable tragedy of Bosnia might be George Bush's revenge on Clinton if he were to lose.

Halberstam credits *Newsday* on-scene reporter Roy Gutman's early-alert dispatches describing Serbian inhumanity against the Muslims as the worst in Europe since the Third Reich. Gutman was beginning to uncover evidence of genocidal crimes at precisely the moment when the incumbent Bush administration, already criticized for being more concerned with foreign policy than domestic issues, was preoccupied by an increasingly difficult reelection drive.

"As Washington dithered over the definition of genocide, Slobodan Milošević, the Serbian president, was allowed to proceed apace in a war that killed more than 200,000 people," Jane Perlez observes wryly. "Just as newspapers were exposing [the Serbs] and an upstart (but not widely watched) TV outfit, CNN, was covering them, experienced network correspondents languished in their expensive European bureaus, unable to get pocket change from their superiors to travel to Bosnia. All this was of a piece with Clinton's recognition that the American people were not eager to know about the persecution of minorities abroad."

War in a Time of Peace rises to its thematic climax with Kosovo, the site of an ancient battle whose implications Halberstam wisely avoids, for the reports on it and other history lessons on the region helped blind Americans and officialdom alike to the carnage there. Only Madeleine Albright, secretary of state not for her qualifications but for her relative lack of disqualifications, kept prodding Colin Powell, always a military dove, to use the ground forces of whose power he was so proud. Her activism nearly gave him an aneuryism, he said. She found him sexist. Compounding the reluctance of the Pentagon to intervene in teapot wars and ethnic skirmishes that the generals, except for NATO chief Wesley Clark, thought posed little threat to the United States was the fact that Clinton was ill at ease with his senior military officers and they with him.

Halberstam finds a sort of Greek *peripeteia*—a point of no return—in the mandate finally recognized by the United States and Britain that they must defeat Milošević, the latter-day Hitler. Milošević finally capitulated on June 3, 1999, an event, according to Halberstam, that "proved a war can be won by air power alone." Jane Perlez demurs, claiming that the author "underplays a result of not using [ground] troops: that Milošević was emboldened to send some 40,000 Serbian forces into Kosovo for ethnic cleansing, leading to the expulsion of nearly a million Albanians."

Kosovo brings to a close Halberstam's monumental story of a decade. In his Author's Note, he never mentions his 1993 book, *The Fifties*. Surely that relatively placid decade, despite its portents of revolutions to come, posed fewer problems. Near the close of his sign-off, Halberstam—modest, almost diffident—hints at the challenge of the present book: "I had what was at best a layman's knowledge of the Balkans, and one of the hardest parts of this assignment was getting up to speed on that complicated part of the world. . . ."

Richard Hauer Costa

Sources for Further Study

Booklist 97 (August, 2001): 2046.
Commentary 113 (January, 2002): 58.
The New York Times Book Review 106 (September 30, 2001): 8.
The New Yorker 77 (October 15, 2001): 217.
Publishers Weekly 248 (August 13, 2001): 298.

THE WARDEN OF ENGLISH
The Life of H. W. Fowler

Author: Jenny McMorris (1946-   )
Foreward by Simon Winchester
Publisher: Oxford University Press (New York). Illustrated. 272 pp. $27.50
Type of work: Biography and language
Time: 1833-1940
Locale: Tunbridge Wells, Rugby, Oxford, Sedbergh, London, Guernsey, Hinton St. George, and other areas of England

∾

The first full biography of Fowler, author of the classic reference A Dictionary of Modern English Usage, *from his parentage through his lengthy career in teaching and lexicography*

∾

Principal personages:
> HENRY WATSON FOWLER (1858-1933), author of *Fowler's Modern English Usage*
> FRANCIS GEORGE FOWLER (1870-1918), his brother and lexicographical collaborator
> JESSIE MARIAN WILLS FOWLER (1861-1930), his wife

Many who care deeply about using the English language in its most correct and effective manner have often depended on *A Dictionary of Modern English Usage* (1926) to help resolve phrasing difficulties or to persuade colleagues of sticky points. Jenny McMorris, archivist for the Oxford English Dictionaries, has delved deeply into the Dictionaries' archives and others to produce a biography of Henry Watson Fowler, author of that classic reference.

The ten pages of endnotes list much personal correspondence between Fowler and his friends, family, and publishing associates, along with century-old newspapers, army records, and Oxford archives. The letters, especially, bring life to the descriptions of Fowler's attitudes, opinions, and behavior. Prominent among these are the letters of Fowler's lifelong friend Gordon Coulton. Along with the story of Fowler's life, the book describes the publishing of several important books, including *The King's English* (1906), *A Dictionary of Modern English Usage*, and *The Concise Oxford Dictionary* (1911). Its publication coincides with the seventy-fifth anniversary of the first publication of *A Dictionary of Modern English Usage*, which has never been out of print, although it has been revised twice, in 1965 and 1996.

There is also a forward by Simon Winchester, author of *The Professor and the Madman: A Tale of Murder, Insanity, and the Making of the* Oxford English Dictionary (1998). *The Warden of English* appears to be a natural follow-on to *The Professor and the Madman*, which described the beginnings of the massive *Oxford English Dictionary*, its founding editor James Murray, and a mysterious contributor, Dr. W. C. Minor. The two histories are not at all alike, however. Where *The Professor and the Madman* is written in a

Jenny McMorris became the archivist for the Oxford English Dictionaries at Oxford University Press in 1985. She studied at Westfield College, London University, and the School of Librarianship and Archives, University College London.

novelist's style, developing its characters and following a plot, *The Warden of English* has a more scholarly tone. Each of the fifteen chapters has copious endnotes, mostly pointing to the Oxford archives. McMorris quotes liberally from the various letters and publications, not only giving some of the flavor of the times but also lending the book the air of a thesis.

She faced a daunting task in researching the life of Henry Fowler, with no cache of family papers or albums and hardly any survivors remaining alive to be questioned, only a few people who still remember when, as children, they were taken to see old "H. W." Fowler had very little social life, and he even turned down an invitation to attend a celebratory dinner with Prime Minister Stanley Baldwin. As a rule, the closest he came to getting out into society was writing letters to *The Times*.

McMorris has pieced together Henry Fowler's story as thoroughly as it can be done, given those restrictions. She begins with several pages of biographical information about Fowler's parents, Robert and Caroline. Fowler, twenty-one when their father died of typhoid, was the oldest of eight children; he had to help his mother sort out the family's affairs. Two of the youngest boys, Frank (then nine) and Arthur (then eleven), were later to be Fowler's collaborators.

When he was a student at Rugby, he began his lifelong enthusiam for both cross-country running and swimming. He ran and swam every day of his life, where possible, until his dying years. He also excelled at Latin and Greek. Although he won a scholarship to Balliol College, Oxford, he earned only mediocre marks there.

He taught for two terms in Scotland, then moved on to Sedbergh School, in Yorkshire, where he taught for seventeen years. He invented a system of cards to help small boys unravel the intricacies of syntax, a system that was used for years after his departure. It was also at Sedbergh that he developed lifelong friendships with Coulton, Bernard Tower, Henry Hart, and other men.

He eventually left the school, partly because he was unable in good conscience to prepare boys for religious confirmation. For some time he was careful to conceal that he was no Christian, but he also disapproved of the arrogance of an agnostic friend. When he married, he acquiesced to having a church wedding. While his wife attended church regularly, he did not. Still, he always made sure that she could do so—even, when her health failed, escorting her to the church steps and returning to escort her home again.

Once, describing his "religious position," he wrote: "I can mark it off in decades clearly enough; thirty years ago I thought religious belief true; twenty years ago doubtful; ten years ago false; and now it is (for me, of course) merely absurd." Later, he drew criticism when his *Concise Oxford Dictionary* defined "Pope," "Jesuit," and "Jew" in ways that offended the affected groups. While some amendments were made in the second edition, Fowler's defense of his entries was that his duty was to record what people actually said, not what he thought they should say. The defining factor was whether the word was current, not whether it was offensive.

After Sedbergh, Fowler went to London to earn his living writing essays for the *Spectator* and other publications. He made new friends there, including some in the Inns of Court Volunteers, a military group that he joined. That same year Frank Fowler, twelve years younger than his brother, moved to Guernsey in the Channel Islands to help a friend grow tomatoes. Four years later, in 1903, Fowler moved there, too. Soon, the brothers were collaborating on translating the second century Greek satirist Lucian for the Oxford University Press.

After that, they worked together on a new manual of English composition, using many quotations from journalists and other writers as bad examples. Published in 1906, *The King's English* drew heavy critical attack, but sold briskly. Oxford then proposed that they handle two different abridgements of the great *Oxford English Dictionary*, which at that time was itself little more than half-finished.

Meanwhile, Fowler, who had been known as a shy soul all his life, met Jessie Wills, who ran a Guernsey nursing home where an old friend of his was being treated. It took only a few months for him to propose, and they were married on his fiftieth birthday, ten days later. By all accounts they were quite different—he was trim, she was plump; she had a mass of prematurely white hair, he had just a fringe; she was loquacious, he was taciturn. He recited their many differences in a clever 1911 poem, but nevertheless, he had begun a devotion to her that would last the rest of his life.

After preparing an abridged version of *The King's English*, the brothers got back to their dictionary work. Oxford dropped the smaller of the two dictionaries, and the two plowed on through the new *Concise Oxford Dictionary*, which was published in 1911. Also in that year, Frank Fowler married a woman half his age, Una Godfrey. Henry Fowler had developed a case of "misolexicography" and wanted nothing to do with the next dictionary project, so Frank began alone what eventually was published as the *Pocket Oxford Dictionary*, while Henry soon got going on a book that he had thought about for years, describing idiomatic usage.

When World War I came, the two brothers managed to enlist in the army. Frank was just under the age limit of forty-five, but Henry had to lie about his age, with encouragement from the recruiter. His daily running and swimming had kept him trim, and he sometimes outperformed some of the younger soldiers. They had only the narrowest exposure to the front lines, however. Through Fowler's daily letters to his wife, McMorris provides detailed accounts of his constant exasperation at bureaucratic confusion and crude military camps in France. It was even more of a struggle for his younger brother, who took ill early on. Fowler also ailed, with the gout, and was sent home in 1916. Frank Fowler remained in the military hospital, where he died of tuberculosis in 1918.

Back on Guernsey, Fowler resumed work both on his brother's *Pocket Oxford Dictionary* and on his own *Dictionary of Modern English Usage*. He finished the former in 1922 and the latter in 1924. His final major project, the *Oxford Dictionary of Modern English*, was unfinished when he died in 1933.

Fowler was never rich, yet he appeared to be utterly devoid of greed. On various occasions he complained about having been offered too much money for some job or other. For instance, a United States publisher insisted on two small additions to the copies of *The Dictionary of Modern English Usage* that he intended to sell, and Fowler agreed to provide the new information. Kenneth Sisam, assistant secretary of the Oxford University Press, said he would send five pounds (a significant amount in 1926). Fowler said that was "ridiculous" and asked for two pounds instead. Sisam eventually persuaded him to take the five pounds, however.

A few years later, Sisam suggested paying Fowler two hundred pounds a year for five years for preparing a lengthy new dictionary of modern English, plus a bonus upon completion, but Fowler replied that "you seem to be offering me the chance of a subsidized sojourn in lotusland for several years." He suggested halving the amount and doubling the time, but eventually accepted the highter amount with a characteristically glib quip: "If you insist on making a millionaire of me, do so."

Terminology difficulties crop up in *The Warden of English* for United States readers who are not familiar with British idioms. At Rugby, Fowler was included in a special "form" (a grade or special group in British secondary schools), won a prize for reading his translation of Shelley into Greek in his last "Speeches" (an annual day in some British schools with formal talks and prizes), and later became head of his "house" (a tight-knit grouping of a British school's children for sports and other competitions).

Oxford was the site of the first printing of a book in England, in 1478, but it was two hundred years later that the Oxford University Press began to develop in a recognizable form. McMorris persistently refers to it as the Clarendon Press, a name that it changed at the end of the nineteenth century after nearly two centuries of use. Nonetheless, the details of the Fowler brothers' written conversations with Oxford authorities, the piecing together of details of the English language, and the reactions of the public to these classic reference books can be entrancing to anyone who embraces this language.

J. Edmund Rush

Sources for Further Study

Booklist 97 (August, 2001): 2065.
The Christian Science Monitor, September 20, 2001, p. 16.
Library Journal 126 (September 1, 2001): 179.
Publishers Weekly 248 (September 3, 2001): 73.
The Washington Post Book World, October 7, 2001, p. 15.

WHERE THE STRESS FALLS
Essays

Author: Susan Sontag (1933-   )
Publisher: Farrar, Straus and Giroux (New York).
   351 pp. $27.00
Type of work: Essays and literary criticism
Time: 1982-2001

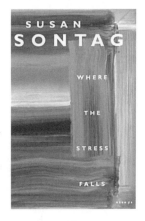

≈

*A collection of critical and intellectual essays covering
two decades and ranging over a wide variety of literary,
artistic, and cultural subjects that highlight Sontag's eclec-
tic and catholic tastes, as well as her moral commitments*

≈

In this collection of forty-one essays, published thirty-five years after the collection *Against Interpretation* launched Sontag's reputation as one of the most important American intellectuals, Sontag reaffirms her commitment, as she says of the painter Howard Hodgkin, "to work on behalf of, in praise of, beauty." Sontag comes not to bury but to praise what she has encountered in her travels through books, museums and galleries, darkened theaters, dance and music halls, and even foreign geographies, where she has sought out such exotica as garden grottoes and volcanoes. Although many of the individual essays take up and articulate the sensual and intellectual riches of a particular subject simply for the sake of celebrating its creation, the essay collection as whole can also be seen as a kind of *apologia pro vita sua* for Sontag's own vocation as a consummate mental traveler who is "interested in everything," and who has continually pursued what might be termed the voluptuousness of artistic experience and knowledge.

Although most of the essays are preoccupied with delineating the small and large pleasures of her aesthetic encounters, Sontag also shares her worries about what she sees as the threatening demises of what she holds most dear—books, the art of reading as the inculcation and nurturing of the inward self, high critical seriousness, the cinema, and even "the idea of Europe." Moreover, while there are spirited defenses of modernism and modern art throughout the essays, the collection ultimately reveals Sontag's investment in the Romantic ideal that art should be a vehicle for self-transcendence. Not all of the essays in the collection are equally strong, and there are quite a few of them that are too thin or too occasional—some pieces were originally written for gallery exhibition catalogues and performance programs, some are all too brief prefatory appreciations, and there is even one "note," on Miguel de Cervantes's *Don Quixote de la Mancha* (1605-1615), written for a National Tourist Board of Spain catalogue. Moreover, much of the writing gathered here could be faulted for

lacking the focus, power, and originality of Sontag's earlier expository writings; nevertheless,
quite a few of the essays more than amply demonstrate what Sontag believes emerges in the writing of Roland Barthes—"a vision of the life of
the mind as a life of desire, of full intelligence
and pleasure."

By way of exemplifying the multiple levels
of her aesthetic sensibility, Sontag has divided
the collection into three sections, "Reading,"
"Seeing," and "There and Here," each of which
encapsulates a distinctive mode for encountering world culture: reading, seeing, and traveling.
The first section, therefore, is mainly comprised
of writing on literature in a variety of shorter and
longer forms—critical essays and appreciations,

∽

Susan Sontag's novel In America
*won the National Book Award for
fiction in 2000, and in 2001 she
was awarded the Jerusalem Prize
for the body of her life's work,
which has included other novels
such as* The Volcano Lover
*(1992); a collection of short
stories,* I, etcetera *(1978); a play,*
Alice in Bed *(pb. 1993); as well as
nonfiction works, among them* On
Photography *(1977) and* Illness as
Metaphor *(1978).*

∽

as well as book forewords and introductions. As is typical with most of Sontag's forays into literature, the emphasis is on the work of Continental writers, such as W. G.
Sebald, Roland Barthes, and Danilo Kiš, and on lesser-known international writers.
Only the title essay, "Where the Stress Falls," an exposition of the modern techniques of narrative perspective in the novel originally written for *The New Yorker*, focuses on American writing—that of the little-known novelist Glenway Wescott as
well as the more renowned authors Ford Madox Ford, Randall Jarrell, and Elizabeth
Hardwick.

The essays in this section perform a variety of critical functions. In some cases,
Sontag simply wishes to introduce the work of an author whom she feels has been little appreciated, and therefore she has included some short essays that originally
served as prefaces in editions of an author's work. For example, there is a spirited introduction to the little-known Latin American "masterpiece," *Memórias póstumas de
Brás Cunas* (1880), an imaginary autobiography by Joaquim Maria Machado de
Assis, which Sontag believes is as noteworthy and "modern" as Laurence Sterne's
The Life and Opinions of Tristram Shandy (1759-1767), and upon which she bestows
the title of "greatness" because it is "one of those thrillingly original, radically skeptical books that will always impress readers with the force of a private discovery."
Likewise, she lavishly praises the storytelling talents of Mexican author Juan Rulfo
(1918-1986) who, although famous in his home country in his lifetime and highly influential upon other Spanish-speaking authors, was relatively unknown in the United
States until Sontag arranged for a new English translation of his novel *Pedro Páramo*
(1955) in 1994.

In other cases, the appreciation of an author's work is an occasion to articulate the
pleasures and insights to be gained from slightly larger subjects. Therefore, in her introductions to prose works by the Russian poet Marina Tsvetaeva and the Polish poet
Adam Zagajewski ("A Poet's Prose" and "The Wisdom Project"), she is also writing
about the importance of the role of "the poet as the avatar of freedom," of literature as

"soul nourishment," and about the idea that, for writers who live in "lacerated" parts of the world, the recovery of historical memory is an ethical obligation. In the case of her essay, "A Mind in Mourning," on the career of the late German novelist W. G. Sebald, already much lauded and admired in the world of literary letters, Sontag's deeper subject, which comes very close to her own image of herself as a writer, is the writer as ideal *promeneur solitaire*—a mentally restless, relentlessly curious wanderer who is the citizen of no country and whose life is a series of tours and peregrinations through what might be called the interior cities of world culture. Finally, two of the essays in this section, "Where the Stress Falls" and "On Writing: Roland Barthes," although ostensibly written in order to elucidate the literary enjoyments and human wisdom to be afforded by particular authors and works, are really extensive expositions of the art of writing itself and of the writer's vocation.

"On Writing: Roland Barthes," perhaps the strongest piece of writing in the entire collection, deserves special mention. Originally written as a preface to *A Barthes Reader* (1982) shortly after Barthes's untimely death in 1980, the piece is both a eulogy for Barthes's career as an eminent man of letters and cultural philosopher and a passionate exaltation of the vocation of writer as theorist of the mind. Although Sontag has never committed herself to writing an essay on a subject about which she is less than enthusiastic, it would be difficult to find another essay by Sontag as exuberant as this one in its admiration for its subject, whom Sontag asserts will one day appear "a greater writer than even his more fervent admirers now claim." Much of what Sontag expresses here regarding Barthes's style and aims as a writer could just as easily be applied to her own *oeuvre*. For example, she praises Barthes's supple prose style as "recognizably French," as well as "comma-ridden and colon-prone," "idiosyncratic," "fearlessly mandarin," and "irrepressibly aphoristic," all of which descriptions are characteristic of Sontag's work as well. While the essay is largely at pains to carefully illumine Barthes's important work as a semiologist and formalist critic and to explain his unique contributions to postmodern criticism, Sontag's primary motive is the desire to put forward and defend the idea of a particular kind of cultural critic—in this case, Barthes, but she is clearly defending her own canon of work as well—as an artist whose supreme achievement is revealing the "mobility of meaning" and the "kinetics of consciousness." Furthermore, Sontag uses her appreciation of Barthes's career to defend a certain practice of writing—again, similar to hers—that is playful and sensuous, and that allows the author to project himself into his subject, thereby fulfilling what Sontag sees as France's "great national literary project, inaugurated by Montaigne: the self as vocation, life as a reading of the self." Although some, after reading this essay, might be discomfited by the self-aggrandizing gestures being played out upon the corpus of Barthes's work—arguably, a far more important writer than Sontag—the essay is ultimately a moving evocation of not only one author's life and work but also of the idea of writing as the loving embrace of subject and object.

The second section of the collection, "Seeing," is perhaps the weakest in the book, mainly because many of the pieces were written to accompany art exhibits and theater performances and therefore are somewhat lacking in context. Occasionally they do not make sense at all without the accompanying visual references, as is the case with the rather cryptic and too elliptical (and sometimes silly) catalogue notes written for a 1989 exhibit at a London gallery that featured the American painter Jasper Johns' *Dancers on a Plane* series. As always, Sontag is at her best when elucidating narrative art, and thus her essay on the German filmmaker Werner Fassbinder's fifteen and one-half hour epic film, *Berlin Alexanderplatz* (1983), the plot of which she compares with Frank Norris's *McTeague* (1899), is a lucid contemplation of cinema as a hybrid art that brings theater and the novel beautifully together. Likewise, her program essay for a 1987 production of Wagner's opera *Tristan und Isolde*, "Wagner's Fluids," is not only a smart literary explication of the opera's plot through a close analysis of the functions of its fluids—water and blood, medicinal balms and poisons—but is also an occasion for Sontag yet again to laud the Romantic ideal of art as emotionally excessive, extravagant, and erotically troubling. When Sontag takes the time to explore pictorial art in exhaustive detail, as she does with the paintings by seventeenth century Dutch artist Gerard Houckgeest ("The Pleasure of the Images") and modern American painter Howard Hodgkin ("About Hodgkin"), the results are a ravishing representation of the power of language to conjure up striking visual images and to illumine a painter's vision. Other essays in this section treat the subjects of modern dance and American ballet, modern and contemporary photography, the avant-garde theater of Robert Wilson, and even the history of garden grottoes.

The final section of the book, "Here and There," is quite possibly the strongest, representing some of Sontag's most thoughtful explorations of what it means to be an intellectual, a writer, and a mental and actual world journeyer. "Homage to Halliburton," which opens this part of the book, is Sontag's loving (albeit brief) tribute to the American writer who first inspired in her, when she was seven, a desire to be a traveler and writer. Anther essay, "Questions of Travel," also addresses the various junctures between writing, traveling, and the aesthetic life, and there are two essays, "The Idea of Europe (One More Elegy)" and "'There' and 'Here,'" which lament, respectively, the passing of "the Europe of high art and ethical seriousness" and America's neglect of the situation in mid-1990's Bosnia. Still other essays explore the nuances of what it means to be a writer and intellectual ("Singleness," "Writing as Reading," and "Answers to a Questionnaire"). Also included is a preface to a 1996 Spanish translation edition of Sontag's first collection of critical writings, *Against Interpretation* (1966), in which Sontag appraises what she perceives to have been the strengths as well as the shortcomings of that earlier volume.

Additionally, there is an essay on the Russian poet and old friend Joseph Brodsky, as well as the reprint of a speech, "On Being Translated," that Sontag delivered at a conference on translation held at Columbia University in 1995. The longest and most important essay Sontag includes here is "Waiting for Godot in Sarajevo," in which Sontag shares the story of her staging of Beckett's play in war-ravaged Sarajevo and redefines what has always been her moral commitment to speak out against social injustice—in this case, genocide—and to do more than simply "bring the news to the outside world." Ultimately, the essay reveals the power of art to bring solace, and even enlightenment, to the darkest corners of the world, while also illustrating

Sontag's commitment to embrace, in her life as well as in her work, the strenuous process of *deracinement* entailed in the vocation of the truly cosmopolitan and secular public intellectual.

Eileen A. Joy

Sources for Further Study

Booklist 97 (August, 2001): 2077.
Houston Chronicle, September 28, 2001, p. 7.
Library Journal 126 (October 15, 2001): 76.
Publishers Weekly 248 (August 20, 2001): 72.

WHY DID I EVER

Author: Mary Robison (1949-   )
Publisher: Counterpoint (Washington, D.C.). 200 pp.
  $23.00
Type of work: Novel
Time: The late 1990's
Locale: Hollywood and a small southern town

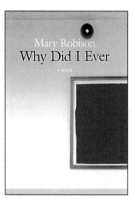

≈

*A fragmented first-person account of a woman with at-
tention-deficit disorder (ADD) coping with her condition,
her two grown children, and her Hollywood script doctor
job*

≈

Principal characters:
> MONEY BRETON, a woman with attention deficit disorder who works as
>   a script doctor for Hollywood studios
> MEV, her grown daughter, a methadone addict
> PAULIE, her grown son, under police protection after being the victim of
>   a violent sexual attack
> HOLLIS, a male friend
> THE DEAF LADY, her neighbor
> DIX DIDIER, her wealthy new boyfriend

Mary Robison is credited—along with Bobbie Ann Mason, Raymond Carver, Ann
Beattie, and others—for reviving the short story as a serious literary form in the
1980's. Her best-known collection, *An Amateur's Guide to the Night* (1983), which
contains several of her most anthologized stories, such as "Coach," "The Dictionary
in the Laundry Chute," and "Yours," made her an influential force in the so-called,
but misnamed, minimalist literary movement.

Robison is also the author of two novels, *oh!* (1981) and *Subtraction* (1991), the
latter receiving mixed reviews, with some critics arguing that Robison had lost control of her material. (One reviewer cutely concluded that *Subtraction* did not add up to
very much.) In *Why Did I Ever*, her first book in ten years, Robison seems very much
in artistic control, even if her persona, Money Breton, seems on an out-of-control diatribe about everything from Hollywood, to her three ex-husbands, to the IRS, to the
food at the International House of Pancakes.

Robison has never really found a wide audience for her work. In an interview she
once admitted she was quite baffled about that, failing to understand why she has been
called weird and inaccessible. Robison, only half seriously, insisted she did not see
any difference between her audience and that of Ann Beattie. Claiming she was as
accessible as Beattie, Robison said she keeps asking herself why her audience is

Mary Robison is the author of two previous novels and three highly acclaimed short-story collections. She is a graduate of The Johns Hopkins University and has received a Guggenheim Fellowship as well as PEN and Authors Guild awards.

one two-hundredth of Beattie's. "If I am leaving something out," complains Robison, "or if making it hard, would someone give me the formula or tell me what it is and I'll put it in? I'll be happy to oblige."

However, Robinson knows that the problem with her lack of widespread popularity is that she does leave things out, shifting responsibility to the reader. Robison has said she prefers to be called not a minimalist but a "subtractionist," because that term implies a little effort and some intention, as though something has been taken out rather than just left out. Robison takes a great many chances in her fiction by not explaining things, by focusing on seemingly insignificant everyday events, and by writing in a nonmetaphoric, bone-clean prose with no exposition. If she has never had the audience she deserves, it is because she makes great demands on her readers.

Consisting of 536 diary-like short entries, with little plot and a central character with the high-strung, frenetic voice of a woman with attention-deficit disorder (ADD), *Why Did I Ever* (there is no question mark) will probably not make Robison's audience grow much larger, for her often desperate central character and the fragmented structural method of the book are not calculated to lull readers into either a familiar world or a pleasant escape.

However, it is easy to believe her publisher's claim that the book is a big hit at readings, for such short staccato bursts of clever one-liners are perfect for a stand-up performance, and Robison herself is more than a little wide-eyed and highly wired in person. Money Breton is precisely the sort of persona an audience would find it hard to resist, with such lines as "'Something tells me I need a nap,' I say. 'That would be your brain,' says Hollis."

Why Did I Ever is a character novel; it is the voice that keeps the reader reading. Once the rhythm of it is caught, it is addictive. It is not a plotted novel; what story there is is simply this: Money Breton is a script doctor for a number of Hollywood studios, most of which have fired her. She is undermedicated, out of Ritalin for her ADD and unable to get more. She has a daughter who is a methadone addict and a son who has been sexually assaulted in New York City and is being guarded by policemen. She flies back and forth from her small southern town to Hollywood, all the time complaining about the absurd script changes the studio insists upon to make a movie project more popular and profitable.

When she is at home, she often drives around in the early morning hours, sometimes all night long, visiting Laundromats, IHOPs, and anyplace else she can escape her ex-husbands, her new boyfriend, her daughter, and the real and imaginary demons that haunt her. Her natural state, like that of a hummingbird, is in motion, physically and verbally. When her friend Hollis reads her the definition of "oscillate" from the dictionary—"a vibrating motion as things move backward and forward, vary or vacillate between different conditions and become stronger and weaker"—she says, "Well, but that describes me."

Most of the "action" of the novel consists of Money (a name she picked for herself) talking to herself and doing funny little disturbing/endearing things such as attaching "solid gold" labels to all sorts of objects with a glue gun, throwing her sunglasses out of her car and running over them thirty-nine times, and signing herself as Mrs. Sean Penn. She says she is always thinking, thinking, thinking, but that most of it is gobbledygook. However, it is hard to resist someone who refuses to give turn signals because she insists, "Why should you get to know where I'm going? I don't;" or who looks at herself in the mirror and says "That face needs cheekbones" and then tells her hands, "Quit shaking, people can see."

It is also hard not to like someone who forges famous paintings for her living room walls and writes inscriptions from famous writers in her books, who paints everything in her house gold, and creates photomontages of herself with Albert Camus and Joan Didion. The reader almost feels like cheering when, after getting fired from one of her banal studio jobs, Money fills the bathtub and drops her fax machine, her modem, and her beeper into the water. Although one might not ordinarily care that someone says they have watched Blockbuster videos of *Little Dorrit*, parts 1 and 2, with Money that bit of trivial information is simply added to all the other bits she gradually reveals; after a while the reader knows her so well that every thing she does and thinks is endearing. It is no surprise when her sweater button sequence is off by two, simply the cause of smile in recognition; when she eats Fritos in her dreams, what else would the reader expect. How can she be blamed for scorning the Hollywood big-wigs who insist that she work on a script about Big Foot? How could the reader not like someone who says the best music she has ever heard is Little Stevie Wonder's "Fingertips, Part 1," adding, "Fingertips, Part 2" made her even happier.

A neighbor she simply calls the "Deaf Lady" (although the woman is hardly deaf), never really knows if Money is faking or not. Indeed, the reader is never quite sure whether the things Money says and does are signs of mental instability, symptoms of her medical condition, or clever, funny bits just for the hell of it. When she unsuccessfully tries to check herself in to a mental hospital, she says, "This is not my real life. My real life is coming up." However, what this book is about is precisely the question of what constitutes a "real life." Money does not know who she is or where she is going and is never quite sure how to escape what presses on her at any given time, asking plaintively, "What kind of drug can I take to get out of this moment?"

Although at one point Money says, "The only thing I have going for me is my attention deficit," it seems the only thing that keeps her going is her concern for her two children and her cat. When the cat disappears for a time, she leaves pieces of her clothing at street corners all over town, hoping the cat will be drawn to the scent, have a seat, and wait for her. Although she is lonely, she does not tell her boyfriend her address. However, on one of her all-night driving jaunts, she sees a fat man driving around with his little pooch and muses: "Now why don't I know him . . . or someone like him? That man, I bet, could make me very happy."

There is a lot of satire in this book about the Hollywood scene, which Robison obviously knows well for she has herself written for the screen, but the Hollywood scenes with agents, producers, writers, and the whole Hollywood panoply are not as intriguing and interesting as the manic voice of Money and her efforts to get control of her life and have some sort of sense of normality, a state which seems constantly to evade her. She worries about her son Paulie and feels helpless to assist her daughter Mev, who seems as out of control as she is herself. If she could only focus strongly enough, concentrate steadily enough, stay in some semblance of order and continuity long enough, she could direct her attention outside herself enough to feel normal. As it is, she is like Fyodor Dostoyevsky's Underground Man, never really sure who she is, never able to escape self-consciousness, never really knowing whether to curse or pray. In one of the most poignant one-liners in the book, she says to herself, "Damn you, damn you, God help you, help you, help."

What Robison has done in this novel is to use the device of a woman with ADD as a metaphor of the failure to find a sense of self when one is fragmented so terribly that there is no sense of an immediate past and no way to plan for the future. The result is a fascinating characterization of a woman about whom one can never really be sure. She is either quite mad or quite funny, either out of control or satirically superior to everyone else. Because she exists only in moments, the novel can be told only in moments. There is no historical continuity for Money Breton.

At the end of the novel, she is, in Joan Didion fashion, still driving around, finally with her cat, which she has found dead in an alleyway. She drives on the concrete strip where there are no other cars in the way, thinking that if her cat gets cold, she could wrap it in her shirt and she would be fine in just her bra. "Are you alone?" she asks herself. "All alone," she answers. She feels she would say to her cat that there is no place safe for anyone anymore, adding, "I'm obliged to you for bringing that home to me."

Why Did I Ever is a very funny, very sad anatomy of a woman, who, in spite of the fact that she is constantly ready to jump out of her skin, is able to cast a sharply satirical look at her splintered self and the fragmented world she lives in.

Charles E. May

Sources for Further Study

Library Journal 126 (October 1, 2001): 143.
Milwaukee Journal Sentinel, October 28, 2001, p. 08E.

WIDE AS THE WATERS
The Story of the English Bible and the Revolution It Inspired

Author: Benson Bobrick (1947-   )
Publisher: Simon & Schuster (New York). Illustrated.
   379 pp. $26.00
Type of work: Religion and literary history
Time: 1380-1611
Locale: London, Oxford, and Cambridge, England; Antwerp, Geneva, Douai

~

Traces the history of the English Bible in the Middle Ages and Renaissance and examines the religious and political consequences of translation

~

Principal personages:
   JOHN WYCLIFFE, Oxford scholar, first medieval translator of the Bible into English
   WILLIAM TYNDALE, Protestant martyr and translator of the Bible
   HENRY VIII, king of England from 1509-1547
   MILES COVERDALE, priest and friend of Tyndale
   ELIZABETH I, queen of England from 1558-1603
   JAMES I, king of England from 1603-1625

In the beginning, "the Word" was in Hebrew and Aramaic and Greek. In the third century B.C.E. the Old Testament was translated into Greek for Jews of the Hellenistic diaspora. In the second century C.E. an "Old Latin" translation appeared for Christians who lacked Greek, and in the late fourth century C.E. St. Jerome produced another Latin version (the Vulgate) for western Christians. By the late Middle Ages, Latin, too, had become unfamiliar to most of the laity and even to some of the clerisy. Nevertheless, the Catholic Church objected to further translation because it feared misinterpretation. Moreover, Church doctrines relied heavily on nonscriptural sources such as the Decretals (papal decisions) and the writings of church fathers.

The fourteenth century Oxford scholar and religious reformer John Wycliffe opposed papal authority, argued for a religion based solely on Scripture, and favored widespread knowledge of the Bible. An English translation of the Old and New Testaments would serve all these ends, and in 1380, Wycliffe began work on an English Bible. Wycliffe's effort coincided with an upsurge of English nationalism and antipapal sentiment prompted by the Hundred Years' War against France; France's war effort was being financed in part by money from the papal treasury. The period also saw a flowering of English in the poetry of Geoffrey Chaucer, William Langland, John

~

Wide as the Waters *is the seventh book by Benson Bobrick, who earned his Ph.D. from Columbia University. His previous works include* Labyrinths of Iron *(1981), a sociological study of subway systems;* Fearful Majesty *(1987), a biography of Ivan the Terrible; and* Angel of the Whirlwind *(1997), a widely acclaimed history of the American Revolution. A freelance writer, Bobrick lives in Brattleboro, Vermont.*

~

Gower, and the Pearl-Poet. In 1362, Parliament opened in English for the first time since the Norman Conquest of 1066.

While Wycliffe's timing seemed auspicious, the Peasants' Revolt of 1381 linked church and state in the effort to suppress dissent. In 1394, the Catholic Church attempted to ban Wycliffe's translation. John of Gaunt, uncle to King Richard II, opposed the move, but he died in 1399. In 1408, Thomas Arundel, Archbishop of Canterbury, drafted the Constitutions of Oxford, barring unauthorized translations. Four years later, Arundel denounced Wycliffe and his English Bible.

No further attempt was made to translate the Bible into English until the early sixteenth century, when William Tyndale undertook the task. Because the Constitutions of Oxford remained in force, he withdrew to the Continent. In late 1525 or early 1526, Peter Schöffer of Worms printed Tyndale's New Testament, and copies soon were being smuggled into England. Unlike Wycliffe, Tyndale worked from the original Hebrew and Greek, though he consulted Erasmus's Latin translation, the Vulgate, and Martin Luther's German version. Tyndale used Hebrew syntax: "Song of Songs" and "holy of holies" instead of the more conventional English "best song," "holiest place." He retained Hebrew compounds such as "scapegoat" and translated phrases verbatim, such as "to die the death." The result was at once accurate, stately, and readable. As testimony to Tyndale's linguistic skills, the King James Bible's New Testament is essentially his.

Yet Tyndale's timing, like Wycliffe's, was unfortunate, because in 1526 Henry VIII was still Catholic and rejoicing in the pope's having named him "Defender of the Faith" in 1521 for attacking Martin Luther. Tyndale's translation adopted Protestant views. He rendered the Greek *ekklesia* as "congregation," a group of worshipers, rather than as "church," a gathering of clergy. *Presbyter* he translated as "senior" (later as "elder"), a leader chosen by the congregation, rather than "priest," someone anointed by the religious hierarchy. *Metanoia* appears as "repentance" rather than "penance." Penance, as Bobrick notes, provided revenues to the Church through the sale of indulgences. Repentance was free. Tyndale attacked the Catholic Church again in his 1530 translation of a portion of the Old Testament, and the preface to his 1534 revised New Testament declared that salvation comes through faith, not works. Though he was safe as long as he remained in the independent city of Antwerp, on May 21, 1535, he was kidnapped and imprisoned near Brussels. On October 6, 1536, he was executed.

By then, Henry VIII had broken with Rome over his desire to marry Anne Boleyn, who supported the Reformation. She owned a sumptuous copy of Tyndale's 1534 edition of the English New Testament. In December, 1534, the English bishops petitioned Henry VIII to authorize an English translation of the Bible. Henry agreed. Thomas Cromwell, Henry's lord chancellor, turned to Miles Coverdale, who had assisted Tyndale, to produce a new version. Coverdale lacked Greek and Hebrew and so relied on the Vulgate, Luther's German Bible, and Tyndale's text. To minimize controversy, he eschewed notes but did provide chapter summaries. His Bible appeared in 1535.

In 1537, two revised versions of Coverdale's Bible were printed, as was "Matthew's Bible," which in fact was Tyndale's complete text as edited by John Rogers, to whom Tyndale had given the manuscript of Joshua to II Chronicles, previously unpublished. Thomas Cranmer, archbishop of Canterbury, urged Cromwell to approve this Bible, "until such time that we, the Bishops, shall set forth a better translation, which I think will not be till a day after doomsday!" Cromwell showed this translation to Henry, who approved of it. Within a year of Tyndale's Bible and Tyndale himself being burnt, his translation was appearing under royal license. In 1539 Coverdale oversaw the printing of a revised Matthew's Bible, called the Great Bible because of its large format. Henry decreed that every church in England make the Great Bible accessible to all parishioners.

When Mary Tudor, Henry's oldest child and a Catholic, came to the throne in 1553, Protestant scholars fled to the Continent. Those in Geneva published a new translation of the New Testament in 1557 and of the entire Bible in 1560. This, the first English Bible to be divided into verses and the first printed in roman rather than gothic type, influenced the rhythms of William Shakespeare's plays. John Milton's poems *Paradise Lost* (1667) and *Samson Agonistes* (1671) are indebted to the Geneva Bible's notes. When the pilgrims sailed for America, this was the Bible they carried with them. Immensely popular, between 1560 and 1644 the Geneva Bible went through 140 editions.

This translation was accurate but embarrassing to the Anglican establishment. Its notes attacked the observance of Easter and Whitsuntide and criticized "worldly subtle prelates." In 1568 a new version, prepared by sixteen translators, appeared. This Bishops' Bible, so-called because most involved in the project were bishops, lacked the elegance of its predecessor. Queen Elizabeth I refused to sanction it, but in 1571 the bishops in convocation ordered that every church and every bishop should own a copy.

Just as Protestants had fled England under Mary, so Catholics moved to the Continent after Elizabeth succeeded her sister in 1558. Many settled in Douai, Flanders. Here they began a new, Catholic translation, thus rejecting the 1546 decision of the Council of Trent opposing vernacular versions of the Bible. This Douay Bible (New Testament, 1582; Old Testament, 1609-1610) was based largely on the Vulgate, which the Council of Trent had declared more accurate than those in the original languages, though the translators in fact consulted Hebrew and Greek texts as well as Protestant Bibles in English.

In trying to remain Latinate if not Latin, the Douay Bible enriched the English language with such words as "acquisition," "adulterate," "advent," "allegory," "character," and "coagulate." It also created obscurity with such phrases as "concorporat and comparticipant" (of the same body, and partakers, Ephesians 3:6) or "coinquination and spottes, flowing in delicacies" (spots they are, and blemishes, sporting themselves with their own deceivings, 2 Peter 2:13). This opacity was intentional. In a note to 1 Corinthians 14:26-33, where Paul discusses speaking in tongues, Richard Bristow wrote in the Douay Bible, "The vertue of the Sacraments and Service consisteth not in the peoples vnderstanding."

Both Catholics and Puritans hoped for support from James I when he succeeded Elizabeth in 1603. Both were to be disappointed. In January, 1604, James hosted the Hampton Court Conference to hear—and reject—Puritan petitions. He did, however, accede to the request of John Reynolds, Puritan president of Corpus Christi College, Oxford, to authorize a new translation of the Bible. Work began late in 1604 and continued for six years. Changes from earlier English versions are often slight, but these illustrate the truth of Mark Twain's observation that the difference between the right word and the nearly right word is the difference between lightning and a lightning bug. Tyndale had written in 2 Samuel 1:27, "How are the mighty overthrown." The King James version reads, "How are the mighty fallen." Tyndale's Genesis 1:1 reads, "In the beginning God created heaven and earth." The King James verse is almost identical: "In the beginning God created the heaven and the earth." With the addition of two articles a stroll has become a procession. In the Bishops' Bible the 23rd Psalm begins, "God is my shepherd, therefore I can lose nothing." The King James version turned this ordinary passage into the unforgettable "The Lord is my shepherd; I shall not want."

Puritans still clung to the Geneva Bible, Catholics to the Douay, but over time the King James Bible, also known as the Authorized version, though it was authorized by neither king nor Parliament, eclipsed all others in English. The nineteenth century historian Thomas Babington Macaulay declared, "If everything else in our language should perish it would alone suffice to show the whole extent of its beauty and power." The rhythms and language of the King James Bible can be heard in the prose of John Bunyan's *Pilgrim's Progress* (1678) and D. H. Lawrence's *The Rainbow* (1915), in the long lines of James Macpherson's Ossian poems (1760-1763) and Walt Whitman's *Leaves of Grass* (1855), in the Gettysburg Address (1863), in African American spirituals, and in the speeches of Martin Luther King, Jr. Newer translations have sought to supplant the King James Bible, such as the Revised Version (1885), the American Standard Version (1901), and the Revised Standard Version (1952). H. L. Mencken pronounced on the futility of such attempts: "Many learned but misguided men have sought to produce translations that should be mathematically accurate, and in the plain speech of everyday. But the Authorized Version has never yielded to any of them, for it is palpably and overwhelmingly better than they are."

Bobrick offers a detailed yet readable account of the translations undertaken from 1380 to 1611. Perhaps he claims too much for the English Bible when he credits it with the establishment of democracy and the spirit of free inquiry. Still, he tells a good story about the creation of one of the enduring monuments of English literature.

Joseph Rosenblum

Sources for Further Study

Booklist 97 (March 1, 2001): 1210.
Library Journal 126 (February 15, 2001): 174.
The New York Times Book Review 106 (April 8, 2001): 8.
Publishers Weekly 248 (February 19, 2001): 78.
Reason 33 (December, 2001): 73.
The Washington Times, April 15, 2001, p. B8.

THE WILD BLUE
The Men and Boys Who Flew the B-24's over Germany

Author: Stephen E. Ambrose (1936-   )
Publisher: Simon & Schuster (New York). 303 pp.
  $26.00
Type of work: History
Time: 1944-1945
Locale: The United States, Italy, and Germany

~

Famed World War II historian Ambrose examines the deeds of the young men who flew the B-24 Liberator bombers against Germany, with special emphasis upon future U.S. senator and presidential candidate George S. McGovern and his crew

~

Principal personages:
   GEORGE S. MCGOVERN, a B-24 bomber pilot in World War II
   RALPH "BILL" ROUNDS, his copilot
   KENNETH HIGGINS, his radioman
   CARROLL WILSON "C. W." COOPER, his navigator
   ISADOR IRVING SEIGAL, his tail gunner
   WILLIAM "TEX" ASHLOCK, his waist gunner
   ROBERT O'CONNELL, his nose gunner
   MIKE VALKO, his flight engineer
   WILLIAM MCAFEE, his ball turret gunner
   SAM ADAMS, his bombardier and navigator
   MARION COLVERT, his navigator
   JOHN B. MILLS, his tail gunner

Given the time that has elapsed since the end of World War II, and the countless books that have been written about that conflict, one would think that little would be left to say about the subject. *The Wild Blue* was written as a means of correcting two errors in the collective popular memory of World War II. One concerns the prosecution of the air war by the United States and the other concerns a participant in that aspect of the war. Ironically, the book became the focus of criticism when it appeared that Ambrose had incorporated sections of other writers' published works in his text; the data were credited to their authors in footnotes but not enclosed within quotation marks to indicate that the material was a direct quote. The cases uncovered in *The Wild Blue* led to analyses of other Ambrose books and revealed a similar pattern of attribution without indicating direct quotation. It is hard to regard this as a case of straightforward plagiarism, since the original authors are noted, but it does appear to indicate sloppy scholarship. Ambrose and his publisher promised to correct the lack of quotation marks in subsequent printings of the books.

It is well known that the air war in Europe was conducted simultaneously through two very different approaches by Great Britain and its former colony. England used its famous four-engine Lancaster heavy bombers against Germany only during night raids, having deemed daylight bombing too risky. Massed formation bombing is by its very nature highly inaccurate, and bombing by night even more so. Aside from the fact that it is militarily ineffective, it exacts a horrendous toll in civilian casualties. Indeed, American military planners considered nighttime bombing to be little more than terrorism. The American solution—precision daylight bombardment of German military, industrial, and transportation targets—degraded the enemy's ability to fight even as it subjected the United States' mighty war birds to appalling casualties. All of this is well known to the public, and such films as *Twelve O'Clock High* (1949) dramatized the feats of the Eighth Air Force as its B-17 bombers made daily runs from bases in England against Adolf Hitler's war machine. There is a certain undeniable appeal in the image of waves of elegant B-17's, beautiful in their terrible symmetry, taking flight from their numerous concrete runways throughout Britain. That, however, is only part of the story.

Stephen E. Ambrose, winner of a National Humanities Award, is one of the most popular historians of the European theater of operations in World War II. His best-selling books on the common soldier include Band of Brothers *(1992) and* Citizen Soldiers *(1997).*

Much of the bombardment of Germany and its military sites elsewhere originated in Italy and was conducted under the most primitive of conditions. Runways were often dangerous, patchwork affairs, the former farmland covered with steel matting. The result was a precarious arrangement that left precious little room for error by the pilots, who were expected to sleep in tents and consume wretched food. Though the B-17 is the plane that is best remembered and preserved from this period, it was the squat, ugly "Flying Box Car"—the B-24—that was built and used in far greater numbers. Ambrose's book is designed in part to tell the story of this all-but-forgotten plane and the men who flew it. He does this by focusing upon the life of one particular B-24 pilot and his crew: that of George S. McGovern. The latter, a long-time friend of the author, was often portrayed as a coward by conservatives during the presidential campaign of 1972, and Ambrose aims to set the record straight. This tendentiousness is not history in the usual sense of the word, and Ambrose makes it clear from the beginning that this is not a disinterested account of the air war. Nevertheless, Ambrose's approach does have a distinct advantage. He balances the necessary facts about the war—the number of planes that took part, the cost in human life, and the effects of the bombing campaign—with a sustained account of McGovern's experiences and those of a few other individuals. Though this is less objective a history than the usual fare, it brings a heightened sense of drama to what would otherwise be a simple tale of carnage.

In terms of structure, Ambrose prefaces the actual history with a prologue and cast of characters, and concludes with an epilogue. The remainder of the book consists of eleven numbered chapters, beginning with a description of the origins of the men who participated in McGovern's last mission in April, 1945. Like a good dramatist—the book relies heavily upon extensive interviews with veterans—Ambrose allows the participants to tell their own stories of how they came to make war; in so doing he gives the reader a palpable sense of what it was like to be there. The participants were volunteers, they came from every conceivable place in the nation, and many were from areas so isolated they had never traveled from home or seen an airplane. What they all had in common was the desire to fly and their youth, and it is daunting to think that many of those massive bombers were flown by pilots who had not even reached the age of twenty. Ambrose seems especially surprised by this, but traditionally wars have been fought by the very young. Even the word "infantry,"which many associate with the image of an older, battle-hardened soldier, alludes to the youth of participants in war.

Before these children could face the prospect of battle, they had to be trained, and one of the highlights of *The Wild Blue* is the emphasis it places on the preparation for war. As Ambrose correctly observes, the Army Air Force became the world's largest educational institution. It was forced to do this because the United States lacked an effective air force at the beginning of the war: In order to send the bombers against Germany, it needed to train pilots, gunners, navigators, bombardiers, radiomen, and mechanics. In terms of numbers, the Army Air Force progressed from a minuscule 20,000 personnel at the time the United States entered the war to 2.4 million by 1944. For George McGovern, the training began with a typical army boot camp and progressed to a physically and academically rigorous ground school, where education ranged from push-ups to navigation. After months of this conditioning, he was allowed to begin his flight instruction on a single-engine trainer, then trained on twin-engine aircraft, where he learned the finer points of flying a multiengine aircraft at night. It was only after completing this segment of his training that he received his wings and went on to learn how to fly B-24's.

The Army failed many of its would-be bomber pilots in training due to the unforgiving nature of aerial bombardment. The B-24, by almost every account, was far more difficult to pilot than any other allied aircraft in World War II. Ambrose gives an excellent description of the cockpit: "There were twenty-seven gauges on the panel, twelve levers for the throttle, turbocharger, and fuel mixture, four on the pilot's side on his right, four on the copilot's side on his left. The wheel, or 'yoke' as it was called, was as big as that on a large truck. There were over a dozen switches, plus brake pedals, rudders, and more." This is a vivid characterization of the B-24's instrumentation, and with a bit of imagination, the reader can picture what a challenge a young pilot would face. However, it would have been far more effective had Ambrose enhanced his text with additional photographs or simplified technical drawings.

What Ambrose does convey well is the very special character of life as it was lived on this nearly forgotten plane. Unlike the other branches of the service or even the Army's ground forces, Army Air Force personnel did not salute on the airfield, freely fraternized in clubs that were nominally restricted to either officers or enlisted men, and generally placed less emphasis upon distinctions in rank. This was a discrete culture within the armed forces, and the reason for the difference had to do with the nature of their mission. Although bombers flew in massed formations, the men on board had to function as a cohesive unit: The pilot had the most responsibility in guiding his plane safely to the target, often through heavy antiaircraft fire, and back; he in turn relied upon the flight engineer, the navigator, the gunners, and the bombardier. A mistake by a single crew member could mean disaster for his plane and the nearby planes.

Though some may wish to romanticize the image of American war birds preying upon a ruthless foe, the actual air campaign against Germany was both far more mundane and more dangerous. It is here that Ambrose's extensive interviews with surviving veterans bear fruit. Every aspect of a typical bombing mission was fraught with danger. This was not the usual takeoff that one associates with a modern airport. A B-24 pilot pushed his 1,200-horsepower Pratt & Whitney engines to full throttle and held the brakes down until it was his turn to go. He was required to follow the plane in front of him closely as it took off, and he had to apply the brakes to the wheels again after the plane left the ground and before the landing gear retracted. If he hit the brakes too soon, the bomber—laden with explosives and high-octane aviation fuel—would crash and explode on impact. McGovern's own plane, which he called the *Dakota Queen*, once rolled into a ditch because his flight engineer was not paying attention to the runway.

Once airborne, the pilot was expected to bring his plane into a tight formation as it passed over a bombing target. Flying in clumped groups was vital for two reasons: first, it concentrated the area of bombardment and thus increased the chances of hitting the target. Second, such close formation flying allowed the heavy bombers to ward off fighter attacks with their 50-caliber machine guns. Death came suddenly, violently, arbitrarily. Ambrose reveals the truly shocking nature of aerial bombardment. Some planes failed to hold their place in formation and collided with their fellow bombers; others drifted slightly and dropped their bomb loads on other B-24's; and some just exploded for no apparent reason, with the 8,000-pound load all but vaporizing the plane. Most dangerous of all was the enemy's response to the bombers: flak. Since bombers flew in massed formations, Germany's antiaircraft guns had ample time to fire exploding shells at the oncoming planes. To the pilot approaching his target, a heavily defended area could very well shower a plane with shards of jagged metal. On one of his early bombing missions, McGovern narrowly escaped death as a piece of metal flew through the windshield and swept over his right shoulder. The only real armor on the bomber was the cast iron in the seats of the pilot and copilot; the crew relied upon flak jackets. Mission after mission, pilots were expected to follow the lead plane, stay on course, and fly through an atmosphere thick with detonations. In effect, the bombers themselves became targets.

McGovern did not take the easy way out in the war. The young officer deliberately chose a dangerous but vitally important target for his thirty-fifth and final mission rather than select an easier route on the "milk run." Despite the loss of an engine and hydraulics (the landing gear had to be cranked down) McGovern brought both plane and crew safely home. If anyone ever had doubts about George McGovern's deeds in war, Ambrose's book dispels them for all time.

Cliff Prewencki

Sources for Further Study

Booklist 97 (May 1, 2001): 1594.
Library Journal 126 (May 15, 2001): 138.
Publishers Weekly 248 (August 27, 2001): 17.
The New York Times Book Review 106 (September 9, 2001): 12.

THE WILKOMIRSKI AFFAIR
A Study in Biographical Truth

Author: Stefan Maechler (1957-   )
First published: Der Fall Wilkomirksi, 2000, in Switzer-
land
Translated from the German by John E. Woods
Publisher: Schocken Books/Random House (New York).
496 pp. $16.95
Type of work: History
Time: 1941-1995
Locale: Poland and Switzerland

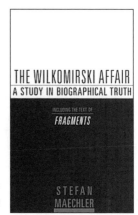

~

A riveting account of the author's investigation of Fragments, *a Holocaust memoir first hailed as a masterpiece
and then attacked as a fraud*

~

Principal personages:
> BINJAMIN WILKOMIRSKI (also known as Bruno Grosjean), author of a
> controversial Holocaust memoir
> THE DÖSSEKERS, Bruno Grosjean's adoptive parents
> EVA KORALNIK, Wilkomirski's literary agent
> DANIEL GANZFRIED, a Swiss journalist who was the first in print to re-
> pudiate *Fragments*
> ELI BERNSTEIN, an Israeli psychiatrist and close friend and supporter of
> Binjamin Wilkomirski
> VERENA PILLER, Wilkomirski's life partner
> KAROLA, a Holocaust survivor who contradicts Wilkomirski's use of her
> story in *Fragments*
> STEFAN MAECHLER, a historian assigned by Wilkomirski's publisher to
> investigate the authenticity of *Fragments*

In 1995, *Fragments*, a short Holocaust memoir written in a staccato style, was published in Germany. Binjamin Wilkomirski, its author, presented his account as virtually a verbatim report of his fragmentary memories of a childhood at two concentration camps, Majdanek and Auschwitz, both in Poland. Wilkomirski made no claims
for his book as literature; indeed, he emphasized that he could provide only a literal
picture of the shards of his memory. However, these shards, he maintained, were absolutely authentic. They had remained a vivid part of his life and had been uncor-
rupted by his subsequent experiences. Shortly before publication of *Fragments*, another publisher alerted Wilkomirski's publisher that Wilkomirski's claims were, at
the least, open to doubt, but the power of his story and Wilkomirski's own affirmation that he had researched his life over several decades overrode any qualms his sup-

861

~

Stefan Maechler studied history and German literature at the University of Zurich. Maechler was commissioned by Wilkomirski's publisher to do a full investigation of their author's life.

~

porters had, and then the reviews and public response seemed to ratify and strengthen his case. Eva Koralnik, his literary agent, had a distinguished history of publishing survivor literature, and her own troubled childhood background resonated with Wilkomirski's story, especially his account of how he discovered in Poland that he was related to the Wilkomirski family and took their name as his own after the war. He received honors from both Jewish and psychological organizations that were impressed with the sincerity of his writing and with his efforts to assist other Holocaust survivors in recovering and articulating their memories.

Then, in 1998, journalist Daniel Ganzfried wrote a series of articles pointing out that Wilkomirski could not document a single one of his experiences as a Holocaust victim. Indeed, Ganzfried believed Wilkomirski had assumed a false identity—that in fact he was Bruno Grosjean, an adopted child of a Swiss couple, the Dössekers. Ganzfried had obtained documents that seemed to clinch his case. Other journalists also began to cast doubt on Wilkomirski's memoir, and his publisher and agent felt compelled to employ Stefan Maechler, a historian of the Holocaust, to investigate the sources of *Fragments*. Remarkably, Wilkomirski was also a party to the investigation and promised to cooperate fully with the historian's inquiry.

Maechler's book emulates, in so far as is possible, the process of his research. He begins with "The Story of Bruno Grosjean," an opening chapter that basically confirms Ganzfried's research and adds even more details from Maechler's investigation, including accounts of his interviews with Bruno's (Binjamin's) mother's brother, which help Maechler to pin down how Bruno came to be adopted by a Swiss family. At this point, it is not clear how Wilkomirski could possibly maintain he is not Bruno Grosjean.

Maechler next presents "Wilkomirski Tells His Own Story," a compelling defense culled from Wilkomirski's own words in letters and in interviews with Maechler and others. Wilkomirski points out that many children of the Holocaust were given false identity papers and to this day cannot definitively reestablish their identities. What is more, Wilkomirski does not deny having been brought up by the Dössekers; rather, he claims that he was the child exchanged for Bruno Grosjean and given Grosjean's identity papers. Other discrepancies and contradictions in *Fragments* are just that, Wilkomirski asserts—that is, they are the stumbling, incomplete efforts of a man attempting to reconstruct past events that bewildered and traumatized him as a child.

Rather than challenging Wilkomirski and simply presuming he is a liar—as Ganzfried did—Maechler explores "The Origins of *Fragments*," a memoir he sees as growing out of a childhood that was indeed harrowing and which led to the story of a boy who lost his mother at the age of four and then found himself at the mercy of an abusive adoptive parent, Frau Dösseker, who assaulted his identity in ways that led Bruno to identify with the Jewish survivor children of the Holocaust. In other words, the thesis that Maechler tentatively advances in this section is that Bruno Grosjean had to find a story and an identity that provided a more vivid and satisfying explanation of his sense of victimization and loss.

"A Global Literary Event," the next section of Maechler's book, is a brilliant analysis of how the press, many readers, and organizations contributed to belief in the story of Binjamin Wilkomirski. Holocaust survivors, for example, embraced him because his story articulated so many of their own horrifying experiences. Israeli psychiatrist Eli Bernstein (not a Holocaust survivor) was impressed with Wilkomirski's behavior and knew him years before his book was published. Bernstein observed Wilkomirski living the life of a Holocaust survivor. Similarly, Verena Piller, Wilkomirski's life partner, observed how he shuffled his feet at night in bed as he relived the terrifying scenes of concentration camps where rats had gnawed at his limbs. How could so much involuntary affect—some of it occurring in Wilkomirski's sleep—be fraudulent, his intimates wondered. At the same time, Maechler points out that there were doubters from the beginning. One reviewer close to Wilkomirski's agent and publisher expressed her reservations in private but could not bring herself to challenge his overpowering story in print. Others, such as Holocaust scholars Lawrence Langer and Raul Hilberg, were skeptical, the latter pointing out that Wilkomirski almost certainly could not have been in both Majdanek and Auschwitz. Other details rang false, as well. There were no rats in the camps, Hilberg noted. Yet the need to believe—especially among Holocaust survivors whom Wilkomirski sought out—suppressed skepticism. Jewish organizations were moved by his story and afraid of what challenging it might do in a climate that now included Holocaust deniers. Certain psychologists prized Wilkomirski's memories as another triumph of recovered memory in child abuse cases. All of these different individuals and groups unwittingly conspired to make *Fragments* "a global literary event."

Then in "The Plunge into the Abyss—Autobiography or Fake?" Maechler comes full circle to squarely face the brutal but accurate process by which Daniel Ganzfried exposed the inauthenticity of *Fragments*. Ganzfried's case becomes more and more compelling as Wilkomirski is pictured withdrawing from public debate, taking refuge in the intensity of his feelings but failing to provide any fresh documentation or even a better rationale for believing his claims. Indeed, Wilkomirski begins to say that he never demanded from readers that they believe his story; in other words, *Fragments* was a true record of his memories but it was never meant to be taken as a verifiable historical document. Perhaps most detrimental to Wilkomirski's case is Maechler's frequent mention that Jerzy Kosinski's novel *The Painted Bird* had had a profound influence on Wilkomirski's decision to write *Fragments*. Kosinski had also asserted that his novel was his own experience and, like Wilkomirski, he began to abandon his autobiographical avowals as soon as his story began to be contested.

"Tracking Down the Truth—The Historical Research," the climax of Maechler's investigation, explodes Wilkomirski's case for himself. No one in the community or in the Dösseker family can remember the exchange of boys that involved Binjamin Wilkomirski taking on Bruno Grosjean's identity. Even worse, Karola, the woman whom Wilkomirski says he befriended in Majdanek and later saw again in a Krakow orphanage, repudiates *Fragments* and tells Maechler that Wilkomirski has stolen her

Holocaust story for his own purposes. Her testimony is especially damning because Wilkomirski has told Maechler all along that he cannot divulge Karola's whereabouts because he does not want to involve her in controversy. Wilkomirski himself claimed to have had to honor her objections by changing Karola's name to Mila in his story.

In two concluding sections, "The Truth of Biography" and "The Truth of Fiction," Maechler confronts what remains of significance in *Fragments* now that it has been exposed as a fraud. On the one hand, he argues that the book is authentic insofar as it renders the inner turmoil that Binjamin Wilkomirski, otherwise known as Bruno Grosjean, genuinely experienced during the war years and their aftermath. What is more, because Wilkomirski steeped himself in histories of the Holocaust and befriended its survivors, his book includes a considerable quotient of authentic narrative about the Holocaust experience. On the other hand, Maechler is aghast that such a mediocre literary work should have stirred readers so profoundly. Nothing in the style or structure of the book merits the high praise or awards it received. Indeed, Maechler goes so far as to suggest that as soon as the reader realizes the book is a fiction, much of its power is attenuated. Yet here he may underestimate the book, since his own research shows that Holocaust survivors and others have continued to believe in the worth of Wilkomirski's perceptions even as they concede he may not have been a Holocaust survivor.

Fragments itself is included in Maechler's book, so readers will be able to make their own determination about the story's strength as an evocation of the Holocaust experience for a child. In some ways, Maechler's fine book might have been improved by putting *Fragments* first—exposing first-time readers to the experience of the story and then allowing them to analyze it. Similarly, as soon as Maechler approaches the section "Tracking Down the Truth," he relegates many of Wilkomirski's comments on Maechler's research to the footnotes—a not-so-subtle suggestion that Wilkomirski's defense is now a secondary matter, given that his story cannot possible be true. It might have been better if Maechler had included another section consisting of Wilkomirski's rebuttal, however weak, which would have paralleled the second section, "Wilkomirski Tells His Own Story."

Aside from these tentative reservations, it must be said that Maechler has produced a masterpiece fully justifying his subtitle, "A Study in Biographical Truth." Maechler provides not only detailed notes that authenticate every aspect of his investigation, he also provides numerous descriptions of his informants and explains how he went about conducting his investigation. The result is that he not only establishes an authentic record, he accounts for what is inauthentic, thereby showing how closely related the truth of biography and the truth of fiction can be.

Carl Rollyson

Sources for Further Study

The New Republic 224 (April 30, 2001): 35.
The Washington Post Book World, April 15, 2001, p. 8.

THE WIND DONE GONE

Author: Alice Randall (1960-   )
Publisher: Houghton Mifflin (Boston). 210 pp. $22.00
Type of work: Novel
Time: 1845-1877
Locale: Atlanta, Georgia; Tata, a cotton plantation (Tara
  of *Gone with the Wind*); Washington, D.C.

∽

A retelling of Margaret Mitchell's Gone with the Wind
from the perspective of Scarlett O'Hara's mulatto half sis-
ter, Cynara

∽

Principal characters:

> CYNARA BROWN, also known as Cindy or Cinnamon, twenty-eight-year-
> old mulatto daughter of Mammy and Planter, Other's half sister, R.'s
> mistress
>
> MAMMY, sixty-year-old mother of Cynara and Other's nurse, Mammy of
> *Gone with the Wind*
>
> R., also called Debt Chauffeur, Other's husband, Cynara's lover, Rhett
> Butler of *Gone with the Wind*
>
> OTHER, daughter of Planter and Lady, half sister of Cynara, wife of R.,
> Scarlett O'Hara of *Gone with the Wind*
>
> LADY, Other's mother, Ellen O'Hara of *Gone with the Wind*
>
> PLANTER, Other and Cynara's father, Gerald O'Hara of *Gone with the*
> *Wind*
>
> MISS PRISS, Other's maid, Prissy of *Gone with the Wind*
>
> GARLIC, Planter's valet, Pork of *Gone with the Wind*
>
> MRS. GARLIC, mother of Miss Priss, Dilcey of *Gone with the Wind*
>
> BEAUTY, lesbian madam of the whorehouse R. frequents, Belle Watling
> of *Gone with the Wind*
>
> DREAMY GENTLEMAN, homosexual husband of Mealy Mouth, Ashley
> Wilkes of *Gone with the Wind*
>
> MEALY MOUTH, wife of Dreamy Gentleman, Melanie Wilkes of *Gone*
> *with the Wind*
>
> JEEMS, former slave and Cynara's childhood friend, Jeems of *Gone with*
> *the Wind*
>
> THE CONGRESSMAN, African American politician from Alabama who
> fathers Cynara's baby

The Wind Done Gone sparked heated argument even before it was published. The
estate of Margaret Mitchell, author of *Gone with the Wind* (1936), filed suit in March,
2001, to block publication, claiming that Alice Randall's book is an unauthorized
sequel to Mitchell's classic romance and tribute to the antebellum South. Estate law-

*Alice Randall is an established
country songwriter, the only African
American woman to have written a
number-one country song. The
Wind Done Gone is her first novel.*

yers claiming copyright infringement charged that Randall stole *Gone with the Wind*'s plot, characters, settings, and scenes and even plagiarized some passages. Randall and her publisher argued on appeal that her book is a literary parody of *Gone with the Wind*. In May, the Atlanta Federal Court of Appeals agreed and overturned the lower court's decision. Houghton Mifflin began shipping the books in June, but Mitchell's estate fanned the flames of controversy by filing an appeal.

The *Wind Done Gone* is indisputably a sequel of a kind. It begins about a month after *Gone with the Wind* ends, with Cynara making her first entry in the diary she has just received as a twenty-eighth birthday present from R, who is recently separated from Other. Cynara's diary will go on to chronicle, among other things, her ongoing relationship with R. and the ultimate fates of Mammy, Other, and Tata, all fit subjects for inclusion in a sequel. Atypical of traditional sequels, however, is the book's radical shift in point of view and voice. *Gone with the Wind* presents its romantic portrayal of the Old South through third person omniscient narration from the point of view of the Southern aristocracy. *The Wind Done Gone* tells another aspect of the same story through a former slave's first person narration. The book further eludes easy categorization in a manner reminiscent of Jean Rhys's *Wide Sargasso Sea* (1966), a "prequel" to Charlotte Brontë's *Jane Eyre* (1847) that describes how Rochester meets and marries his Creole bride, who is fated to become the insane shut-in whose existence and identity is hidden from Jane Eyre. In *The Wind Done Gone*, Cynara's diary accounts of her childhood at Tata serve a similar purpose by extending into the past the reach of the original.

Whether or not *The Wind Done Gone* should be called a literary parody is subject to debate. Where it inverts Mitchell's story so that the masters are the puppets and the slaves are the puppeteers, it is an ahistorical, wish-fulfilling fantasy. Where it attempts to undermine the racist stereotypes of *Gone with the Wind*, it is a critique, once again recalling *Wide Sargasso Sea* with its negative depiction of British colonial practices in the West Indies. The most common definition of parody refers to a caricature of the original work, a lampoon or burlesque where the style of the original is imitated and exaggerated for humorous or satirical effect. With the exception of a few isolated passages and the characters' altered names, the style of Randall's novel does not fit that definition. In common with most parodies, however, understanding and appreciation of *The Wind Done Gone* is dependent upon familiarity with the earlier work. R., Mammy, and the other characters derived from *Gone with the Wind* are flat and undeveloped. The plantation and Atlanta are only sketchily drawn. Moreover, the outline for Cynara's life story is provided by Mitchell's plot, with many of her most emotion-drenched recollections based on some of Mitchell's most memorable scenes. There is one crucial difference, however. *Gone with the Wind* contains only one fleeting reference to white slave owners having sex with their slaves. Miscegenation becomes the overriding focus of *The Wind Done Gone*.

Cynara's diary opens with her childhood memories of life in the plantation house, Tata. Cynara bitterly recounts how Other monopolizes the attention of her own mother, Mammy, while Mammy ignores her. Lady, Other's mother, becomes her solace for a while to such an extent that a complete role reversal takes place, with Other nursing from Mammy and Cynara nursing from Lady. Whether Lady allows such unlikely familiarity because she is jealous of Other's love for Mammy or of her husband Gerald's lust for Mammy is unclear. In any case, the unorthodox arrangement ends when Cynara reaches puberty and is sold for one dollar to a nearby plantation owner to save her from becoming the mistress of Other's future husband. Gerald, Cynara's father, prefers that she become Mammy's equivalent there as mistress to his neighbor's future son-in-law rather than as mistress to his own, apparently because he worries that Other's charms would suffer by comparison with Cynara's.

Before Gerald's plan has time to become a reality, fate in the form of influenza intervenes. The neighbor dies in the epidemic, and, at the age of fourteen, Cynara finds herself on the auction block. Beauty, an old flame of R.'s, buys her to work as a maid and laundress at her brothel. R. takes her for his mistress when she reaches fifteen, a lucky break as it turns out because R. is not only a considerate lover who introduces her to the pleasures of the flesh, he becomes her mentor in other subjects, too, teaching her to read and write and sending her on a grand tour of Europe. While Cynara fills her diary with fond memories of her student days with R. and painful incidents from her childhood, she is mute on events that might have occurred during most of the time period covered by *Gone with the Wind*. Left untold is how she spent the war or reacted to freedom. Indeed, for most of the book, Cynara's interests seem relatively narrow, chiefly confined to her relationships with R. and Mammy and envious comparisons with Other's more fortunate circumstances. One of those circumstances, Other's romance with R., actually comes about because Cynara tells R. about Other as a test of his love and loyalty. R. fails the test when he meets Other and is smitten. This, along with Mammy's apparent preference for Other, confirms Cynara's belief in her own inferiority.

Shortly after Cynara receives her diary, Mammy dies without seeing her daughter. Other's death soon follows from a suicidal fall down the stairs subsequent to her disfigurement by smallpox. Not long thereafter, R. gives Cynara a packet of old love letters from the fifteen-year-old Lady to her cousin Feleepe. The letters reveal that Lady and her cousin shared a black ancestor. By the South's one-drop-of-Negro-blood miscegenation rule, they were thus rendered black themselves. R. then introduces Cynara to the attractive African American Congressman. The latter two events begin to weaken Cynara's lifelong inferiority complex as she realizes not only that Other was actually black like her but that she is attracted to the Congressman not in spite of but because he is black—and successful. Cynara's self-esteem begins to grow when R. shows her a note Mammy had sent him shortly before her death begging that he marry "mah little gal." With these words, Cynara realizes that her mother really loved her, so she begins to love herself, giving her the strength to first reject R.'s proposal that they live in London where she can pass as white and eventually to reject R. himself. Already pregnant by her Congressman before she abandons R., Cynara finally sets off to live life on her own terms as a truly free person should. Her Congressman loses his seat with the end of Reconstruction; nonetheless, the story eventually arrives at a happy conclusion when her great-grandson mortgages Tata to finance a victorious run for Congress.

Identity and how it is determined is a prominent theme in *The Wind Done Gone*. That race and miscegenation should be of major concern in a work that critiques a Southern classic about its peculiar institution is no surprise. That the complexities of sexual and social roles and relationships between men and women should be explored is obvious; *Gone with the Wind* is one of the defining romances of the twentieth century. That convoluted family histories of betrayals and secrets and sudden revelations should sometimes take center stage is to be expected in a tale about both the literal and figurative ties that bind. Identity politics, however, is another matter and is jarringly out of place here. If *The Wind Done Gone* purports to seriously address corrosive issues raised by *Gone with the Wind*, that effort is marred by the inclusion of a seemingly gratuitous dollop of homosexuality. The sensitive, musical, impractical Ashley Wilkes of *Gone with the Wind*, succumbing to the common stereotype, is transformed into the homosexual Dreamy Gentleman in *The Wind Done Gone*. Meanwhile, Cynara has a lesbian encounter in Europe, cavorts with the prostitutes at the whorehouse after hours, and flirts with Beauty, the madam. While homosexuality undoubtedly existed in the Old South, in *The Wind Done Gone*, its inclusion merely distracts.

The Old South portrayed in *The Wind Done Gone* is a strangely benign place considering its sullied reputation. In fact, Mealy Mouth, Dreamy Gentleman's wife, is the only character responsible for white on black violence when she has Miss Priss's homosexual brother beaten to death after he becomes her husband's lover, to preserve Dreamy Gentleman's reputation. Otherwise, it is black characters who instigate violence against whites. Miss Priss kills Mealy Mouth; Mammy may or may not have killed Lady's three sons. From time to time, Cynara's diary does allude to historical episodes of violence toward blacks. Far from contradicting Mitchell's sentiments, however, her remarks sometimes seem to echo Mitchell's about the horrors of Reconstruction compared to the good old days of slavery: "It's the boil on the body of Reconstruction, whites killing blacks. They didn't kill us as often, leastways not directly, when they owned us."

Cynara writes in her diary: "I read *Uncle Tom's Cabin*. I didn't see me in it." Ironically, *Uncle Tom's Cabin* is undoubtedly a more brutally accurate albeit highly melodramatic rendition of antebellum reality than is *The Wind Done Gone*. Slaves were rarely taught to read; in fact, it was against the law to do so. Young slave girls were not likely to be given their own houses or sent on tours of Europe by fawning white lovers. Nor was it likely that white men would marry their mulatto mistresses, even after the slaves were set free. Given that the *Wind Done Gone* aims to correct the unrealistically affectionate portrayal of relations between masters and slaves depicted in *Gone with the Wind*, these inexplicable passages can only serve to undermine that goal.

While the premise of *The Wind Done Gone* holds promise, ultimately, the book does not satisfy. Interest lags not only because of instances of inauthenticity or implausibility. Lack of sustained interaction between characters deflates dramatic tension. For example, Cynara and Other rarely even speak to one another. Plot devices such as Cynara's mysterious case of the autoimmune disease lupus can be confusing, unconvincing, or unnecessary. The prose style is uneven and sometimes opaque: "I couldn't say more. But I was racing 'round the furniture in my mind, trying to find a chair to sit on. Why do I always think of it just that way? Is thinking truly like housecleaning?" Despite its faults, however, *The Wind Done Gone* deserves attention as part of the ongoing and essential conversation about race in America.

Sue Tarjan

Sources for Further Study

Booklist 97 (May 1, 2001): 1595.
Library Journal 126 (May 1, 2001): 128.
Los Angeles Times Book Review, June 24, 2001, p. 1.
National Review 53 (August 20, 2001): 44.
The New York Times, May 3, 2001, p. F1.
The New York Times Book Review 106 (July 1, 2001): 16.
Time 157 (May 7, 2001): 74.
The Washington Post Book World, June 24, 2001, p. 3.

WITH THE STROKE OF A PEN
Executive Orders and Presidential Power

Author: Kenneth R. Mayer (1960-   )
Publisher: Princeton University Press (Princeton, N.J.).
   293 pp. $39.95
Type of work: Current affairs and history
Time: Primarily the 1930's to the late 1990's
Locale: Mostly Washington, D.C.

~

The most comprehensive study to date of executive orders and presidential power in the United States

~

Principal personages:
> HERBERT HOOVER, thirty-first president of the United States
> FRANKLIN DELANO ROOSEVELT, thirty-second president
> HARRY S. TRUMAN, thirty-third president
> DWIGHT DAVID EISENHOWER, thirty-fourth president
> JOHN FITZGERALD KENNEDY, thirty-fifth president
> LYNDON BAINES JOHNSON, thirty-sixth president
> RICHARD MILHOUSE NIXON, thirty-seventh president
> GERALD R. FORD, thirty-eighth president
> JAMES EARL CARTER, JR., thirty-ninth president
> RONALD W. REAGAN, fortieth president
> GEORGE HERBERT WALKER BUSH, forty-first president
> WILLIAM JEFFERSON CLINTON, forty-second president

In this, the most comprehensive study to date of the uses American presidents have made of executive orders, Kenneth R. Mayer, professor of political science at the University of Wisconsin at Madison, focuses on eighty-eight specific executive orders and discusses thirty-two of them in considerable depth and detail. He has chosen for his scrutiny a representative sampling from a broad range of presidential administrations. His greatest emphasis is on the use of such orders by presidents from Franklin Delano Roosevelt, who served from 1933 until his death in 1945, and the presidents that followed him up to and including Bill Clinton.

Mayer uses William Safire's definition of executive order from *Safire's Political Dictionary* (1980): "Action that can be taken by a Chief Executive without legislative action." Executive orders exemplify a behavioral paradigm first articulated by Richard Neustadt in *Presidential Power* (1960), a book that influenced the presidency of John F. Kennedy considerably and was influential in the administrations of succeeding presidents.

The most influential presidents are characterized by their persuasive ability. In

Neustadtian terms, such presidents are leaders actively involved in political bargaining. Mayer cites Franklin Delano Roosevelt and Harry S. Truman as examples of leaders in the sense that Neustadt defines effective leadership. He ranks Dwight D. Eisenhower the lowest of recent presidents in demonstrating this quality.

Executive orders have often been viewed as the means presidents have of accomplishing on their own what Congress refuses to give them. Presidents who are dealing with congresses dominated by the opposing party routinely find it necessary to resort to this method of getting things done and of accomplishing their political aims.

∽

Kenneth R. Mayer is a professor of political science at the University of Wisconsin at Madison. His previous book, coauthored with David Canon, was Dysfunctional Congress? The Individual Roots of an Institutional Dilemma *(1999). He is also the author of* The Political Economy of Defense Contracting *(1991).*

∽

One of the major strengths of the United States Constitution is that it sets up a system of checks and balances and clearly articulates the separation of powers that the founding fathers envisioned through the establishment of relatively autonomous legislative, judicial, and executive branches of government. Presidents who do not use executive powers judiciously may well overstep—and in notable cases have overstepped—the limits placed upon them by the Constitution. A number of political scientists regard the wholesale use of executive orders as a weakness, a failure on the part of a chief executive to use persuasive skills to influence Congress.

Presidents have often used executive orders because they had no alternative. Notable among the use of such orders were those relating to the integration of the South and to the implementation of affirmative action. Presidents from Harry S. Truman to Lyndon Johnson worked to bring about a new society in which racial discrimination would not be countenanced officially. To overcome some legislative tactics, such as the filibuster, aimed at scuttling the implementation of legislation to assure all citizens equal rights under the Constitution, presidents between 1945 and 1980 frequently used executive orders.

Mayer notes that Franklin Delano Roosevelt was the modern president who made the greatest use of executive orders. He fails to mention, however, that Roosevelt served as president during the United States' involvement in World War II (1941-1945) and that he also held office longer than any other U.S. president ever had or ever would, being elected to four consecutive terms as president, the last of these terminated by his death in 1945, only months after his inauguration.

Major questions of constitutional interpretation arise regarding the legal bases for presidents to issue executive orders. On one hand, the legal ramifications can be disputed endlessly. On the other hand, the legal considerations are often overwhelmed by the political considerations surrounding the exercising of this presidential privilege. Many argue that gradually the president has become much more powerful than the framers of the Constitution envisioned when they drew up that document. As society has gained in complexity, the dynamics existing between presidents and the law have become more complicated than the founding fathers foresaw.

Mayer laments that, before 1895, there was no systematic method for gathering and cataloguing executive orders. In that year, the federal government began printing such orders in "slip" form so that they could be collected in loose-leaf binders. Ten years later, the Department of State established a repository for executive orders and requested that agencies of the executive branch submit their archives to this repository.

In 1907, the Department of State organized the collection chronologically and assigned numbers to each executive order. The classification system was confusing because some agencies discovered old stashes of executive orders after they had submitted earlier collections, and these newly discovered documents were numbered in such a way as to suggest they were much more recent than they actually were.

It is estimated that at least fifty thousand executive orders have been issued throughout the history of the United States presidency, but by December, 1999, the numbered entries in the repository came to 13,144, suggesting that something over 35,000 such orders were missing from the collection. In 1929, the first year of his presidency, Herbert Hoover issued Executive Order (EO) 5220, which required the submission of all such orders to the Department of State, but this order essentially went unheeded by many agencies. Certainly not all of the many executive orders Franklin Roosevelt issued have been catalogued as ordered by Hoover.

All chief executives find themselves poised between two opposing poles: If they are too strong, as anyone who seeks and wins the office of president may well appear to be, there is the risk that they will move toward the kind of monarchy that led to the Revolutionary War and from which the founding fathers were consciously distancing themselves as they framed the Constitution. If chief executives are weak, however, the danger is that the government will fall into chaos and paralysis, leaving it vulnerable to a takeover from those who would like to wrest power from the prevailing administration.

When chief executives come under extreme pressure, as Ronald Reagan did over the Iran-Contra affair beginning in 1986, which involved attempts to circumvent restrictions on U.S. arms being sold to Nicaraguan rebels and Iran, and as Richard Nixon did over the cover-up of connections to the Watergate break-in at the Democratic National Party's headquarters, they can use executive orders to deflect attention from the immediate problems that threaten them. In the case of Bill Clinton's sexual involvement with intern Monica Lewinsky, the possibility existed that the whole administration would come tumbling down if the president resigned or if he was adjudged guilty in the impeachment hearings.

In August, 1997, before the Lewinsky story broke, Clinton used executive power to launch an attack on Iraq after Saddam Hussein attacked Kuwait. A congress with a Republican majority overwhelmingly supported the president's order in this case. On December 16, 1997, however, as news of the Lewinsky affair became headline news in most of the nation's newspapers, Clinton, using an executive order, launched another attack on Iraq, ostensibly because Hussein had defied the efforts of United Nations arms inspectors to inspect his country for arms and chemical weapons. This time, Congress publicly deplored both the timing and the policy involved in Clinton's executive order, understandably viewing it as a strictly political move.

The institutional model of government that Mayer spells out in the first two chapters of this book lead him to predict that as society continues to grow in complexity, it will undergo a gradual increase in presidential power. The speed with which events frequently happen in modern society often leave little time for the notoriously slow wheels of legislative action to arrive at feasible solutions for many critical problems. Mayer implies that the very nature of contemporary society, for many eminently practical reasons, leads inevitably to the usurpation of individual rights and of constitutional guarantees.

He writes, "The president occupies an office beset by contradictory impulses, or ambivalence (to use Harvey Mansfield's term): The occupant 'innovates and imitates' at the same time that he seeks to portray himself as merely an agent of the popular will, 'now subordinate, now independent.'" Regardless of how powerful an office the presidency is, in the final analysis, presidents serve at the pleasure of the electorate, so they must constantly be conscious of how their actions will affect the public will.

When new presidents take office, particularly if they are of a different party from their predecessors, they often issue a flood of executive orders during their first weeks on the job in an effort to distance themselves from the preceding administration. In the second week of his term, Bill Clinton issued Executive Order 12836, which revoked two executive orders, unpopular with labor unions, that George Bush had issued earlier. This is a clear case of using executive privilege for purely political reasons, but it is a widespread practice of both parties.

During his last few months in office, Gerald Ford issued a number of executive orders without going through the usual channels. Typically, all such orders are cleared by both the Office of Management and Budget and by the Office of Legal Counsel in the Department of Justice. Ford bypassed this established protocol. His order to pardon the former president, Richard Nixon, was highly controversial and cast suspicion upon Ford's motives, although his act has since been perceived as a courageous move that was necessary to heal a nation that had been grievously divided over Watergate, the ensuing hearings, and finally President Nixon's resignation.

Presidents may well resort to chicanery in the issuance of executive orders designed to achieve their ends but contrary to established policies. Mayer cites as an example how Harry S. Truman, shortly after the end of World War II, paved the way for the establishment of the Central Intelligence Agency (CIA). During World War II, intelligence activities rested in the Office of Strategic Services (OSS). William Donovan, coordinator of information since July 1941, pressed for the establishment of an independent intelligence agency that would not come under the control of any agency or military department but would have a direct line of communication with the Executive Office of the President. In November, 1944, Donovan drafted an executive order for Franklin Roosevelt to consider. When the president died in April, 1945, the OSS still existed and the agency for which Donovan was pressing had not yet been established.

President Truman issued an executive order in September, 1945, abolishing the OSS and dividing its responsibilities between the Departments of State and War. By

January, 1946, Truman had established by executive order the Central Intelligence Group (CIG), which had representatives from the Departments of State, War, and Navy and was headed by a director appointed by the president. Truman had to be very careful about the semantics of this executive order "to get around legislative restrictions on funding independent executive branch agencies in the absence of legislative authorization." By designating the new office a group rather than an agency, Truman assured that his executive order fell within the letter of the law.

Mayer has rendered a valuable service in writing this book, which is carefully documented. It has a serviceable index and, although it does not have a bibliography, the extensive notes will lead scholars to relevant sources that will aid their research.

R. Baird Shuman

Sources for Further Study

Choice 39 (December, 2001): 761.
Presidential Studies Quarterly 31 (September, 2001): 547.

WITTGENSTEIN'S POKER
The Story of a Ten-Minute Argument Between
Two Great Philosophers

Authors: David Edmonds and John Eidinow
First published: 2001, in Great Britain
Publisher: Ecco Press/HarperCollins (New York). Illustrated. 340 pp. $24.00
Type of work: Biography and philosophy
Time: 1889-1994
Locale: Cambridge, England; Vienna

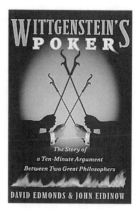

≈

The story of a clash of tempers—and temperaments— between Ludwig Wittgenstein and Karl Popper at Cambridge University in 1946 is skillfully expanded into an account of their lives and the philosophical milieus in which they flourished

≈

Principal personages:
> LUDWIG JOSEF JOHANN WITTGENSTEIN, engineer, village schoolmaster, mathematician, war hero, and regarded by many as one of the most brilliant philosophers who ever lived
> KARL RAIMUND POPPER, a believer in genuine philosophical problems who disputed Wittgenstein's sneering dismissal of philosophic1al questions as mere puzzles
> BERTRAND RUSSELL, eminent philosopher and mathematician who championed the early Wittgenstein but deplored the later one

The time was 8:30 in the evening of Friday, October 25, 1946. The place was a set of rooms in the Gibbs Building of Cambridge University. The occasion was the weekly meeting of the Cambridge Moral Science Club, gathered to hear a paper by Dr. Karl Popper on the topic, "Are There Philosophical Problems?" A program that would ordinarily, on most campuses and with most participants, provide a sedate evening of academic chatter exploded in a verbal firefight between two extraordinarily sharp thinkers, Popper and Ludwig Wittgenstein. The questions that remain today are what, exactly, was Wittgenstein's intent when he waved a poker taken from the fireplace, and what did Popper say to him and when did he say it.

The most prominent member of the audience was Bertrand Russell, who had supported Wittgenstein's early work but by the time of the meeting had lost faith in him. Wittgenstein found Russell "glib" and quick, but superficial. Russell lauded Popper's *The Open Society and Its Enemies* (1945) for its attack on Plato's political philosophy, but never quite reciprocated Popper's intense admiration for him. As much as

875

David Edmonds and John Eidinow are award-winning journalists with the BBC. This book, their first, has been translated into more than a dozen languages.

Popper wanted to demolish Wittgenstein in debate, he surely wanted to impress Russell at the same time. Indeed, it has been suggested that Russell instigated Popper's attack, but the evidence is slight.

Besides Russell, the thirty members present that night included Sir John Vinelott, one-time English High Court judge; Stephen Toulmin, who became a distinguished philosopher himself; Wasfi Hijab, the club secretary and one of Wittgenstein's most devoted disciples; Richard Braithwaite, who occupied H3, the meeting rooms at apartment 3, staircase H; Peter Munz, formerly a student of both Popper and Wittgenstein; Michael Wolff, who was to become a Victorian specialist; and Peter Geach, a postgraduate student married to a Wittgenstein follower, Elizabeth Anscombe. Reconciling their accounts is difficult.

Geach recalls Wittgenstein demanding of Popper, "Consider this poker," which he held up but soon dropped on the fireplace tiles. Braithwaite then spirited the poker away and Wittgenstein left with no ceremony. Wolff's memory is of Wittgenstein holding the poker absentmindedly before exchanging sharp words with Russell, who told him, "You're mixing things up, Wittgenstein. You always mix things up." Munz remembers Wittgenstein waving the poker—red-hot—in Popper's face and Russell barking, "Wittgenstein, put that poker down at once," at which point Wittgenstein obeyed Russell and stalked out slamming the door. Toulmin recollects only that Wittgenstein picked up the poker to illustrate a point about causation and later left quietly. But as Popper has told the story, Wittgenstein was waving the poker and demanding an example of a moral principle, prompting Popper to reply, "Not to threaten visiting lecturers with pokers," at which retort Wittgenstein hurled the poker into the fireplace and slammed the door on his way out. Others say that Popper uttered this statement of principle only after Wittgenstein's departure. Vinelott suggests that Popper was merely joking and that Wittgenstein left—with no slamming of doors—out of contempt for Popper's facetiousness. There are other differences in details, but on the key question of which came first, Popper's remark or Wittgenstein's departure, Geach insists that Popper just plain lied and that Wittgenstein left the meeting before Popper's quip.

Understanding this bizarre incident requires some knowledge of what brought these two intense Vienna-born assimilated Jewish intellectuals together at Cambridge University, and of the philosophical currents that bore them to prominence.

Wittgenstein was born April 26, 1889, the eighth and last child of the Austrian millionaire industrialist Karl Wittgenstein and his wife Leopoldine, née Kalmus. After completing his early schooling at Linz in 1906, Wittgenstein studied engineering for two years in Berlin before moving to Manchester University, where he read Bertrand Russell and Alfred North Whitehead's *Principia Mathematica* (3 vols., 1910-1913). In 1911, Wittgenstein introduced himself to Russell, astonishing the philosopher with his brash genius, and in 1912 entered Trinity College, Cambridge. In August, 1914,

Wittgenstein joined the Austro-Hungarian army and, after recovering from a wound in an artillery workshop, volunteered for front-line duty in Galicia, Bukovina, and Italy, where he was awarded the Distinguished Military Service Medal with Swords before becoming a prisoner of war in 1918. During these hectic years, Wittgenstein finished his first work, the *Tractatus Logico-Philosophicus*, finally published in 1922, by which time Wittgenstein had given his inherited fortune to his sisters, begun teaching in rural schools, and undertaken a 5,700-word dictionary for schoolchildren.

Wittgenstein renewed his philosophical pursuits in 1927, when he met Moritz Schlick and several other members of the Vienna Circle of logical positivists; and in 1929, after becoming engrossed in studying the foundations of mathematics, he received the Ph.D. from Cambridge University for his *Tractatus*. Through the 1930's, Wittgenstein divided his time between Cambridge and Norway, became professor of philosophy at Cambridge in 1939, and assumed the chairmanship of the Moral Science Club in 1944 before resigning his professorship in 1947. After final visits to Vienna and Norway, Wittgenstein returned to Cambridge and died of cancer in 1951.

Born in Vienna on July 28, 1902, to the lawyer Dr. Simon Popper and his wife Jenny, née Schiff, Popper was no war hero and he had none of the astonishing power to bewitch people that came naturally to Wittgenstein. (John Maynard Keynes said of Wittgenstein, "God has arrived. I met him on the 5:15 train.") Nevertheless, Popper was an intimidating intellectual presence himself, a Viennese Jew like Wittgenstein and subject to many of the same influences. Popper entered the University of Vienna in 1918 as a nonmatriculated student, studied at the Vienna Conservatoire, apprenticed himself to a cabinetmaker for two years (1922-1924), taught briefly in a primary school, and in 1928 completed his doctorate in the history of music, philosophy, and psychology.

Popper's own introduction to the Vienna Circle came in 1929, and with Herbert Feigl's support he worked on what became *The Logic of Scientific Discovery* (1934). In 1930, he married Josefine Anna Henninger and began teaching in secondary school. On leave in 1935-1936, Popper twice visited England, where he met a constellation of star philosophers and gave his first paper at the Cambridge Moral Science Club. In 1937, he accepted a position at Canterbury University College, Christchurch, New Zealand and began two important books, *The Poverty of Historicism* (1944) and *The Open Society and Its Enemies*. Popper returned to England in 1946, was granted British citizenship that same year, and became professor of logic and scientific method at the London School of Economics in 1949. Popper was knighted in 1965 and continued to write almost till his death in London in 1994.

Both Wittgenstein and Popper had significant ties to the Vienna Circle of logical positivists. This group, upward of twenty members, included Moritz Schlick, a scientist trained under Max Planck; Rudolf Carnap, a logician; and the mathematician Kurt Gödel, whose theorems unsettled the foundations of Russell and Alfred North Whitehead's *Principia Mathematica*. These brilliant academics met in weekly gatherings and were sometimes joined by such visitors from abroad as A. J. Ayer from Britain, whose *Language, Truth, and Logic* (1936) remains the best-known product of the Circle's lucubrations. The members were united by their conviction that the free-ranging speculations of German idealism identified with Immanuel Kant and Georg Wilhelm Friedrich Hegel should be subordinated to the scientific method. The Viennese judged Kant and Hegel's metaphysics "a combination of obfuscation, mumbo jumbo, and muddleheadedness," say Edmonds and Eidinow, who quote Gilbert Ryle on philosophy in Austria and Cambridge: "Philosophy was regarded in Vienna as a blood-sucking parasite, in England as a medicinal leech."

Wittgenstein's opinion of metaphysics emerges in his remark: "Reading the Socratic dialogues one has the feeling: What a frightful waste of time!" This dismissal of Plato helps explain why, for the Viennese, Wittgenstein would come to be "a deity to them all," in Ayer's words, and why the Circle offered him a membership, which he rejected although he met occasionally with Schlick and several others in 1927. Wittgenstein had argued in the *Tractatus* that mathematical proofs and analytic statements were tautologies that advance no new knowledge, and he had proclaimed— famously, as it turned out—that we must not speak of what we do not know. The Vienna Circle took all this to heart and assumed the appellation of logical positivists from their conviction that all meaningful statements must be analytic (assertions such as "a bachelor is an unmarried man") or capable of empirical verification. Edmonds and Eidinow point out, however, that "what many in the Circle misunderstood was that Wittgenstein did not believe that the unsayable should be condemned as nonsense. On the contrary, the things we could not talk about were those that really mattered." For whatever reason, Wittgenstein chose to keep a safe distance from his Circle admirers.

For Popper, though, the Circle was one he would gladly have joined had he been invited, but as it turned out he was dubbed by one of the members, Otto Neurath, the "official opposition." Popper's exclusion came, say Edmonds and Eidinow, from Schlick's anger at Popper for having attacked Schlick's hero Wittgenstein at a meeting of the so-called Gomperz Circle in 1932. Schlick had been on Popper's dissertation committee, and he edited the series in which Popper hoped to publish his first book, but Popper's pugnacity prohibited any restraint in his blistering contempt for Wittgenstein's orphic pronouncements. Beyond the contretemps over Wittgenstein, however, Popper destroyed the logic of the Circle's fundamental premise that knowledge could be indubitably advanced by empirical observation. Like David Hume two centuries earlier, Popper challenged the certainty of inductive reasoning, and he demonstrated that the Circle's verifiability principle was itself not open to proof by observation. In its place, Popper substituted his own principle of "falsification"—that is, if it is impossible to test a theory, then it is not a scientific theory.

Russell's contemplation of statements such as "The King of France is bald" had led to his Theory of Descriptions, in which he demonstrated by analysis that the absurdity of such statements lay in their false premises. Wittgenstein's *Tractatus* employed a similar method of logical atomism to derive his picture theory of language— that facts and propositions somehow present true pictures of the world. However, the Wittgenstein of the poker incident had come to see language as a tool that individuals can use as they please, with the consequence that there is no private language, only a public language governed by rules of our own devising. Descartes's famous "*Cogito ergo sum*," for instance, loses its significance for not being supported by a universal definition of thought, and it follows that in straining for generalizations that explain philosophical problems, philosophers are chasing a will-o'-the-wisp. The problems of philosophy are puzzles, not problems, mere conundrums produced by the use of language. Wittgenstein's famous metaphor for the value of philosophy was "to show the fly the way out of the fly bottle," and even he conceded that as, human language users, we cannot always escape the fly bottle.

So this was the Wittgenstein that Popper was intent on debunking that evening in H3. Popper certainly thought there were many problems for philosophers to contend with, the enemies of an open society, for instance. These philosophical differences nonetheless are far from the whole story about Popper's contempt for Wittgenstein, for there are understandable human motives for Popper's attitude. Both were assimilated Viennese Jews, but they did not come from quite the same side of the tracks. Whereas Wittgenstein came from an enormously wealthy family that was able to buy its way out of the camps, Popper was forced to leave Austria for New Zealand in 1937. Wittgenstein's seemingly privileged life must have been intolerable for Popper to witness, and how much more painful it must have been for Popper in his last years to see his own reputation among the giants fading while Wittgenstein was still commonly being ranked close to Aristotle, Plato, and Kant.

Frank Day

Sources for Further Study

Booklist 98 (October 1, 2001): 270.
The New York Times Book Review 106 (December 30, 2001): 10.
Publishers Weekly 248 (October 1, 2001): 45.
Time 158 (November 19, 2001): 141.

THE WORLD BELOW

Author: Sue Miller (1943-   )
Publisher: Alfred A. Knopf (New York). 275 pp. $25.00
Type of work: Novel
Time: The early 1900's and the late twentieth centuy to
  2000
Locale: Maine, Vermont, and California

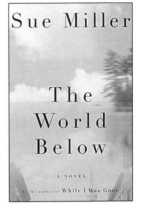

∼

*Miller's stories of two women, grandmother and grand-
daughter, reveal parallels and differences in the women's
lives and poignantly demonstrate the past as prologue, always influencing that which comes after*

∼

Principal characters:
> GEORGIA RICE, a young woman in Maine in 1919 when she is sent away
> to the Bryce Sanatorium to recover from tuberculosis, six months that
> change her life
> CATHERINE "CATH" HUBBARD, Georgia's granddaughter, who, after two
> failed marriages in California, returns to the old house in Vermont
> where her grandparents lived
> SEWARD WALLACE, a young man in the sanatorium who becomes Geor-
> gia's first lover
> JOHN HOLBROOKE, Georgia's husband, a country doctor several years
> her senior
> PETER, Catherine's first husband and father of her three children, Karen,
> Jeff, and Fiona
> JOE, Catherine's second husband, who leaves her to marry Edie
> RUE RICE, Catherine's aunt, who wills her parents' house in Vermont to
> Catherine and her brother Lawrence
> SAMUEL ELIASSON, a widower Catherine meets when she goes back to
> Vermont
> JESSIE, Catherine's first grandchild, born prematurely

In the present of the novel, at the end of the twentieth century, Catherine Hubbard
is a fifty-two-year-old mother of three grown children. Only the oldest, Karen, lives
anywhere close by. Twice-divorced and at loose ends when she learns that she and her
brother Lawrence have inherited their grandparents' house, Catherine leaves San
Francisco to go back to the territory of her childhood, specifically to the old house in
West Barstow, Vermont, where her grandparents lived for many years.

Catherine is unclear whether this is an escape from her old life in urban California
or the making of a new life in small-town New England. Truly, she risks little by making this change, taking a leave of absence from her job and hedging about how long

she will stay. Ultimately the novel portrays little change in her, although she has had an engrossing few months learning more about her decidedly interesting grandmother, Georgia.

When Georgia is still a teenager, her mother dies after a long and painful struggle against cancer, leaving Georgia, the eldest daughter, in charge of the household. Her father is a hardware salesman gone from home five days a week. Georgia feels isolated but content with her role. Suddenly, the family doctor, John Holbrooke, pronounces that she has tuberculosis and sends her to a sanatorium to recover. Later, after Dr. Holbrooke and Georgia marry, he admits that she may not have had the disease after all, but that he thought she was stifling in her family situation.

Sue Miller is the best-selling author of several novels, including While I Was Gone *(1999),* The Distinguished Guest *(1995),* For Love *(1993),* Family Pictures *(1990), and* The Good Mother *(1986).*

Georgia has "secrets" to reveal to her husband as well. In the "san," she became aware of patients sneaking around for sexual encounters, and soon she and Seward Wallace, who at seventeen is three years her junior, are going into the woods or a shed to make love. The sexual encounters are exciting but not very satisfactory for her. Seward urges her to run away with him to Denver, or anywhere, to marry and be free from the restrictions of the "san." Georgia is flattered by his need for her, but she intuits that he is dying and she knows she does not love him in the same way he loves her. She tells him she must stay in the "san" and get well. He leaves, and not long afterward she returns home, where her father is about to marry a local widow. Dr. Holbrooke promptly asks Georgia to marry him. Before she accepts, she confesses that she is "damaged goods," which he interprets as a reference to her tuberculosis. When he later learns she meant her sexual liaison with Seward, it takes him some time to recover. Later, when she is eight months pregnant with their first child, she learns from Seward's sisters that he has died and that they want to bring his body back to Vermont for burial. Georgia secretly tucks away money she gets from her husband and sends them the money they need for this, and on her own she drives John's car to Seward's dismal funeral in the rain. Afterward, she reports this to John, which again stirs his jealousy. Despite all this, they reach a level of mutual acceptance and have a long and relatively happy marriage. He precedes her in death by several decades, and she lives on until age eighty-eight, apparently content.

Catherine pieces together bits about her grandmother's life from diaries that Georgia had kept meticulously over the years, diaries Catherine finds in a trunk in the attic of the old house. This gathering of a life preoccupies Catherine for the few months she lives there. It becomes her mission to understand both the grandmother and the grandfather that she had loved.

Catherine had lived with Georgia and John for a while after her mother was taken to a psychiatric hospital, and she credits them with kindness and attention to her needs. They were the ones who urged her to spend a summer in Paris with their daughter Rue, giving Catherine an excuse to break away from the high school boy with whom she was having an unsatisfactory sexual affair. Years later, divorced from her first husband, Peter, she brings her three children across the country to Vermont to her grandparents' house for a few months of that same comfort and sense of stability she had found there as a teenager.

Georgia's diaries are factual but neither detailed nor informative about how Georgia felt about the events she records. Thus, much of the story of her life is interpreted and indeed invented by Catherine. Sometimes Catherine is the first-person narrator speaking of Georgia's life, and at other times Georgia's life is written from a third person omniscient point of view.

Interspersed with the sections focusing on Georgia are details from Catherine's own life, past and present. Often what she is learning and thinking about her grandmother leads her to comment about her own history. Both had mothers who were felt as "absent" except for their very tangible presence as victims of lingering illness. Both mothers died when their daughters were teenagers. Their fathers were likewise "absent," although dictatorial when present. When Georgia's mother died, her grandmother wanted to take and raise the children, but their father would not let her; when Catherine's mother committed suicide, Grandmother Georgia did take care of Catherine and her brother. Both girls as teenagers saw these changes after the deaths of their mothers as the beginning of their own maturation. Each of them, while still young, had a premarital and sexually unsatisfactory love affair, Georgia without guilt despite the restrictive mores of 1919, Catherine feeling pressured into it because of the permissive attitudes of the 1960's. Problems that arose in Georgia's marriage were eventually resolved and the marriage remained intact. Catherine and her first husband divorced when he became disillusioned with family burdens. Her second, Joe, had enjoyed his niche as stepfather in a bustling and noisy household, but when the children grew up and left home he soon left Catherine to marry Edie, who had young children.

Catherine almost starts a romantic relationship in Vermont with Samuel Eliasson, a retired professor who had been renting her grandparents' house and had lived there with his wife until she died. What ends that possibility for Catherine is Samuel's insistence that she is wrong about something she remembers seeing long ago. When Catherine was sixteen, she and her grandfather had been out in a small fishing boat. Below the surface of the lake she saw buildings, eerie ghost houses and streets, what had been a town now flooded over. Samuel is currently researching the very subject of the demise of the small town in New England. He insists that when dams were built, all the villages that were to be covered with water were completely torn down and even bodies from the cemeteries moved before the flooding occurred. Catherine knows what she had seen. The fact that later Samuel admits that he had been wrong, that he has learned that the houses and buildings in one village were indeed flooded over, is of no use to Catherine except for restoring her pride. By that time she is back in San Francisco. Her daughter Karen's first child, Jessie, was born very prematurely and is likely to be kept in the hospital for many weeks. Catherine had been ready to leave Vermont, and now she feels needed by her daughter and son-in-law Robert.

The image of that submerged village gives the novel its title. To Catherine it had represented the hidden mystery of lives past, just as later she tries to understand her grandmother's life by finding the depths under the surfaces recorded in the diaries. The village was the literal image of something "Grand, somehow" because "it was gone forever but still visible, still imaginable, below us. . . . Sad and beautiful too. . . . the lostness of the world down there, the otherness of it. It was like being able to look at memory itself." Catherine thinks at the time, "I felt a kind of yearning for everything past, everything already gone in my life."

The feeling of things already gone that Catherine experienced at age sixteen has become the dominant motif of her quest at age fifty-two to understand the past and its influence on the present. It shapes her acceptance of the uncertainty of baby Jessie's situation: "It's all too unknown anyway, what becomes of one's children. What *we* become, for that matter. . . . it doesn't seem any harder to me not to know about Jessie than not to know what will happen to each of [my children]."

The novel, filled with shifts, seems choppy at times with its tales from two eras. No matter which one of the two women's lives is being traced, it is hard not to be impatient for more revelations about the other one. Especially, the reader wants to know more about Georgia. Perhaps this is inevitable since Catherine yearns to know more about her, too. Maybe Catherine can dramatize and portray her grandmother's life more easily than her own precisely because Georgia's is fixed in the past and has a known end. In any case, the language sparkles most in the sections about Georgia, whether told by Catherine or by the third-person narrator.

A notable strength of the novel, and a true tribute to memory, is the particularity of details: Georgia setting the spark and throttle before the car is cranked to start the engine; Karen setting the automatic timer, then dashing to join the rest of the family as they "stood in the horizontal late-day light and squinted at the camera"; Catherine emptying a medicine cabinet, "throwing away the Mercurochrome I found there, the rusted bobby pins in a little cup, the ancient-looking bottle of aspirin."

The written word, arguably more than any other artifact, is a key to holding memories of the past. Sue Miller's words remind readers of the importance of the past and its impermanence, simultaneously speaking of "lostness" and endless continuity. Catherine's new little granddaughter will be shaped not only by the inherited genes of numberless generations, but by what she learns about that past, how she learns to see herself in that flow of continuity. Yet as Catherine muses, "But what lasts, after all? What stays the same through the generations? Boundaries shift, refugees die or flee with what they can carry, the waters slowly fill in behind the dams, and what was once there is lost forever, except in dreams and memories."

Lois A. Marchino

Sources for Further Study

Kirkus Reviews 69 (August 15, 2001): 1156.
Library Journal 126 (September 14, 2001): 114.

A WORLD MADE NEW
Eleanor Roosevelt and the Universal Declaration of Human Rights

Author: Mary Ann Glendon (1938-   )
Publisher: Random House (New York). 333 pp. $25.95
Type of work: History and law
Time: 1945-1948
Locale: New York, London, Paris, Geneva, Washington D.C., and elsewhere

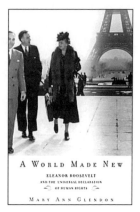

∾

A narrative account of how Eleanor Roosevelt chaired and inspired the committee of the United Nations that drafted the Universal Declaration of Human Rights (UDHR) and then successfully achieved its adoption by the General Assembly

∾

Principal personages:
> ELEANOR ROOSEVELT, former first lady who effectively chaired the Human Rights Commission
> RENÉ CASSIN, French jurist who organized and drafted much of the final version of the Universal Declaration of Human Rights
> CHARLES MALIK, Lebanese philosopher who had considerable influence in its formation
> PENG-CHUN CHANG, Chinese philosopher who also exercised great influence
> JOHN HUMPHREY, United Nations official from Canada who wrote the first rough draft of the document
> ALEXEI PAVLOV, Soviet delegate who attempted to make it reflect the Marxist-Leninist viewpoint
> HARRY S. TRUMAN, United States president who appointed Mrs. Roosevelt as delegate to the United Nations

Since its adoption by the United Nations (U.N.) General Assembly in 1948, the Universal Declaration of Human Rights (UDHR) has often served as an inspiration and as a standard for judging the extent to which the governments of the world have upheld the rights, liberties, and fundamental needs of their citizens. Students of international relations disagree about how effective the instrument has been. Critics, on one hand, can point to countless violations of its provisions, and they ask whether it is really helpful to say that governments should not do the terrible things that they, in fact, continue to do. Supporters of the document, however, contend that the UDHR has gradually had an impact on public expectations, and that, in any case, the option of an enforcement mechanism was an impossible dream in the period just after World War II.

Professor Mary Ann Glendon has written a fascinating and important story about the small group of persons who had primary responsibility for writing and winning the adoption of the UDHR. Her book *A World Made New* should become the definitive work on the topic. Glendon has a wonderful ability to describe individual personalities, their ideas, and their actions. In addition to revealing previously unknown details, she has demonstrated a keen eye for interesting and revealing anecdotes. Examples include the occasional pettiness of outstanding diplomats and Mrs. Roosevelt's almost complete indifference to food. While explaining the origins of the UDHR, Glendon also provides insight into other important things that were happening at the time, including the beginning of the Cold War and the creation of the new state of Israel.

Mary Ann Glendon is a professor of law at Harvard University. She was the first woman to lead a Vatican delegation to an international conference, and has been featured on Bill Moyer's World of Ideas. *She is author of many award-winning books, including* Abortion and Divorce in Western Law *(1987),* The Transformation of Family Law *(1989),* Rights Talk *(1991), and* A Nation Under Lawyers *(1994).*

Although she clearly admires Eleanor Roosevelt and believes that the UDHR was a good thing, she maintains a centrist point of view and avoids excessive polemics. To the left-wing critics who charge that the UDHR defends only Western and capitalistic values, she points out that non-Western diplomats were actively involved in its formation, and that non-Western countries have sometimes been among its most outspoken proponents. To right-wing critics who assert that the document was inspired by communist ideology, she emphasizes that the Soviet Union and other Eastern-bloc countries abstained in the final voting on the document. Some American conservatives, nevertheless, will take notice of Glendon's observation that the Anglo-American individualistic tradition had less influence on the final document than did the "dignitarian rights tradition" of continental Europe and Latin America, which generally envisioned rights within the context of the family and citizens' duties.

A World Made New is based upon a prodigious amount of research in both published and unpublished sources. Almost fifty pages of documentary notes reveal that Glendon utilized the diaries, letters, interviews, and memoirs of the participants, including her exclusive access to the papers of Lebanese philosopher Charles Malik. She made abundant use of the United Nations archives, including verbatim transcripts of the meetings of Roosevelt's committee. Glendon was also able to find a great deal of interesting information in the archives of the Soviet Politburo that were becoming declassified at about the same time that she was doing her research. Finally, she obtained considerable help from the large number of secondary works, such as the numerous books by Joseph Lash on Eleanor Roosevelt and John Humphrey's earlier history of the UDHR and its influence.

Glendon begins the story with the creation of the United Nations toward the end of World War II. Although Franklin Roosevelt had favored a general reference to human rights in the Dumbarton Oaks meeting, his emphasis was on trying to prevent the international aggression of countries. At the end of the war, the United States and several countries modified their policies with the revelations of the Holocaust and other Nazi atrocities. In its final form, as completed in the San Francisco Conference on June 26, 1945, the United Nations Charter reaffirmed the important of human rights, the dignity of the individual person, and the concept of equality in three separate places, but the Charter did not provide any additional guidance about the nature of the rights and liberties that were to be protected, and one of the key clauses of the Charter stipulated that the United Nations would not intervene "in matters which are essentially within the domestic jurisdiction of any State." President Harry S. Truman nevertheless said that he looked forward to the framing of an "International Bill of Rights."

Shortly after the San Francisco Conference, President Truman appointed Eleanor Roosevelt as a member of the U.S. delegation to the United Nations. Despite her lack of experience in international affairs, Truman wanted to keep the prestige of the Roosevelt name with his administration, and he was keenly aware of Eleanor Roosevelt's longstanding commitments to humanitarian reforms and social equality. In January, 1946, at the first meeting of the General Assembly in London, her hard work and quickness in grasping technical material made a very favorable impression on the other delegates. In June, 1946, therefore, she was selected to be the American representative to the newly formed Commission on Human Rights, which had the initial task of putting together an international bill of rights. When the commission held its first meeting in January, 1947, Roosevelt, because of her enormous prestige, was unanimously elected the chairperson.

Glendon shows that the representatives to the commission included several remarkable personalities. The four persons most responsible for the drafting of the UDHR were René Cassin, who had been chief legal counsel in Charles de Gaulle's resistance; Peng-chun Chang, a Renaissance man with extensive knowledge of Asian traditions; Charles Malik, a professional philosopher from the Middle East; and John Humphrey, the hard-working director of the Human Rights division of the United Nations. Other significant participants included Carlos Romulo, a fiery anticolonialist from the Philippines; Hansa Mehta of India, who insisted on highlighting the rights of women; and Alexei Pavlov of the Soviet Union, who unsuccessfully tried to convince the other representatives to minimize the notion that individual citizens have rights contradictory to the interests of socialist governments.

One of the commission's most important decisions was to formulate a nonbinding bill of rights at the same time that it worked on legally binding conventions. Eleanor Roosevelt strongly supported this decision. Remembering the U.S. Senate's earlier refusal to approve American participation in the League of Nations, she advocated a cautious, step-by-step approach. Endorsing the wisdom of this approach, Glendon observes that the two binding conventions—one devoted to political and civil rights, the other to economic and social rights—were completed only in 1966, and that it took another ten years for them to actually go into effect. Even then, individual countries had to agree to follow the conditions of the treaties, and many have refused to do so.

As chairperson, Roosevelt did not do much of the actual drafting of the UDHR. Glendon makes it clear, nevertheless, that her work was vitally important to the success of the commission. She kept the project moving and was able to work toward consensus and compromise. With her particular vision of New Deal liberalism, she was able to help the members arrive at a synthesis between the Anglo-American tradition, emphasizing individual freedom, and the welfare-state paradigm, which asserts that governments have some positive obligations for meeting the needs of citizens. Glendon notes that Roosevelt had to spend considerable time convincing American officials to accept as much of the welfare-state concept as they did.

Humphrey and Cassin, in their later writings, sometimes made contradictory statements about who wrote the first draft of the Universal Declaration, which has led to considerable confusion. Based on U.N. records, Glendon finds that Humphrey did the research and drafting of the first draft, listing the rights that had been recognized in a large variety of traditions. Cassin, who had much experience as a legal draftsman, then used Humphrey's draft as a foundation for a more elegant and logically organized document, so that it could be called a declaration rather than a bill of rights.

On December 10, 1948, the General Assembly approved the UDHR, with forty-eight countries voting their approval, eight abstentions, and none opposed. Among those abstaining, South Africa was unwilling to accept the idea of racial equality, Saudi Arabia strongly rejected the idea that people had a right to change their religion, and the Soviet Union and several Eastern European countries refused to recognize many principles in the document, especially the rights to emigrate and to express ideas considered hostile to workers' interests. A number of countries voted against the inclusion of particular items. Most of the Muslim countries, for instance, disagreed with the idea of gender equality in marriage. Glendon recognizes that all of the voting representatives knew that the United Nations Charter specified that the organization would not have the authority to intervene in the domestic affairs of the member countries. If the Universal Declaration had threatened to substantially limit national sovereignty, it simply would not have been approved by the General Assembly, at least not in 1948.

In spite of the many reservations and disagreements, Glendon writes: "Where basic human values are concerned, cultural diversity has been exaggerated." Thus, she strongly disagrees with those who assert that the UDHR is an illegitimate attempt to impose Western values on other cultural traditions. She notes that Roosevelt's committee discovered in its research "that a core of fundamental principles was widely shared in countries that had not yet adopted rights instruments." Although different cultures strongly disagreed about foundational theories, the committee discovered general agreement that certain practices, such as mass murder and denial of due process, are "so terrible in practice that no one will publicly approve them." Endorsing this perspective, Glendon quotes a statement by Daniel Lev: "The idea of universal human rights shares the recognition of one common humanity, and provides a minimum solution to deal with its miseries."

Glendon probably minimizes the importance of cultural differences in regard to the rights asserted in the UDHR. The country with the largest population in the world, China, for instance, has never had a tradition of tolerating meaningful dissent from official policies, and numerous countries of the Middle East are religiously opposed to allowing freedom for religious dissidents. To some extent, it depends on whether one looks at the people in power or the victims of oppression. Certainly all oppressed people would like to enjoy freedom and equality. If and when these oppressed people gain power, unfortunately, they are frequently unwilling to give other people the rights and liberties that they demanded for themselves. The cycle continues.

Although the UDHR provides aspirational guidelines rather than legally binding obligations, Glendon is convinced that it has helped make the world a better place. Like Eleanor Roosevelt, she expresses faith in the long-term effects of education and public opinion. Although admitting that progress has been painfully slow, Glendon finds that the Declaration helped promote several progressive changes during the second half of the twentieth century, including the end of Jim Crow laws in the American South, the framing of the Helsinki Accords of 1975, and the end of apartheid in South Africa. She finds, moreover, that institutional guarantees of free expression and trials based on due process are more prevalent than in any earlier time in history. Yet atrocious violations of human rights continue. Glendon is among those who prefer to look upon the glass as half full rather than half empty.

Thomas Tandy Lewis

Sources for Further Study

America 184 (June 18, 2001): 26.
Booklist 97 (March 1, 2001): 1221.
First Things 114 (June/July, 2001): 43.
Foreign Affairs 80 (September/October, 2001): 55.
The New York Review of Books 48 (April 26, 2001): 32.
Publishers Weekly 247 (December 11, 2001): 69.

YELLOW
Stories

Author: Don Lee (1959-   )
Publisher: W. W. Norton (New York). 255 pp. $22.95
Type of work: Short fiction
Time: The 1970's to the 1990's
Locale: California, Japan, and Boston

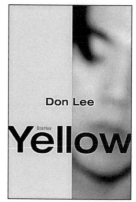

~

The lives and loves of several Asian Americans (mostly Korean American men) from a predominantly white California small town

~

Principal characters:
  DEAN KANESHIRO, furniture maker
  HANK LOW KWON, public defender
  ALAN FUJITANI, boat owner
  ANNIE YUNG, computer programmer
  PATRICK FENNY, high school student
  DUNCAN ROH, philanderer
  EUGENE KIM, oncologist
  DANNY KIM, management consultant

Don Lee's first book, *Yellow: Stories*, presents an engrossing collection of psychologically intricate characters realized in a supple, elegant prose and woven into intriguing plots spiced with suspense and irony. The action and protagonists of these eight stories are located or originate in Rosarita Bay, a small town on the seacoast south of San Francisco. (Although the name Rosarita Bay is fictional, the town is recognizably Half Moon Bay.) *Yellow*, then, is a short story cycle (or composite novel) like Amy Tan's *The Joy Luck Club* (1989) and Louise Erdrich's *Love Medicine* (1984). However, by having location as a unifying device, *Yellow* is more like *Winesburg, Ohio* (1919), by Sherwood Anderson, and *Dubliners* (1914), by James Joyce. Indeed, like Joyce and Erdrich, whose protagonists are of specific ethnic groups, Lee's protagonists in these stories are all Asian Americans—even though some were originally non-Asian when the stories first appeared in periodicals. Just as *Dubliners* departs from the norm by closing with the novella-length classic "The Dead," so *Yellow* closes with the ambitious novella-length "Yellow."

Lee's volume leads off with "The Price of Eggs in China," a lighthearted yet uneasy courtship tale involving a triangle of Asian Americans that also includes racial stereotyping, deception, criminality, and aesthetics. Dean Kaneshiro, a Japanese American, is a consummate artist of furniture making. At age thirty-eight he already

Don Lee's stories have appeared in many periodicals, and he has held fellowships from St. Botolph Club and Massachusetts Cultural Council. He has edited the literary journal Ploughshares *for more than a decade. A third-generation Korean American, his father was a State Department officer. Lee attended the University of California, Los Angeles, and Emerson College.*

has a chair collected by the New York Museum of Modern Art. His techniques and materials originate in the vanished pre-Meiji Japan. Eschewing nails and glue, he aspires to a Zen experience in furniture making. Dean is in love with unsuccessful poet Caroline Yip, to whom an insensitive reviewer has attached the ethnic slur of "Oriental Hair Poet No.1." Her arch rival in love and art is successful Marcella Ahn, reviewed as "Oriental Hair Poet No.2." (By this enumeration of the women, Lee not only mocks the ethnic stereotyping that the literary establishment falls into but also reminds his reader of the sorry history of Asian polygyny.) No. 2 has ordered a chair from Dean. As Dean sizes up No. 2's buttocks for his work, Don Lee provides a sample of his own piquant, crisp, tongue-in-cheek prose: "He squatted and stared at it for a full ten seconds. It was a good butt, a firm, StairMastered butt, a shapely, surprisingly protuberant butt." No. 1 becomes jealous of No. 2. To secure No. 1's love, Dean (a mystery novel buff) frames No. 2 by perpetrating an elaborate crime on his collection of precious wood. Although all ends well enough, Lee's intricate plot leaves Dean ironically unsure whether No.1 did not also frame No. 2 in such a way as to manipulate Dean into carrying out his framing scheme. In this wittily plotted, lighthearted, and elegantly told tale, love indeed triumphs, though deception must be practiced and the artist must sacrifice the material, if not the form, of his art.

The second story, "Voir Dire," strikes a considerably more somber note. Hank Low Kwon is an idealistic public defender in the uncomfortable position of defending a cocaine-addicted child killer. Hank's lawyer ex-wife, a Kuppie (Korean yuppie), scorns his idealism. His current girlfriend, Molly, is a blonde Amazon surfer and diving instructor able to floor Hank with a friendly punch, who announces that she is pregnant. Hank had wanted a child with his ex-wife, who preferred professional success instead. He is unsure he wants a child with Molly, whose biological clock is ticking away at thirty-five. He feels as co-opted in love as in work. In the closing scene, Molly challenges him: "Admit it. You want this baby." When he protests feebly, she mounts the trampoline beside her bed "and bounded into the air. Her back was arched, arms swept out in a swan dive. She was coming right at him. He watched her, staying still. . . . Eventually, she would crush him."

These first two stories portray men in relationships where they are controlled or manipulated by women. Variants of this dynamic recur in several other stories. In "Widowers," Alan Fujitani is a forty-something widower who has lost confidence in himself in any lasting relationship since his wife's death twenty years ago. He becomes acquainted with a strong-minded twenty-three-year-old widow, Emily. One evening, she urges him to go for a swim. In the ocean, Alan asks Emily to lie on her back so that he can buoy her shoulders. As she complies, "he could feel his doubts pass . . . he held her above the swells . . . as if nothing could ever disrupt their tender and elegant suspension." Yet as the reader knows, the man's feeling of confidence and strength is founded on delusion—for a woman floating on her back floats by herself. Alan is only being allowed by Emily to feel he supports her. Even in a story like "The Lone Night Cantina," where the protagonist is Annie Yung, a sympathetic woman cruising a cowboy bar, the man who is her objective turns out to be controlled by another woman, his recently dead wife. When Annie beds him, the hoped-for cowboy turns impotent, overcome by the guilt and uncertainty laid on by his wife's legacy of fifty thousand dollars.

Similarly, in "The Possible Husband," Duncan Roh is a successful forty-one-year-old restauranteur and roué who has racked up a hundred conquests (more or less), seemingly a confirmed philanderer impossible to imagine as being married. Indeed, his story is subdivided into four parts, each named after a season of the year, and each recounting his affair with a different woman, creating the impression that Duncan's exploits are a never-ending annual cycle. However, in the final episode, Duncan's love of surfing lures him into a bomb of a wave in which he is trapped and pummeled. The story ends as he starts to black out and hallucinates that he is describing the colors of the water to his current girlfriend, the painter Lily Kim, who thinks that all men are pigs. It is only two stories later that Lee offhandedly reveals Duncan's capitulation to marriage with Lily: Ironically, his near-death surfing experience has broken his seemingly endless cycle of philandering, only to result in marriage to a man-hater.

The only story which does not revolve around a man-woman relationship is "Casual Water," perhaps the most affecting piece in the book. Here the relationship is between two Amerasian boys and their well-meaning but ne'er-do-well golfer father. Their Filipina mother abandoned them eight years ago. Their father, who feels that he must leave his sons to take his last chance at the Professional Golfer's Association tour, deserts them. It is the summer when Patrick Fenny, the elder son, is eighteen and has been offered his dream of attending Annapolis, but Brian, who is eleven, faces the nightmare of foster homes if his brother leaves. The excruciating choices that father and sons make are handled by Lee with scrupulous fairness and penetrating empathy. The reader is relieved when Lee resolves their dilemma by showing the support available from Rosarita Bay's Asian American community.

Two other brothers are each the protagonists of the last two stories. In "Domo Arigato," Eugene Kim, a Korean American oncologist, catches sight of his former Stanford girlfriend, Nikki Keliher, in an airport lounge and reflects on his break-up with her twenty years ago. Nikki had taken him to meet her parents, then living in Japan, where her father was a Central Intelligence Agency officer. Whereas Eugene is drawn to Japan yet feels alien in it, Mr. Keliher knows things Japanese like aikido and sashimi fresh from a twitching fish, yet at the same time commits faux pas and pronounces that "the Japanese are the most duplicitous people I've ever known" (this from one whose profession is guile). During Eugene's visit, it becomes clear that his habitual circumspection is ill-suited to Nikki's energetic spontaneity. Nonetheless, when Nikki eventually breaks up with him, Eugene wonders how much of it was due to Nikki's spirit of spontaneity and how much to their racial difference—for Nikki's mother had cautioned him weeks before, "She's planning to break up with you. . . . [Marriage is] easier with someone your own kind." Lee seems to make a stinging indictment of the duplicity of race relations in America as Eugene assesses his present marriage to a black Asian American and parallels his town to Nagano: "They were happy in Rosarita Bay . . . not unlike that little mountain village in Japan. The people here were civil and polite . . . . Out of kindness, they never said what they meant. It didn't matter to Eugene what was really in their hearts, as long as they could live, side by side, in quiet disregard."

Unlike its companion stories, which focus on a relatively brief time span (a one-night stand, a year's philandering), "Yellow" stretches over more than twenty years. It might, in fact, be read as an account of the rise of an Asian American yuppie. Danny Kim (brother to characters in "Domo Arigato" and "The Possible Husband") is the protagonist of this novella. Perhaps more so than the other stories, it deals overtly with the stereotypes over which Asian American males stumble. It opens with a bedroom scene where one of Danny's white girlfriends belittles his "Oriental" manhood even after a night of good sex. It then flashes back to Danny's teen years when he takes up boxing to bulk up his physique and self-respect, but he becomes such a good fighter that he is overmatched in a championship bout and is then called "yellow" after being disqualified for butting his opponent. At the University of California at Los Angeles in the 1970's, despite his good looks, excellent grades, and flawless sexual performance, he is nagged by feelings of "self-loathing and doubt" exacerbated by racial incidents: He winces when another Asian sees him with a white girl and calls him a "banana" (an Asian who thinks him/herself white), he is shocked when a white girl turns him down for a date because of his race. He has a passionate affair with a white coed after winning her away from a French film director. After she introduces him to her Minnesota family, who obtusely address him as an immigrant or a refugee, Danny breaks up with her, accusing her rather unreasonably of not wanting his children. After going on to Harvard and completing an M.B.A., Danny finally dates an Asian American woman and marries her. He settles into a management consultancy firm in Boston. It is the 1980's, and anti-Asian sentiment is rising across America. By 1991, Danny has risen in his firm to the point where he is competing with a white colleague for a partnership. Overtaken by paranoia, Danny imagines racism everywhere and in every remark, and feels sure that his rival will prevail because of his race. To his astonishment, Danny is named partner. His rival, whose marriage is breaking up, attempts suicide in the Charles River, but Danny saves him after a suspenseful struggle. Ironically, the maneuver for which he was once called "yellow" now makes him a hero. More importantly, in saving his rival he breaks the stereotypes they both had of each other; Danny realizes his rival's fears and woes—his humanity, in short—and thereby Danny realizes his own humanity.

Lee's *Yellow* is an entertaining and thought-provoking read that opens a knowing and revealing window into the lives of middle-class Asian Americans. Realism is its mode. Lee's protagonists are not eponymous veterans of wars nor survivors of immigration odysseys. They tend to be average citizens, often hedonistic, mostly yuppie, sometimes the weaker links of humanity. Many are merely seeking to have a life. On that quest, some may accidentally stumble upon a meaning to life, and Don Lee tells this as it is.

C. L. Chua

Sources for Further Study

The Boston Globe, June 17, 2001, p. F5.
The Denver Post, May 20, 2001, p. I3.
The New York Times Book Review 106 (July 15, 2001): 6.

YONDER STANDS YOUR ORPHAN

Author: Barry Hannah (1942-   )
Publisher: Atlantic Monthly Press (New York). 336 pp.
  $24.00
Type of work: Novel
Time: The present
Locale: Points in and around Eagle Lake, Mississippi

≈

Truman Capote once called Hannah "the maddest writer in the USA," and in Yonder Stands Your Orphan, *Hannah delivers the goods: a novel of madness and mayhem that lives up to and even exceeds Capote's claim*

≈

Principal characters:

MAN MORTIMER, a pimp and gambler, the man around whom most of the events of the novel revolve

DEE ALISON, Mortimer's main love interest, a nurse and single mother of four

FRANK BOOTH, the man who, with Mortimer, shares an affection for Dee Allison

Yonder Stands Your Orphan, Barry Hannah's first novel in ten years, brings together a cast of Mississippi misfits who are, in Hannah's words, "orphans from normal." The novel is presided over by the king orphan himself, a man by the name of Man Mortimer, a man with a longing for days of old, when knives gripped by one's bare hands were the weapon of choice. Man Mortimer is a man with a mission. It is his aim in life to make the folks he comes into contact with "face the music of their essential selves . . . Men and women in this nation were changing," is how Man Mortimer sees it, "and he intended to charge them for it." A pimp by vocation, a smooth-talking womanizer who in high school was a "dead ringer for Fabian but in recent years was verging toward the dead country star Conway Twitty," Man Mortimer has built for himself a nouveau Southern empire made up of shiny sports utility vehicles that serve as brothels on wheels. At the center of this empire, Man Mortimer sees himself as being untouchable, and thereby pardoned of his role in these and other illicit activities.

The law could not touch him because his bordello was spread in myriad chambers throughout the suburbs and even underpasses in giant, newish sport utility vehicles with flattened rear seats, good mattresses, sunroof s tinted by creamy smoke and fine stereo systems, the aphrodisiacs of new-car smell and White Diamond mist working side by side.

It is only the realization that he is sharing with another man the affections of his woman, Dee Allison, that sends Mortimer spinning off his Mississippi axis and out of control. When Mortimer finds out about Frank Booth, Dee Allison's other lover, he takes a stiletto knife and he rams it into Booth's left side. "This was the side of the liver . . . . The liver brought quick death. He did not expect it to go in so smoothly. Booth, he thought, was suddenly a cadaver." But here, Mortimer is dead wrong. Booth "withdrew the knife from his side and rammed it back to its owner, . . . straight through his root and went then into one testicle." Not since Ernest Heming-

Barry Hannah is the author of many books, including the collection of stories Airships *(1978), which is regarded as a contemporary classic, as well as the novels* Geronimo Rex *(1972), which was a finalist for the National Book Award, and* Ray *(1980), which was nominated for the American Book Award. He is the writer-in-residence at the University of Mississippi.*

way's *The Sun Also Rises* (1926) has a wound of this sort taken on such symbolic weight. Now Man Mortimer is put in a position where he, too, is forced to face down his own essential self. Instead, Mortimer turns away from this mirror and turns his attentions, his bloodlust for vengeance, on the citizens who call Eagle Lake, Mississippi, their home. Now a man newly maimed, Mortimer's mission "to get people to face the music of their essential selves" begins to take shape.

The characters in *Yonder Stands Your Orphan* are on a "common run back and forth from ruin." Hannah places Mortimer at the center of this universe, the sun of this crooked cosmos, yet it is the planets that spin around Mortimer—that is, the other principal players (and there are plenty to keep track of)—that make this novel more than just the story about the disintegration of one man's kingdom. Hannah is a master at offering readers a vivid sense of each character's personal life history, as if they are secretly looking through someone's photo album, or better yet a video documentary that the characters themselves never even knew was being filmed. Listen, for instance, to what Hannah says about Ulrich, a peripheral character at best,

> A bombardier out of England and over Germany for the Eighth Air Force, and a puttering aeronaut ever since, a tinkering veteran (though his only personal flight had been without an engine, some fifty yards during Hurricane Camille in 1969), he had thought science his whole life. But recently he had erupted in mourning over man's treatment of animals. And without gratitude to them either, a holocaust without a ceremony!

The local sheriff is summed up: "Besides acting in local theater, the sheriff rode a Norton motorcycle. The people of the county were not clear on what man they had. He was handsome and very verbal. These things were measured against him."

To Hannah's way of thinking, no bit of information is too minor or even too trivial to pass along to the reader, and the technique works. The characters rise up off the page as creatures fully realized. However, in a review published in *The New York Times Book Review*, Hannah's methods were criticized, claiming that "you never get the feeling that these people exist in relation to one another. Nothing feels integrated. A character arrives, stays for a few pages, then exits, and you forget about him until his next appearance." It is true that characters almost haphazardly appear and then disappear, with sometimes chapter-long stretches passing before they are brought back to figure in to the novel's dramatic action. The claim that basic relationships fail to exist between these characters is a short-sighted failure on the part of the reviewer to examine exactly what is the common link between the people who bring Hannah's Mississippi so richly to life.

Hannah's shipwrecked Mississippi is more of an emotional landscape than it is a physical one divided into counties. The state of Mississippi itself—that geographical place that exists also on a map—is not common ground enough to serve as this bridge. What connects the characters to and with each other is Man Mortimer himself, a man who, even though he is wounded (both physically and emotionally) and even though he is not a native son to Eagle Lake, does move (and dangerously so) through this landscape and through the lives and minds of Eagle Lake and its inhabitants, men and women who like to gather at the end of the Eagle Lake pier to share snippets of small-town gossip and to pass judgment on those who pass by the viewfinder that is the pier itself.

Like all eleven of Barry Hannah's previous books, the main character always is language itself. The way that a story is told, the acoustics of the sentence, the voice— these are the elements that make Hannah's fiction uniquely his own. Hannah allows the words themselves to preside over the composition of his books: not plot, not even the narrative action (of which there is always an abundance in his work). What is quintessential to understanding and appreciating the work of Barry Hannah is knowing that one is reading a writer who subverts narrative and the "what" in a novel in favor of voice and the "how" that is always lurking behind a novel's narrative situation.

Hannah says of his methods of narratology: "I approach my work with humility and supplication, begging for that without which nothing budges, nothing moves: voice. You might have a swell tale that might bring in and hold folks of some intelligence around a campfire for thirty minutes or upwards to two hours, but you will have only junk if you don't find the voice—inevitable, urgent, necessary. . . ." Hannah later confesses: "I have never had any interest in form, structure, or technique." What makes Hannah even more of a force is that not only does he find the voice—which is always lingually juiced—he also spins a wild and swell tale that is structured much like a piece of freeform jazz, with its wild riffs and off-the-beaten-path solos that at times make the listener wonder, where is this man going? How is he ever going to make it back to where it all started? These are questions that the reader will likely and understandably ask during the experience of reading *Yonder Stands Your Orphan*. Hannah's narrative arc is more vertical than it is horizontal, the pace of the action siding on the slow side, with the cadences of his sentences—rhythms that are both baroque and biblical—serving as the engine torque that moves the narrative into forward drive. Some words of advice to the reader who is coming brand new to the world of Barry Hannah: Drive with both hands on the wheel, and with both eyes fixed straight ahead, and be on the lookout for the unexpected to dart out of the dark road that Hannah likes to travel, a world that is itself an orphan from middle America, a world that is defined by the never-before.

Barry Hannah is, like fellow Mississippian William Faulkner, a difficult writer, a writer whose books cannot be reduced down to a one-sentence synopsis, a writer of books whose plot is oftentimes hard to pin down or even follow during an initial reading. It is during a follow-up reading that the events in *Yonder Stands Your Orphan* begin to make sense and relationships between characters coalesce and fall into place. As the novel works toward its violent end, as heads literally begin to roll and bodies are hanged and crucified, the reader is left alone to fend for themselves, and all that can be said here at the end is what one of the peripheral characters says when asked, "What were you doing while all this was going on?" His response mirrors the role of the reader: "All I can brag to is I was around, in a corner or under a stage or in the projector room or the broom closet, and sometimes I held the scareder little ones on my lap." When Mortimer's own mother is murdered near the novel's end, Mortimer's transformation into a state of orphanage is complete. Here at this end, there is a feeling of newfound relief on Mortimer's part, a sense that he is ready, at long last, to be left alone with himself.

Peter Markus

Sources for Further Study

Booklist 97 (June 1, 2001): 1841.
Library Journal 126 (June 1, 2001): 216.
Publishers Weekly 248 (June 25, 2001): 51.
The Washington Post Book World, August 19, 2001, p. 6.

ZUÑI AND THE AMERICAN IMAGINATION

Author: Eliza McFeely (1956-   )
Publisher: Hill and Wang/Farrar, Straus and Giroux
  (New York). 204 pp. $24.00
Type of work: Anthropology and history
Time: 1879-2001
Locale: The United States, with an emphasis on the Zuñi
  Pueblo, New Mexico

~

*Examining the lives and work of Matilda Stevenson,
Frank Hamilton Cushing, and Stewart Culin, McFeely explores the nature of anthropological study at the turn of
the nineteenth century with special reference to the Zuñi
Pueblo in New Mexico*

~

Principal personages:
  JAMES STEVENSON, officer in charge of the first Bureau of American
    Ethnology field expedition
  MATILDA STEVENSON, wife of James Stevenson, who befriended
    We'wha, a berdache from Zuñi, and authored a 1904 study of the
    Zuñi Pueblo
  FRANK HAMILTON CUSHING, the single participant of the Stevenson field
    expedition who stayed on to live at Zuñi for five years, and success-
    fully insinuated himself into Zuñi society
  STEWARD CULIN, innovative curator of the Brooklyn Museum and tire-
    less collector of Zuñi and other American Indian artifacts
  JOHN HILLER, photographer of the Stevenson field expedition
  WE'WHA, friend of Matilda Stevenson, a Zuñi berdache made famous by
    becoming a kind of living exhibit in Washington's National Museum

Despite the title *Zuñi and the American Imagination*, Eliza McFeely's book is not
really an in-depth study of Zuñi history, culture, religion, or ethnography. Nor is it a
comprehensive study of the American imagination, although it does make passing
reference to the ways in which Aldous Huxley (in *Brave New World*, 1931) and Robert Heinlein (in *Stranger in a Strange Land*, 1961) used the idea of Zuñi in their famous science fiction novels, novels which inspired generations of Americans to question modern commercial culture and long somewhat unrealistically for an imagined
peaceful, agrarian, communal American past.

McFeely quickly dispatches the history of the Zuñi Pueblo itself in chapter 1,
"Finding Zuñi." In a few brief pages, she covers the "discovery" of the Pueblo in
1539, the various Spanish occupations, the dramatic Pueblo Uprising, and finally

Zuñi's acquisition by the United States through agreements made after the Mexican War of 1858. She is then free to focus on her real interests, the careers of Matilda Cox Stevenson, Frank Hamilton Cushing, and Stewart Culin, the self-made anthropologists who dominated the study of Zuñi from the first federally funded expedition by the Bureau of American Ethnology in 1879 to the Brooklyn Museum's magnificent Zuñi exhibit mounted by Culin in 1925.

~

Zuñi and the American Imagination *had its origins in Eliza McFeely's Ph.D. dissertation at New York University. This is her first book.* McFeely *currently teaches American history at the College of New Jersey in Ewing*

~

Examining each adventurer/ethnographer/collector in turn, McFeely creates a lively picture of the careers of these early observers of Zuñi. Unfettered by modern-day university or scholarly standards of anthropology, each of these intrepid explorers studied Zuñi in the way that most fitted his or her own particular interests and personality. While they all shared certain general ideas about "primitive" cultures, they each brought unique talents and frailties to the work, creating a legacy of information which is, ironically, largely discredited by the modern academic community, yet frequently consulted by the Zuñis themselves for keys to their past.

In chapter 3, "Two-Fold One-Kind: Matilda Stevenson," McFeely explores the sympathies between Matilda Stevenson, a Victorian lady working in the hyper-masculine West in a field dominated by men, and her Zuñi friend We'wha, a berdache, or Zuñi male who had chosen to live his life following the ways of the women of his tribe, joining a third gender which the Zuñi believed could mediate between the male and female, one they referred to as "two-fold one-kind."

Like most of her contemporaries, Matilda Stevenson was strongly influenced by Darwin's *On the Origin of Species* (1859), which many read to include a kind of social evolution among peoples, and Lewis Henry Morgan's theory of cultural evolution espoused in his book *Ancient Society* (1877), which contended that all human societies went through three identical phases (savagery, barbarism, and civilization), and that, more important, since all cultures inevitably solved similar problems in similar ways, contemporary primitive societies could be studied as representative of primitive societies of all times and places. These ideas led to Stevenson's belief that Zuñi was a magnificent example of the second stage of Morgan's evolutionary scheme, "barbarism," and that her studies at Zuñi would therefore have a universal application. She held an equally strong personal belief, however, that evolution to the final stage of "civilization" would be denied the Zuñis, who were destined to be overwhelmed by American society, which would increasingly encroach on them and influence them for the worst. Her task then, as she saw it, was to make a painstaking record of the spiritual and social customs, the medical practices, the rituals, the crafts, and the lifestyles of what she considered a soon-to-be-extinct American Indian tribe. As a woman, with We'wha as a special confidante, she was able to amass a wealth of information which she published in her 1904 study of the Pueblo, a study that was meticulous in its detail and curiously devoid of interpretation. More prone to reflection was We'wha, whom Stevenson brought to Washington, D.C. (where she hoped he might pick up the habit of eating with a knife and fork, thereby hastening his tribe's development toward "civilization"), but We'wha's scrutiny of American culture sent him back to the Pueblo an even more staunch defender of Zuñi ways—ways which have proven over time to be even more robust than Stevenson's own ethnographic work.

In chapter 4, "A Place of Grace," McFeely turns her attention to Frank Hamilton Cushing who, armed with some of the same general anthropological notions as Matilda Stevenson, decided that the only way to study Zuñi would be from the inside. Cushing let the Stevenson expedition return to the East without him, and he followed a program of total immersion, believing that if he practiced the Zuñi arts, if he explored every inch of their landscape, if he could induce them to initiate him into their arcane rituals, he could report not only on what the Zuñi do, but why they do it. A natural storyteller who loved to be the hero of his own tales, Cushing was remarkably successful in realizing his dreams of infiltrating Zuñi society. He lived in a Zuñi household, ate Zuñi food, adopted Zuñi dress, and soon believed that he understood the Zuñi better than they did themselves. Cushing succeeded in penetrating the ritual life of Zuñi's kivas (ceremonial structures) and sacred sites in a way that has never been equaled, finally becoming a member of the Priesthood of the Bow. Using Morgan's ideas of the universality of cultures and his own powers of analogical thinking, Cushing created prodigies of empathy and folly in his popular and scholarly writings. His "going native," so well shown in Hiller's photographs of him in Zuñi regalia, was both the strength of his early reputation and the ultimate cause of his modern devaluation. McFeely's book is nothing if not a trenchant study of the vicissitudes of anthropological dogma at any given time, and their retrospective effect on the perceived careers of the early practitioners in the field.

Neither Stevenson nor Cushing would probably be remembered at all today if they had not combined their observations and their writings with avid collection and expatriation of Zuñi art and artifacts to the East. Both early students of Zuñi culture were also skilled salvage anthropologists, who used means both fair and foul to divest the Zuñis of wagons full of pottery, masks, fetishes, games, tools, kachinas, ritual items, and even scalps. Museums all over America coveted such items because they were beautiful, exotic, magical, and they helped extend American history into a richer past, which could be explored with the same studiousness as the British might look into their Roman prehistory. Removing artifacts from Zuñi under the guise of conservation, these early explorers of the Pueblo gave Eastern museum curators the raw material out of which to extract a well-organized and scientifically verifiable American past—one displayed neatly in glass cupboards, labeled and categorized, safe from the ravages of time or constant use.

Stewart Culin, the first curator of ethnology at the Brooklyn Institute of Arts and Sciences opened a hall at that museum in 1905 devoted to the southwestern United States with an emphasis on Zuñi, which was distinguished not only by the comprehensiveness of the collection but also the skill of its presentation. While Culin had been to Zuñi on collecting missions, most of his contacts were with white traders, and his acquisitions were often done through others who were closer to the Zuñis, such as

Cushing. His contribution was not so much in the acquisition of firsthand knowledge through traveling personally to Zuñi; his genius was in transporting the Southwest, and Zuñi in particular, back to his museum visitors in Brooklyn. By the time his massive collection of Zuñi artifacts was reinstalled for a second exhibit in 1925, Culin had not only removed more items from the Pueblo than anyone else, but he had also adopted the methods of Barnum & Bailey and Madison Avenue to make them infinitely more interesting to the American public. Sterile glass cases with neatly typed labels were replaced by dioramas backed with dramatic photographs of the Pueblo. Artifacts were grouped together to give the feeling of everyday Zuñi life. His exhibits became more and more aesthetic and less and less scientific. It became impossible to tell which artifacts were ancient and which were recent creations crafted expressly to fill out Culin's collection. Culin's interest in the art of museum display overwhelmed his weaker interest in ethnology. His reputation predictably suffered. Once again, an early explorer of Zuñi had been mousetrapped by his own egotism.

In her conclusion, "Zuñi Legacy," McFeely brings her study up to the present. She shows how modern anthropology, practiced by experts with university affiliations and degrees, has moved away from the idea of a universal pattern of mind and fixed stages of human development. Its focus is more clearly on the uniqueness of all human societies and the interconnectedness of human cultures, which can be uncovered, hopefully, by less invasive means, such as tracing pottery patterns and comparing migration routes and deoxyribonucleic acid (DNA). This means that a new battalion of anthropologists has been deployed to discover the truth about Zuñi, armed with new methods, new technologies, and different theories from their predecessors: theories such as those expressed in Ruth Benedict's *Patterns of Culture* (1934), which divides the world's cultures neatly into Dionysian and Apollonian types, terms which will turn out to be no doubt as useful, and as misleading, as Morgan's "savage" and "barbarian."

In the midst of all this intense observation, Zuñi, the Pueblo, has shown itself to be much less fragile than its early explorers could ever have imagined. It remains relatively intact in the New Mexico desert, waiting to show yet another wave of Americans anthropologists something about an older, quieter, enduring way of life.

Cynthia Lee Katona

Sources for Further Study

Booklist 97 (March 1, 2001): 1223.
Library Journal 126 (February 1, 2001): 103.
The New Republic 224 (June 11, 2001): 47.
Publishers Weekly 248 (March 5, 2001): 73.

MAGILL'S
LITERARY ANNUAL
2002

BIOGRAPHICAL WORKS BY SUBJECT

1977-2002

ABEL, LIONEL
  Intellectual Follies (Abel) (85) 451
ABERNATHY, RALPH DAVID
  And the Walls Came Tumbling Down
    (Abernathy) (90) 39
ACHEBE, CHINUA
  Home and Exile (Achebe) (01) 408
ACHESON, DEAN
  Dean Acheson (McLellan) (77) 197
ADAMS, ABIGAIL
  Descent from Glory (Nagel) (H-84) 121
ADAMS, CHARLES FRANCIS
  Descent from Glory (Nagel) (H-84) 121
ADAMS, HENRY
  Descent from Glory (Nagel) (H-84) 121
  Five of Hearts, The (O'Toole) (91) 295
  Letters of Henry Adams, 1858-1892, The
    (Adams) (84) 441
  Letters of Henry Adams, 1892-1918, The
    (Adams) (90) 516
ADAMS, JOHN
  Descent from Glory (Nagel) (H-84) 121
  Faces of Revolution (Bailyn) (91) 279
  John Adams (Ferling) (93) 413
  John Adams (McCullough) (02) 444
ADAMS, JOHN G.
  Without Precedent (Adams) (H-84) 497
ADAMS, JOHN QUINCY
  Descent from Glory (Nagel) (H-84) 121
  John Quincy Adams (Nagel) (98) 472
ADAMS, MIRIAM "CLOVER"
  Five of Hearts, The (O'Toole) (91) 295
ADLER, MORTIMER J.
  Philosopher at Large (Adler) (78) 654
AGEE, JAMES
  James Agee (Bergreen) (85) 473
AGEE, JOEL
  Twelve Years (Agee) (82) 854
AIKEN, CONRAD
  Conrad Aiken (Butscher) (89) 207
  Selected Letters of Conrad Aiken (Aiken) (79) 652
AKHMATOVA, ANNA
  Akhmatova Journals, 1938-41, The
    (Chukovskaya) (95) 19
  Anna Akhmatova (Reeder) (95) 38
  Nightingale Fever (Hingley) (82) 555
ALABI, PANTO
  Alabi's World (Price) (91) 10
ALBEE, EDWARD
  Edward Albee (Gussow) (00) 199
ALEXANDER
  Search for Alexander, The (Lane Fox) (81) 712
ALI, MUHAMMAD
  King of the World (Remnick) (99) 453
ALLEN, FRED
  Province of Reason (Warner) (H-85) 368
ALLEN, PAULA GUNN
  I Tell You Now (Swann and Krupat,
    eds.) (88) 413

ALLENDE, SALVADOR
  Overthrow of Allende and the Politics of Chile,
    1964-1976, The (Sigmund) (78) 630
ALS, HILTON
  Women, The (Als) (98) 874
ALSOP, JOSEPH "JOE"
  Taking on the World (Merry) (97) 802
ALSOP, STEWART
  Taking on the World (Merry) (97) 802
AMIS, KINGSLEY
  Kingsley Amis (Jacobs) (99) 457
AMIS, MARTIN
  Experience (Amis) (01) 290
ANDERSON, SHERWOOD
  Sherwood Anderson (Anderson) (85) 820
  Sherwood Anderson (Townsend) (88) 817
ANGELOU, MAYA
  All God's Children Need Traveling Shoes
    (Angelou) (87) 25
  Singin' and Swingin' and Gettin' Merry like
    Christmas (Angelou) (77) 738
ANGERMEYER, JOHANNA
  My Father's Island (Angermeyer) (91) 614
ANTHONY, SUSAN B.
  Elizabeth Cady Stanton, Susan B. Anthony,
    Correspondence, Writings, Speeches (Stanton
    and Anthony) (82) 214
  Not for Ourselves Alone (Ward and
    Burns) (00) 580
ANTIN, MARY
  Province of Reason (Warner) (H-85) 368
ARBUS, DIANE NEMEROV
  Diane Arbus (Bosworth) (96) 174
ARENDT, HANNAH
  Between Friends (Arendt and McCarthy) (96) 73
  Hannah Arendt (Hill, ed.) (80) 395
  Hannah Arendt (Young-Bruehl) (83) 322
  Passionate Minds (Pierpont) (01) 694
ARLETTY
  Six Exceptional Women (Lord) (95) 724
ARNOLD, MATTHEW
  Life of Matthew Arnold, A (Murray) (98) 500
  Matthew Arnold (Honan) (82) 518
ARTAUD, ANTONIN
  Antonin Artaud (Artaud) (77) 52
  Antonin Artaud (Esslin) (78) 68
ARVIN, NEWTON
  Scarlet Professor, The (Werth) (02) 727
ASHE, ARTHUR
  Days of Grace (Ashe and Rampersad) (94) 213
ATHENS, LONNIE
  Why They Kill (Rhodes) (00) 843
ATTLEE, CLEMENT
  Attlee (Harris) (H-84) 33
AUDEN, W. H.
  Auden (Davenport-Hines) (97) 79
  Later Auden (Mendelson) (00) 475
  W. H. Auden (Carpenter) (82) 923
  W. H. Auden (Osborne) (80) 860

BIOGRAPHICAL WORKS BY SUBJECT

BIOGRAPHICAL WORKS BY SUBJECT

WEBSTER, DANIEL
Daniel Webster (Bartlett) (79) 143
Daniel Webster (Remini) (98) 221
Great Triumvirate, The (Peterson) (88) 363
One and Inseparable (Baxter) (H-85) 339
Province of Reason (Warner) (H-85) 368

WEEKS, EDWARD
Writers and Friends (Weeks) (83) 928

WEIGL, BRUCE
Circle of Hanh, The (Weigl) (01) 190

WEIL, SIMONE
Simone Weil (Fiori) (90) 738
Simone Weil (Nevin) (93) 736
Utopian Pessimist (McLellan) (91) 838

WEISSTEIN, NAOMI
Working It Out (Ruddick and Daniels, eds.) (78) 937

WEIZMANN, CHAIM
Chaim Weizmann (Reinharz) (86) 111

WELCH, DENTON
Journals of Denton Welch, The (Welch) (85) 504

WELCHMAN, GORDON
Hut Six Story, The (Welchman) (H-83) 201

WELLES, ORSON
Orson Welles (Leaming) (86) 709

WELLS, H. G.
Great Friends (Garnett) (81) 386
Group Portrait (Delbanco) (83) 312
H. G. Wells (West) (85) 380
Invisible Man, The (Coren) (94) 410
Rebecca West (Rollyson) (97) 684

WELTY, EUDORA
Conversations with Eudora Welty (Prenshaw) (85) 137
Eudora (Waldron) (00) 240
Eudora Welty's Achievement of Order (Kreyling) (81) 288
One Writer's Beginnings (Welty) (85) 663
Passionate Minds (Pierpont) (01) 694

WERFEL, FRANZ
Franz Werfel (Jungk) (91) 313

WEST, DOROTHY
Richer, the Poorer, The (West) (96) 641

WEST, JESSAMYN
Woman Said Yes, The (West) (77) 928

WEST, MAE
Passionate Minds (Pierpont) (01) 694

WEST, REBECCA
Rebecca West (Glendinning) (88) 732
Rebecca West (Rollyson) (97) 684
Young Rebecca, The (West) (83) 932

WHARTON, EDITH
Feast of Words, A (Wolff) (78) 314
Letters of Edith Wharton, The (Wharton) (89) 475
No Gifts from Chance (Benstock) (95) 544

WHITE, E. B.
E. B. White (Elledge) (85) 209
Letters of E. B. White (White) (77) 413

WHITE, KATHARINE S.
Onward and Upward (Davis) (88) 630

WHITE, PATRICK
Flaws in the Glass (White) (83) 257
Patrick White (Marr) (93) 619
Patrick White (White) (97) 656

WHITE, STANFORD
Evelyn Nesbit and Stanford White (Mooney) (77) 260

WHITE, T. H.
Great Friends (Garnett) (81) 386

WHITE, THEODORE H.
In Search of History (White) (79) 314

WHITEHEAD, ALFRED NORTH
Alfred North Whitehead, 1861-1910 (Lowe) (86) 5
Alfred North Whitehead, 1910-1947 (Lowe) (91) 20

WHITMAN, WALT
Walt Whitman (Kaplan) (81) 883
Walt Whitman (Zweig) (85) 984
Walt Whitman's America (Reynolds) (96) 806

WHITNEY, DOROTHY PAYNE
Whitney Father, Whitney Heiress (Swanberg) (81) 921

WHITNEY, WILLIAM COLLINS
Whitney Father, Whitney Heiress (Swanberg) (81) 921

WIDEMAN, JOHN EDGAR
Brothers and Keepers (Wideman) (85) 57
Fatheralong (Wideman) (95) 227

WIDEMAN, ROBBY
Brothers and Keepers (Wideman) (85) 57

WIESEL, ELIE
All Rivers Run to the Sea (Wiesel) (96) 18
And the Sea Is Never Full (Wiesel) (00) 22

WILBERFORCE, WILLIAM
Wilberforce (Pollock) (79) 862

WILDE, OSCAR
Oscar Wilde (Ellmann) (89) 630

WILDE-MENOZZI, WALLIS
Mother Tongue (Wilde-Menozzi) (98) 567

WILDER, THORNTON
Enthusiast, The (Harrison) (84) 272
Journals of Thornton Wilder, 1939-1961, The (Wilder) (86) 491
Thornton Wilder (Simon) (80) 815

WILHELM II
Last Kaiser, The (Tyler-Whittle) (78) 509

WILLIAM, DUKE OF CLARENCE
Mrs. Jordan's Profession (Tomalin) (96) 465

WILLIAMS, CHARLES
Charles Williams (Hadfield) (84) 153

WILLIAMS, GEORGE WASHINGTON
George Washington Williams (Franklin) (86) 332

WILLIAMS, TENNESSEE
Five O'Clock Angel (Williams) (91) 291
Memoirs (Williams) (77) 494
Tom (Leverich) (96) 756

WILLIAMS, TERRY TEMPEST
Leap (Williams) (01) 513

WILLIAMS, WILLIAM CARLOS
Lives of the Modern Poets (Pritchard) (81) 520
Pound/Williams (Pound and Williams) (97) 675
William Carlos Williams (Mariani) (82) 946

WILLS, CHERYLE
I've Known Rivers (Lawrence-Lightfoot) (95) 384

BIOGRAPHICAL WORKS BY SUBJECT

933

CATEGORY INDEX

1977-2002

ANTHROPOLOGY. *See* SOCIOLOGY,
ARCHAEOLOGY, and ANTHROPOLOGY

ARCHAEOLOGY. *See* SOCIOLOGY,
ARCHAEOLOGY, and ANTHROPOLOGY

AUTOBIOGRAPHY, MEMOIRS, DIARIES, and
LETTERS
Abba Eban (Eban) (78) 1
Accidental Autobiography, An (Harrison) (97) 1
Adieux (Beauvoir) (85) 1
Aké (Soyinka) (83) 10
Akhmatova Journals, 1938-41, The
(Chukovskaya) (95) 19
Albert Einstein (Einstein) (80) 19
All God's Children Need Traveling Shoes
(Angelou) (87) 25
All Rivers Run to the Sea (Wiesel) (96) 18
Always Straight Ahead (Neuman) (94) 11
Amateur, The (Lesser) (00) 10
Amazing Grace (Norris) (99) 40
America Inside Out (Schoenbrun) (H-85) 22
American Chica (Arana) (02) 35
American Childhood, An (Dillard) (88) 25
American Life, An (Reagan) (91) 24
American Requiem, An (Carroll) (97) 38
And the Sea Is Never Full (Wiesel) (00) 22
And the Walls Came Tumbling Down
(Abernathy) (90) 39
Angela's Ashes (McCourt) (97) 43
Anne Sexton (Sexton) (78) 54
Another World, 1897-1917 (Eden) (78) 59
Answer to History (Mohammad Reza Pahlavi) (81) 47
Antonin Artaud (Artaud) (77) 52
Anything Your Little Heart Desires (Bosworth) (98) 68
Arna Bontemps-Langston Hughes Letters, 1925-1927
(Bontemps and Hughes) (81) 57
Around the Day in Eighty Worlds (Cortázar) (87) 45
Arrivals and Departures (Rovere) (77) 62
As I Saw It (Rusk) (91) 56
Asking for Trouble (Woods) (82) 28
Assault on Mount Helicon (Barnard) (85) 27
Atlantic High (Buckley) (83) 29

Autobiography of a Face (Grealy) (95) 56
Autobiography of Values (Lindbergh) (79) 43
Basil Street Blues (Holroyd) (01) 64
Becoming a Doctor (Konner) (88) 77
Becoming a Man (Monette) (93) 62
Berlin Diaries, 1940-1945 (Vassiltchikov) (88) 95
Bernard Shaw, 1856-1898 (Holroyd) (89) 89
Bernard Shaw, Collected Letters, 1926-1950
(Shaw) (89) 84
Better Class of Person, A (Osborne) (82) 45
Between Friends (Arendt and McCarthy) (96) 73
Beyond the Dragon's Mouth (Naipaul) (86) 56
Blessings in Disguise (Guinness) (87) 71
Blind Ambition (Dean) (77) 96
Bloods (Terry) (H-85) 48
Blooming (Toth) (82) 55
Blue-Eyed Child of Fortune (Duncan, ed.) (93) 91
Body Toxic (Antonetta) (02) 97
Born on the Fourth of July (Kovic) (77) 115
Borrowed Time (Monette) (89) 112
Boston Boy (Hentoff) (87) 84
Boswell (Boswell) (78) 140
Boyhood (Coetzee) (98) 134
Breaking Ranks (Podhoretz) (80) 101
Breaking with Moscow (Shevchenko) (86) 81
Broken Cord, The (Dorris) (90) 76
Bronx Primitive (Simon) (83) 80
Brothers and Keepers (Wideman) (85) 57
Burning the Days (Salter) (98) 138
Byron's Letters and Journals, 1822-1823
(Byron) (81) 108
Cassandra (Wolf) (85) 74
Chance Meetings (Saroyan) (79) 92
Charles Darwin's Letters (Darwin) (97) 148
Cherry (Karr) (01) 181
Chief, The (Morrow) (86) 121
Childhood (Sarraute) (85) 89
China Men (Kingston) (81) 137
Chinabound (Fairbank) (H-83) 61
Christopher and His Kind (Isherwood) (77) 158
Circle of Hanh, The (Weigl) (01) 190
Clear Pictures (Price) (90) 104
Clinging to the Wreckage (Mortimer) (83) 127

CATEGORY INDEX

CATEGORY INDEX

939

CATEGORY INDEX

CATEGORY INDEX

945

CATEGORY INDEX

CATEGORY INDEX

CATEGORY INDEX

CATEGORY INDEX

CATEGORY INDEX

CATEGORY INDEX

CATEGORY INDEX

CATEGORY INDEX

966

CATEGORY INDEX

CATEGORY INDEX

CATEGORY INDEX

CATEGORY INDEX

CATEGORY INDEX

975

CATEGORY INDEX

CATEGORY INDEX

CATEGORY INDEX

TITLE INDEX

1977-2002

TITLE INDEX

TITLE INDEX

TITLE INDEX

TITLE INDEX

TITLE INDEX

Passion of Emily Dickinson, The (Farr) (93) 610
Passion of Michel Foucault, The (Miller) (93) 614
Passion Play (Kosinski) (80) 649
Passionate Apprentice, A (Woolf) (92) 607
Passionate Minds (Pierpont) (01) 694
Passionate War, The (Wyden) (H-84) 330
Passwords (Stafford) (92) 612
Past, The (Kinnell) (86) 727
Past Is a Foreign Country, The (Lowenthal) (87) 645
Past Masters, The (MacMillan) (77) 610
Pasternak (Hingley) (84) 673
Pastoral (Phillips) (01) 699
Pastoralia (Saunders) (01) 703
Patchwork Planet, A (Tyler) (99) 624
Path Between the Seas, The (McCullough) (78) 636
Path to Power, The (Thatcher) (96) 573
Patients Are People Like Us (Baruk) (79) 532
Patrick O'Brian (King) (01) 707
Patrick White (Marr) (93) 619
Patrick White (White) (97) 656
Patrimony (Roth) (92) 615
Patriots and Liberators (Schama) (78) 642
Paul Celan (Colin) (92) 619
Paul Celan (Felstiner) (96) 577
Paul Klee (Lanchner, ed.) (88) 668
Paul Revere's Ride (Fischer) (95) 604
Paul Robeson (Duberman) (90) 652
Pause and Effect (Parkes) (94) 615
Peace Breaks Out (Knowles) (82) 621
Peace Brokers, The (Touval) (H-83) 335
Peace Like a River (Enger) (02) 626
Peace to End All Peace, A (Fromkin) (90) 657
Peacock Spring, The (Godden) (77) 614
Pearl Harbor (Prange, Goldstein, and Dillon) (86) 732
Pearl S. Buck (Conn) (97) 661
Peckham's Marbles (De Vries) (87) 650
Peerless Flats (Freud) (94) 618
Pencil, The (Petroski) (91) 656
Penitent, The (Singer) (84) 678
People and Uncollected Stories, The
  (Malamud) (90) 661
People of the Lake (Leakey and Lewin) (79) 535
People Shapers, The (Packard) (78) 649
People's Emperor, The (Wilson) (81) 645
Percys of Mississippi, The (Baker) (84) 682
Perestroika (Gorbachev) (88) 677
Perfect Recall (Beattie) (02) 631
Perfect Spy, A (le Carré) (87) 654
Periodic Table, The (Levi) (85) 682
Perjury (Weinstein) (79) 540
Perón (Page) (H-84) 336
Perpetrators, Victims, Bystanders (Hilberg) (93) 624
Pershing (Smythe) (87) 660
Persian Nights (Johnson) (88) 683
Persistence of the Old Regime, The (Mayer) (82) 626
Personal History (Graham) (98) 629
Personal Impressions (Berlin) (82) 632
Personal Injuries (Turow) (00) 605
Personal Politics (Evans) (80) 655
Perspective of the World, Vol. III, The (Braudel) (H-85) 353
Peter Paul Rubens (White) (88) 690
Peter the Great (Massie) (81) 651
Phantom Empire, The (O'Brien) (94) 622
Phenomena (Hankla) (84) 686
Philadelphia Fire (Wideman) (91) 661
Philip Larkin (Motion) (94) 626
Philosopher at Large (Adler) (78) 654
Philosopher's Demise, The (Watson) (96) 581
Philosopher's Pupil, The (Murdoch) (84) 690
Philosophical Explanations (Nozick) (82) 638
Philosophy in the Twentieth Century (Ayer) (83) 592
Phoenicians, The (Moscati, ed.) (90) 665

Phony War, 1939-1940, The (Shachtman) (H-83) 338
Pickup, The (Gordimer) (02) 636
Picture Bride (Song) (84) 695
Picturing Will (Beattie) (91) 665
Pieces and Pontifications (Mailer) (83) 597
Pieces of Life (Schorer) (78) 657
Pieces of Soap (Elkin) (93) 629
Pigs in Heaven (Kingsolver) (94) 631
Pilgrim in the Ruins (Tolson) (93) 633
Pilgrims in Their Own Land (Marty) (H-85) 358
Pillar of Fire (Branch) (99) 628
Pioneer Women (Stratton) (82) 642
Pitch Dark (Adler) (84) 699
Pitcher's Story, A (Angell) (02) 641
Pity of War, The (Ferguson) (00) 609
Place in Space, A (Snyder) (96) 585
Place I've Never Been, A (Leavitt) (91) 670
Places in the World a Woman Could Walk
  (Kauffman) (85) 688
Plague Dogs, The (Adams) (79) 546
Plagues and Peoples (McNeill) (77) 618
Plain and Normal (Wilcox) (99) 632
Plains Song (Morris) (81) 655
Plainsong (Haruf) (00) 614
Planning a Tragedy (Berman) (H-83) 343
Platte River (Bass) (95) 609
Plausible Prejudices (Epstein) (86) 737
Players (DeLillo) (78) 661
Playgoing in Shakespeare's London (Gurr) (88) 696
Playing for Keeps (Halberstam) (00) 618
Pleading Guilty (Turow) (94) 636
Pleasure-Dome (Madden) (80) 659
Pleasures of the Imagination, The (Brewer) (98) 634
Plowing the Dark (Powers) (01) 711
PM/AM (Pastan) (83) 603
Poe Log, The (Thomas and Jackson) (88) 701
Poems (Knott) (90) 669
Poems, 1968-1998 (Muldoon) (02) 645
Poems, The (Yeats) (85) 692
Poems New and Selected, 1962-1992 (Van
  Brunt) (94) 641
Poems of Paul Celan (Celan) (90) 673
Poems of Stanley Kunitz, 1928-1978, The
  (Kunitz) (80) 665
Poet and Dancer (Jhabvala) (94) 645
Poet as Journalist, The (Whittemore) (77) 623
Poetical Works of Federico García Lorca (García
  Lorca) (93) 637
Poetics of Aristotle, The (Halliwell) (88) 706
Poetry and Repression (Bloom) (77) 627
Poetry into Drama (Herington) (86) 742
Poetry of Tennyson, The (Culler) (78) 665
Poets in Their Youth (Simpson) (83) 608
Poets, Poetics, and Politics (Humphries) (93) 642
Poet's Work (Gibbons, ed.) (80) 668
Poet's Work, The (Nathan and Quinn) (92) 623
Point, The (D'Ambrosio) (96) 589
Polish Complex, The (Konwicki) (83) 611
Polish Officer, The (Furst) (96) 593
Political Liberalism (Rawls) (94) 649
Political Life of Children, The (Coles) (87) 665
Political Repression in Nineteenth Century Europe
  (Goldstein) (H-84) 342
Politician, The (Dugger) (H-83) 348
Politics and Ideology in the Age of the Civil War
  (Foner) (81) 661
Politics in Black and White (Sonenshein) (94) 654
Politics of Energy, The (Commoner) (80) 671
Politics of Recovery, The (Romasco) (H-84) 347
Politics of Rich and Poor, The (Phillips) (91) 674
Polonaise (Read) (77) 632
Pop Internationalism (Krugman) (97) 666
Pope's Rhinoceros, The (Norfolk) (97) 671

1013

TITLE INDEX

TITLE INDEX

TITLE INDEX

AUTHOR INDEX

1977-2002

AUTHOR INDEX

AUTHOR INDEX

AUTHOR INDEX

AUTHOR INDEX

AUTHOR INDEX

AUTHOR INDEX

AUTHOR INDEX

ROAZEN, PAUL
Helene Deutsch (86) 402
ROBB, GRAHAM
Balzac (95) 60
Rimbaud (01) 736
Victor Hugo (99) 838
ROBB, PETER
M (01) 549
ROBBINS, CARLA ANNE
Cuban Threat, The (H-84) 106
ROBBINS, TOM
Half Asleep in Frog Pajamas (95) 287
ROBERTS, DAVID
Jean Stafford (89) 414
Newer World, A (01) 627
ROBERTS, JANE, and MARTIN KEMP, with PHILIP
STEADMAN
Leonardo da Vinci (90) 505
ROBERTS, JOHN MORRIS
History of Europe, A (98) 383
ROBERTSON, JAMES I., JR.
Stonewall Jackson (98) 736
ROBERTSON, JAMES OLIVER
American Myth, American Reality (81) 39
ROBERTSON-LORANT, LAURIE
Melville (97) 568
ROBINSON, DAVID
Chaplin (86) 116
ROBINSON, JANICE S.
H. D. (83) 331
ROBINSON, KIM STANLEY
Antarctica (99) 48
Gold Coast, The (89) 316
Red Mars (94) 688
ROBINSON, MARILYNNE
Death of Adam, The (99) 226
Mother Country (90) 586
ROBINSON, PHYLLIS C.
Willa (84) 945
ROBINSON, ROXANA
Georgia O'Keeffe (90) 289
ROBISON, MARY
Amateur's Guide to the Night, An (84) 16
Why Did I Ever (02) 847
ROCHLIN, GENE I.
Trapped in the Net (98) 773
RODENBECK, MAX
Cairo (00) 117
RODGERS, DANIEL T.
Work Ethic in Industrial America, 1850-1920,
The (79) 904
RODRIGUEZ, ABRAHAM, JR.
Boy Without a Flag, The (93) 96
Spidertown (94) 760
RODRIGUEZ, RICHARD
Days of Obligation (93) 204
Hunger of Memory (82) 377
ROGERS, GUY MacLEAN, and MARY R.
LEFKOWITZ, editors
Black Athena Revisited (97) 114
ROLLIN, BETTY
First, You Cry (77) 291

ROLLYSON, CARL
Lillian Hellman (89) 511
Lives of Norman Mailer, The (92) 445
Nothing Ever Happens to the Brave (91) 639
Rebecca West (97) 684
ROLLYSON, CARL E., and LISA O. PADDOCK
Susan Sontag (01) 805
ROMASCO, ALBERT U.
Politics of Recovery, The (H-84) 347
ROOKE, LEON
Shakespeare's Dog (84) 784
ROOT-BERNSTEIN, ROBERT SCOTT
Discovering (90) 186
ROREM, NED
Knowing When to Stop (95) 427
RORTY, RICHARD
Truth and Progress (99) 799
ROSE, JONATHAN
Intellectual Life of the British Working Classes,
The (02) 418
ROSE, PHYLLIS
Parallel Lives (84) 662
ROSE, STEVEN
Lifelines (98) 508
ROSE, STEVEN, R. C. LEWONTIN, and LEON J.
KAMIN
Not in Our Genes (H-85) 329
ROSEN, JONATHAN
Eve's Apple (98) 299
ROSEN, ROBERT
Nowhere Man (01) 661
ROSENBAUM, RON
Explaining Hitler (99) 273
ROSENBERG, DAVID, editor
Congregation (88) 189
ROSENBERG, TINA
Haunted Land, The (96) 330
ROSENBERG, WILLIAM G., and MARILYN B.
YOUNG
Transforming Russia and China (H-83) 426
ROSENFIELD, ISRAEL
Invention of Memory, The (89) 400
ROSENGARTEN, THEODORE, editor
Tombee (87) 875
ROSENKRANTZ, LINDA
My Life as a List (00) 554
ROSENTHAL, M. L., and SALLY M. GALL
Modern Poetic Sequence, The (84) 570
Sailing into the Unknown (79) 632
ROSS, LILLIAN
Here but Not Here (99) 360
ROSSABI, MORRIS
Khubilai Khan (89) 432
ROSSNER, JUDITH
Attachments (78) 77
ROTH, HENRY
Diving Rock on the Hudson, A (96) 190
From Bondage (97) 319
Mercy of a Rude Stream (95) 482
Requiem for Harlem (99) 654
ROTH, JACK J.
Cult of Violence, The (81) 215
ROTH, MICHAEL S., ed.
Freud (99) 311

AUTHOR INDEX

AUTHOR INDEX

SILLITOE, ALAN
  Her Victory (83) 340
  Lost Flying Boat, The (85) 579
  Second Chance and Other Stories, The (82) 747
  Widower's Son, The (78) 904

SILVERMAN, KENNETH
  Edgar A. Poe (92) 174
  Life and Times of Cotton Mather, The (H-85) 256

SIME, RUTH LEWIN
  Lise Meitner (97) 526

SIMIC, CHARLES
  Night Picnic (02) 592

SIMMONS, CHARLES
  Wrinkles (79) 918

SIMON, HERBERT
  Models of My Life (92) 519

SIMON, JEFFREY
  Cohesion and Dissension in Eastern Europe (H-84) 91

SIMON, JOHN
  Singularities (77) 742

SIMON, KATE
  Bronx Primitive (83) 80
  Renaissance Tapestry, A (89) 708
  Wider World, A (87) 985

SIMON, LINDA
  Genuine Reality (99) 329
  Thornton Wilder (80) 815

SIMON, NEIL
  Rewrites (97) 692

SIMPSON, EILEEN
  Poets in Their Youth (83) 608

SIMPSON, HELEN
  Getting a Life (02) 334

SIMPSON, LOUIS
  Best Hour of the Night, The (85) 42
  Collected Poems (89) 180
  Revolution in Taste, A (80) 709
  Searching for the Ox (77) 706

SIMPSON, MONA
  Anywhere but Here (88) 42
  Lost Father, The (93) 487
  Regular Guy, A (97) 688

SINCLAIR, ANDREW
  Jack (78) 454

SINCLAIR, CLIVE
  Brothers Singer, The (84) 127

SINGAL, DANIEL JOSEPH
  War Within (83) 873
  William Faulkner (98) 850

SINGER, IRVING
  Nature of Love, The (89) 585

SINGER, ISAAC BASHEVIS
  Collected Stories of Isaac Bashevis Singer, The (83) 135
  Death of Methuselah and Other Stories, The (89) 231
  Image and Other Stories, The (86) 461
  King of the Fields, The (89) 441
  Lost in America (82) 485
  Old Love (80) 614
  Penitent, The (84) 678
  Shosha (79) 677

SINGH, PATWANT
  Sikhs, The (01) 774

SÎN-LEQI-UNNINNÎ
  Gilgamesh (85) 324

SINYAVSKY, ANDREI. See TERTZ, ABRAM

SIRICA, JOHN J.
  To Set the Record Straight (80) 822

SISMAN, ADAM
  Boswell's Presumptuous Task (02) 120

SISSMAN, L. E.
  Hello, Darkness (79) 264

SISSON, C. H.
  Avoidance of Literature, The (80) 40

SITKOFF, HARVARD
  Struggle for Black Equality, 1954-1980, The (82) 822

SKIDELSKY, ROBERT
  John Maynard Keynes, 1920-1937 (95) 400
  John Maynard Keynes, 1937-1946 (02) 453

SKLAREW, MYRA
  Science of Goodbyes, The (83) 694

SKOCPOL, THEDA
  Protecting Soldiers and Mothers (94) 671

ŠKVORECKÝ, JOSEF
  Bass Saxophone, The (80) 54
  Engineer of Human Souls, The (85) 227
  Miracle Game, The (92) 509

SLATER, LAUREN
  Lying (01) 545

SLAVIN, JULIA
  Woman Who Cut Off Her Leg at the Maidstone Club and Other Stories, The (00) 855

SLAVITT, DAVID R.
  Cliff, The (95) 123
  Lives of the Saints (91) 530
  Rounding the Horn (79) 608
  Walls of Thebes, The (87) 936

SLAYTON, ROBERT A.
  Empire Statesman (02) 248

SLOAN, JAMES PARK
  Jerzy Kosinski (97) 470

SLOAT, WARREN
  1929 (80) 591

SLOMAN, JOEL
  Stops (98) 741

SLOTKIN, RICHARD
  Fatal Environment, The (86) 264

SMILEY, JANE
  Age of Grief, The (88) 6
  All-True Travels and Adventures of Lidie Newton, The (99) 32
  Greenlanders, The (89) 326
  Horse Heaven (01) 412
  Moo (96) 473
  Ordinary Love and Good Will (90) 642
  Thousand Acres, A (92) 817

SMITH, BRADLEY F.
  Reaching Judgment at Nuremberg (78) 695
  Road to Nuremberg, The (82) 695
  Shadow Warriors, The (H-84) 403

SMITH, BRADLEY F., and ELENA AGAROSSI
  Operation Sunrise (80) 631

SMITH, DAVE
  Cuba Night (91) 179
  Goshawk, Antelope (80) 380
  In the House of the Judge (84) 374
  Roundhouse Voices, The (86) 775

SMITH, DENIS MACK. See MACK SMITH, DENIS

SMITH, GADDIS
  Morality, Reason, and Power (87) 577

AUTHOR INDEX

TANIZAKI, JUN'ICHIRŌ
Naomi (86) 640
TANNER, TONY
Jane Austen (87) 435
TARTT, DONNA
Secret History, The (93) 711
TATE, JAMES
Collected Poems, 1919-1976 (78) 188
Constant Defender (84) 202
Viper Jazz (77) 888
Worshipful Company of Fletchers (95) 895
TAUBMAN, WILLIAM
Stalin's American Policy (H-83) 400
TAYLOR, ANNE
Annie Besant (93) 23
Visions of Harmony (88) 932
TAYLOR, CHARLES
Sources of the Self (91) 763
TAYLOR, ELIZABETH, and ADAM COHEN
American Pharaoh (01) 34
TAYLOR, GARY
Cultural Selection (97) 187
Reinventing Shakespeare (90) 685
TAYLOR, HENRY
Compulsory Figures (93) 192
Flying Change, The (86) 293
TAYLOR, INA
Woman of Contradictions, A (91) 909
TAYLOR, NICK, with JOHN GLENN
John Glenn (00) 443
TAYLOR, PETER
In the Tennessee Country (95) 363
Smoke Ring, The (H-85) 415
TAYLOR, PETER HILLSMAN
Old Forest and Other Stories, The (86) 673
Oracle at Stoneleigh Court, The (94) 590
Summons to Memphis, A (87) 832
TAYLOR, TELFORD
Munich (80) 555
TELUSHKIN, JOSEPH, and DENNIS PRAGER
Why the Jews? (H-84) 481
TENNANT, ROBERT
Joseph Conrad (82) 412
TERKEL, STUDS
Good War, The (H-85) 173
TERRAINE, JOHN
To Win a War (82) 850
TERRILL, ROSS
Future of China After Mao, The (79) 240
Mao (81) 549
White Boned Demon, The (H-85) 495
TERRY, WALLACE
Bloods (H-85) 48
TERTZ, ABRAM
Goodnight! (90) 314
Little Jinx (93) 473
Strolls with Pushkin (95) 773
Voice from the Chorus, A (77) 892
TERVALON, JERVEY
Understand This (95) 823
TESNOHLIDEK, RUDOLF
Cunning Little Vixen, The (86) 204
TEVETH, SHABTAI
Ben-Gurion, 1886-1948 (88) 90
THACKARA, JAMES
Book of Kings, The (00) 90

THANT, U
View from the UN (79) 809
THATCHER, MARGARET
Downing Street Years, The (94) 248
Path to Power, The (96) 573
THERNSTROM, STEPHAN, and ABIGAIL THERNSTROM
America in Black and White (98) 31
THEROUX, ALEXANDER
Primary Colors, The (95) 613
THEROUX, PAUL
Collected Stories, The (98) 194
Consul's File, The (78) 215
Family Arsenal, The (77) 274
Half Moon Street (85) 338
London Embassy, The (84) 472
Millroy the Magician (95) 491
Mosquito Coast, The (83) 496
Old Patagonian Express, The (80) 619
O-Zone (87) 631
Riding the Iron Rooster (89) 726
Sir Vidia's Shadow (99) 711
THOLFSEN, TRYGVE R.
Ideology and Revolution in Modern Europe (H-85) 225
THOMAS, D. M.
Alexander Solzhenitsyn (99) 24
Ararat (84) 36
White Hotel, The (82) 932
THOMAS, DONALD
Robert Browning (84) 741
THOMAS, DWIGHT, and DAVID K. JACKSON
Poe Log, The (88) 701
THOMAS, DYLAN
Collected Letters of Dylan Thomas, The (87) 132
THOMAS, DYLAN, and JOHN DAVENPORT
Death of the King's Canary, The (78) 238
THOMAS, ELIZABETH MARSHALL
Reindeer Moon (88) 748
THOMAS, EMORY M.
Confederate Nation, The (80) 156
Robert E. Lee (96) 645
THOMAS, HUGH
Armed Truce (88) 57
THOMAS, KEITH
Man and the Natural World (84) 492
THOMAS, LEWIS
Medusa and the Snail, The (80) 533
THOMAS, MERLIN
Louis-Ferdinand Céline (81) 529
THOMPSON, E. P.
William Morris (78) 913
THOMPSON, JEAN
Who Do You Love (00) 830
THOMPSON, JOHN M.
Revolutionary Russia, 1917 (82) 679
THOMPSON, KENNETH W.
Winston Churchill's World View (H-84) 493
THOMPSON, LEONARD
History of South Africa, A (91) 408
THOMSON, GEORGE MALCOLM
First Churchill, The (81) 344
THOMSON, PETER
Shakespeare's Professional Career (93) 728
THOMSON, RUPERT
Air and Fire (95) 15

1091

AUTHOR INDEX

AUTHOR INDEX

AUTHOR INDEX

WURTS, JAY, with LE LY HAYSLIP
When Heaven and Earth Changed Places (90) 879

WYATT, DAVID
Fall into Eden, The (87) 253

WYATT-BROWN, BERTRAM
Southern Honor (H-83) 396

WYDEN, PETER
Bay of Pigs (80) 59
Day One (H-85) 104
Passionate War, The (H-84) 330

WYMAN, DAVID S.
Abandonment of the Jews, The (H-85) 1

WYND, OSWALD
Ginger Tree, The (78) 349

XUE LITAI, SERGEI N. GONCHAROV, and
JOHN W. LEWIS
Uncertain Partners (95) 809

YA'ARI, EHUD, and ZE'EV SCHIFF
Intifada (91) 461

YAGODA, BEN
About Town (01) 1

YALOM, MARILYN
History of the Breast, A (98) 391

YANKELOVICH, DANIEL
New Rules (82) 548

YATES, RICHARD
Easter Parade, The (77) 247
Liars in Love (82) 453

YEAGER, CHUCK, and LEO JANOS
Yeager (86) 974

YEATES, MARIAN, and JOAN HOFF
Cooper's Wife Is Missing, The (01) 218

YEATS, WILLIAM BUTLER
Collected Letters of W. B. Yeats, 1865-1895,
The (87) 142
Poems, The (85) 692

YEATS, WILLIAM BUTLER, and MAUD GONNE
Gonne-Yeats Letters 1893-1938, The (94) 368

YEHOSHUA, A. B.
Five Seasons (90) 263
Journey to the End of the Millennium, A (00) 453
Late Divorce, A (85) 530
Mr. Mani (93) 527

YERGIN, DANIEL H.
Prize, The (92) 645
Shattered Peace (78) 766

YERGIN, DANIEL H., and JOSEPH STANISLAW
Commanding Heights (99) 204

YEROFEYEV, VIKTOR, et al., editors
Metropol (84) 533

YEVTUSHENKO, YEVGENY
Collected Poems, The (92) 104

YGLESIAS, HELEN
Family Feeling (77) 277

YORK, HERBERT F.
Advisors, The (77) 27

YOSHIMOTO, BANANA
Kitchen (94) 445

YOUNG, HUGO
Iron Lady, The (90) 429

YOUNG, MARGUERITE
Harp Song for a Radical (00) 358

YOUNG, MARILYN B., and WILLIAM G.
ROSENBERG
Transforming Russia and China (H-83) 426

YOUNG, PHILIP
Hawthorne's Secret (85) 358

YOUNG-BRUEHL, ELISABETH
Anna Freud (89) 23
Hannah Arendt (83) 322

YOURCENAR, MARGUERITE
Abyss, The (77) 1
Dark Brain of Piranesi and Other Essays,
The (85) 152
Fires (82) 275
Oriental Tales (86) 706

YOVEL, YIRMIYAHU
Spinoza and Other Heretics, Vol. I and Vol.
II (91) 768

ZAGORIN, PEREZ
Francis Bacon (99) 303

ZAKARIA, FAREED
From Wealth to Power (99) 315

ZEE, A.
Old Man's Toy, An (90) 628

ZEITLIN, JUDITH T.
Historian of the Strange (94) 393

ZERUBAVEL, EVIATAR
Seven Day Circle, The (86) 807

ZIEGLER, PHILIP
King Edward VIII (92) 403
Mountbatten (86) 629

ZIFF, LARZER
Return Passages (02) 698
Writing in the New Nation (92) 924

ZIMMER, CARL
At the Water's Edge (99) 69

ZINSSER, WILLIAM
Willie and Dwike (85) 1036

ZIOLKOWSKI, THEODORE
German Romanticism and Its Institutions
(91) 347

ZUBOFF, SHOSHANNA
In the Age of the Smart Machine (89) 377

ZUKOFSKY, LOUIS
"A" (80) 1
Complete Short Poetry (92) 114

ZURAVLEFF, MARY KAY
Frequency of Souls, The (97) 315

ZWEIG, PAUL
Walt Whitman (85) 984

ZYSMAN, JOHN, and STEPHEN S. COHEN
Manufacturing Matters (88) 529